Corporate Governance, The Firm and Investor Capitalism

NEW PERSPECTIVES ON THE MODERN CORPORATION

Series Editor: Jonathan Michie, *Director, Department for Continuing Education and President, Kellogg College, University of Oxford, UK*

The modern corporation has far reaching influence on our lives in an increasingly globalised economy. This series will provide an invaluable forum for the publication of high quality works of scholarship covering the areas of:

- corporate governance and corporate responsibility, including environmental sustainability;
- human resource management and other management practices, and the relationship of these to organisational outcomes and corporate performance;
- industrial economics, organisational behaviour, innovation and competitiveness;
- outsourcing, offshoring, joint ventures and strategic alliances;
- different ownership forms, including social enterprise and employee ownership;
- intellectual property and the learning economy, including knowledge; and
- transfer and information exchange.

Titles in the series include:

The Modern Firm, Corporate Governance and Investment
Edited by Per-Olof Bjuggren and Dennis C. Mueller

The Growth of Firms
A Survey of Theories and Empirical Evidence
Alex Coad

Knowledge in the Development of Economies
Institutional Choices Under Globalisation
Edited by Silvia Sacchetti and Roger Sugden

Corporate Strategy and Firm Growth
Creating Value for Shareholders
Angelo Dringoli

The Internationalisation of Business R&D
Edited by Bernhard Dachs, Robert Stehrer and Georg Zahradnik

Corporate Governance, The Firm and Investor Capitalism
Legal-Political and Economic Views
Alexander Styhre

Corporate Governance, The Firm and Investor Capitalism

Legal-Political and Economic Views

Alexander Styhre

School of Business, Economics and Law, University of Gothenburg, Sweden

NEW PERSPECTIVES ON THE MODERN CORPORATION

Cheltenham, UK • Northampton, MA, USA

Published by
Edward Elgar Publishing Limited
The Lypiatts
15 Lansdown Road
Cheltenham
Glos GL50 2JA
UK

Edward Elgar Publishing, Inc.
William Pratt House
9 Dewey Court
Northampton
Massachusetts 01060
USA

A catalogue record for this book
is available from the British Library

Library of Congress Control Number: 2016942175

This book is available electronically in the **Elgar**online
Business subject collection
DOI 10.4337/9781785364020

ISBN 978 1 78536 401 3 (cased)
ISBN 978 1 78536 402 0 (eBook)

Typeset by Columns Design XML Ltd, Reading
Printed and bound in Great Britain by TJ International Ltd, Padstow

Contents

Preface   vi
Acknowledgements   ix

Prologue: the Great Recession *Durcharbeitung*   1
Introduction: the nature of the firm and its governance   8

PART I   INSTITUTING THE FIRM

1. Corporate law and the legal environment of the firm   29
2. Managerialism, the problem of principal–agent relations, and free
    market advocacy   60

PART II   RETHINKING THE FIRM

3. The agency theory model of the firm and its implications   107
4. Investor capitalism and the nexus of contract view of the firm:
    assessing the consequences   165
Epilogue: neoclassical economic theory and ideology   219

Bibliography   236
Index   273

Preface

The finance market collapse of 2008 has inspired many scholars and pundits to spill much ink, and some have argued that the events of 2008 were the 'Berlin Wall moment' of free market capitalism (at times referred to as neoliberalism). In my view, that characterization is a misnomer, as the Berlin Wall coming down was the culmination of a long-term process where a politico-economic regime finally came to the end of the road as it could no longer uphold itself and satisfy even the most elementary human needs. In contrast, the financial market collapse of 2008 has led to few structural changes and the finance industry per se has been most successful in both pushing the costs for its restoration onto other actors (most notably national states, now operating under 'austerity schemes'; see, for example, Major, 2014; Schui, 2014; Blyth, 2013) and further entrenching their own interests, leading to an even more salient oligarchic structure of the finance industry. Rather than being a Berlin Wall moment, the 2008 events were more like the Harrisburg or Chernobyl nuclear plant accidents: they made us all aware of the risks and revealed some of the costs of the system but, after all, when the dust had settled, they changed very little. In the case of nuclear energy, the underlying nuclear physics theories, the regulatory work, or the market for nuclear energy did not change in any decisive way. In the case of the 2008 financial market collapse, the underlying neoclassical economic theory framework justifying the practices in the finance industry, the regulatory and legal framework (becoming increasingly more lenient and liberal), and the demand for credit and financial services did not change in any decisive way. In both cases, too many people had too much to gain from justifying and further reinforcing these advanced but ultimately fragile and thus potentially harmful energy and financial systems. In both cases, these were 'man-made disasters' and what Charles Perrow (1984) calls 'normal accidents'. Humans made and built these systems but apparently failed to keep them under full control; even more importantly, after the fact, when the harm had already been done, there were few possibilities for abandoning these systems despite their hazardous risks.

Perhaps future historians will address these two disasters – one environmental, polluting the life world of humans and other forms of life, one socio-economic, leading to enormous social costs in terms of increased economic inequalities (but also, indisputably, provided many merits in terms of increased supply of credit) – as evidence of the learned helplessness of advanced, capitalist human societies, building techno-scientific and socio-economic systems to serve these societies but eventually no longer being able to run them as humans may wish as they become too complex to slow down and monitor, even when the risk of derailment becomes too high, or even acute. From my own perspective, the latter type of 'normal accidents', that of socio-economic systems such as the global finance industry, is part of my jurisdictional domain as a management researcher and business school scholar. The underlying politico-theoretical framework that justified and served to construct and fortress the present finance industry arguably deserves systematic scholarly attention. During the last few years, I have published three research monographs addressing the shift from managerial capitalism to investor capitalism. The first volume, *Management and Neoliberalism* (2014), addressed the political changes and free market activism beginning in the New Deal era during the 1930s. The second volume, *The Financialization of the Firm* (2015), examined the consequences for the individual corporation when it was no longer treated as a site where production capital was integrated and monitored under one single management and the board of directors, but was now better seen as 'a bundle of financial assets'. The third volume, *Leadership Varieties* (2016, co-authored with Thomas Johansson), discussed how the concept of leadership is strongly informed by the shift from managerial capitalism to investor capitalism, and how the fiduciary duties of former corporate elites have been gradually displaced by rational choice-informed incentives and compensation packages. In addition, the emergence of a market for corporate control has gradually undermined the very idea of the firm as an economic and social team production unit dependent on various forms of professional expertise for its functioning.

This fourth volume in this series of investigations focuses more explicitly on corporate governance and corporate law, and how neoclassical economic theory has by and large misunderstood, ignored, marginalized or trivialized not only management theory but also legal theory and corporate law when advocating its favoured contractarian theory of corporate governance. That is, this volume adds to the previous three volumes the analysis of how primarily legal theory and neoclassical economic theory in many cases are irreconcilable or complementary, and how much of the free market advocacy that has been integral to the politico-economic project to overturn managerial capitalism and to advocate free market capitalism – a project propelled by the political objective to restore capital owner interests – is factually wrong or seriously flawed regarding the assumptions made and propositions stated. This may sound like a bold declaration, but in order to understand corporate governance the analyst must recognize legal theory, corporate law and the day-to-day practices in corporations. In other words, rather than being neatly derived from deductive reasoning on the basis of neoclassical economy theory propositions regarding, for example, market efficiency and individual decision choices, corporate governance is social and economic practice seated in legal traditions and political objectives that have evolved over time. Free market protagonists may wish the world looked differently (and I do not in any way deny them the right to think so), but they must recognize, like any other researcher and scholar, that their preferences are not the same thing as factual conditions. What is the case in the best of all possible worlds may, sadly, not be the world that we inhabit and try to operate within. Unfortunately, the world that managers, shareholders, regulators, politicians, customers and so on, inhabit and operate within and govern and regulate is far more messy and non-linear than neat models and parsimonious theories of economic activity may suggest, and consequently the tendency to cut theoretical corners easily obscures and leads astray to a higher extent than is recognized.

Alexander Styhre
Melbourne, December 2015

Acknowledgements

I am grateful to Francine O'Sullivan, Commissioning Editor at Edward Elgar Publishing, for being given the chance to publish this research monograph. I would also like to thank my colleagues at the Department of Business Administration, and the faculty of the Organization and Management section, School of Business Economics and Law, University of Gothenburg, for upholding and caring for an intellectually stimulating environment. Finally, I would like to thank the Department of Management and Marketing, Faculty of Business and Economics, University of Melbourne, and Professor and Head of Department Leisa Sargent and Professor Bill Harley in particular, for inviting me to spend some time in this exciting place and providing me with some time to work on this volume.

Prologue: the Great Recession
Durcharbeitung

> Capitalism does not invent hierarchies, any more than it invented the market, or
> production, or consumption; it merely uses them. In the long procession of
> history, capitalism is the later-comer. It arrives when everything is ready.
>
> Fernand Braudel (1977: 75)

The Annales school historian Emmanuel Le Roy Ladurie (1983) remarks that in the period of 1350 to 1750 there was only a modest population growth in Europe. The continent was held captured by a military-state apparatus, dominated by the aristocracy, and with the monarchy as a largely military institution, implicated in the European balance of power (Le Roy Ladurie, 1983: 15). To maintain the power balance, constant wars and skirmishes tortured the European population and prevented economic development and population growth for more than four centuries. 'From the fourteenth to the seventeenth century inclusive, the economy was servant not master', Le Roy Ladurie (1983: 23) writes. Only after the beginning of the industrialization process, itself derived from the advancement of the bourgeoisie at the expense of the aristocracy and its primary institution the monarchy, could the economy start to grow. In this case, the facts by and large speak for themselves: '[i]n 1328, the French population stood at 17 million; it was 19 million in 1700 – still about the same. But by 1879, it had reached 27 million and had risen to almost 40 million by the time of the Franco-Prussian war of 1870' (Le Roy Ladurie, 1983: 25). Roughly after 1750, midway between the glorious English revolution and the French and American revolutions, population growth could finally be reported. In Le Roy Ladurie's (1983) perspective, a series of reforms, institutional changes and new ideas contributed to the decline of the aristocratic-military state:

> The forces of renovation included the State, the modernized Church, the educational system – all more repressive and more efficient; a more plentiful money supply; a more sophisticated nobility and bourgeoisie; better-run estates; greater literacy everywhere; a more rational bureaucracy; more active trade; and urbanization at what eventually became an irresistible rate, forcing

1

nations (whose productivity was not keeping pace) to produce more peasants in order to feed the new mass of townspeople. (Le Roy Ladurie, 1983: 25)

In the contemporary political affairs literature and debates, there are many worried concerns about regions in the Middle East and in the Maghreb being stuck in cycles of outbursts of violence and war and calmer periods, very much being 'medieval' in their nature. The lack of economic growth and work opportunities creates unrest and disappointment, and it is seemingly very complicated to change the downward spiral of escalating violence. Historians remind us that this was very much the situation on European soil for centuries, but today the wars have been canalized into other competitive activities such as commerce and sports.

In the transformation of the European feudalism into modern states with growing economies (Bloch, 1962), the bourgeoisie and what was eventually called the middle class played a key role. The aristocracy has always enjoyed inherited privileges and has therefore opposed change and shown little interest in enterprising activities. For the aristocrat, the bourgeoisie striving to accumulate capital and to make a better living was not only unnecessary for the economically favoured class, tightly bound up in a network of reciprocal relations that ensured the highest possible economic welfare also for the coming generation, but this very idea was also the vulgar ambition of the parvenu. While the aristocracy was a leisure class, the bourgeoisie lived in accordance with what Gay (2001) refers to as the Gospel of Work, which prescribed hard and diligent work as a principal virtue. Virgil had written that '*Labor omnia vincit improbus*', that 'persistent labour conquers all' (cited in Gay, 2001: 192), and this became the leitmotif of the bourgeois way of life. 'The gospel of work was emphatically and almost exclusively a bourgeoisie ideal. By and large, aristocrats did not value it and the working poor did not need it', Gay (2001: 198) writes. Needless to say, out of historical necessity, the aristocracy did not commit to the bourgeois way of life. The multitude, the poor and the penniless, the rural classes and the 'little people' in the towns, endured living conditions that effectively prevented them from nourishing any ambition to create a better life for themselves. Only occasionally did the aristocracy and the working classes create venturesome and enterprising individuals who managed to escape the shackles of a class society that was far from dynamic and meritocratic. This new venturesome and diligent social class, the bourgeoisie, representing a 'distinctive combination of striving and straitening, desire and self-denial, hedonism and frustration' (Fourcade and Healy, 2013: 568), became a formidable challenge for the aristocracy to keep at bay. At the end of the day and after many rivers have been crossed, it was the bourgeoisie that created Western capitalism, rooted in the idiosyncratic blend of a risk-taking attitude and the close monitoring of resources, enabling both economic ventures and the regulation of economic affairs, specific for the Western capitalist economy. To allude to Winston Churchill's famous bon mot, capitalism, the ultimate and lasting triumph of the liberal bourgeoisie over the conservative and self-destructive aristocratic-monarchic medieval state, is the 'least bad' of economic systems; it has beyond doubt demonstrated a remarkable capacity to accumulate economic wealth, but has been less trustworthy when it comes to the distribution of such benefits and in maintaining its stability over time.

The great financial market meltdown and the accompanying economic decline, widely referred to as the 'Great Recession' in the literature, was an event that caused much debate and discussion in both the media and academic circles (Eichengreen, 2015). The 2008 crash represented a 'Berlin Wall moment' of free market advocacy, Peck (2010: 9) argued, while for others, the events were little more than bumps in the road of the neoclassical prescription of the economic system. One of the most intriguing books being published in the period – the 2008 events produced an entire literary sub-genre, whereof, for example, Blinder's (2013) *When the Music Stopped* is one exemplary piece of scholarship and commentary – was Richard A. Posner's (2009) *A Failure of Capitalism*. Written by a judge and legal scholar with conservative and libertarian political convictions and preferences, Posner (2009) did not sugarcoat his pills regarding the causes and consequences of the finance market collapse. 'The depression[1] is the result of normal business activity in a laissez-faire economic regime – more precisely, it is an event consistent with the normal operation of economic markets', Posner (2009: 235) says.[2] Formerly being committed to free market capitalism advocacy, one can only speculate about the frustration Posner must have felt when writing these lines. Nevertheless, Posner (2009: 240) insists, '[t]he financial crisis is indeed a crisis of capitalism rather than a failure of government'. In addition, the crisis is 'systemic' (Posner, 2009: 236) and one of the principal consequences is that capitalism '[m]ay survive only in a compromised form' (Posner, 2009: 234). Posner also addresses which groups are responsible for the new situations, and the list becomes quite extensive before Posner is done with this job. First of all, the 'economic libertarians' were hit in 'the solar plexus' as the crisis was not a consequence, as they have regularly stated, 'of the government's overregulating the economy and by doing so fettering free enterprise', but derived from 'innate limitations of the free market' (Posner, 2009: 306).

In brief, the free market advocacy was based on faulty premises and the wrong idea about the nature of unregulated and free markets. In addition, economists and especially finance professors should carry their share of the responsibility, Posner (2009: 257) says. Part of the problem is that these scholars are also actively working in the finance industry and therefore they try to combine two roles that are essentially incompatible and/or potentially violating professional scholarly norms: '[Professors of finance] are consultants, investors, and sometimes money managers; many of them, either before joining a university faculty or during leaves of absence from the university, have worked for the Federal Reserve, the International Monetary Fund, or other nonacademic institution' (Posner, 2009: 258–9).

In fulfilling such multiple and diverse roles, finance professors, being the leading advocates of free market capitalism and the deregulation of finance markets, mix up their responsibilities in culpable ways: '[i]f they [professors of finance] criticize the industry and suggest tighter regulations, they may become black sheep and lose lucrative consultantships' (Posner, 2009: 259). In addition, the Federal Reserve's two chairmen during the period, Alan Greenspan and Ben Bernanke, two conservatives, operated for too long on the basis of misconceived ideas regarding the nature of the finance market and thus failed to stem the tide once the levees broke. Finally, the Bush Administration accomplished little more than to deliver a 'cascade of blunders' (Posner, 2009: 308).

These are quite harsh words, especially as they are written by one of the allies of free market advocators. Posner's (2009) disappointment and anger is present on every single page of his book, and we may therefore pay attention to the claim made that capitalism may only survive in a 'compromised' and revised form. At the height of the last system-wide capitalist crisis, the Great Depression, the Harvard Law School professor Merrick Dodd (1932) addressed the question regarding to whom salaried managers are accountable and advocated what would eventually become known as corporate social responsibilities. When reading Dodd's text, more than eight decades after its publication, the issues addressed by Posner (2009) seem oddly familiar:

> Concentration of control of industry in a relatively few hands has encouraged the belief in the practicability of methods of economic planning by which such security can be achieved in much greater degree than at present. This belief is no longer confined to radical opponents of the capitalistic system; it has come to be shared by many conservatives who believe that capitalism is worth saving but that it cannot permanently survive under modern conditions unless it treats the economic security of the worker as one of its obligations and is intelligently directed so as to attain that object. (Dodd, 1932: 1151–2)

Plus ça change. Still today, conservatives believe capitalism is 'worth saving', but there are few distinct ideas about how that can be accomplished on a basis of the predominant regime of investor capitalism. Perhaps we are witnessing, as Fligstein (2005) suggests, the decline of the shareholder welfare and finance industry dominance era, but there are many who doubt competitive capitalism is at the crossroads.

Despite the 2008 finance market debacle, competitive capitalism remains a magnificent engine in terms of its ability to maximize economic value creation. This engine is much worse in terms of *sharing* and *distributing* this value (as indicated by the conspicuous growth of economic inequality in most OECD countries and elsewhere; see, for example, Perugini et al., 2016) and it is certainly not capable of 'self-regulating' as free market advocators have persistently claimed since at least the interwar period. Despite these 'systemic' features, competitive capitalism remains the least bad economic system, but it is a system that needs to be kept under tight control and to be understood as what serves societies and human beings. Fernand Braudel, one of the leading economic historians of the twentieth century, emphasizes that capitalism cannot exist without its surrounding and supportive society: 'capitalism is unthinkable without society's active complicity. It is of necessity a reality of the social order, a reality of the political order, and even a reality of civilization. For in a certain manner, society as a whole must more or less consciously accept capitalism's values' (Braudel, 1977: 63–4). While Braudel's (1977: 61) claim that one of capitalism's 'greatest strengths' is its ability to adapt and to change (capitalism is 'conjunctural', Braudel says), capitalism nevertheless 'only triumphs when it becomes identified with the state, when it is the state' (Braudel, 1977: 64).

The hard-liners of free market advocacy, claiming that 'economic freedom' is privileged above and beyond any political idea about freedom (that is, they reject Braudel's thesis about the role of society and the state – the formalized and bureaucratized organization of society – out of hand), and who want to subsume any human activity under market evaluations and pricing, may not be in the best position to justify competitive capitalism for the wider population. For these staunch defenders of free market capitalism, there is no escape from the purifying and all-encompassing cleansing of market pricing. Any human decision, no matter how small, is uncompromisingly evaluated and thereafter priced by the market. Rather than God seeing all, knowing all, it is now the market, the supreme calculator and information processor, that executes such a function. Similarly, just as God lets us all be held responsible for our choices and behaviour in the Christian liturgy, so too does the market reward and punish choices and behaviour, free market protagonists argue. The works of, for example, Alan Blinder (2013) and Richard Posner (2009), independent of their previous role in creating the existing system of competitive capitalism, are indicative of a willingness to, perhaps for the first time since the mid-1970s, one more time discuss the economic system of competitive capitalism and to try to figure out how this remarkably efficient economic engine can be embedded in a society that both creates and reproduces this economic system while also being the primary beneficiary of its functioning.

Part of that story, it is claimed here, consists of how the corporation has been enacted over time and how it has been supported by and reformed by legislation, law enforcement, regulation, and the advancement of economic theories that shape and influence the object of analysis. The common term for all these different practices and engagement is *corporate governance*, here denoting the broad concern regarding how companies – incorporated business charters – are to be understood within society and the economy in which they are operating. In addition, to fully recognize the shifts and changes in the discourse on corporate governance, beginning in the latter half of the nineteenth century, a historical perspective is taken in this volume, starting around the Great Depression and the Wall Street crash of 1929, and moving on into the new millennium. Only from this bird's-eye view can corporate governance practices and their influence in the economy be fully recognized and understood.

NOTES

1. Posner (2009) refuses to use the concept of 'recession', in his view a euphemism that seeks to blindfold the public in an attempt to trivialize the causes and consequences of the crisis. Hence the use of the more eye-catching term 'depression'.
2. The term 'normal operation' used by Posner (2009) deserves some attention. Greenwood and Scharfstein (2013) argue convincingly on the basis of solid empirical evidence that it was the combination of new asset management practices and the expansion of credit, primarily in the form of mortgages, which fuelled the swift growth of the finance industry after the mid-1990s (see Chapter 4 for an extended argument). While the output from 'traditional banking' as a percentage of GDP was 'roughly the same in 2007 as it was in 1997' (Greenwood and Scharfstein (2013: 19), a substantial share of this growth occurred in 'transactional services', which in turn were 'largely reflected in fees associated with deposits, residual loan origination, and the catchall category of "other products supporting financial services"' (Greenwood and Scharfstein, 2013: 19). In short, 'non-traditional banking' took off in the period after the mid-1990s. The increased securitization of financial assets also 'went hand-in-hand with the growth of "shadow banking"' (Greenwood and Scharfstein, 2013: 21) and what Engel and McCoy (2007) call 'predatory lending' (substandard lending aimed at distributing risks through securitization), wherein key functions of traditional banking are provided outside of the traditional financial entities that

do not benefit from central bank liquidity or public sector credit guarantees (Greenwood and Scharfstein, 2013: 21). Shadow banking is a thinly veiled approach to circumvent regulatory control and therefore also increases the instability of the financial system. '[T]he shadow banking system that facilitated this expansion [of mortgage credit] made the financial system more fragile', Greenwood and Scharfstein (2013: 26) conclude. Cole and White (2012) also examine the causes of the finance industry collapse of 2008 and their data suggest a run-of-the-mill, indigenously produced, man-made crisis that was more or less following previous patterns for such events:

> [M]ost banks in the current crisis are failing in ways that are quite recognizable to anyone who has studied the hundreds of bank failures that occurred during the 1984–1992 period; hence the phrase 'déjà vu all over again' … Banks that invest heavily in commercial real estate loans, including construction and development loans, non-residential mortgages, and multifamily mortgages, are taking levels of risk that are not simply captured by existing capital requirements, just as they were back in the 1980s. (Cole and White, 2012: 27)

As Greenwood and Scharfstein (2013: 26) remark, this recurrent pattern very much runs counter to the traditional 'functional' view of finance (apparently not able to adjust itself to emerging empirical evidence), wherein 'a primary function of the financial sector is to dampen the effects of risk by reallocating its efficiently to parties that can bear risks the most easily' (Greenwood and Scharfstein, 2013: 26). That is, the 2008 financial crisis was not a bit unusual or indicative of an emerging irregular pattern, but was in an everyday sense of the term perfectly 'normal'. Still, the question remains as to why yet another finance industry crisis occurred when theoretical prescriptions render the finance industry the capacity of self-correction and stabilization. Fahlenbrach and Stulz (2011) and Hagendorff and Vallascas (2011) both stress the incentive structure underlying executive compensation in financial institutions, in turn derived from a shareholder primacy ideology now widely entrenched in large domains of the world of business. '[C]EOs with better incentives to maximize shareholder wealth took risks that other CEOs did not. Ex ante, these risks looked profitable for shareholders. Ex post, these risks had unexpected poor outcomes', Fahlenbrach and Stulz (2011: 25) conclude. '[L]inking executive compensation policy to align the interest of shareholders and management in banking is likely to lead to excessive risk-taking', Hagendorff and Vallascas (2011: 1094) add. Banks and other financial institutions that theoretically, practically and legally enjoy the jurisdictional discretion to spread and minimize risks in the economic system through financial operations were instead incentivized to become sites where such systemic risks were fabricated on an industrial basis (for a recent review of the literature on corporate governance and risk management in banks, see Ellul, 2015). From the mid-1990s and onwards, this became the new conventional wisdom – what Posner (2009) refers to as 'normality' – of the finance industry.

Introduction: the nature of the firm and its governance

ASSUMPTION AND PROPOSITIONS

This volume is based on one assumption and two propositions. This assumption and the two propositions are the recurrent themes which this volume purports to address and whose significance will be demonstrated. For the sake of clarity, they should therefore be defined at this early point:

- *Assumption*: The recent thoroughly demonstrated and researched growth of economic inequality and economic stagnation in Western capitalism cannot be explained by individual activities or policy changes, idiosyncratic events, or by sheer *force majeure* beyond the influence of informed policy-making, but needs to be examined as institutional changes in what can best be described as the infra-structure of the corporate system of Western capitalism. More specifically, these infrastructural changes in the corporate system are most accurately described as questions pertaining to corporate governance. Corporate governance here includes '[a]ll the devices, institutions, and mechanisms by which corporations are governed' (Macey, 2008: 2). Ultimately, corporate governance denotes decision-making regarding the value creation and value extraction in the corporate system, and, more specifically, within a focal firm, under the influence of market-based competition, legislation, and existing regulatory frameworks.
- *Propositions*: (1) Managers do not, by and large (even though noteworthy exceptions are reported), shirk or act incompetently in *predictable ways* when seeking to navigate in competitive environments to create economic value accruing to their stakeholders and when submitting to extant legal frameworks and institutionalized regulatory control. (2) If they did (which is counterintuitive and unsupported by empirical evidence regarding the degree of economic value creation in the corporate system of Western capitalism), it would still not induce agency costs in relationship to other

comparable costs (a) to the extent proposed by agency theorists and contractarians, and/or (b) to the extent that it would justify legal and regulatory reform to further channel economic resources to a limited number of organizational stakeholders, most noteworthy the shareholders.

ECONOMICS IN BOOKS AND IN REAL LIFE

Max Weber (1949) remarked in his seminal book on the methodology of sociological inquiry that a new science is in the first place a form of social organization of joint intellectual pursuits, and only in the secondary instant can a new science address practical concerns in the surrounding world: '[i]t is not the "actual" interconnections of "things" but the *conceptual* inter-connections of problems which define the scope of the various sciences. A new "science" emerges where new problems are pursued by new methods and truths are thereby discovered which open up significant new points of view' (Max Weber, 1949: 68, emphasis in original). The same idea was later expressed by Georges Canguilhem (1989: 30): '[t]he history of science concerns an axiological activity, the search for truth. This axiological activity appears only at the level of questions, methods and concepts and nowhere else'. A science is therefore a shared explanatory framework which from time to time, but not always, manages to predict outcomes or to explain certain previously puzzling phenomena. But such benefits are only secondary to the very formation of the discipline's internal organization. Teece and Winter (1984: 117) address the difference between managerial work and its dependence on explanatory frameworks capable of guiding decisions and the neoclassic economic theory framework and its inability to provide such heuristics and rules of thumb: '[m]ost management problems are ill-structured. They are messy, involving complex interdependencies, multiple goals, and considerable ambiguity, and their nature is much dependent on the conceptual lens through which they are viewed'. In contrast, neoclassic economic theory, formalist and mathematized, in turn, is 'shaped by a concern with problems that are very different from the management problems just described' (Teece and Winter, 1984: 117). As a consequence, Teece and Winter (1984) reason, neoclassical economic theory has many benefits but it is by and large not very practically useful for managers in need of more straightforward decision-making tools and heuristics to act professionally within their domain of practice.

This difference between neoclassical economic theory and the professional field of management and its scholarly branch, management studies, is a standing concern in the business school setting. Economists treat management studies as a form of anecdotal storytelling devoid of methodological rigour and systematic accumulation of robust, verified know-how; management scholars tend to dismiss economic theory as mathematized nonsense that by and large fails to predict or even explain managerial behaviour or even aggregated economic phenomena. This mutual resentment is unfortunate as it prevents a fruitful collaboration between the various branches and schools in economic thinking (including also economic sociologists, legal scholars, economic historians and political scientists). If there could be a better understanding of the benefits and weaknesses of individual research programmes, the ability to handle practical problems and challenges would have been improved. Unfortunately, as we learn from Weber (1949), scholarly and disciplinary boundary work counteracts such collaborative efforts. By and large, the line of demarcation between neoclassical economic theory and management studies is that the former follows a rational choice theory model based on individual decision-making, while the latter subscribes to a behavioural theory of collective decision-making. Just as the philosopher of science Norwood Hanson (1958) claimed that the two astronomers, Tycho Brahe and Johannes Kepler, adhering to different explanatory theories and operative methods, saw things differently when they turned their eyes to look at the moon to make 'theory-laden observations', so too can economists and management scholars only observe what their favoured explanatory theoretical frameworks permit them to see. The economist sees forms of calculative thinking derived from self-interest; the management scholar sees human behaviour being shaped by the thick institutional framework wherein the actor operates.

Economics may be, as suggested by Thomas Carlyle, 'the dismal science' (Trigilia, 2002: 24), but that does not make the discipline incapable of contributing to the operational functionality of the economic system. While economists are fond of portraying their discipline as being a hard science in the Newtonian tradition, regulated by laws and theorems, it has proved time and again to be more like an engineering science based on skilled and calculated judgement. As Downer (2011: 748) remarks, 'engineers have long understood that they cannot perfectly deduce technological performance from models, algorithms, and blueprints'.[1] Similarly, an economist (cited in Reay, 2012: 64) argues that 'good economics requires a lot of judgment, because the answers are never cut and dry'. The economist continues: '[t]hese are not simple, "look it up" kinds of answers. If you could look it up, we would've given you a book and you wouldn't need us. But you can't look it up' (Economist, cited in Reay, 2012: 65). In this 'messy reality' (Downer, 2011: 740), laws, theorems and algorithms are heuristics that guide analysis and decision-making, but they can never fully accommodate all the contingencies and local variation which they purport to describe.

In this volume, the concept of corporate governance will be examined as a field of intense interest for economists, legal scholars and management researchers. While the term *management* commonly denotes the day-to-day administrative and leadership work conducted in corporations and public sector organizations, *corporate governance* addresses the role of the firm in its wider social, institutional and financial setting. The principal issue in managerial activities is to secure the long-term survival of the firm and to produce economic value that benefits the wider society. For most of the post-World War II period, the incorporated business managed by professional managers, that is, the conventional firm, has served as the principal institution in what has been called *managerial capitalism* (Chandler, 1984). Marris (1964: 1) defines managerial capitalism as '[a] system in which production is concentrated in the hands of large joint-stock companies'. Marris (1964: 15) defines management as '[t]he particular in-group, consisting of directors and others, which effectively carries out the functions legally vested in the board'. More specifically, these joint-stock companies are dependent on professional managerial skills, provided by a category of salaried executives, and managers who have the competence needed to run and oversee such companies. In Marris' (1964) account, managerial capitalism denotes an economic system wherein most of the economic activities are no longer undertaken by 'the classical entrepreneur' but by managers and corporations. The corporate governance theorists' concern is that this new professional group '[c]an wield considerable power without necessarily holding equity, sharing profits or carrying risks' (Marris, 1964: 1). That is, in contrast to the enterprising entrepreneur or the capital owners holding stocks in the corporation, managers have a weaker professional legitimacy as they are by definition salaried employees in the chartered business. 'A manager is a different type of person from an entrepreneur, with different ideals and different personal values', Marris (1964: 6) writes. This condition implies an agency problem, Marris (1964: 5) proposes: 'it is by no means obvious that action intended to maximize the utility of a company's stockholders is consistent with maximizing the utility of the action-takers, i.e., of management'. In a corporate governance perspective, the institution of the incorporated business (for example, the public company with dispersed ownership), serving as the principal vehicle for economic production and economic well-being in the capitalist economic system, needs to be examined in great detail to avoid sub-optimization, malfunctioning or mere fraud. The concept of the firm per se – its juridical, economic and practical nature – is of key interest in the corporate governance perspective.

The renowned economist Kenneth Arrow (1974: 33) defines the firm as a decision-making community: '[t]he purpose of organization is to exploit the fact that many (virtually all) decisions require the participation of many individuals for their effectiveness. In particular ... organizations are a means of achieving the benefits of collective action in situations in which the price system fails'. In addition to this view – firms exist because they make collaborative efforts and joint decision-making more effective – there are many different views of the elementary nature of the firm, ranging from the firm as being an economic entity with the lowest level of transaction costs (Demsetz, 1988; Alchian and Demsetz, 1972), a bundle of legal contracts (Jensen and Meckling, 1976), a repository of knowledge (Spender, 1996; Foss, 1996), or a site where entrepreneurial capacities can be combined (Foss and Klein, 2012). Today the firm is no longer, practically speaking, a free-standing entity but economic value is increasingly generated in networks of organizations where the boundaries between firms become porous. Davis (2013: 294) speaks about 'the postcorporate economic organization', which indicates the increased collaborative efforts in contemporary competitive capitalism. One of the consequences of this post-corporate economic organization is the decline of the *public corporation*, the large-scale stock company with relatively distributed ownership:

> Many accounts attribute the current situation to the unfettered power of large corporations. In reality, the reverse is true: our current problems of higher inequality, lower mobility, and greater economic insecurity are in large part due to the collapse of the traditional American corporation. Over the past generation, large, public traded corporations have become less concentrated, less interconnected, shorter-lived, and less prevalent: there are fewer than half as many public corporations today as there were fifteen years ago. (Davis, 2013: 284)

From a corporate governance perspective, this shift from the large-scale firm to the network-based economic organization represents a major shift in the morphology of competitive capitalism (Powell, 2001). In order to sketch the changes over time of the view of the firm, there is a need for a historical perspective on corporate governance, treating the firm as being a different vehicle for economic activities during periods of time. While the firm was initially regarded as a juridical solution taming the unregulated capitalist system and structuring it into free-standing legal entities, subject to regulation and taxation, the firm is today in the era of investor capitalism regarded in entirely different terms, being a bundle of financial assets managed to generate a cash flow benefiting its share-holders (Useem, 1996). In order to fully understand the shift in perspective and, by implication, the regulatory and managerial practices derived from this novel view, corporate governance practices must per se be understood as what is situated in a historical setting, including social, political, economic and cultural conditions and interests. Therefore, this volume will address the following issues:

- How was the firm initially incorporated in the early period of ownership or personal capitalism?
- How was corporate governance affected by the political and economic changes that promoted what is widely labelled as managerial capitalism, dominating in the 1945–70 period of time?
- How was free market advocacy and the critique of managerial malfeasance in, for example, agency theory articulated from the mid-1970s contributing to the shift in corporate governance in the 1980s and 1990s?
- In what way were corporate governance practices influenced by the deregulation and expansion of the national, regional and global finance industry beginning in the 1980s and continuing into the new millennium?

This volume examines how corporate governance is both informed by wider social, economic and political interests and objectives at the same time as corporate governance (for example, corporate law) has been a vehicle or a means to accomplish such objectives. That is, there is a recursivity between corporate governance theory and the development of the economic organization of society that needs to be untangled and subject to scholarly attention.

ECONOMIC IDEAS AND POLICY-MAKING

If there is a such a thing as an integrated economy (which is assumed here) and that the economy is an assemblage of free market activities and pricing and the legal and regulatory control of the market-based economy, then there is reason to believe that the very policy-making work is embedded in predominant economic ideas and that these economic ideas gain their impetus from a variety of economic, political and cultural conditions per se being bound up with the existing economic system. More specifically, this volume examines how the very idea of the firm as the principal vehicle for economic value creation is based on certain economic ideas.

Blyth (2002: 11) remarks that 'economic ideas' provide agents with 'interpretive frameworks' that 'describe and account for the workings of the economy by defining its constitutive elements and ... "proper" (and therefore improper) interrelations'. As a great deal of political decisions and policy-making occur in contexts where ambiguity, uncertainty and bounded rationality are the constitutive conditions of the joint work, such 'economic ideas' are in many ways taken as maps that help navigation in a territory (Simmons et al., 2008):

> Without theories of how economic, political, and social worlds work – theories that vary among groups and over time – it will not often be clear what policy options will help advance one's interests, and thus what actions one should take. These theories, moreover, are not absolute truths, but can be contingent, evolving, and the product of larger worldviews' (Berman and Pagnucco, 2010: 366)

When moving from being heuristics and aids and gradually becoming reified as doctrines and ideologies, economic ideas – regardless of their theoretical inconsistencies of lack of robust empirical substantiation – become 'blueprints of new institutions' (Blyth, 2002: 11). Expressed differently, 'economic ideas' allow agents to 'reduce uncertainty, propose a particular solution to a moment of crisis, and empower agents to resolve that crisis by constructing new institutions in line with these new ideas' (Blyth, 2002: 11). Canguilhem (1989: 380) adds that institutions are based on shared values: '[e]very social institution embodies a human interest; an institution is the codification of a value, the embodiment of value as a set of rules'. Economic ideas are therefore embedded in certain values, brought forward as rules.

Keynes (1953: 383) points out that the ideas of economists and political philosophers, regardless of their accuracy and internal consistency, are 'more powerful than is commonly understood'. In fact, Keynes contends, 'the world is ruled by little else'. Hyman Minsky (1986: 139–40), advancing the finance capitalism instability hypothesis, said that 'theory lends legitimacy to policy': '[t]he neoclassical synthesis [that is, neoclassical economic theory] put blinders on policy makers by restricting the legitimate options to manipulating government spending and taxation and operating upon the money supply'. In these accounts there is a strong performative impetus in abstract economic ideas (Svetlova, 2012; Ferraro et al., 2005; MacKenzie, 2004), in many cases having the capacity to shape policy-making regardless of their logical consistency and empirical accuracy.

CORPORATE GOVERNANCE AND THE ROLE OF ECONOMIC IDEAS

As indicated above, economic ideas do play a role in how policy-making, legislation and regulatory issues are handled. The topic of this book, the enactment of the firm during different regimes of predominant and competing economic ideas, is centred on the issue of governance and, more specifically, corporate governance. As will be discussed below, corporate governance is a key issue in all economic systems based on private ownership, while at the same time there are quite distinctively divergent views regarding how economists, economic sociologists and management scholars define corporate governance. These differences are in turn embedded in the different theoretical frameworks and methodo-logical traditions and epistemologies of the scholarly disciplines, and therefore it is complicated to once and for all reach an agreement regarding the nature and role of corporate governance.

The Neoclassical Economic Theory View

Shleifer and Vishny (1997: 737) suggest that corporate governance 'deals with the ways in which supplies of finance to corporations assure themselves of getting a return on their investment'. More specifically, such corporate governance practices to protect investments made are 'typically exercised by large investors' (Shleifer and Vishny, 1997: 739). While these are the basic lines of demarcation for corporate governance as theory and practice, Shleifer and Vishny (1997: 737) do agree that there are legal and practical difficulties involved in this work, principally derived from the difficulty involved in writing too detailed contracts that would enable efficient law enforcement: 'the contracts that the managers and investors sign cannot require too much interpretation if they are to be enforced by outside courts'. In addition, in many cases, when firms demand funding from many investors, there is a minority shareholder problem, where holders of small stocks of shares are exposed to the economic-political activities of large investors (Shleifer and Vishny, 1997: 737). This makes the corporate governance practices costly and potentially inefficient.

La Porta et al. (2000: 4) define corporate governance in similar terms, 'as a set of mechanisms through which outside investors protect themselves against expropriation by the insiders'. Again, it is the finance market investors (for example, private shareholders, mutual funds, institutional investors) and their interests and rights that are in focus in the formal definition. Curiously, La Porta et al. (2000: 4) here invoke law rather than free market efficiency as being the principal underlying resource for this enactment of the firm and corporate governance practices: '[t]he legal approach to corporate governance holds that the key mechanism is the protection of outside investors – whether shareholders or creditors – through the legal system, meaning both laws and their enforcement'. This is a theme Hermalin (2013: 734) addresses, defining corporate governance as '[t]he means by which the externalities that controlling parties generate are regulated'. In this view, again giving priority to shareholders as the key principal, 'shareholders elect the board to act on their behalf, and the board in turn monitors top management and ratifies major decisions', Hart (1995: 681) argues. This is the standard neoclassical argument, that shareholders hold contracts granting them the right to the so-called *residual cash flow* (the money generated that remains after all other costs and investments are covered) and that shareholders use the board as their vehicle to monitor top management decision-making. Still, being by and large a matter of contracting between shareholders, directors and managers, Hermalin (2013: 735) claims that 'one cannot wholly ignore the state – or at least the law – with respect to corporate governance'; the state *does play* a role, but it should preferably be minimized to merely providing rules for incorporation, leaving the contracting parties on their own to sort out their interests, rights and liabilities through contracting. Other neoclassical economic theorists are less tolerant of the influence of the state and are at pains to discredit any governmental attempts to define the rules of the game of corporate governance and accompanying monitoring and law enforcement activities. Hart (1995: 686) himself advocates what he calls 'the familiar "Chicago argument"' that proposes that the market economy can achieve better corporate governance quality if the government ceases to intervene. Using the case of the founders of the firm making the decision regarding what corporate governance practices suit their interests, Hart (1995: 686) argues that the founders can select the optimal 'mix' of corporate governance activities: '[company founders] have an incentive to choose selection procedures for the board of directors, the mix of executives and nonexecutives directors, the structure of audit and remuneration committees, disclosure rules concerning takeovers, etc. ... They therefore have the incentive to choose corporate governance rules that maximize total surplus' (Hart, 1995: 686).[2] This argument is again that the firm's principal objective is to maximize its economic value and output (its 'surplus'), which in itself is an assumption embedded in the neoclassical understanding of corporate governance practices rather than being a free-standing and legally justifiable proposition. Hart continues to draw his line of reasoning to a conclusion: '[a]ccording to the Chicago view, then, there is no need for statutory corporate governance rules. In fact statutory rules are almost certain to be counterproductive since they will limit the founders' ability to tailor corporate governance to their own individual circumstances' (Hart, 1995: 686).

The idea that mandatory corporate governance rules can be dropped altogether is a quite far-fetched conclusion, anchored in the free market advocacy that lies at the very core of the neoclassical argument. As we will see next, economic sociologists take an entirely different view of corporate governance, making it more manifold and diverse than merely defining a strict shareholder/board of directors/management relation, and locating the firm within a wider set of constituencies and interests.

The Economic Sociology View

O'Sullivan (2000) defines corporate governance accordingly:

> Corporate governance is concerned with the institutions that influence how business corporations allocate resources and returns. Specifically, *a system of corporate governance shapes and makes investment decisions in corporations, what types of investments they make, and how returns from investments are distributed.* (O'Sullivan, 2000: 1, emphasis in the original)

In this view, the perspective shifts from the finance market actors (that is, shareholders), treating the firm as a site where salaried executives potentially threaten to squander the economic value that the shareholders are legally entitled to (according to the nexus of the contracts view of the firm), to a from-within-the-firm perspective where managers are not so much the subjects of monitoring and disciplining as they are legitimate actors in the business charters, recruited by the board of directors. Moore and Rebérioux (2011: 85), speaking more broadly about the 'social sciences', say that corporate governance is '[p]rincipally an enquiry into the causes and consequences of the allocation of power within large economic organizations'. More specifically, Moore and Rebérioux (2011: 85) continue, corporate governance scholars tend to be '[p]rimarily concerned with "public" or listed corporate entities, whose securities are traded on regulated liquid investment markets', and which therefore exhibit the '[i]nstitutional characteristic known popularly as "the separation of ownership and control"'. Here, corporate governance is a 'system' of activities and practices that ensure good decision quality, but that also handles the question of how what Hart (1995) calls the 'surplus' should preferably be allocated. In the neoclassical argument, it is beyond doubt the shareholders that should receive the residual cash flow, but within the economic sociology model of corporate governance, the firm needs, in order to remain competitive and to ensure its long-term survival, to pay attention not only to one group of principals (that is, the shareholders) and recognize a wider set of stakeholders. This is an essentially *sociological view*, thinking of the firm as an incorporated business in the first place instituted within society, not only an 'economic engine' but also a site of other societal benefits, including, for example, employment and a long-term commitment to innovation and economic renewal. As O'Sullivan (2000) makes clear, for economists trained in the neoclassical tradition (as the bulk of the leading economists are), such an argument violates the free market efficiency proposition and the primacy of economic efficiency, suggesting that (1) markets are by definition more effective in generating and allocating economic resources than other comparable mechanisms, and (2) the firm's principal (some would say the only) role is to create economic value. In this view, economists would retort, the sociological view of corporate governance adds unnecessary complications to the definition and therefore prevents a meaningful view of what corporate governance is, thereby blocking the firm from making what it is best fit to accomplish, namely to create economic value. Such critiques still miss the mark, as economic sociologists do not share the belief in the benefits of the free market, nor do they think the firm is solely incorporated to create wealth for only one constituency, the owners of stock.

Practically speaking, for economic sociologists, the corporate governance system is not one single law or model but is instead a practice based upon a patchwork of legal texts, regulations, political solutions and agreements, all adding bits and pieces to the legal environment (discussed in more detail in the next chapter) wherein the firm can fulfil some of its social and economic roles. As the so-called *varieties of capitalism* literature suggests (for example, Hall and Thelen, 2009; Allen, 2004; Dore et al., 1999), there are many different governance systems in different regions and countries that have their own benefits and shortcomings, but there seems to be an agreement today that there is 'no one best way' to structure a corporate governance system (Fligstein and Choo, 2005). Fligstein and Choo (2005: 63) define three distinct elements of the corporate governance system, including: (1) *corporate law*, which 'defines the legal vehicles by which property rights are organized'; (2) *financial market regulation* that sets the rules for how firms can obtain finance capital for their operations, leading to a legal-regulatory system that defines the relations between firms, banks, financial institutions and 'public equity and debt markets'; (3) *labour law* that 'defines how labour contracts will operate in a particular society'. For free market advocates, much of the work done in these three domains involves activities that impose additional costs and sources of inefficiency on the firm, and therefore, for example, labour law is a deviation from the individual–firm contract that would better, free marketeers claim, define the particular relations between specific parties. This is again the free market argument that economic sociologists are not willing to subscribe to, and they evade such criticism by citing the empirical studies that show that countries and regions with, for example, a high degree of labour market regulation, are in fact demonstrating a more stable and solid economic growth than countries with a lower degree of labour protection (Sarkar, 2013: 1345). Neoclassicists in response tend to treat such evidence as being unreliable and at best anecdotal or a temporary condition, and therefore it is difficult to reconcile the two views of the role of the firm and the nature of corporate governance.

The Management Studies View

A third view of corporate governance that can possibly be said to stand midway between the viewpoints of neoclassicists and economic sociologists is that held by management scholars, who tend to subscribe to a behavioural theory of the firm view in the Herbert Simon tradition (Cyert and March, 1963; March and Simon, 1958; Simon, 1947). In contrast to economic sociologists, management scholars do not think that the claim of shareholders' enrichment is of necessity illegitimate, but they are apt to stress the risks and unintended consequences of managerial opportunism and inefficiencies that derive from corporate governance practice benefiting shareholder welfare. In addition, management scholars do not share the proposition that the market a priori is capable of effectively measuring and thus monitoring managerial efficiency, nor the idea of the central proposition in agency theory that managers act opportunistically in predictable ways. In other words, management scholars share some of the worries and concerns regarding the efficiency of corporate governance and managerial discretion, but they tend to arrive at different conclusions and policy recommendations. Above all, efficiency in corporate governance is a human accomplishment, not a benefit derived from free markets being some ultimate processor of information and the pricing of commodities and human resources, including professional managerial skills.

'[C]orporate governance designates the legal and factual framework for managing and supervising the corporation', Werder (2011: 1346) writes. Based on this definition, Werder (2011: 1347) defines corporations as '[a] network of actors (or stakeholders) that are characterized by specific opportunism option and opportunism risk profiles'. Hambrick et al. (2008: 384) define corporate governance broadly as '[t]he structures and processes by which an organization's assets and activities are overseen'. Like many other management scholars do, Hambrick et al. (2008) stress that the extant literature 'typically viewed governance as a principal–actor problem between shareholders and management' (see, for example, Sundaramurthy and Lewis, 2003). 'The overwhelming emphasis in governance research has been on the efficacy of the various mechanisms available to protect shareholders from self-interested whims of executives', Daily et al. (2003: 371) suggest. Still, management scholars tend to side with economic sociologists in making the assumption that corporate governance should preferably include more relationships and connections than merely that between the shareholders and the board of directors and management. In fact, Werder (2011) defines a number of stakeholders including suppliers, clients, employees and the wider public that all should be considered in the governance work. Based on this stakeholder theory of the firm, Werder (2011: 1353) suggests that one of the functions of corporate governance is to reduce the influence of what Werder refers to as *stakeholder opportunism*:

> [T]he main managerial implication of the notion of stakeholder opportunism is that management also has to consider the potential options and risk of opportunistic behavior that all stakeholders face … [m]anagement also has to consider that – in a way, as specific kinds of objectives – stakeholders are also interested in not being expropriated by other stakeholders' opportunism.

For management scholars, shareholders are one important constituent of the firm, but they are not the stakeholder given the authority to dictate corporate governance practices singlehandedly.

Kogut (2012: 8) argues that governance can be separated into two distinct, yet related sets: one set of practices such as the election of independent directors on the board of directors, and one set of institutions 'constituting the social and political system'. These institutions define and dictate the rules for governance but they are still always loosely coupled with governance practices; thus systems and practices are 'surely though imperfectly connected', Kogut (2012: 8) contends.

This view of corporate governance is not entirely different from, for example, Feldman and Pentland's (2003) view of organization routines as being composed of an *ostensive* (prescribed routines) and a *performative* component (routines as they unfold as a series of practices). However, these two 'sets' (in Kogut's term) are never perfectly matched; there is always a deviation between the map and the territory. Expressed differently, for adherents to the behavioural theory of the firm, the deviation between the ostensive and performative components of corporate governance is nothing surprising or uncommon. It is rather the rule in organizational settings, riddled with ambiguities and inconsistencies, while for neoclassical economic theorists, following a more strictly rational choice theory model that is less tolerant of such inconsistencies, the inability or unwillingness to follow rules is frequently understood as the outcome of either poor legislation or poor managerial skills and competencies. So what the neoclassical economic theorists regard as an act of incompetence on the part of policy-makers, regulators or managers is treated more leniently by management scholars, paying attention to a wider set of issues and concerns that the practising manager needs to handle (Werder, 2011). In other words, the neoclassical corporate governance model renders the scope of the activities a unidirectional relation between shareholders and managers and applies a smaller set of performance measures to assess the efficiency in goal fulfilment, but the proponents of this governance model are consequently also more prone to pass judgement regarding the adequacy and efficiency of the performative aspect of corporate governance.

In an attempt to renew the research agenda and to discard the neoclassical shareholder welfare doctrine, Hambrick et al. (2008: 384–5) suggest that researchers should examine *why* governance arrangements look the way they do, and explore *how* governance arrangements affect managerial and corporate outcomes. That is, rather than being stuck with the assumption that corporate governance is by and large operating in the shadow of endemic managerial malfeasance, there is a need for a renewal of how corporate governance is studied. In this volume, corporate governance is one field of research that is part of a wider theoretical debate, that of the nature of the firm and what economic ends the firm serves. In order to understand fully how the firm has shifted from being understood more or less as a socially embedded institution, being a vehicle for many social and economic activities and interests in the era of managerial capitalism, to become reduced to being understood as a bundle of financial assets in the era of the present regime of investor capitalism, there is a need to understand legal and regulatory traditions pertaining to the incorporation of businesses within the realm of the state.

Such an understanding needs to recognize the role of political and ideological mobilization, and the practical work to govern and manage organizations within the specific conditions of the focal firm, differing greatly among various industries. In brief, the enactment of the firm is thus not strictly a matter of corporate governance theory, nor the political mobilization to criticize, for example, collectivist tendencies in the economy, nor only enacted through the performances of practising managers, but is instead the outcome of all these joint activities. In this volume, the enactment of the firm will be examined on the basis of such an analytical framework.

OUTLINE OF THE BOOK

This volume examines how the corporate system and the theory of the firm (to use the neoclassical economic theory parlance) has been re-defined and altered under the influence of free market advocacy. The foremost consequence of this shift from a legal-political view of the firm, dominating in the regime of managerial capitalism, to the economic definition of the firm is the change in corporate governance practices in the new regime of investor capitalism and more specifically its trade-mark, the fortification of shareholder welfare as the conventional wisdom regarding what firms should strive to accomplish. This narrative under-lines the 'ideational struggle' between neoclassical economic theory, legal theory and legislative practice (court rulings and so on), and management theory. This struggle does not, however, take place in a social vacuum, but is strongly influenced by various financiers participat-ing in and funding intellectual work (for the want of a better word), political initiatives and doctrines, the work of lobbyists and interest groups, and, ultimately, the ups and downs in the economic cycle, that is, present macroeconomic conditions.

This story is structured into four chapters and one epilogue. In Chapter 1, the legal system enabling the incorporation of a business within the realm of the state, being developed in the latter half of the nineteenth century but having roots stretching back to the medieval period, is discussed. In addition, Chapter 1 addresses how the 1930s' New Deal politico-economic programme to restore the faith in the economic system of capitalism included reforms of this corporate law system and thus implemented new legislation and regulatory oversight pertaining to, for example, the finance industry. In Chapter 2, the focus shifts from the New Deal programme per se to the emerging free market advocacy, focused on the 'efficiency' of the economy and individual enterprising initiatives rather than the economic and social stability that the New Dealers promoted. In the eyes of the forming community of free market protagonists, led by the economist and political writer Friedrich von Hayek, the fears of 'collectivism', understood as virtually all forms of state interventions into supposedly efficient and self-regulating markets – the supreme pricing mechanism, according to Hayek and his followers – was a broad, yet unifying description of an accurate and pressing problem. Despite consolidating intellectual and financial capital in the joint cause, the post-World War II period was a disappointment for the free market protagonists as their declarations regarding the evils of collectivism sharply contrasted against the strong economic growth, the reduction of economic inequality, the development of welfare state provisions, and the political stability of the period, anchored in a steadfast monitoring state apparatus and the efficacy of the Keynesian economic theory dominating the economic policy. For the free market protagonists, the post-World War II period was the long march up to the mid-1970s period where they were once again given the chance to speak about collectivism as a threat to the 'economic freedom' they cherished.

Chapter 3 discusses the 1970s' economic and political turmoil (especially in the US) leading to the mobilization of the pro-business community to finance academic researchers and think-tank pundits to develop novel theoretical descriptions of the firm. In this new period of time, when the previously robust Keynesian economic theory seemed unable to explain emerging economic conditions, nor was it able to provide any guidance for how to deal with the new economic situation, neoclassical economic theory was used to advance the idea, inherited from the New Dealer Adolf A. Berle but somewhat modified to suit their interests, that the firm should be understood as a 'legal fiction' and as 'a bundle of contracts', and that it was the shareholders ('the principals' in the new vocabulary) that legitimately claim the so-called residual cash flow generated by the firm. As examined in detail in Chapter 3, this agency theory prescription is not consistent with corporate law, nor does it recognize the difficulties involved in acquiring and coordinating the production factors needed to generate economic value. Agency theory and the idea of shareholder primacy is thus based on wishful thinking (contrasting corporate law and the factual evidence of court rulings) and a gross idealization of the virtues and capacities of market-based control and a miscalculation of the costs of acquiring production factors in the market and coordinating the uses of such resources (in relationship to management theory). This leaves us with a theoretical prescription that singlehandedly favours one corporate constituency, that of capital owners qua shareholders. At the same time, the theoretical consistency and empirical evidence supporting the efficacy of this prescribed corporate governance model remain unsatisfying. Fortunately, for free market protagonists (assuming that the regime of shareholder primacy is the closest one can get in terms of 'pure market based control and pricing'), robust empirical evidence and logical consistency are desirable but not mandatory features when making a theory practically useful as long as there are influential groups that benefit from the consequences of such faulty yet operative prescriptions or if emerging economic conditions call for novel theories and models. In the case of agency theory and its shareholder primacy, capital owners and the new pro-business political leadership in Washington and Downing Street jointly picked up the ideas and actively contributed to the advancement of the new regime of investor capitalism, rendering, for example, managers as a class of subcontractors serving the interests of the finance industry.

In Chapter 4 the more recent (that is, in the new millennium) scholarly discussions regarding corporate governance are examined. This reiterates that the nexus of the contract view of the firm underlying agency theory is inconsistent with existing corporate law, making the idea of shareholder welfare an ideological statement regarding capital owners' alleged rights and privileges rather than a proposition grounded in legal theory and court ruling. In the second half of the chapter, the long-term consequences of the new corporate governance practices in combination with other free market reforms are examined. Contrary to what, for example, Friedrich von Hayek predicted in the 1930s and 1940s, the free market and its 'economic freedom' has led to lower economic growth, higher unemployment, a lower degree of investment in R&D, increased economic inequality (not of necessity an undesirable outcome for free market protagonists, though), and a shortage of venture capital to finance entrepreneurial activities in the economy (whereof the bulk of the capital is still provided by the state – the *bête noire* of free market protagonists (Mirowski, 2011; Mowery, 2009). The sheer growth of the finance industry indicates that capital owners, entering emerging industries primarily when most of the risks are discounted (Roy, 1997), have reinvested their return on capital in the finance industry rather than in production capital and human resources. If these are the principal and long-term features of 'economic freedom', free market protagonists are facing a challenge in convincing the majority of the population in advanced, (post)industrialized and democratic economies that they should put their faith in the virtues of this regime of economic freedom.

In the Epilogue, the ideology of neoclassical economic theory is addressed against the background of the material presented in this volume. Unlike other scholarly disciplines, economists have fortified a unified theoretical framework and have erected a barrier against adjacent disciplines to effectively exclude research findings in, for example, management studies, legal theory, the behavioural sciences and economic sociology, all adding to the understanding of the complexity of economic systems and their entities. The consequence is an insular and in many ways cloistered discipline that favours deductive reasoning, mathematical formalism and parsimonious theories at the expense of predictive capacities (the pièce de résistance these days is the failure of economists to anticipate the 2008 finance industry meltdown). Using Karl Mannheim's (1936) distinction between *utopian ideas* and *ideologies*, wherein the former term denotes ideas and reform programmes that benefit socially subordinate groups (for example, salaried workers) and the latter term denotes ideas and reforms that operate in the interests of socially dominant groups, the Epilogue argues that the neoclassical economic theory that served to overturn managerial capitalism is thoroughly ideological. Economists would naturally shun such ideas, speaking of the solid methods used (frequently quantitative) and their system for peer-review to certify ideas and theories. However, in the case of, for example, agency theory there is little evidence of any critical self-correction – a principal mark of scientific inquiry – in the face of emerging evidence or at least a recognition of even the most elementary legal strictures or empirical research findings in management studies being relevant to the arguments advanced. That is, rather than being a scientific theory, agency theory is an engineered conceptual apparatus developed to instrumentally justify and prescribe how the economic value generated in corporations should accrue to one single corporate constituency (capital owners) rather than many (for example, co-workers, clients, subcontractors, the wider society). In the words of Mannheim, agency theory is not a scientific theory but an ideological prescription of how certain groups wish the world would be if they had the authority to dictate its operative rules. Speaking *ex cathedra* (and, let us remember, backed by wealthy financiers), agency theorists, despite the conspicuous fragility of their theoretical model, were in fact granted such privileges, at least for a period of time. We are now in the position of being able to oversee the long-term consequences of such privileges.

NOTES

1. Downer (2011: 748) argues that engineers have understood that they cannot 'perfectly deduce technological performance from models, algorithms, and blueprints', and therefore they rely on a combination of experimental data and data collected from 'real world events' (for example, car crashes, failing bridges and other engineered artefacts ceasing to function

as predicted) to better adjust their predictive capacities and their design of the artefacts (see also Harvey and Knox, 2010; Vinck, 2003). Some of the tools engineers employ in their work are forms of standardization and the reproducibility of experiments, but both these tools are useful only when they are stripped of data from 'extraneous variables' so the engineer's vision can be narrowed to a few key variables. This procedure, in turn, may include the elimination of relevant phenomena within what is under investigation, making the data potentially misleading or even faulty (Downer, 2007: 18). Therefore, technology is not so much about 'universality' as it is about being able to construct functional technologies that work in 'concrete, complex situations' (Brian Wynne, 1988, cited in Downer, 2007: 20. See also Simakova, 2010; Smith, 2009, on the predicament of potential failure, always accompanying engineers and product designers). This means that the work of engineers (and scientists too, operating on the basis of 'engineered nature' created in the laboratory setting; see, for example, Rheinberger, 1997; Lynch, 1985; Knorr Cetina, 1981; Latour and Woolgar, 1979) is 'not so much a matter of *interrogating* the world as *calibrating* it' (Downer, 2007: 21, emphasis in original). The consequence is that engineers learn that they need to make a 'subjective judgment' about which data that is of relevance for their pursuits (Downer, 2011: 748; Petroski, 1996).

In analogy, studies of economic theory and finance markets instruments such as algorithms suggest that economic theory too has performative capacities (MacKenzie et al., 2007; MacKenzie, 2006; 2004; MacKenzie and Millo, 2003) and that the tools and resources used by finance traders are based on the ability to calibrate (using Downer's, 2007, term) the value of financial assets within the pricing mechanism of the continuously fluxing and volatile global finance markets (MacKenzie and Spears, 2014a, 2014b; Beunza and Stark, 2004). Moreover, finance traders, using models and algorithms derived from finance theory (here assumed to be the most practically oriented and most immediately verifiable of all neoclassical economic theory provisions) rely, just like engineers in Downer's (2011) account, on subjective judgement (for example, Chong and Tuckett, 2015; Zaloom, 2006; 2003). Taken together, therefore, the engineering method to calculate and predict outcomes on basis of models, algorithms and subjective judgement, and to continually include emerging information into the assemblage of resources in use, is also of relevance for the economists' work. This does not in any way undermine the authority of economic theorizing as a social and scientific practice, but it poses a sceptical view of the deductive reasoning on the basis of axiomatic principles that characterize, for example, agency theory. An economic theory devoid of critical self-correcting mechanisms, capable of accommodating emerging data (also from outside the core discipline) becomes stale and useless over time, stuck in inherited doctrines and dogma. Such a theoretical framework will fail to provide guidelines and recommendations that work in 'concrete, complex situations' in predictable ways.

2.   In Hart's account (1995), the founder of the firm is given considerable decision-making authority, but in corporate law and in most cases, it is the board of directors who are granted the authority to conduct business decisions, including the selection of the CEO and other top executives, to set their compensation arrangements, and to monitor firm strategies and performance. The board of directors have the right to replace the CEO and other executives if necessary and to respond to, for example, acquisition offers, also here operating with '[t]he full right to accept or reject executives' recommendations' (Bebchuk, 2007: 680).

PART I

Instituting the firm

1. Corporate law and the legal environment of the firm

INTRODUCTION

'Society is produced by our wants, and government is produced by our wickedness; the former promotes our happiness *positively* by uniting our affections, the latter *negatively* by restraining our vices. The first is a patron, the last a punisher', Thomas Paine (1995: 5, emphasis in original) writes in his influential pamphlet *Common Sense*, published in 1775–76. In his *Two Treatises of Government* (first published in 1690), another foundational work for the liberal, modern society, John Locke emphasized that law making is ultimately based on 'the public good':

> Political power, then, I take to be a right of making laws with penalties of death, and consequently all less penalties, for the regulating and preserving of property, and of employing the force of the community, in the execution of such laws, and in the defence of the commonwealth from foreign inquiry; and all this only for the public good. (Locke, [1690] 2003: 10; Book II, §3)

In these liberal treatises, man is a creature capable of both creation and destruction, and therefore society needs to be built on constitutional rights and legislation that effectively combine liberating and controlling features, yet obey the principle of common good. Following Mannheim's (1986) argument, Paine's position is exemplary of a liberal view, locating law at the centre of the constitutional rights that are capable of protecting the individual from the sovereign or other actors granted legislative powers. In contrast, Mannheim (1986: 56) says, conservatism is based on what he calls *mythical transcendence*, the reliance on notions such as 'the nation', 'the monarchy', 'the people', or – in our case – 'the market' as being what can serve as a warrant for individuals' rights and well-being. 'Liberal theory is based on the mentality of the Eighteenth-century Enlightenment, while conservative theory rests primarily on romanticism', Mannheim (1986: 55) suggests. While conservatives are prone to justifying beliefs and practices on the basis of abstract (mythical, in Mannheim's parlance) terms, 'liberal-bourgeois thought' sets the problem of liberty and well-being 'predominantly upon a juristic plane, specifically in conjunction with natural law', Mannheim (1986: 56) argues: '[t]he *legitimacy of a form of rule* is justified by means of purely ideological constructions, which generate the meanings required, always at *the juristic level of validity* (social contract)' (emphasis in original). One of the earliest accounts of such a legalistic view of constitutional rights is Spinoza's ambition to separate religious doctrines from the wider social contract, today widely recognized as a key constitutional feature (the right of 'religious freedom') but being nothing short of heresy even in the liberal and culturally sophisticated seventeenth-century Amsterdam. Says Spinoza (2009: 195): '[i]f men were naturally bound by the Divine law and right, or if the Divine law and right were a natural necessity, there would have been no need for God to make a covenant with mankind, and to bind them thereto with an oath and agreement'. While this distinction between the mythical transcendence of conservatism and the legalistic orientation of 'liberal-bourgeois thought' may appear as an archetypal procedure of academic hair-splitting, it is in fact of relevance for the forthcoming discussion, as corporate governance is widely understood as what is embedded in either the rule of law or the rule of the market, or, in most cases, a combination thereof.

As the economy, the totality of economic value creation and distribution activities, is a central element of any advanced and differentiated society, Thomas Paine's (1995) proposition regarding government is applicable also in economic organization, by definition outside of political and regulatory bodies. Institutional economic theory in particular emphasizes the role of legal, regulatory and law-enforcing agencies that monitor and thus shape economic life. Douglass North (1991: 97) defines institutions as 'the humanly devised constraints that structure political, economic, and social interaction. They consist of both informal constraints (sanctions, taboos, customs, traditions, and codes of conduct), and formal rules (constitutions, laws, property rights)'. In North's neoclassical view of institutions, their primary role is to 'reduce transactions and production costs per exchange' so that trade can be realizable. That is, institutions' role is to secure operative economic relations (for example, markets) that better exploit differences in production factor costs and the benefits of division of labour. In North's (1991: 98) view, institutions include both political and economic institutions. Ultimately, the value and *raison d'être* of these institutions is derived from their ability to lubricate the economy and to promote the production of economic value and growth. More specifically, North (1991: 105) lists three types of institutional innovations: (1) 'those that increased the mobility of capital', (2) 'those that lowered information costs', and (3) 'those that spread risks'. In practical terms, such institutional innovations include, for example, forms of market creation, the establishment of regulatory control that prevents and punishes opportunistic behaviour, and activities that increase the supply of financed capital.

Neoclassical economic theory is generally speaking uneasy when it comes to the role of regulatory agencies. As unregulated markets are *ex hypothesi* the most efficient way to process information, to discount risks, and to price commodities and services, any regulatory initiative is suspiciously treated as an unnecessary complication and the presence of polity within strict economic undertakings. As a consequence, much research on institution-building is located in disciplines such as economic history, political science and economic sociology, more receptive to the idea of the need for monitoring markets and assuming that markets are not naturally occurring phenomena but human accomplishments. In other words, much research is directed towards understanding how policy-making (as a form of institution-building in North's use of the term) is structured in accordance with certain norms and beliefs. Campbell (2002) here introduces the term *cognitive parading* in policy-making work, being defined as '[t]aken-for-granted descriptions and theoretical analyses that specify cause and effect relationships, that reside in the background of policy debates and that limit the range of alternatives policy makers are likely to perceive as useful' (Campbell, 2002: 22). In addition, Campbell (2002: 27) speaks more narrowly about *frames* in policy-making, being '[n]ormative and sometimes cognitive ideas that are located in the foreground of policy debates'. In a similar vocabulary, Schmidt (2008: 306) emphasizes the role of *cognitive ideas* in policy-making, being certain dominant ideas that 'provide the recipes, guidelines and map for political action and serve to justify policies and programs by speaking to their interest-based logic and necessity'. In addition to the cognitive ideas, Schmidt (2008: 307) suggests that *normative ideas* also shape the policy-making work: '[n]ormative ideas instead attach values to political action and serve to legitimate the policies in a program through references to their appropriateness'. Such concepts underline how policy-making is an ongoing process of creating meaningful scenarios for how policies can influence and shape, for example, economic activities in ways that are desirable for the policy-makers and their constituencies (for example, voters). Campbell (2002: 30) portrays the policy-makers as *epistemic communities* being 'networks of professionals and experts with an authoritative claim to policy-relevant knowledge, who share a set of normative beliefs, causal models, notions of empirical validity, and a common policy enterprise'. While such an epistemic community is likely, like any other professional community (for example, scientists, professional musicians), to become a self-regulating social world unto itself, policy-making is exposed to detailed media attention that, at least in theory, makes them responsive to public opinions and wider social interest. 'In order for their policy programs to be adopted, political elites strategically craft frames and use them to legitimize their policies to the public and each other', Campbell (2002: 27) writes.

Studies of policy-making and policy-enforcing organizations such as the IMF, the World Trade Organization (WTO), the World Bank and central banks reveal that the work in these organizations is a complex, politicized and in many ways slow process to align heterogeneous interest and objectives (Fernández-Albertos, 2015; Chwieroth, 2010; Conti, 2010; Chorev and Babb, 2009; Griffin, 2009; Neu et al., 2006). In many cases policy-making unfolds on the basis of predominant frames and cognitive and normative ideas, political as well as economic, but they are fundamentally moulded by emergent political interests of member organizations (for example, nation states). This makes policy-making on the international level a time-consuming and in many ways tedious process that provides a test of the tenacity of the participants. In some cases, the political inertia of such organizations is treated as evidence of an innate inefficiency of these organizations, but the slowness of the advancement of regulatory frameworks should probably not be interpreted as an indication of regulatory value.

One specific form of institution in competitive capitalism is the corporate charter, the incorporation of businesses (originally) within the realm of the state as a principal vehicle for economic activities. Corporate law is one of the most central juridical–political innovations in the institutional framework of competitive capitalism and yet, as will be demonstrated in this volume, economic theory in many ways ignores or diminishes the influence of corporate law as being one of the fundamental innovations in the capitalist economy. Once instituted, many legal–juridical innovations become infrastructural, that is, they are ignored 'as long as they work', and there is thus the risk of making a category mistake (using Gilbert Ryle's apt term) when assuming that free market capitalism is a naturally occurring economic condition while in fact it is buttressed by a variety of legal framework and regulatory procedures. This fallacy of treating efficient markets not so much as human accomplishments but as some original, primordial natural state will be subject to critical analysis in this volume.

DEVELOPING BUSINESS CHARTERS AND CORPORATE LAW

The rise of the 'corporate organizational form', Kaufman (2008: 402) argues, has long been regarded as 'one of the defining innovations of the modern era'. The 'corporate system' (Eisenberg, 1989: 1523) in turn relies on the enactment of corporate legislation and the possibility to incorporate businesses, a legal innovation that was one of the major institutional innovations of the eighteenth and nineteenth centuries. These business charters instituted by corporate law and granted by the legislators offered a number of benefits for the promoters: '[c]orporate assets are legally protected from both shareholders and creditors in many cases, thus creating a legal shield between corporate actors and corporate responsibilities. In the contemporary context, corporate assets are also subject to different taxation and regulation schemes than unincorporated businesses' (Kaufman, 2008: 403).

If nothing else, the sheer growth in numbers of business charters in the American states that passed corporate laws testifies to their usefulness for entrepreneurs and promoters. By the year 1800, 'only 335 charters had been issued in the United States for business corporations'; by 1890, there were 'nearly 500,000 business corporations' (Blair, 2003: 389, footnote 3). In addition to empirical evidence, Kaufman (2008: 405) suggests that the history of incorporation and corporate law is '[k]ey to understanding the relationship between the state and the public and private spheres'. That is, corporate law (and other relevant legislation) serves to define and establish boundaries between the rights of the state and the rights of the individual in quite specific ways.

The history of corporate law thus needs to be examined in detail to render latter-day debates regarding trust versus market control in the corporate governance literature meaningful. Siding with a number of prominent legal theorists and economic historians, Kaufman (2008) argues that corporate law has medieval roots and that the very concept of *the corporation* is a relatively recent complement to a wider socio-economic governance problem of how to legitimize and monitor business ventures. In fact, in the early period of incorporation, most of the business charters were not given to corporations but to a diverse set of organizations:

> The legal structure of the modern corporate form derives from efforts in medieval Europe to grant legal autonomy to universities, towns, and ecclesiastical institutions. Trade guilds and commercial monopolies were also

granted corporate status in special circumstances. Even the earliest corporations thus represent the delegation of state authority to subsidiary entities, a form of power-sharing that raised questions about the extent and limit of the powers of both the incorporator and the incorporated. (Kaufman, 2008: 403)

In post-revolutionary America, the new republic now hosted a number of organizations (including the President and Fellows of Harvard College, the oldest business charter on the continent, dated to 1650, 14 years after its inception) that had been granted business charters under English law. After 1776, the individual states strategically employed business charters to constitute themselves as autonomous, sovereign legislators separated from the federal state. But again, just as in the case of Europe, '[t]he majority of private corporations chartered between 1780 and 1810 were not business concerns at all; they were churches, townships, schools, and voluntary organizations' (Kaufman, 2008: 404). In fact, of the incorporations registered in Massachusetts (the leading state in terms of the nominal number of incorporations and with the oldest corporate legislation – Rhode Island had more incorporations per capita measured in terms of 'white males') during the period 1791–1800, only 4 per cent were 'non-infrastructure businesses' (while 24 per cent of all business charters were granted to 'infrastructure companies'). Handlin and Handlin (1945) stress that corporations were originally regarded as a government agency, serving the public interest:

> At its origin in Massachusetts the corporation was conceived as an agency of government, endowed with public attributes, exclusive privileges, and political power, and designed to serve a social function for the state. Turnpikes, not trade, banks, not land speculation, were its province because the community, not the enterprising capitalists, marked out its sphere of activity. (Handlin and Handlin, 1945: 22)

In addition to the relatively minor role of companies in the legislative practices and law making, the 'institutional success' of corporate law was not, Lamoreaux (2009: 17) argues, immediately secured as the federal parliament and thereafter the state courts were prone to use business legislation as a political resource: '[a]fter the American Revolution, responsibility for chartering corporations had devolved on the various state legislatures. These bodies initially assumed that they had powers akin to those of Parliament to alter or revoke charters, and they did not hesitate to meddle in corporate affairs'. A decisive change came about in 1819, finally separating business charters from the state legislatures, when the US Supreme Court ruled in favour of the Dartmouth College trustees who had filed a lawsuit challenging an act of the New Hampshire legislature. Writing for the Court, Chief Justice John Marshall declared that state legislatures '[d]id not inherit Parliament's boundless powers over corporations but, rather, had to acknowledge the superior authority of the Constitution' (Lamoreaux, 2009: 18). From now on, business charters were protected by the federal constitution, widely interpreted as a Supreme Court decision favouring market-based control of incorporated business ventures:

> Over time, state and federal courts not only upheld the notion of freedom of incorporation but also began to defend the sanctity of the private corporation from state interference ... Arguably, judges expanded their conception of the public good to embrace America's increasingly brisk economy. Private gain was heralded as a key component of the public good, a rationalization that would subsequently come to undergird all American political-economic policy. (Kaufman, 2008: 419)

Taken together, Kaufman (2008) argues, it would be inadequate to think of corporate law as what was initially developed to maximize efficiency and transparency in business ventures. Instead, Kaufman (2008: 406) argues, '[n]ew legal doctrines form without conscious design but are instead post hoc responses to social and legal conditions that change and cumulate over time'. The common law, within which corporate legislation was originally enacted, rendered the corporation as '[a] relatively undifferentiated organizational form' that could be used for a variety of purposes (Kaufman, 2008: 420). It is therefore historically inconsistent to project today's corporate system and legislation onto the legal statutes of the earliest corporate laws. Corporate law is frequently the outcome of reactive responses to emerging problems leading to court ruling; the responsiveness and agility of the legal system is thus a better explanatory factor when it comes to understanding the statutes of corporate law than to adhere to a rationalist credo assuming that corporate law is formulated under the favourable conditions of certainty and the capacity to anticipate latter-day governance problems. 'Courts and legislatures have not always been consistent in their vision of the American private corporation, but the long-term trend has been toward greater corporate autonomy, except in cases where the openness of markets is at stake', Kaufman (2008: 421) summarizes.

THE ROLE OF CORPORATE LAW

In many cases, there is a confusion regarding the corporate law and economic theories of the firm more broadly in the literature. While economists tend to think of the firm as a vehicle for economic value creation and economic value extraction within the domain of the market economy, legal scholars generally take a wider and more socially embedded view of the firm. Legal scholars treat the firm as a legal entity being incorporated within the social organization to benefit wider social and political objectives rather than merely providing a more narrow range of benefits including, for example, shareholder value creation. Bratton (1989a: 1471), a legal scholar, stresses that for economists, the firm 'is a legal fiction that serves as a nexus of contractual relationships among individual factors of production'. This view, where the firm is understood as a black box that transforms input production factors to output goods and services, is addressed by Bratton (1989a: 1472) as the 'contractual view of the firm'. As will be discussed in more detail in Chapters 2 to 4 in this volume, contractual theory of the firm represents one quite specific legal tradition that is not always of necessity compatible with the claims made by, for example, agency theorists. In contrast to the contractual view, legal theory assumes that the firm is more than a bundle of contracts; instead, the corporation is granted rights from the state and should therefore be seen in a wider socio-political and economic context than the contract view implies (Bratton, 1989a: 1475). Kaufman and Zacharias (1992) argue that the difference between the contractual view of the corporation and the semi-professional view of management based on fiduciary duties in corporate law represents a deep-seated concern regarding autonomy and accountability in American society: 'American and legal theorists have looked at the market, liberty's principal arena, for an important supplement to democratic rule. By delineating the private from the public sphere, the market allegedly created a social space in which individuals could determine their life stories from public or government influence' (Kaufman and Zacharias, 1992: 524).

Even after World War II, in the era of managerial capitalism and where the efficiency of large firms and management's technical competence were evident to most commentators, these anxieties regarding the privileges and discretion of managerial elites persisted. The legitimation crisis of the professionally managed corporation was cushioned by corporate law, capable of 'reconciling management's dictatorial control with the nation's constitutional ideals' (Kaufman and Zacharias, 1992: 528), and corporate law provided a vocabulary for articulating management as a profession. More specifically, this vocabulary '[c]ame largely from fiduciary doctrines that held the responsibilities of trustees to be morally more arduous than conventional market relationships' (Kaufman and Zacharias, 1992: 528). That is, corporate law endowed professional managers with fiduciary duties and discretion that by and large protected them from market-based evaluations.

Eisenberg (1989) stresses that, in practice, the corporation is governed on the basis of a combination of legal rules and rules derived from market conditions:

> A corporation is a profit-seeking enterprise of persons and assets organized by rules. Most of these rules are determined by the unilateral action of corporate organs or officials. Some of these rules are determined by market forces. Some are determined by contract or other forms of agreement. Some are determined by law. (Eisenberg, 1989: 1461)

Eisenberg (1989) here distinguishes three basic categories of rules: (1) *enabling rules*, which 'give legal effect to rules that corporate actors adopt in a specific manner'; (2) *suppletory* or *default rules*, which 'govern defined issues unless corporate actors adopt other rules in specific manner'; and (3) *mandatory rules*, which 'govern defined issues in a manner that cannot be varied by corporate actors' (Eisenberg, 1989: 1461). In addition, in the practical day-to-day work in corporations, Eisenberg (1989) argues, it is useful to distinguish between (1) *structural rules*, which 'govern the allocation of decisionmaking power among various corporate organs and agents'; (2) *distribution rules*, which 'govern the distribution of assets (including earnings) to shareholders'; and (3) *fiduciary rules*, which 'govern the duties of managers and controlling shareholders' (Eisenberg, 1989: 1462). When speaking about corporate law, it is thus important to keep in mind that some rules are mandatory, not open to negotiations, while other governance rules rely on the managers' and directors' ability to adopt rules that best fit the intentions of the legislators to promote business venturing. Taken together, corporate law is a non-trivial domain of jurisdictional expertise that cannot easily be understood on the basis of, for example, economic theory frameworks or, more generally, preferences regarding alleged efficient governance principles.

Eisenberg (1989) notes that corporate law can be applied somewhat differently in the three cases of (1) closely held corporations, having few shareholders frequently being directly involved in the management of the firm; (2) publicly held corporations, for example, listed companies with widely dispersed ownership; and (3) firms that are to be introduced to the stock market through IPOs (Initial Public Offerings) (Eisenberg, 1989: 1463). Despite these differences, the corporate law system is in all three cases based on the same principles of the corporate system that have been established over time in the American society and the legal system, Eisenberg argues (1989):

> The American economy is a corporate system, in the sense that control of the economic factors of production and distribution is vested largely in the hands of privately appointed corporate managers. This system is legitimated on three major bases. The first is the belief that the shareholders, as the owners of the corporations, have the ultimate right to control it. The second is the belief that corporate managers are accountable for their performance. The third is the belief that placing control of the factors of production and distribution in the hands of privately appointed corporate managers, who are accountable for their performance and who act in the interest and subject to the ultimate control of those who own the corporation, achieves a more efficient utilization of economic resources than that achievable under alternative economic systems. (Eisenberg, 1989: 1523)

Blair (2003) argues that business historians have identified three plausible explanations for the popularity of the corporate form: (1) it amassed 'large amount of capital'; (2) it provided 'limited liability' for the investors (representing one decisive legal innovation in the modern period, Handlin and Handlin, 1945: 11, notice, as there was 'no clear precedent from Roman law' and 'early English law knew nothing of limited liability')[1]; and (3) it centralized the control of the corporation (Blair, 2003: 389). Blair (2003: 390) adds a fourth factor as being a 'critical advantage of the corporate form': '[t]he ability to commit capital, once amassed, for extended periods of time – for decades or even centuries'. Blair explains that not only did the owners of a new business charter need to protect the corporation from the investors' creditors to enable long-term stability to promote economic growth, the corporate form justified the establishment of a 'pool of assets that was not subject to being liquidated or dissolved by any of the individual participants who might want to recover their investment' (Blair, 2003: 392). In other words, the corporate form not only protected investors ('participants' in the business charter, in Blair's parlance) from the individual investors' creditors, potentially harming the interest of less indebted investors, but it also provided a mechanism that protected the investors from their own proclivity to use the corporation as a form of deposit: '[t]he commitment of capital by shareholders ... helped protect the at-risk investments made by other corporate participants', Blair (2003: 392) writes. This mechanism is of great importance for the analysis of the institutionalization of the corporate form as a legal entity as it strongly undermines the claim that, for example, shareholders have the right to command resources amassed within the corporation. By the legal strictures of corporate law, directors (and, *de jure*, the managers hired by the directors) are given an autonomous position to manage the 'pool of assets' controlled by the corporation; the basic legal principle underlying US corporate govern-ance, stated in §141(a) of Delaware General Corporation Law, is that '[t]he business and affairs of every corporation ... shall be managed by or under the direction of a board of directors' (cited in Moore and Rebérioux, 2011: 96). Says Blair (2003):

> Incorporating a firm created a governance mechanism which separated the role of contributing financial capital from the role of operating the business and making regular decisions about the use of assets in the business. When the corporation is formed, initial investors not only commit a pool of capital to be used in the business, but they also yield control over the business assets and activities to a board of directors that is legally independent of both shareholders and managers. (Blair, 2003: 393)

In other words, the success of corporate law derived not only from its ability to legitimize the social role and status of professional managers, but also less abstractly, because it enables incorporated business charters to operate efficiently as corporate prescribed shared rules, procedures and obligations for all partners and stakeholders:

> The corporate form ... provided a more reliable basis for building organ-izational capital than did either an individual proprietorship or partnership. To build sustainable organizations, individuals with sufficient talent and expertise to run a business operation had to be induced to give up their own entrepreneurial aspirations in order to work in a business in which they would not be independent and might now share directly the potential business profits. The corporate form gave stability to the business enterprise, which helped ensure those professional managers that their firm-specific investments would be protected, along with the dedicated physical and financial capital, and that they would have substantial input in how the business would be run. (Blair, 2003: 427).

Corporate law was therefore a principal vehicle for taming opportunistic behaviour and for aligning various stakeholders' – most notably the business partners' – own interests within one single legal entity.

The Growth and Differentiation of the Corporation

In the latter half of the nineteenth century, American railroad companies were incorporated and they developed large hierarchies and dispersed ownership, leading to the need to formulate corporate laws that enabled this modern type of organization to operate as smoothly as possible

(Bratton, 1989a: 1486). As Hilt (2014) makes clear, the corporate law was not so much establishing the firm as a set of contracts between business partners and their owners (holders of stock) or creditors, as it was a contract between the state and the business partners; the firm is from the very beginning incorporated within the socio-economic realm of the state. In the period after 1880, the railroad company model of the managerial firm was widely spread in the growing American economy (Perrow, 2002), leading to the development of a new class of professional management workers and executives:

> Hierarchies of salaried executives dominated these new corporations. Success-ful mass production required long-term policy commitment and substantial investment; professional, salaried managers were designated to make these formulations and to direct production. Actors on the capital markets withdrew from active participation in corporate management because they saw them-selves as lacking necessary expertise. (Bratton, 1989a: 1487)

In this period, the modern corporate firm was instituted, relying on a combination of hierarchical organization, salaried professional managers and dispersed ownership. Quite early on it was evident that influential capital owners and venturesome executives found ways to create oligar-chies and monopolies, and such tendencies were counteracted by political activism leading to new legal frameworks. The Sherman Antitrust Act of 1890 'outlawed restraints of trade by existing monopolies and any attempt to create a new monopoly' (Cassidy, 2009: 128), and the Clayton Antitrust Act of 1914 'proscribed price discrimination, exclusive dealing contracts, and other predatory tactics that the trusts had used to boost their profits' (Cassidy, 2009: 128). By and large, there was substantial political support for the state regulating and monitoring industry through corporate law, antitrust legislation, regulations and law enforcement in the period.

During the depression following the great Wall Street crash of 1929 and in the New Deal era, it was widely debated whether this combination of legislation, regulation and law enforcement was enough to curb the oligarchic tendencies in competitive capitalism, and many scholars, policy-makers and politicians spent a significant amount of time ponder-ing how to balance different interests in the economy (Hawley, 1966). The Glass–Steagall Act of 1933 and the Securities Act of 1934 that created the Securities and Exchange Commission (SEC), the agency monitoring the finance industry, were two New Deal products aimed at strengthening the control of the state over private enterprises (Hilt, 2014: 8.16). The period from the mid-nineteenth century to the decade before the outbreak of World War II was thus a period wherein corporate law was instituted as a means for the state to balance private enterprising and public interests. As Hilt (2014: 8.17) remarks, the legal environment of the privately owned or public firm was the outcome from the legal, political and regulatory engineering of a system that aimed to balance various interests and objectives: 'the solutions to [corporate governance problems] have sometimes been sought in legal innovations, and in other cases, institutional or market-based solutions emerged'. Speaking in legal terms, the American corporate law system could be seen, Hilt (2014: 8.18) argues, as a 'partially codified hybrid of common-law institutions and indigenous innovations'. Eisenberg (1989: 1525) shares this view, that corporate law is best understood as an assemblage of various types of legal rules, market-based rules and managerial decisions jointly combined to accomplish the highest possible efficiency, transparency and stability in the corporate system:

> [b]elieving that just because markets are not perfect, mandatory rules would be better ... However, the converse proposition is also true: just because mandatory rules are imperfect does not mean that markets would be better ... The brute facts are that most markets are not perfect and most mandatory rules are perfect; that even imperfect markets and legal rules may have positive effects; and that the question in any given case is to determine which of these two imperfect mechanisms is better, or, if possible, to determine how these two imperfect mechanisms can be shaped to reinforce each other. Taken separately, neither markets, morals, nor law, are in themselves sufficient to curb traditional and propositional conflicts. Taken together, markets, morals, and law have shown themselves capable of achieving that objective. (Eisenberg, 1989: 1525)

In other words, legislative practice, an attention to market conditions, and moral standards are all important elements in the development of the corporate system that is a key mechanism in competitive capitalism and that supports enterprising activities at the same time as stability and transparency is enabled. As with many other successful institutional innovations, gradually becoming 'infrastructural' inasmuch as they are no longer even recognized as once being quite innovative or even radical mechanisms and practices as they become taken for granted and even deemed to be of minor interests, the innovation of corporate law suffers from this ignorance, Blair (2003: 393) suggests:

> The corporate form does not now seem so unique and remarkable, so that its benefits might seem trivial. But it is worth exploring what it was that made the corporate form so attractive to business organizers as the US economy moved from an agrarian, small-scale production economy to a large and modern industrial economy. (Blair, 2003: 393)

The corporate system instituted and contributed to the building of competitive capitalism, and yet – as we will see in the following chapters of this volume – it was from the 1970s widely regarded by agency theorists as in fact inhibiting the efficient use of resources.

CORPORATE LAW AND REGULATIONS

One important distinction in corporate governance is between law and regulations. Wherein the former specifies legal entities and their relations as a juridical condition that remains relatively stable over time, regulation is a political tool to accomplish certain objectives and goals within existing legal frameworks. Posner (1974: 335) argues that regulation refers to 'taxes and subsidies of all sorts as well as to explicit legislative and administrative controls over rates, entry, and other facets of economic activity'. Among free market protagonists such as Posner (1974), regulations are by and large undesirable as policy-makers intervene in supposedly self-regulating markets and thus bias the competition, which in turn reduces the overall market efficiency. George Stigler (1971: 3) suggests that, 'as a rule', regulation is '[a]cquired by the industry and is designed and operated primarily for its benefit'. Regulation is thus here the outcome from industry putting pressure on policy-makers and regulators to establish non-market-based subsidies and other benefits being in their own interests. Trade barriers and import quotas are typical examples of such regulations that can protect domestic producers from external competition. Stigler (1971: 16) argues that regulation therefore is beneficial for *some* but *not all* actors in an economy, and therefore regulations are undesirable as they grant certain groups benefits that others are denied: '[w]hen an industry receives a grant of power from the state, the benefit to the industry will fall short of the damage to the rest of the community'.

Despite such criticism from free market advocates, regulation is widely popular in political quarters, primarily because politicians and policy-makers are engaged with a wider set of social and economic interests than to ensure optimal market efficiency, and regulations provide them with political tools that help them fulfil their political agendas and promises. The regulation studies literature points at many different effects, benefits and unintended consequences of regulation and deregulation, making regulatory factors a key issue to consider for corporations. One body of literature emphasizes how corporate interests and lobbying strongly influence regulatory procedures, which therefore risks influencing the political process to regulate markets and industries (Hiatt and

Park, 2013; Abraham and Sheppard, 1999). In some cases, such as the levels of executive compensation, there may be a political will to establish a regulatory framework, and yet there are difficulties involved in regulating industry (Suárez, 2014). One of the factors to consider is the lobbying industry and the flow of finance capital between industry and the policy-making community in, for example, Washington DC and Brussels.

Thornburg and Roberts (2008) study the enactment of the Sarbanes–Oxley Act, the foremost consequence of the Enron bankruptcy and the evidence of corporate crime in the American energy company, and they find that the accounting industry contributed heavily both to political candidates ($15 354 056 to 'federal candidates during the 2000 election cycle') and lobbyists ($21 777 432) (Thornburg and Roberts, 2008: 233) and that the primary recipients of these donations were incumbent legislators who were members on committees 'having jurisdiction over SOX' (Thornburg and Roberts, 2008: 245). This flow of finance capital suggests, Thornburg and Roberts (2008: 245) conclude, that '[p]olitical strategies focus more on interests of business and its members than on the interests of the broader public'. Mian et al. (2010) observe a similar pattern in the case of the American Housing Rescue and Foreclosure Prevention Act (AHRFPA) and the Emergency Economic Stabilization Act (EESA) that followed the declining sub-prime mortgage market (for details, see Mian and Sufi, 2014; Dymski, 2013; MacKenzie, 2012; Levitin and Wachter, 2012; Engel and McCoy, 2007. For a more personal account of the consequences of the unregulated home mortgage industry, see Andrews, 2009). The *Wall Street Journal* described AHRFPA as '[t]he most important piece of housing legislation to come along in a generation' (Mian et al., 2010: 1971), as there were large economic interests being affected by the new legislation. Mian et al. (2010: 1969) found that 'a strong predictor of voting behavior on EESA is the amount of campaign contributions from the financial service industry'. Mian et al. (2010: 1969) say this finding is 'consistent with anecdotal evidence suggesting that the financial industry lobbied heavily to shape the EESA and get it passed'. The causality between campaign contributions and voting behaviour is thus linear in Mian et al.'s (2010: 1969) empirical material, at least for 'politicians running for reelection', but not for 'retiring politicians'. Mian et al. (2010) also identified a correlation between a conservative ideology and voting behaviour, where Republicans were more sceptical regarding the regulatory control of the state intervening in market activities. The finance industry – the 'mortgage industry', in Mian et al.'s (2010) vocabulary – was also quite precise in how they allocated their donations, targeting politicians from districts with a 'high fraction of subprime borrowers' (Mian et al., 2010: 1997). Both Thornburg and Roberts (2008) and Mian et al. (2010) show how the regulatory political process is easily becoming a case of 'vending machine politics' (Froud et al., 2004: 905) as campaign donations and other forms of economic support can easily and legitimately find their way to policy-makers in democratically elected political bodies. Under all conditions, in periods of economic and financial instability, the regulatory process becomes pervaded by specific interest and the money such interests bring with them, making an already complicated process even more difficult to handle (Humphrey et al., 2009).

Regulation and Innovation

In addition to the imbrication of financial interest and the regulatory process, there is a body of literature that emphasizes how innovation activities may benefit from regulatory standards (Faulkner, 2009; Ashford et al., 1985), but that also shows how innovations can undermine regulation. Faulkner (2009) argues that the field of tissue engineering benefits from clearer regulatory frameworks, and that the European Union should actively engage in regulating the emerging field of research and venturing to help the actors coordinate themselves within the grids of regulatory practices and standards. On the other hand, Phillips et al. (2011) argue that *too much* regulation can make it complicated for actors to get the leeway they need to innovate effectively. In the finance industry, subject to waves of regulation and deregulation over the last decades (for example, Lépinay, 2011; Abdelal, 2007; Singer, 2007; Hammond and Knott, 1988), and where a substantial body of literature regards regulatory failure in combination with excessive risk-taking as the two main factors explaining the finance industry meltdown in 2008 (Jarsulic, 2013; Silvers, 2013; Friedman and Kraus, 2012; Campbell, 2010), innovations have played a key role in making the old regime of regulatory control obsolete or at least less efficient. A scholarly research question worthy of some attention is thus how and why the regulation failed.

Martinez-Moyano et al. (2014) observe what they refer to, following Vaughan (1999), as the 'normalization of deviance' in the finance industry. Including a sample of 70 regulators, Martinez-Moyano et al. (2014) found evidence of 'flexible rule following' operating within its very own political economy of risk and benefits, granting organizations the possibility to follow regulatory rules when it suited their interests: 'organizations attend to rules depending on the salience, time horizon, and relative certainty of the benefits of production compared with those of compliance' (Martinez-Moyano et al., 2014: 332). One of the factors contributing to the normalization of deviance from rules, Martinez-Moyano et al. (2014) argue, is the short-term perspective taken by organizations where the short-term benefits of flexible rule-following tend to win over medium to long-term risks of being punished for not respecting the regulatory framework.

> In some areas, including financial markets, rule enforcement erodes when the short-term benefits of production diminish concerns about unspecified, distant risks from rules or procedural violations ... Beliefs, cognitive assumptions, formal and informal procedures, and rewards for completing transactions versus maintaining tight internal controls reinforce the bias towards completing transactions and away from equally mindful enforcement of rules. (Martinez-Moyano et al., 2014: 333)

Clark and Newell (2013) use the term *complicit decoupling* to denote a policy drift that occurs when organizations that collaborate and rely on each other (for example, rating agencies and firms issuing bonds) gradually lower the standards for professional integrity and change the role as providers of objective and neutral information. The long-term consequences of such complicit decoupling between the formal relations of two or more parties and their actual collaborations lead to a gradual decline in the efficiency of regulatory frameworks, and therefore also harm the efficiency of market transactions. In other words, regulation is always of necessity socially embedded inasmuch as it presupposes that certain values and norms, not of necessity made explicit in the regulatory statutes, are internalized by relevant actors (Bozanic et al., 2012).

Such policy drifts and complicit decoupling do not only occur when self-serving actors choose to act opportunistically to benefit their own interests, but they are also caused by innovations. In the field of life science innovation, Niezen et al. (2013) demonstrate how the structuring of databases has informed the regulation of the pharmaceutical industry. Lenglet (2011) shows how the use of algorithmic trading and the work of 'quants' – skilled mathematicians employed in the finance industry – have shaped finance industry regulation. In the finance industry, Frame and White (2004) suggest, financial innovations can be grouped into (1) *new products* (for example, 'adjustable-rate mortgages, exchange-traded index-funds'); (2) *new services* (for example, 'online securities trading, Internet banking'); (3) *new 'production' processes* (for example, 'electronic record-keeping for securities, credit scoring'); and (4) *new organizational forms* (for example, 'a new type of electronic exchange for trading securities, Internet-only banks') (Frame and White, 2004: 118). Frame and White (2004: 121) also say that 'some forms of regulation must inhibit innovation', but also recognize that 'innovation can arise from efforts to circumvent regulation'. At the end of the day, it is 'impossible *a priori* to assign a positive or negative sign to the connection between the stringency of regulation (however measured) and the pace of financial innovation' (Frame and White, 2004: 121). Under all conditions, Frame and White (2004: 118) argue that financial innovations that lead to the improvement of the finance industry will have 'direct positive ramifications throughout the economy'.

Funk and Hirschman (2014: 670) argue that financial innovations serve to undermine existing regulatory frameworks inasmuch as new financial interests such as swaps resist the categories of existing regulatory frameworks and therefore gradually render regulations ineffective in monitoring financial transactions and the level of risk-taking. Funk and Hirschman (2014: 671) define regulation as '[l]imitations on the products a firm can offer, the price at which it may offer those products, or the location where it may do business'. Over time, the deregulation of the markets, beginning in the late 1970s and early 1980s, was first propelled by consumer interests, serving, for example, to increase the supply of credit in the US finance market. From the late 1980s and onwards, industry interests substituted consumer interest (Funk and Hirschman, 2014: 671). In the finance industry, the standard explanation for the substantial deregulatory efforts is, in Suárez and Kolodny's (2011: 77) formulation, that the '[r]egulatory environment of the late 1990s can only be understood through the political behavior of individual firms and of the membership organizations that represented them in Washington'. The deregulation of the finance industry is thus the outcome of the activism of pro-business communities and lobbyists, and political mobilization is the primary driver for the changes in regulatory oversight. Funk and Hirschman (2014: 673) add that regulation and business activities (including innovation) maintain a 'dialectical relationship': 'just as businesses respond to regulation by complying with regulation (or not) and innovating (or not), regulators and legislators respond to changes in the behaviors of business by enforcing existing regulations (or not) or creating new ones (or not)' (Funk and Hirschman, 2014: 673).

Examining the case of the repeal of the Glass–Steagall Act of 1933, Funk and Hirschman (2014: 677) proposed that the finance industry first try to alter established regulatory frameworks through 'traditional lobbying efforts', but as the efforts were only moderately successful, they had the incentive to develop innovations that were ambiguous and 'ill-defined with respect to contemporary regulatory categories'. As, for example, swaps became widely used in the finance industry, accompanied by new more lenient principles for how existing regulatory rules should be interpreted, more or less derived from a more generous pro-business and pro-finance industry attitude of the late 1990s, the balance of power between regulators and finance industry actors changed, paving the way for the overturning of the Glass–Steagall Act (Funk and Hirschman, 2014: 692). In other words, while the finance industry deregulation of the late 1990s, with the repeal of the New Deal regulation of the Glass–Steagall Act, certainly benefited from political activism and lobbying and the pro-business climate, the practical work to create new financial assets became the *coup de grâce* for the extant regulatory framework as these innovations escaped the existing interpretative framework and thus undermined its efficacy and legitimacy.

The question is then how well 'laws in books' and 'laws in real life' are aligned – whether the map accurately depicts the territory – or if there is room for local interpretations and enactment of corporate law. There are reasons to believe, based on studies of policy-making processes in organizations such as the IMF and the World Bank, that there is a loose coupling between policy-making in practice and scholarly ideas about, for example, market efficiency. Babb (2013) discusses how what she calls *policy paradigms* (that is, free market efficiency theories) may be partially influenced by 'scholarly ideas', but ultimately the outcome is shaped by the political processes developed within the organizations that negotiate various policy programmes: 'although policy paradigms are both inspired and legitimated by scholarly theories, they are also shaped by politics' (Babb, 2013: 271). That is, policy-making and regulations are not collected from scholarly treatises and journal articles and implemented en bloc but are shaped and moulded by the procedures for political policy-making. Despite the inertia and bargaining of policy-making, policies do after all become enacted, and they gradually trickle down to the level of everyday work in organizations: policies become part of the legal environment of the firm.

LAW IN BOOKS AND LAWS IN REAL LIFE

Institutional theorists and legal scholars argue that laws are enacted by the legislator to be followed but also to accomplish other benefits, for example, to signal what society tolerates and regards as appropriate and desirable behaviour. In addition, legislation is shaped by the possibilities of enforcing the law in practice, making certain legislation most cumbersome to handle from a practical perspective. Halliday and Carruthers (2007: 1142, 1146) make an important distinction between 'law making' – '*law in the books*' – and 'law implementation' – '*law in practice*': '*Law in practice* refers to behavior and institutions that constitute and enact law as it actually is experienced by those it regulates' (Halliday and Carruthers, 2007: 1146). While law in the books per se may be subject to debates and interpretations and animated discussions regarding their interpretation and applications, law in practice is even more complicated, being operationalized and rolled out as a variety of activities that are more or less loosely coupled with the underlying legal strictures. 'Law on the books and law in action are two quite different things', Halliday and Carruthers (2007: 1196) summarize. Among legal scholars and institutional theorists, there is an ongoing and lively debate regarding the intersection of law and institutions and the various implications thereof. Edelman and Suchman (1997: 493) distinguish between a material (a 'functionalist') and a 'cultural view' on law, suggesting that '[c]ultural perspectives see law as a pervasive belief system that permeates the most fundamental morals and meanings of organizational life'. The functionalist views tend to regard legal texts as an expression of a 'common will' in society or the consent among informed legislators regarding the law in a specific domain of interest. The cultural view, in contrast, recognizes that all legislation is the outcome of bargaining and negotiations wherein various groups express their own interests and concerns regarding the legislation in the making: 'legal regulations are often "enacted" ... at a fairly local level, with intraorganizational professional constituencies playing a significant part in determining which institutional norms and scripts get reflected in organizational structures and practices', Edelman and Suchman (1997: 499) say. In this view, where laws are regulated, specific professional communities (for example, lobbyists) serve at times to amplify and reify 'legal threats that may have little to do with reality', Edelman and Suchman (1997: 500) suggest. Edelman et al. (2011) introduce the term the *legal field* to denote the various organizations and professional communities that actively participate, directly or indirectly, in the legal work: '[l]egal fields comprise courts, legislatures, administrative agencies, legal academia, and all legal actors, as well as the various parties that enter into the legal system on an occasional basis' (Edelman et al., 2011: 900).

More specifically, regardless of whether the material or cultural view of legislation work is the most adequate description of the process, legislation recursively both influences the organization and is influenced by the organization's activities. Edelman and Suchman (1997: 507) thus follow Edelman's (1990) seminal paper and use the term *legal environment* to denote how laws 'create, constrain, shape, enable, and empower organizations'. This is the very core of the institutional view of law, the idea that 'laws in books' are translated into legal environments ('laws in practice') that in various ways shape and inform how an organization acts under certain conditions. Seen in this view, there is relatively loose coupling between law, regulatory practices and organizational activities: '[r]egulatory environments place law in the posture of seeking to control organizations, but much regulation grows out of organizations' actions and agendas, and organizational responses to regulations often define the meaning of compliance' (Edelman and Suchman, 1997: 507). In Edelman et al.'s (2001) account, the process when formal legislation is trickling down to practical managerial work is referred to as the *managerialization of law*, the work of managers to interpret and 'reify' legal texts as practices that preferably suit their own interests.

The Managerialization of Law

Edelman et al. (2001: 1592) define the managerialization of law as '[t]he process by which conceptions of law may become progressively infused with managerial values as legal ideas move into managerial and organizational arenas'. This is a term that denotes how laws in books are translated into the legal practices seated within the firm, and thus become aligned with the interests of organization actors. This process is also mediated by legal experts and consultants who work on behalf of the companies to interpret the existing legislation to capture and accommodate the intentions of the legislators:

> Because law is broad and ambiguous and is rarely read directly by employers, most organizational actors rely at least indirectly on the legal profession for information about legal requirements. Lawyers often run workshops for personnel professionals or write for their professional periodicals, and personnel professionals in turn communicate the law to their employers and others who make organizational policy. As law is communicated by and among professionals, it is filtered through a variety of lenses, and colored by different professional backgrounds, training, and interests. (Edelman et al., 2001: 1595)

Legal texts are often complex documents; on the one hand they seek to bridge and bond all the interests, issues and concerns that the legislators need to take into account, and on the other hand the law needs to be intelligible for lay audiences and so that it can be enforced by the state and international organizations. Legal texts are thus complicated to decode and there may be many interpretations of them. This interpretation and translation of law into practice therefore demands specialized expertise. In addition, not only are the legal documents per se far from trivial to decode, but the very act of decoding the legal text is embedded in an environment where, for example, organizational actors interpret a new legal document in their own interests, Edelman et al. (2001: 1598–9) suggest:

> Managers tend to understand law – and the legal environment more broadly – as a set of constraints upon the range of possible management styles that will achieve organizational goals ... Thus, *as legal ideas move into managerial and organizational arenas, law tend to become 'managerialized', or progressively infused with managerial values.* (Edelman et al., 2001: 1598–9, emphasis in the original)

The very process of the 'managerialization of law' thus occurs as '[m]anagement consultants rhetorically refashion legal ideas that challenge traditional managerial prerogatives and suggests new ideas, which they claim are more innovative, more rational, and more progressive' (Edelman et al., 2001: 1592). In short, the managerialization of law is to some extent the component of a 'reframing of law' in ways that 'make it appear more consistent with traditional managerial prerogatives' (Edelman et al., 2001: 1592). This may sound as if legal counsellors and consultants can freely choose to interpret the law as they or their clients wish, but much of the legal texts provide possibilities for interpretation and interpreting legal texts in terms that favour existing managerial prerogatives, and discretion is a human response to new legal directives. Using a term first introduced by Philip Selznick (1949), Edelman et al. (2001: 1599) say that the law is 'infused with managerial values'.

There are many consequences of the managerialization of law. First, there is no straightforward implementation of legislation in the corporation, but legal texts are always subject to local interpretations and applications that suit local interests and existing practices; there is 'no simple one-to-one causality involved' when laws are implemented, Swedberg (2003: 6) argues. This does not suggest that legislators give managers carte blanche to implement the law as they wish, but there needs to be a reasonable consistency between the *intentions* of the legislator (a key term in legal theory and legal practice) and actual outcomes. In many cases, as we will see below, the degrees of freedom granted when reading the legal texts lead to corporations being more ambitious than the legislators possibly expected or even wanted, leading to unanticipated consequences of law. Second, while formally speaking the legislator monitors and controls the subject of legislation (that is, the corporation), it would be a mistake to regard this as a linear top-down process because legislation can serve, like any other regulation, as a form of subsidy or benefit in the hands of the corporation. From a sociological perspective, Swedberg (2003: 7) says, law is '[c]losely connected to the notion of order, and that order is crucial to society as well as to power elites'. In fact, Swedberg proposes, law can be seen as '[o]ne of the many weapons in the arsenal of power, similar to physical coercion'. The managerialization of law is therefore precisely the process wherein legal texts are appropriated within the firm, partly to regulate and control its activities, and partly to be used to the firm's advantage to further strengthen strategic positions and competitive advantages.

EMPIRICAL STUDIES OF LEGISLATION AND ORGANIZATIONAL AND INDUSTRY RESPONSES

The institutional theory idea of the managerialization of law has been complemented by a series of empirical studies that reveal how legislation leads to both anticipated and desired outcomes and unintended consequences that extend outside the legislators' immediate interests. This latter consequence, the inability to anticipate the full consequences of legislation, is a standard objection to the state and the government intervening into, for example, market-based activities, allegedly biasing the market and redirecting the attention of market actors. Studies of the implementation of law partially support such claims but proponents of legislation and regulation as legitimate means of the state to control the economy and economic activities point to the benefits derived from, for example, stable market conditions, and stress how legislating and regulatory bodies are the market makers of competitive capitalism.

Many studies of the effects of new legislation deal with labour market regulation and industrial relations including, for example, diversity management legislation (Edelman et al., 2001) or sexual harassment legislation (Dobbin and Kelly, 2007), but there are also studies conducted regarding more policy-oriented legislation, including, for example, antitrust legislation (Kelly and Dobbin, 1999). In many cases, there is a loose coupling between legislation and organizational practices, but as long as the intentions of the legislators are understood and the corporations ensure that they have taken action to act in accordance with such intentions, such loose couplings can be tolerated, as, for example, Dobbin and Kelly (2007) argue. For instance, sexual harassment is widely recognized as an unethical and immoral act where one party violates the integrity of the other party, and therefore legislators want to ensure that corporations share this legal-moral view and that they institute routines for the handling of sexual harassment complaints within the firm. However, Dobbin and Kelly (2007) argue that the legislation does not specify in detail *what* routines the corporation should implement. Instead, it is a general compliance with the legislator's identified social problem that is the principal outcome from the legal text, Dobbin and Kelly (2007) propose:

> Executives prefer formal bureaucratic remedies that can routinize legal compliance, but it is also the case that the courts have come to reinforce such solutions because they constitute standards that can be applied across cases. What matters, before the courts, is not whether the employer has a system for addressing harassment complaints and preventing harassment that has been proven effective, in the workplace in question or anywhere for that matter, but whether the employer has a system that symbolizes commitment to those ideals. (Dobbin and Kelly, 2007: 1237)

In the legislator's view, the managers are in a better position to decide what 'formal bureaucratic remedies' best respond to local demands, and they thus delegate the responsibility for implementing routines to executives and directors. Therefore, the 'symbolic commitment' to the counteracting of undesirable personal intimacies in the workplace is a principal accomplishment of the existing legislation.

In other cases, new legislation can be interpreted as what is favourable to corporate interests, and therefore corporations choose to be more ambitious and even more progressive than the legislators possibly anticipated or even hoped for, simply because the implementation of new policies may strengthen competitive positions. Baron et al. (1986) examine how the new 'personal administration' legislation in the US, relatively vague in terms of prescribing what actions need to be taken, led to the expansion of human resource management departments and human resource management as a field of professional expertise more broadly. This led to a major shift in American industry where the 'tyranny of the foremen' (see, for example, Jacoby, 1985) was substituted by more formal and transparent labour relations in industry. The federal government had defined high turnover in certain industries as the initial problem and favoured legislation to reduce the turnover problem. The federal government was thus mandating a set of innovations that gradually crystallized into what is today's HRM practices (Baron et al., 1986: 364):

> The number of personnel and labor relations professionals in the United States increased from fewer than 3,000 in 1946 to 53,000 in 1950 and 93,000 in 1969 ... in percentage terms, the growth rate of the personnel profession far outstripped the growth rate of other professions (and of the U.S. labor force as a whole) during the postwar years. (Baron et al., 1986: 375)

In this case, one specific problem and its accompanying legislation, not very precise in its prescribed corporate practices, led to a series of new organizational innovations. HRM thus became established as a response to the problem of high turnover, and was spread through the force of what institutional theorists refer to as *mimetic isomorphism* (DiMaggio and Powell, 1983). These 'unintended consequences of legislation', Kelly and Dobbin (1999: 485) suggest, are a consequence of what they refer to as 'legal ambiguity', an incomplete and to some extent vague legal intention, a form of blank surface onto which legal counsellors and executives can jointly project their perceived solutions to new legislation. This legal ambiguity can therefore, Kelly and Dobbin (1999: 485) say, 'lead to strong corporate responses'. For instance, Kelly and Dobbin (1999: 485) suggest that many American employers implemented maternity leave programmes in the 1970s and 1980s, well before the passage of the Family and Medical Leave Act of 1993, simply because they either saw this legislation coming and wanted to discount the additional cost that the reform and new legislation would induce, or because they saw such benefits as being to their advantage in the competition over qualified co-workers.

A third body of studies show how legislation may have far-reaching consequences that may or may not be anticipated by legislators and policy-makers. Dobbin and Dowd (2000) and Dobbin (1994) discuss how antitrust laws influenced the development of the railway system in, for example, Massachusetts. The antitrust legislation altered the business model of key actors, and as actors demanded many investors to finance the costly development of the railway system, antitrust legislation created a finance market where railway companies could raise finance capital. 'Because firms bought the rivals at fair market prices, ownership was increasingly spread across many investors ... Under the finance model, then, more and more firms had large numbers of shareholders', Dobbin and Dowd (2000: 652) summarize. Dobbin's (1994) research monograph, on the other hand, stresses the connections, no matter how crooked or non-linear, between ideas 'about how economic rationality operates' and the legislation being put to place. Examining the differences between the American, the French and the British railroad systems development, Dobbin (1994) identifies three distinct and locally embedded economic policies regarding the railroad industry:

> Because Americans believed that competition between localities would spur growth and that federal action would merely spawn graft, most American railroads backed state and local government financing but not federal financing. Because the French believed that growth must be orchestrated by the central state, French railroads backed central state financing but eschewed provincial and local financing as irrational. Because the British believed that

all government meddling was inefficient, British railroads opposed government financing of all kinds. These and other ideas about self-interest were
clearly conditioned by national context. (Dobbin, 1994: 214)

Depending on historical conditions, political conditions and the influence
of certain groups, and other socio-economic and cultural conditions,
these three leading industrial nations developed their own idiosyncratic
railway industry policy, but somewhat surprisingly, while choosing
different routes and bringing different equipment to move from A to B,
the three countries eventually arrived more or less at the same point,
Dobbin (1994) says:

> Many policy analysts begin with the assumption that transcendental economic
> laws govern the universe, and take policy to be responsive to those laws ...
> Two kinds of evidence undermine such economic determinism. First, I review
> evidence that *policies organized around widely different economic principles
> produced similar outcomes* in terms of industry growth and prosperity.
> Second, I review evidence that the economic laws these nations discovered
> reflect local institutional history rather than exogenous, transhistorical laws.
> (Dobbin, 1994: 222, emphasis added)

In the case of the railway system development as an industrial policy
programme, the idea of the role of the state and private enterprising were
mixed up with local conditions, and there were many cases of how
existing legislation was used to motivate certain decisions. Dobbin (1994)
thus concludes that antitrust legislation is more of a framework wherein
the intentions regarding the favours of free competition expressed by the
legislator can be temporarily compromised if there are other benefits
emerging en route. Violating the law is thus tolerable at times, as long as
it produces beneficial effects, if the violation is only temporal, and if no
single actor can benefit handsomely from such violations. In other words,
the coupling between legal texts and corporate and industrial practice is
at times loose, providing executives and legal advisors with some degrees
of freedom when interpreting a piece of new legislation.

At the end of the day, the role of law and regulation is widely
underappreciated by the public, also including industry representatives,
Dobbin and Dowd (2000: 653) propose: '[d]espite much evidence that
antitrust law revolutionized America's industrial environment, it plays at
best a supporting role in theories of industrial organization'. In the case
of the US, a general sense of the government being all too prone to
meddle with business matters and a general anti-statist sentiment in parts
of American society further breed the idea that federal policy is
inefficient and perhaps even illegitimate in terms of reducing market

efficiency (Kelly and Dobbin, 1999: 457: Campbell and Lindberg, 1990: 642). In addition, organization theorists and management scholars have paid 'scant attention to the role of the state in shaping the behavior of organizations', Kelly and Dobbin (1999: 458) suggest. Against this relatively widespread ignorance regarding legislation and regulatory matters, the institutional theory view of law and the process of the managerialization of law present a more affirmative understanding of how legislation shapes and informs corporations.

THE FIDUCIARY COMPONENT OF CORPORATE LAW

Whenever there is a difference between 'laws in books' and 'laws in real life', there is a need for actors to interpret their practices and to conduct their decisions within the horizon of social interest and wider social objectives (Commons, 1924). 'The businessman should be actuated by the motive of serving society rather than maximizing profit as the sole end of enterprise', Howard Bowen (1953: 39) argued in his work *Social Responsibilities of the Businessman*. Bowen continues: '[t]he business-man should be imbued with respect for the dignity and essential worth of all men and with a spirit of compassion, shown in his relationship with his workers, customers, suppliers, competitors, and others with whom he has business dealings' (Bowen, 1953: 40).

This attitude towards the businessman has radically changed since the early 1950s, today being understood widely as serving a narrower set of stakeholders, but there are legal scholars who maintain that the work of corporate governance and leadership, despite the strong influence of shareholder welfare advocacy, should be understood as a fiduciary duty. Stout (2004) suggests that both executives and directors are given fiduciary duties in managing the corporation so that it benefits society in a broad sense of the term. Rent-seeking and self-serving *homo economicus*-type individuals are thus not attractive to recruit to such positions. Also practising managers such as Sherron Watkins (2003), serving as an executive and whistleblower during the Enron bankruptcy, one of the most emblematic corporate collapses in the post-World War II period (see, for example, Tourish and Vatcha, 2005; Craig and Amernic, 2004; Seeger and Ulmer, 2003), stress the need for emphasizing the fiduciary duties of executives and managers: '[i]n order to flourish, a successful capitalist system must be predicated on fairness, honesty, and integrity. In fact, many scholars describe the capitalist system as a three-legged stool – economic freedom, political freedom, and moral responsibility. A weakness of one and the stool topples' (Watkins, 2003: 122).[2]

Several empirical studies reveal how, for example, 'narcissistic leaders', triggered by the scenario of creating extra-normal profits but indifferent to downside risks, ignore their fiduciary responsibilities and therefore put the corporation's assets at stake (for example, Chatterjee and Hambrick, 2007), thus violating the intentions of the legislators. Such leaders increase levels of risk while producing little additional rent on the basis of this risk exposure: 'although narcissists tend to generate more extreme and irregular performance than non-narcissists, they do not generate systematically better or worse performance' (Chatterjee and Hambrick, 2007: 378). From a mainstream rational choice theory view, the failure to adhere to the fiduciary duties makes these executives unattractive for corporations.

Almandoz (2014) studied the role of founding teams in banks and speaks favourably of what he calls a 'community logic', a term that can be accommodated within the fiduciary duty view of leadership and corporate governance work. The board of directors in banks operating in accordance with a 'financial logic' rather than a 'community logic' were more prone to making use of 'risky deposits', Almandoz (2014: 458) found. In addition, boards containing a larger share of directors with a 'finance career background' increased the risk-taking (Almandoz, 2014: 459). This finding, emphasizing the local community as a beneficiary of qualified and professional leadership work, is consistent with, for example, Kerr and Robinson's (2011: 152) study of Scottish bankers, failing to connect to both the local market and their organizations (that is, their fiduciary duties were more or less abandoned altogether), ultimately leading to the bankers 'destroying the businesses that they were charged with managing'.

SUMMARY AND CONCLUSION

All economic enterprising and business venturing is, more or less explicitly, based on self-interest and some consuming of energy and efforts on part of the founders, entrepreneurs and promoters of a new business. In addition, in a differentiated economy, economic activities include diverse skills and sources of expertise and therefore demand coordination and agreements between participating business partners. Based on these premises, policy-makers and regulators representing the sovereign state face the thorny question of how to protect the business from opportunistic behaviour and fraud, deriving both from outside as well as inside the firm. One solution to this governance problem is to enact legal statutes that specify the roles and rights of the business promoters but also the role of investors who supply the finance capital. A business charter is thus the incorporation of a new firm under the regime of pre-existing state-based or federal legal frameworks. As the legal statutes cannot be too detailed or too complicated to understand – which would undermine the possibilities for law enforcement and court ruling, or make the business partners' and financiers' contract inoperable – corporate law is primarily specifying a general set of rules. At the same time, these rules include quite complex terms such as fiduciary duties, stressing that 'laws in books' and 'laws in real life' in many cases diverge. This leaves room both for interpretation of the intentions of the legislators, but also, critics contend, opens up for what is called *moral hazard*, the risk that participants act in self-interested ways without the risk of being punished for this undesirable behaviour. Ultimately, despite these concerns, corporate law, granting the directors a central role in the firm's corporate governance structure, remains the best protection for the greater number of participants, legalists argue. As will be debated in the succeeding chapters, a contractarian view of the firm advocates 'the market for corporate control' as a more efficient mechanism than legislation and court ruling for reducing the risks of moral hazard and forms of self-serving behaviour, most notably managerial malfeasance. In the contractarian view, the legislative model of corporate governance marginalizes market information and makes legislators – in the case of disputes – the privileged interpreters of such market information. In other words, the discourse on corporate governance is based on the tension between the concept of *trust* and the concept of *contract*, representing two, if not competing, at least complementary governance models.

NOTES

1. Djelic (2013) shows that the development of limited liability as a legal concept was a long and complicated political process. Following a major economic and financial crisis in the United Kingdom, the so-called Bubble Act 1720 reaffirmed that joint stock companies '[c]ould only exist if they were chartered by royal or parliamentary fiat', and this legislation '[s]ignificantly slowed down the progress of legal incorporation in Britain for the rest of the century' (Djelic, 2013: 601). However, as early as 1782, when the corporate form became increasingly popular in the United Kingdom, the independent Irish Parliament enacted the Partnership Act, the first attempt to institute limited liability as a legal statute. The Act had a limited impact on the Irish economy and was ultimately a failure as it did not increase the supply of finance capital in Ireland or otherwise boost the economy. In the mid-nineteenth century, limited liability was still 'a rare and dubious privilege' in the United Kingdom but the Incorporation Act of 1844 and the Limited Liability Act of 1855 served to make limited liability a 'natural attribute' of a corporate charter (Djelic, 2013: 599). These two Acts were 'undeniably liberal victories' (Djelic, 2013: 603) as they encouraged and legitimized the liberalization of the economy and the freedom of investment. In the period, the debate regarding the benefits and risks with limited liability 'was reaching its climax' (French,

1990: 15; Bryer, 1997). Conservatives argued that limited liability was morally wrong inasmuch as it involved 'dishonouring obligations freely undertaken' (French, 1990: 15). Conservatives also worried about the fast pace of the British industrialization and argued that there was no shortage of finance capital in the British economy and that limited liability business charters would easily unleash a wave of dangerous speculation (Djelic, 2013: 610): '[t]he major argument against the introduction of general limited liability into mid-19th century Britain was that there was no need for it, as the rapidly expanding economy was generating a massive surplus of savings which eagerly sought out any investment opportunity', French (1990: 27) writes. That is, conservative commentators referred to what eventually would be discussed as *moral hazard* (Djelic and Bothello, 2013). Others, including John Stuart Mill, for example, proposed that limited liability would '[a]llow capital and profit-sharing schemes where workers and employees had a stake in common' (Djelic, 2013: 603), and more radical debaters and social reformers – including the so-called Chartist social movement and Christian socialists being active in the 1830s and 1840s – claimed that limited liabilities would work in the best interests of labourers or society at large. Taken together, all these activities taking place between around 1720 and 1855 and well beyond the mid-nineteenth century tend to be overlooked and forgotten as we today '[t]end to take for granted both limited liability and its association with the corporate form' (Djelic, 2013: 596).

2.   Watkins does not hesitate to speak up regarding her view of the Enron executives and the CEO Jeffrey Skilling in particular, calling for new legal practices to be able to prescribe sanctions against conspicuous opportunistic behaviour:

> Jeffrey Skilling [...] resigned on August 14th [2001], citing personal reasons that never quite materialized [...] he had about $100 million in the bank and so he basically decided to 'call in rich'. That, to me, is pathetic. I thought there should be the equivalent of a corporate court martial. A Navy battleship captain can't decide in the middle of a skirmish 'I'm tired and I'm going back to land'. He would be court martialed; you can't abandon your crew. (Watkins, 2003: 121)

'Skilling knew that we had hit an iceberg, that we were taking on water, that it was probably lethal, and he was choosing to go home', Watkins (2003: 121) adds, leaving little room for interpretation. Watkins' and other commentators' assessment of the Enron leadership strongly contrast with some pre-bankruptcy accounts, including, for example, Gary Hamel's management guru-style volume *Leading the Revolution* (2000), peppered with enthusiasm over Enron's ability to transform the energy market from being 'stodgy old-boys' clubs' into 'flexible energy markets that meet the everchanging needs of energy-hungry customers' (Hamel, 2000: 211). Hamel (2000: 219) speaks about the 'spectacular success' of Enron, and even explicitly addresses Enron's advanced 'risk management practices' as being one of their core competencies, two statements that were shattered to pieces (and possibly did not exactly boost the credibility of Hamel's academic and consultancy work) once the post-bankruptcy investigations revealed systematic fraud throughout the one-time seventh largest corporation in the US. To further underline how conspicuously the Enron executives and directors ignored their fiduciary duties and other professional norms and standards of decency, Watkins' article can be cited at length:

> [On 3 December 2001] the employees were told to get back to their desks, pack up personal items, and leave [... In contrast] 25 executives received three-months retention bonuses in the last week of November 2001 [...] These 25 executives paid themselves nearly $55 million. One person got $8 million, another $5 million, another $2 million, two more paid themselves $1.5 million, several people received $700,000, $600,000, and $400,000 bonuses. Enron's annual salaries for these managing directors were closer to $300,000 per year – so many of these 'special' bonuses were three to five times annual base pay. (Watkins, 2003: 122)

No wonder the term 'Enronitis', meaning 'a situation in which large corporations fail to secure investment because they are suspected of fraud and mismanagement' (Collins

English Dictionary, accessed 27 May 2015 at: http://www.collinsdictionary.com/dictionary/english/enronitis), is the lasting heritage of Enron. Another consequence is the Sarbanes–Oxley Act.

2. Managerialism, the problem of principal–agent relations, and free market advocacy

INTRODUCTION

In the mid-nineteenth century to the 1920s periods, the modern day capitalist economic system and many of its institutions were established, including not least the hierarchical, divisionalized corporate form that large American corporations such as General Motors developed. The swift growth of, for example, the American economy in the period brought economic prosperity but also led to the concentration of economic value. The oligarchic tendencies in industry and the strong position of finance industry actors were two of the concerns that politicians and policy-makers sought to handle through the means of legislation. The liberal lawyer Louis D. Brandeis published a volume in 1914 wherein he discussed the role of what he referred to as 'the money trust', the influence of finance institutions that imperilled 'industrial and political liberty' (Brandeis, 1914 [1967]: 43). In his critique of the finance institutions, Brandeis had no desire to sugarcoat the pill:

> The goose that lays golden eggs has been considered a most valuable possession. But even more profitable is the privilege of taking the golden eggs laid by somebody else's goose. The investment bankers and their associates now enjoy that privilege. They control the people through the people's own money. If the bankers' power were commensurate only with their wealth, they would have relatively little influence on American business ... The power and the growth of power of our financial oligarchs comes from wielding the savings and quick capital of others ... The fetters which bind the people are forged from the people's own gold. (Brandeis, 1914 [1967]: 12–13)

Also Thorstein Veblen (1916), the economist and social theorist and one of the genuine intellectual outsiders of the twentieth century, addresses the role of finance capital owners in the American industrial system. Speaking about bankers and other finance industry actors as the 'financial captains of industry', this group of investors demonstrate, Veblen (1916: 16) claimed, an 'addiction to abstract and unremitting valuation of all things in terms of price and profit', which leaves them unfit to appreciate the everyday practices of managing a business, a task now being delegated to 'a bureaucratic clerical staff' (Veblen, 1916: 16). Veblen (1916: 16) deplores this authority and argues that finance industry actors are only 'experts in process and profits and financial manoeuvres', but their access to finance capital grants them favourable positions: '[t]he final discretion in all questions of industrial policy continues to rest in their hands', Veblen says (1916: 16). In the American industrial system of the first decades of the twentieth century, Veblen summarizes, the credit system is '[g]athered into a self-balanced whole, closed and unbreakable, self-insured against all risk and derangement' (Veblen, 1916: 27). The works of Brandeis (1914 [1967]) and Veblen (1916) are indicative of the widespread concern regarding the influence of finance industry actors (investment banks, finance institutes, arbitrageurs, speculators, rentiers and so on) in the industrial system of competitive capitalism. Antitrust legislation had already been enacted in the 1890s, but after the Wall Street crash of 1929, there was again a growing suspicion in political quarters that this legislation was not sufficient to counteract the interests of specific groups such as capital owners. In the 1920s and 1930s during the Great Depression, a new regime of managerial capitalism was developed, wherein managers operating the large-scale corporations characteristic of the mass-production-based capitalism that emerged in the post-World War II period were given specific privileges but also responsibilities to act in accordance with wider political ambitions beyond sheer economic value creation. While the New Deal politics of the Roosevelt Administration in many ways managed to push the American economy out of its stalemate, the strong tendency to increasingly locate the initiative to monitor the economy in political organizations and agencies became subject to intense debates and criticism in the 1930s and 1940s. Being branded as a form of 'collectivism' that shared many qualities with the communist planned economies in the eyes of its critics, the New Deal programme was by and large treated as a form of deviation from the free market ideal that classical and what would be known as neoclassical economic theory prescribed as the most efficient way to price commodities and to transfer capital.

THE ROLE OF MANAGERS, THE FIRM, AND THE CRITIQUE OF COLLECTIVISM

Ownership and Control: Adolf Berle's Seminal Problem

Bratton (1989b: 413) remarks that in the economic system of corporate capitalism, where ownership is private and economic activities are centred on corporations, the executives and managers overseeing these corporations have three sources of power. First, they 'determine the processes of production and distribution'. Second, they 'dominate enormous hierarchical bureaucracies and exercise authority over all those lower in the hierarchy'. These two sources of power are essentially located within the structure of the corporation, but as the wider economy takes advantage of these goods and services being produced, especially in the case of monopolies or oligarchies, these intraorganizational sources of power entail extra-organizational influence. In addition, being the third source of power, executives and managers 'impose externalities on those outside the entities' (Bratton, 1989b: 413). Based on these conditions, that executives and managers do have a substantial amount of power to influence the wider society and the economy, there are good reasons for politicians and policy-makers to enact laws and regulations, and to impose practices that balance operational freedom to act on the part of the managers and other social interests. Corporate law and various additional legislation have been the principal tools to accomplish such benefits, but in the 1920s and especially after 1929, there were also reasons to think about the norms, values, attitudes and ideologies of the men (not so many women yet) in the executive suites and how well they conformed with wider social interest and ambitions.

The legal scholar Adolf A. Berle was engaging with this problem in the 1920s, and while liberals such as Louis D. Brandeis tended to argue that antitrust laws should be more effectively enforced to make the economy more efficient, Berle took an entirely different analytical route, arguing that market competition per se was perhaps part of the problem (Bratton and Wachter, 2008: 110). Under all conditions, the Wall Street crash and the following Great Depression, the largest economic crisis of the twentieth century by far, had little to do with ineffective antitrust legislation. In 1934, Berle published *The Modern Corporation & Private Property* together with Gardiner C. Means, a seminal work in corporate governance theory, one of 'the most influential social-scientific works of the twentieth century', in Moore and Rebérioux's (2011: 86) account. Berle and Means (1934) here stressed the difference between the *principals* of the firm, including, for example, stockholders and creditors, and the *agents*, the salaried managers who are granted the operational authority and discretion within the corporations they oversee. This distinction between ownership and practical management has ever since become the most generic relation in the corporate governance literature and in agency theory in particular. Unfortunately, much of the substance of Berle and Means's work has been ignored or misinterpreted. In his writing that preceded the publication of *The Modern Corporation & Private Property*, Berle noticed that in the 1920s, roughly one-third of all the American economic wealth was controlled by the 200 largest corporations, and the executives in these corporations were therefore 'the princes of property', Berle claimed (Bratton and Wachter, 2008: 111). Berle was no Marxist, but a liberal, and one of President Roosevelt's entrusted New Deal advisors, but he was sceptical regarding the concentration of wealth and economic power in the hands of a few executives. For that reason, the role of the executive should be carefully examined. While *The Modern Corporation & Private Property* offered relatively limited recommendations for legal reform, it indicated a strong preference for executives to take on a technocratic and almost semi-political role inasmuch as they should understand that they were managing corporations of pervasive and wide-ranging economic influence. In fact, Berle and Means (1934: 353–6) argued that management should develop into a 'purely neutral technocracy' (Bratton and Wachter, 2008: 121).

In the more recent reading of Berle and Means's work in, for example, agency theory and the so-called contractual theory of the firm (discussed in Chapter 3 in this volume), it is primarily the distinction between principals and agents that has been appropriated and integrated within the agency theory view that managers are the shareholders' agents, working for their benefit. The wider socio-economic and political role of executives and managers is thus defenestrated in the pursuit to find a foundational text for the shareholder welfare agenda of agency theorists. This is a narrow-minded and essentially faulty reading of Berle and Means's work, Bratton and Wachter (2008: 121) argue: '[i]nstead of unrestrained maximization, directors were to maximize the value of the corporation in a way that satisfied societal goals'. Also Mizruchi (2004: 581) stresses the wider significance of the executives' and managers' work in the economy in Berle's work, today mostly ignored by commentators: 'Berle and Means's concern about the separation of ownership from control was not simply about managers' lack of accountability to investors. It was also a concern about managers' lack of accountability to society in general'. For Berle and Means, the unstable and potentially self-destructive nature of competitive capitalism did not derive from, as agency theorists would have it from the early 1970s, the managers of large-scale corporations acting opportunistically to benefit their own interests, but because they fail to see their wider social and societal roles as agents who are accountable not only to shareholders but to all citizens and benefactors of their work: '[f]ar from being an offspring, shareholder primacy contradicts Berle rather than succeeds him', Bratton and Wachter (2008: 151) summarize.

The work of Berle and Berle and Means's book represented the beginning of a theoretico-practical pursuit to critically rethink the role of managers within the regime of competitive capitalism. With competitive capitalism enduring its worst crisis ever in the 1930s and with the communist planned economies reporting strong growth in the period, there were good reasons for intellectuals of all political hues to carefully examine the legal-political and economic rules of the games and the mechanisms of competitive capitalism. Even a dedicated free market economist such as Joseph Schumpeter (1942) was not too sure that the competitive capitalism model would be able to sustain the pressure from alternative economic systems. Far from being hegemonic, in the 1920s and 1930s competitive capitalism seemed vulnerable and unstable. That competitive capitalism was an economic system capable of producing large economic wealth was beyond doubt, but was it a sustainable economic system that could operate in tandem with the wider society? Such questions were addressed by Adolf Berle and his collaborators in the period.

The New Deal and Managerial Capitalism

The progressive era legal reform and the birth of welfare capitalism

After the Wall Street crash of 1929, the American and the global economy plunged into a long-term depression and more abstract academic hair-splitting had to give way to practical work to restore competitive capitalism. Already in the early nineteenth century, social reformers such as Henri de Saint-Simon (1817 [1975]: 160) had advocated an economic model that Saint-Simon referred to as *L'organization industrielle*, an organization that included both 'those who produce and those who safeguard the producers'. This economic organization thus embodied both the production functions of competitive capitalism and its legal and regulatory institutions, agencies and their activities. Such a regulated economic system was less appealing for both capital owners and academic economists, who were more intrigued by the metaphor of the 'invisible hand' proposed by Adam Smith. In this view, it is self-interested and enterprising actors who through their self-serving activities ensure that there is a steady and predictable supply of commodities in the market. What this invisible hand really would be in terms of economic theory and policy remains unclear to this day, but neoclassic economic theorists tend to believe that it is the market per se that is bestowed with such abilities to almost effortlessly coordinate uncoordinated economic activities to the benefit of all social actors. While this Smithean mechanism has become a staple reference within the neoclassical corpus, in practice the invisible hand of the market had by and large been displaced by the most visible hands of salaried managers by the end of the nineteenth century: '[i]n many sectors of the economy the visible hand of management replaced what Adam Smith referred to as the invisible hand of the market forces ... The rise of modern business enterprise in the United States, therefore, brought with it managerial capitalism' (Chandler, 1977: 1).

In the antebellum period, there were few salaried managers in the American economy, but as the corporations grew in size and became geographically dispersed (as in the case of the US railroad companies), the owners were no longer capable of monitoring the activities but had to rely on entrusted salaried managers (Chandler, 1977: 3). While the old regime of *ownership capitalism* or *personal capitalism* did not die out overnight and many autocratic owners such as Henry Ford could maintain their grip of their corporations well into the post-World War II period, by the first decades of the twentieth century the regime of managerial capitalism was by and large in place. The new regime of *welfare capitalism* (Jacoby, 1997; Brandes, 1976) or *corporate welfarism* (Berkowitz and McQuaid, 1978), one of the foremost consequences of the 'rule of professional managers', was based on two parallel developments: one process centred on legal-political reform and emphasized new legislation and effective court ruling, and one process reformed the corporations themselves, propelled by the managers' anxiousness to handle and respond to the souring amount of conflicts between labour, management and capital owners by establishing new labour relations (Jenkins and Brents, 1989).[1] These two attempts to reform the capitalist economic system were endorsed and actively supported by moderate to liberal economists who organized the American Association for Labor Legislation (AALL), including, *inter alia*, the renowned institutionalist John R. Commons (Moss, 1996).

Addressing the first development, Urofsky (1985: 63) stresses that the legal system (and more specifically the courts) by and large, despite being portrayed as the 'enemies of reform' by some progressives, 'upheld the vast majority of the protective statutes it reviewed' (Urofsky, 1985: 63). This faith expressed in the rule of law was based on the belief, as

Richard Hofstadter put it (cited in Urofsky, 1985: 64), that 'industrialized society was to be humanized by law'. More specifically and of interest for the forthcoming discussion, conservatives opposed such legal reform and instead sought to enshrine the laissez-faire rationalism of the nineteenth century in the form of contracts, a specific form of juridical expression based on bilateral agreements rather than comprehensive reforms and legislations benefiting a wider community (Urofsky, 1985: 65). However, the legal system did not approve the contractual solution: '[t]he doctrine of contracts ... was far from triumphant at the state level' (Urofsky, 1985: 88). Instead, the courts basically implemented the progressive reforms in legal institutions, even though the courts carefully balanced a series of interests and concerns:

> Rather than as bastions of reaction, most state courts could be fairly characterized as upholders of the best common-law tradition, attempting to meet the new social and economic conditions of the country. In doing so they did not embrace one doctrine to the exclusion of others but, in most cases, balanced legal doctrines, contracts and police power. (Urofsky, 1985: 88)

In parallel to the legislative reforms and changes, in the first decades of the twentieth century a specific form of paternalist *welfare capitalism* was developed in some of the major American corporations (Brandes, 1976), including the camera manufacturer Kodak in Rochester, New York, and the retailing company Sears, Roebuck & Company in Chicago, Illinois (Jacoby, 1997). Welfare capitalism benefited white, working-class men and to a lesser degree white, working-class women, but few people of colour or ethnic minorities were hired by these companies and fitted poorly into the cultural and social homogeneity and conformism that was the foundation of the welfare capitalist model, rooted in what Graebner (1987) refers to as the 'engineering of consent'. Ultimately, Brandes (1976: 6) argues, welfare capitalism proved to be an unacceptable solution to the crisis of labour–management relations in the period: 'Americans rejected the big stick policy, the idea of social revolution, and welfare capitalism', and opted for the tripartite system developed in the New Deal era and successfully instituted in the postwar period, characterized by 'a continuing tug of war between big labor and big business with government seeking to prevent either side from gaining predominance' (Brandes, 1976: 6).

Roosevelt's New Deal
Adelstein (1991) argues that American managerialism was influenced by the 'social physics' developed in Europe by Auguste Comte and Henri de

Saint-Simon in France, and by the idealistic statism of Georg W.F. Hegel and German historicists, who saw 'the democratic state as the voice and active agent of the social being in the world of affairs' (Adelstein, 1991: 165). In Europe, for centuries tortured by religious and political wars between competing states, the nation state was widely seen as a legitimate vehicle for political stability, modernization and economic growth. In the US, a confederation of former British, French and a few more European colonies, the state had an entirely different meaning as what would threaten the hard-earned freedom of the individual. Many colonialists and migrants had also fled repressive religious authorities and an autocratic aristocracy in Europe, and, more generally, poverty at large to settle in the new continent. Despite these differences between Europe and the US, the American managerialists believed in the active role of the state as a means to secure a functional economy. Adelstein (1991) here described an almost Manichean struggle in America between the dislike of collectivism and the fear of economic oligarchies:

> The intrinsic collectivism of the managerial vision met with strong resistance in an individualistic culture still deeply distrustful of central government. An equally pervasive hatred of monopoly and concentrated economic power led to the Sherman Act of 1890 and bespoke a widespread uneasiness with the apparently inexorable advance of large-scale organization. (Adelstein, 1991: 166)

In the late 1920s and 1930s, when the previously functional capitalist economic system seemed to end up in a deadlock, the Roosevelt Administration embarked on the New Deal economic rescue programme, the National Industrial Recovery Act (NIRA) in the early 1930s (for an authoritative account of the New Deal debates and reforms, see Hawley, 1966). The support for Roosevelt and his politics was overwhelming, and ended decades of Republican dominance in American politics:

> The election of 1932 gave Roosevelt a huge majority. The Democrats' majorities in Congress – 311 to 116 in the House and 60 to 35 in the Senate – were the largest the party had ever received and the largest for any party since 1910. The 1934 and 1936 elections cemented Roosevelt's remarkable victory. The latter is the only midterm election since the Civil War in which the president's party picked up seats in both the House and Senate. This extraordinary electoral sweep was completed in 1936. Roosevelt buried Alf Landon, losing only Maine and Vermont. The lineup in Congress was stunning. In the Senate, Democrats outnumbered Republicans 76 to 16. (Hacker and Pierson, 2002: 296)

Roosevelt was the hope for many in a period of time wherein 'capitalism seemed to have lost its control over the country' (Bellow, 2015: 395). When Roosevelt was elected, Saul Bellow (2015: 317) recalls, aged 17 at the time, his algebra teacher Miss Scherbarth, 'an elderly lady whose white hair was piled in a cumulus formation over her square face and her blue-tinted square glasses, allowed herself a show of feeling and sang "Happy days are here again". Our astonishment was great. As a rule Miss Scherbarth was all business'.

President Franklin D. Roosevelt was a liberal Democratic president but he was not a great friend of collectivism and intuitively understood how the New Deal programme would be received in some quarters. Yet he saw few other options than to infuse the economy with the lifeblood of collectivist economic activities when private enterprise failed to restore economic growth:

> [Roosevelt] intuitively grasped the fundamental problem of central planning in a free society – how to imbue the people with a spirit of common purpose sufficiently powerful to win their submission to the end of the planners and their consent to the intrusive control of day-to-day economic affairs that planning most entails. (Adelstein, 1991: 161)

The New Deal programme included all kinds of economic and social, even cultural, projects, all aimed to restore the American economic system based on private ownership and enterprise accompanied by relatively moderate forms of political regulation of economic affairs. Despite the slow and gradual restoration of the economic system and the faith in it in the 1930s, Roosevelt received a fair share of criticism for worsening rather than restoring economic conditions. While such criticism often was based on deductive reasoning on the basis of economic theory propositions and turning a blind eye to the economic hardship of millions of Americans (of which John Steinbeck's *The Grapes of Wrath* is perhaps the most well-known literary account), Roosevelt's policies and programmes did win in the end in terms of successfully rehabilitating American competitive capitalism.

Despite the critique from primarily free market quarters, Roosevelt's political speeches did not debunk collectivism; instead, it was part of his message, that in times of hardship the business leaders must rise to the occasion and think of themselves as being part of a larger community: '[b]usiness', Roosevelt said, 'must think less of its own profit and more of the national function that it performs. Each unit of it must think of itself as a part of a greater whole, one piece in a larger design' (Roosevelt in a speech in 1932, cited in Adelstein, 1991: 175). Such speeches are indicative of how collectivism had gained a grip on American society, critics contended, and consequently, the New Deal programme became subject to systematic criticism in the business community, which was clear-sighted enough to understand that New Deal-era politics represented a major shift in power, and not to its favour this time:

> More threatening than any piece of legislation were the ideological and political realignments that produced the New Deal itself. Businessmen were no longer seen as national heroes or as guarantors of the nation's prosperity. Instead, the country's hope now lay with Big Labor and Big Government. The proximate cause of these changes was the Depression, whose severity permanently altered the political landscape. (Jacoby, 1997: 193)

Langston (1992) suggests that much of this criticism was unjustified and failed to see the dangers of political passivity, recently demonstrated by Roosevelt's predecessor Herbert Hoover, whose tardy and incompetent response to the Depression paved the way for a long reign of Democratic presidents:

> Franklin Roosevelt's New Deal ... was a triumph of neither socialism nor fascism, bolshevism nor monarchicalism. In discussing Roosevelt's program today, in fact, these terms are useless except as epithets ... [T]o associate the program of an American president with one of these foreign ideologies has always been a favorite ploy of those who would unconditionally damn an administrative effort. The critics of Roosevelt ... made common appeal to the demons of Socialism, Bolshevism, and other heresies. But Roosevelt's critics largely miss their mark, for within the New Deal, the adherents of 'foreign' ideologies were largely irrelevant. (Langston, 1992: 70)

Hawley (1966) argues that there were components of economic planning inherent to NIRA, but the inspiration for this work was for the most part of American origin rather than having foreign influences:

> [A vision] that found its way into the National Industrial Recovery Act was that of a collectivist democracy engaged in purposeful national planning. ... A few drew inspiration from foreign precedents, particularly from the newly inaugurated Soviet Five Year Plan. But the great majority elaborated on a planning ideology that was indigenous to America. One line of inspiration here came from the discipline of scientific management, from the system of ideas developed by such men as Frederick W. Taylor and Henry L.L. Gantt and applied to the economy as a whole by writers influenced by Thorstein Veblen. From Veblen these men drew such concepts as the technological imperative, the work-a-day, matter-of-fact discipline of the machine process, and the distinction between the business interest and the industrial interest. (Hawley, 1966: 43–4)

In addition, during World War I, from which the American economy benefited greatly, the idea of a planned economy had first been established, and as it proved to work better than was perhaps anticipated, there was a certain degree of acceptance among politicians and state officials in Washington for economic planning as a viable governance model. As the free market economy apparently had unattractive features from a policy-maker's view and had proved to be unstable and unable to recover on its own, economic planning did not appear to be devoid of merits from a policy-making perspective. The Roosevelt administration thus encountered the thorny question on how to stitch together a functional model that satisfied the interests and convictions of the key actors participating in the economic recovery work, and how to avoid the Scylla and Charybdis of state-governed central economic planning (being an unattractive alternative, also including many risks) and a return to unregulated free market capitalism (which had proved to function poorly without the oversight of the sovereign state):

> The policy of enforcing competition, said the planners and business rationalizers, was outmoded, intellectually bankrupt, and a proven failure. The vision of a business commonwealth, said the antitrusters and national planners, was only a mask for the proven evils of private monopoly. And the idea of democratic planning, said the antitrusters and business planners, was a contradiction in terms, a policy that could only result in the eventual destruction of political democracy, property rights, individual liberty, and the capitalist system. (Hawley, 1966: 43–4)

Carosso (1970: 428) argues that Roosevelt engaged two groups in the work to restore and revitalize the American economy. One group were the so-called Brandeisian progressives who 'believed in regulation, opposed bigness, and feared monopoly – most of all a money monopoly'. The other group were a set of advisors who were sceptical of free markets and argued for closer business–government cooperation and more national planning. According to Carosso (1970: 428), Roosevelt listened to both sides, 'but in the end decided in favor of regulation', that is, the free, yet regulated market solution won, leaving less space for central agencies to plan and monitor the economy. Despite the unfavourable conditions and circumstances that Roosevelt's advisors had to handle, a preference for free markets accompanied by regulatory procedures and law enforcements and an American enterprising culture still dominated the New Deal programmes and legislation. In fact, as Kaufman and Zacharias (1992: 542) demonstrate, the New Deal corporate legislation was not so much a form of 'collectivist project' undermining competitive capitalism as it effectively reinforced shareholders' rights:

New Deal securities legislation in effect authorizes federal officials to reinforce the shareholder's ownership role under state laws and to reduce the risks of separating ownership from control ... To ensure that shareholders had information adequate to oversee management, Congress required corporations to issue periodic financial reports ... Congress carefully avoided changing the state's powers to charter corporations and to define the substance of the shareholder–management relationship. (Kaufman and Zacharias, 1992: 542)

Carosso (1970: 432–3) argues that the New Deal policies did not harm the finance industry as the securities laws proved to be '[f]ar less fundamental than some of their advocates had expected or many of their opponents had feared'. None of the key practices and legal relations were significantly altered.

Despite the New Deal legislation securing the functioning of competitive capitalism, even in the event of its worst crisis to date in the US, previously benefiting greatly from the World War I economy that strongly contributed to the US taking over the role as the world's leading economy (Ahamed, 2009), free market protagonists and libertarian theorists and pundits and the pro-business community more widely were far from convinced regarding the efficacy and long-term consequences of the New Deal policy. Instead, there was a growing concern that a planned economy that undermined entrepreneurialism and the enterprising American culture was underway. The catchphrase par excellence to denote this new political-administrative culture was *collectivism*, and the idea that trust and fiduciary duties alone would be capable of restoring the economy and its corporations was treated with scepticism:

> Totalitarianism might thus lurk ominously behind trust, and this treat loomed large in postwar writing on the modern corporation. Few could avoid comparing the concentrated power of large corporations and their 'supporting' regulatory apparatus with that of various Soviet counterparts. This comparison was particularly disturbing in regulated industries like energy, communications, and transportation, in which the distinctions between private and public administration were far from clear. (Kaufman et al., 1995: 61)

As will be discussed below, despite their many new solutions to corporate governance problems, the New Deal-era policies gave rise to a new version of free market advocacy, not so much sharing Adolf Berle's concerns that it is the free market capitalism per se that caused the Great Depression as it took the opposed route – to claim that it is the state meddling with economic affairs and more specifically the culture of collectivism that precedes economic decline.

The Concept of Collectivism and the Formation of the Neoliberal Thought Community

In 1937, the well-known writer, political commentator and public intellectual Walter Lippmann, mostly known for his writing about the role of journalism in democratic society, published the book *The Good Society*. The book was written in what many historians regard as the most politically unstable decade of the twentieth century, with Stalin in power in the economically consolidated new communist Soviet federation, fascists strengthening their positions in, for example, Germany and Italy, and with the Depression looming in the US, including conflicts between capital owners and the labour movement such as the large sit-down strike at General Motors in 1936–37 (Fine, 1969) and what would be known as the 'Dearborn Massacre', when Ford Motor Company's so-called 'service men' opened fire on laid-off workers at the River Rouge Plant in Michigan, killing five protesters (Grandin, 2009: 243). Seeing classic economic and political liberalism being hemmed in in many ways, Lippmann criticized what he treated as rampant collectivism that would undermine the Western economies unless it was counteracted by liberals. 'Unless he [the contemporary man] is authoritarian and collectivist, he is a mossback, a reactionary, at best an amiable eccentric swimming hopelessly against the tide. It is a strong tide', Walter Lippmann wrote (cited in Cockett, 1994: 10), indicating his resentment vis-à-vis the new political climate.

Lippmann had originally supported the New Deal as a response to the effects of the 1929 Wall Street crash, serving to restore the belief in the political system's ability to monitor and regulate the economy (Krome, 1987: 57). However, in 1937, Roosevelt initiated a reform of the court system that would strengthen the political control, which Lippmann regarded as a too far-reaching policy that would undermine the constitution and thus be 'incompatible with the tenets of liberal democracy' (Krome, 1987: 59):

> Roosevelt, Lippmann believed, was a man who would operate within the American Constitutional system. The problem was that in his desire to do good, Roosevelt was placing the whole American system in danger. Roosevelt had instituted many precedents. While Lippmann did not believe Roosevelt would abuse them, other leaders might. (Krome, 1987: 60)

Lippmann's critique of collectivism was grounded in his concern for the democratic political system. Lippmann also believed that an active government was a moral, not a political or an economic question (Krome, 1987: 60), and claimed that the government's job would be to 'stimulate, sometimes regulate, and aid the economy in time of need' (Krome, 1987: 60). In other words, unlike some of his European admirers, Lippmann firmly believed in democracy and above all in the American constitution, and he did not oppose an active government intervening in the economy when necessary. For Lippmann, it was democracy per se that needed to be defended against collectivism as it is the most efficient system to translate diverging interests into robust compromises (Krome, 1987: 61).

The Good Society immediately received much attention. In 1938, the renowned Chicago economist Frank Knight published a most positive review of *The Good Society*, including many anti-statist declarations that would become a common thread in the free market advocacy for the rest of the century: '[t]he first and essential function and task of government is to preserve unthreatened its own monopoly of political power, and that means prevention of the development of dangerous power groups outside itself', Knight (1938: 865) argues. When Lippmann states that '[t]here is no way of practicing the division of labor, and of harvesting the fruits of it, except in a social order which preserves and strives to perfect the freedom of the market' (*The Good Society*, p. 297, cited in Knight, 1938: 867), Knight agrees with no reservations, and proposes that the view that 'collectivism means dictatorship is correct beyond reasonable doubt' (Knight, 1938: 868–9). This dictatorship is manifested accordingly, Knight (1938: 868–9) continues: '[t]he authorities of a collectivist state would have to have unlimited power, and security of tenure, and would have to exercise their power ruthlessly to keep the machinery of organized production and distribution running'. For Knight, eventually proving to be one of the more moderate free market protagonists (Van Horn and Emmett, 2015; Jones, 2012), at least in comparison to 'dogmatic supporters of laissez-faire' (Quiggin, 2010: 21) such as Friedrich von Hayek and Ludwig von Mises, Lippmann provided an accurate and timely description of the current situation.

In France, Louis Rougier, Professor of Philosophy in Besançon, organized *Le Colloque Walter Lippmann* between 20 and 30 August 1938 in Paris to bring together academics, intellectuals and possibly also industrialists who shared Lippmann's sense of urgency (Cockett, 1994: 9). For Rougier, Lippmann's book was 'the best exhibit of the evils of our times' ('*La meilleure explication des maux de notre temps*', cited in Cockett, 1994: 9). Many leading middle-right intellectuals participated in *Le Colloque Walter Lippmann*, including the French sociologist Raymond Aron, the Austrian economist Hayek, his mentor and teacher Mises, and the renowned liberal German economist Wilhelm Röpke. When Rougier published the conference proceedings, he prided himself on his accomplishments and was not shy to refer to it as the 'Magna Carta of Liberalism' (Cockett, 1994: 10).

In the UK and more specifically at the London School of Economics where Lionel Robbins and eventually Hayek were located, Lippmann's work was seen as a breath of fresh air into what the LSE faculty regarded as a Keynesian economic hegemony. As Robbins explained in a letter to Lippmann, economists in Europe felt themselves to be intellectually and politically isolated and Robbins even spoke of an 'Elijah complex' (after the Old Testament prophet Elijah), stating: '[o]nly I, of all the prophets of God, remain' (cited in Jackson, 2012: 57). In the era of Keynesian economic policy and increased preferences for collectivist thinking and ideologies, few stood up to defend economic liberalism, Robbins and Hayek argued.[2] Lippmann claimed he had read the works of Hayek and Mises as part of his critique of planned economies, and Hayek himself entertained the idea of writing a similar work to further stress the urgency to counteract collectivism and state-governed economies. In 1944, after facing some difficulties in finding a publisher for this work, Hayek finally published *The Road to Serfdom*, a seminal work in the genre of free market advocacy, wherein he forcefully defended free market economies. The book acquired much interest but the publication of the volume was untimely, being published at the end of the war and at the entry-point of the most significant expansion of the Western economies and economic welfare and equality brought by the Keynesian economic policy, supported by the *Pax Romana* jointly accomplished by capital owners and the labour movement and the expansion of the welfare state. These changes by and large rendered Hayek's work as a text that conspicuously failed to predict the consequences of his anathema collectivism.

> The reason for the lukewarm reception [of *The Road to Serfdom*] may lie in the contrast between Hayek's predictions and the experience of most of his readers … Certain forms of planning such as rationing came to an end [after World War II], but welfare provisions expanded rapidly after the war and monetary and fiscal policy were systematically used to ensure full employment. Hayek had warned that the expansion of planning would be the prelude to a loss of liberty, but many in the Western world had a different experience in this period: by the early 1970s, women had acquired greater freedom than ever before in most Western countries. In the same period, African Americans began to harvest the fruits of their long struggle for civil rights. (Schui, 2014: 134)

The 1950s and 1960s, contrary to Hayek's bleak scenario, became the triumph of the Keynesian economic model. Despite receiving much attention in conservative circles, especially in the US where Hayek's anti-statism struck a chord and turned Hayek into a minor celebrity figure, Hayek's work did not in any way anticipate the consequences of the welfare state.[3]

In 1947, based on a donation from a Swiss businessman (many of the free market protagonists' activities were sponsored by private financiers, indicating their marginal position in the era of Keynesianism; see, for example, Fourcade and Khurana, 2013; Jones, 2012; Peck, 2010), Hayek organized a conference in the alpine resort of Mont Pèlerin in Switzerland, and just as in *Le Colloque Walter Lippmann* nine years earlier, prominent economists (for example, Chicago economists such as Frank Knight, George Stigler and Milton Friedman), social theorists (for example, Michael Polanyi), philosophers (for example, Karl Popper), and industrialists participated. Hayek suggested that what would be known as the Mont Pèlerin Society (MPS) would become 'something halfway between a scholarly association and a political society' (Mirowski, 2013: 43), actively undermining collectivist theories, ideologies and policies. Ultimately, Mirowski (2013: 43) says, 'the project was to produce a functional hierarchical elite of regimented political intellectuals'. As the university system was already entrenched by collectivist-minded academics, liberals and left-leaning scholars who did not share the MPS members' convictions and worries, Hayek and his collaborators thought, the free market protagonists of MPS and elsewhere had little hope that the university would be the best vehicle to advance their programme. Instead, close-knit communities with regulated entries and membership became the model *par préférence*. Despite MPS members eventually claiming a long series of Bank of Sweden's Prizes in Economic Sciences in memory of Alfred Nobel (at times incorrectly called 'the Nobel Prize in Economics'), the Mont Pèlerin Society, Peck (2010: 40) says, was 'struggling and inchoate' and 'was for many years a club of losers'. In the era of the expansion of the welfare state, regulated on the basis of Keynesian economic theories, the free marketeers could do little more than bide their time in resorts generously paid for by wealthy industrialists who shared their concerns regarding the influence of, for example, trade unions in the regime of competitive capitalism.

The concept of collectivism

Apparently, the imprecise term *collectivism* needs to be operationalized to enable an understanding of what exactly it was that made these liberals and libertarians so alarmed regarding its political significance. After all, the post-World War era brought unprecedented economic growth, and that would – in theory at least – possibly cheer up self-declared defenders of 'economic freedom'. There is something beneath the surface of economic considerations that propels the strong sense of resentment vis-à-vis 'collectivism' in, for example, Hayek's work. In the following, the three themes of free market efficiency, elitism and anti-unionism will be examined as interrelated components of the dismissal of collectivism.

First of all, Hayek and his peers were not particularly interested in distinguishing between the various forms and schools of the collectivist programme that they saw in front of them.[4] 'For Hayek, planning, socialism and totalitarianism were part of the same problem', Grocott (2015: 154) says. Cassidy (2009) addresses Hayek's position in *The Road to Serfdom*:

> This was a strange way to portray the European welfare state and Roosevelt's New Deal. From the purist perspective, health insurance, Social Security, state-financed education, and regional development programs were violations of laissez-faire, but none of them impinged on the industrial and financial core of the enterprise system. (Cassidy, 2009: 45)

Even the most rudimentary analysis would have revealed vast differences between, for example, the social democratic or social-liberal welfare state's economic policy in many countries in Europe and its concern for entrepreneurship and private enterprise, and the totalitarian Soviet-style command economy beyond the iron curtain. But what Mirowski (2013), alluding to Ludwik Fleck's (1979) apt term, calls the *neoliberal thought collective* (NTC) was blinded by their staunch belief in the urgency to fight their identified enemies of economic freedom to engage in such more elaborate discussions. Bigotry rather than a scholarly attitude based on reasoning and debate was characteristic of this early stage free market advocacy.

The Euclidean axiom regarding the value of economic freedom was embedded in the idea of the market being what Hayek called a 'spontaneous order' and an 'information-processing unit'. As Burgin (2012: 188) points out, Hayek did not believe that markets per se of necessity rewarded merit, but his market advocacy was rooted in the belief that 'markets provided an ethically neutral arbiter, and that this was preferable to any system that tried to determine outcomes in the basis of a preconceived notion of good'. That is, markets are capable of accommodating all the information available and thus provide a *price function*, that is, the market price effectively embodies if not all, at least most of the public information available. The market thus processes more information than any planning agency, no matter how efficient and well managed, can practically handle. In Hayek and his followers' account, the market offered two key benefits: it promised formal quality and effectively processed information: '[t]he market had great power to reserve, even nurture, individual freedoms. Its rule promised formal equality. They allowed people to solve problems as they saw them and according to their own tastes, instead of forcing everyone to accept collective definitions, priorities and solutions' (Kaufman et al., 1995: 60).

In addition, to make markets function efficiently, that is, to operate 'rationally' with the neoclassical economic theory term, there is a need for *competition*. It is in general, Hayek (1979: 76) asserts, 'not rationality' which is required to make markets work, but 'competition, or traditions which allow competition, which will all produce rational behavior'. As with many other economic propositions, this strong faith in the rationality brought by competition and the many benefits of free market activities such as efficient pricing may appear as parsimonious and logically consistent theories, whereas they do not of necessity work in practice, Konzelmann (2014) notices:

> There is something reassuring to neoliberals – given their fixation with the overarching efficiency of markets – in the assumption that public sector profligacy and private sector parsimony (and vice versa) are interactive. If this was the case the economic system would indeed become self-stabilizing, obviating the need for government intervention. However, there are few signs of any such tendency towards automatic stabilization. (Konzelmann, 2014: 732)

In other words, the Euclidean axiom of the NTC, the idea that markets are efficient, was never true as markets are of necessity not celestial mathematical operators and arenas for original and unbiased competition on an equal footing, but, as shown by economic historians, economists and economic sociologists, they are man-made arenas for economic exchanges and transactions. The so-called *efficient market hypothesis* (EMH) has served as a foundational principle for neoclassic economic theory and what would be called price theory, and even though it has time and again been proved to be incorrect (market efficiency is, at best, weak and market prices therefore do not contain all available information), a long series of ad hoc hypotheses have been added to save this core of the neoclassical theory programme (mostly in terms of listing the undesirable consequences of governments' interventions into markets).

Second, one shared theme of free market advocacy is the elitism that portrays certain individuals as being the victims of their own inability to make adequate assessments of predominant economic conditions. Hayek was himself never fully convinced about the value of democracy and, for example, his approval of the brutal dictatorship of General Augusto

Pinochet in Chile in the 1970s testified to this attitude (Hayek did not hesitate to accuse the democratically elected socialist Salvador Allende, apparently representing a more 'collectivist' political agenda than Pinochet, for 'being the real dictator'; see Grocott, 2015: 157). In *The Road to Serfdom* (p. 165), Hayek questioned whether most people have the capacity for 'independent thought' (Jones, 2012: 66). Intellectual freedom, otherwise cherished among free market protagonists, should instead be granted to a small elite worthy of being graced with such freedoms. Hayek consequently, Mirowski (2013: 75) says, 'harbored a relatively low opinion of the role of education and discussion in the process of learning'. In Mirowski's (2013: 79) view, it is ironic that Hayek is at times portrayed by his admirers as a theorist of the new knowledge economy, as they apparently turn a blind eye to Hayek's own writing.

Third, and as a direct consequence of the preference for elitism, free marketeers and Hayek in particular nourished a strong anti-unionism attitude. For Hayek (1979: 96), 'the real exploiters in our present society' are not rent-seeking capitalists or entrepreneurs, but 'organizations which derive their power from the moral support of collective action and the feeling of group loyalty'. The danger of these groups (for example, trade unions) is that their mobilization to advance their members' interests leads to an 'artificial preponderance over market forces', and this in turn leads to a 'distortion' of the market's 'economic structure', Hayek (1979: 96) ominously declared. In this passage, Hayek (1979) reveals the belief that despite being self-regulating, supreme information arbiters, markets still need to be defended against such 'organized action' as they are easily disturbed by certain groups' interests. These two propositions seem difficult to reconcile within the market efficiency theory advocacy as markets primarily respond to activities and events as *information* to be processed, and therefore the presence of organized interests would *ex hypothesi* be accommodated as yet another set of information to consider in the pricing of assets. Or, on the other hand, if the presence of 'organized action' would actually serve to 'distort the economic structure of markets', then markets are de facto man-made accomplishments which one cannot offhand assume provide auxiliary benefits, including superior information-processing and pricing capacities. Blinded by his belligerence, Hayek's (1979) reasoning is logically inconsistent and theoretically untenable. Still, Hayek (1949) explicitly wages war against the trade unions: '[i]f there is to be any hope of a return to a free economy, the question of how the powers of trade-unions can be appropriately delimited in law as well as in fact is one of the most important of all the questions to which we must give our attention' (Hayek, 1949: 117).

Here it should be noticed that few in the American business elite shared Hayek's concerns. Data from a survey issued by the magazine *Fortune* in 1939 suggested that '[m]ore than 78 percent of the executives responded "yes" when asked whether they agreed with the idea of labor unions' (Mizruchi, 2013: 82; see also Hacker and Pierson, 2002: 309). In fact, the New Deal policies overall '[d]epended heavily on the support of prominent business leaders as well as a "brain trust" of policy intellectuals' (Jenkins and Brents, 1989: 897; see also Quadagno, 1984). The critique from the conservative business bloc did not become a decisive factor until the second phase of the New Deal and the enactment of the Social Security Act in 1935:

> [L]iberal capitalists controlled the formulation of the major proposals [in the New Deal], that capitalist leaders generally supported them, and that concerted opposition emerged late in the policy-making battles because of the formation of a rival conservative bloc that used social security taxes as a secondary theme in its general attack on the New Deal. (Jenkins and Brents, 1989: 894)

By the time of Roosevelt's election, there were no credible alternatives to a broad mobilization to overcome the economic hardship.

Hayek's fierce anti-unionism was one of the issues that Walter Lippmann addressed in his conversations and letters with Hayek. When Hayek wanted to publish an American edition of *The Road to Serfdom*, Lippmann was not very cooperative and even declined to write a preface for the edition (Jackson, 2012: 66). Lippmann was a staunch democrat with an intuitive understanding of the vulnerability of the average citizen and understood the importance and value of *Realpolitik*. By the end of the day, Lippmann was less interested in theoretical hair-splitting and the byzantine defence of abstract principles such as 'economic freedom', separated from actual accomplishments, than Hayek and his collaborators. When Hayek published *The Constitution of Liberty* in 1960, Lippmann again addressed Hayek's *faiblesse* for criticizing trade unions rather than engaging in a more systematic analysis of the production mechanisms and functions of the economy (for example, corporations), potentially much more rewarding to explore for an economist:

> I am puzzled to find that you have one reference to the corporation and nineteen references to labor unions. Does that mean that the index is at fault, or can it be that you think the corporation and its problem rate less than one page in a treatise of this kind? (Walter Lippmann, in a letter to Hayek, cited in Jackson, 2012: 68)

What a careful observer as Lippmann saw was that Hayek, at the very moment of the highest economic growth and political stability of the twentieth century, failed to see little more than what his underlying assumptions afforded, that is, 'that post-world war capitalist economies were dominated by organized labor, with business suffering from the pincer movement exerted by the social democratic state and the unions' (Jackson, 2012: 68).

In summary, Lippmann's harsh critique of the Roosevelt administration for pushing its economic-political agenda too far, to the point where it compromised the constitutional rights that defined the democratic political system, was carefully read by European and North-American economists and liberals. From this work they appropriated the term 'collectivism' that became the leitmotif in the free market advocacy for the rest of the century. Lippmann himself, being a figure of major intellectual stature in the US, appeared to be marginally interested in being some kind of representative for the project initiated by Hayek and his collaborators, and he certainly did not share their disregard for democracy and their elitism. *The Good Society* was therefore a book that was read and interpreted differently from how Lippmann himself would possibly have wished.

THE LONG MARCH OF FREE MARKET ADVOCACY: THE POST-WORLD WAR II ECONOMIC EXPANSION AND THE HEGEMONY OF KEYNESIAN ECONOMICS

Conservatism and the Virtues of Market Competition

Walter Lippmann's critique of the New Deal programmes, followed by the mobilization of the community of free market protagonists, was resounding in conservative quarters in American society. By the twist of history, this conservatism was to some extent the ultimate evidence that the New Deal had been successful, as certain groups could now afford to long for less state intervention in the economy once it was practically restored and stabilized by the means of political initiatives. As Philips-Fein (2011: 731) points out, 'ironically, postwar federal government support for highways and mass homeownership helped create communities that would ultimately prove deeply hostile to New Deal liberalism'. The growth of the suburbs in the postwar period, Philips-Fein (2011: 731) continues, created 'a homeowner's philosophy of individual rights, meritocracy, and property ownership'. The free market advocacy and its emphasis on competition and earning one's own income through hard and honest work nicely fitted into the American identity. The Christian upper middle class, for instance, 'saw belief in business principles and market ideals as natural extensions of their religious faith', Philips-Fein (2011: 733) says.[5]

At the same time as the conservative middle class tended to side with critics of the New Deal programmes, many of the 'most farsighted and liberal of the business leaders' (Philips-Fein, 2009: 8), especially in consumer-oriented industries such as electronics and garments, were early supporters of the Keynesian New Deal programme that Hayek and his colleagues regarded as a principal threat to economic freedom. Business executives and directors understood that the New Deal initiatives would 'raise the wages of workers and hence create more disposable income, stimulating mass consumption' (Philips-Fein, 2009: 8). In contrast, the social Darwinism preached by Hayek and others provided little guidance in how to move out of the Depression. Instead, Philips-Fein (2009: 23) says, free markets, laissez-faire policies, and similar ideas appeared to the majority of the Americans to be little more than the 'folklore of capitalism' – 'fantasies promulgated on behalf of the very rich'.

Despite the postwar boom in the economy and the rise of mass-consumption, certain business conservatives worried about the political mobilization of their workers as such industrial unionization seemed to be bound up with the oligopolistic mass-production regime of managerial capitalism. Echoing Hayek's anti-unionism, in the 1950s the leadership at General Electric were concerned that unions would press for higher social security benefits, more public spending and an expanded welfare state, all leading to higher taxes and costs for the corporation (Philips-Fein, 2009: 89). More specifically, such benefits, business conservatives thought, would create 'the potential economic independence of the worker from the job' (Philips-Fein, 2009: 89). Therefore, trade unions were targeted as a means to undermine New Deal politics.

This anxiety regarding the role of the state and ability of markets to operate outside of government regulation and oversight in industry was also part of the academic debates of the years prior to and after World War II. For free market advocators, the principal adversary and mastermind behind the New Deal programmes was John Maynard Keynes, and consequently, much of the remainder of the twentieth century unfolded as an ongoing intellectual debate between Keynesians (and versions thereof) and free market protagonists (also operating under different banners).

Cambridge University vs. London School of Economics: Keynes and his Critics

As always, it is difficult to write about the history of human accomplishments as being a one-man show. Galilei did not singlehandedly create the scientific revolution and Newton did not institute the scientific and mathematized method all by himself, but they were both part of a wider socio-economic and cultural fabric wherein their individual contributions certainly made a difference. This subject-centred view of history easily obscures the role of collaborative efforts, chance and the role of the windows of opportunity for change that come and go on an irregular and unpredictable basis. Despite these caveats, it is difficult to write about macroeconomic policy and neoclassical economic theory in the twentieth century without placing John Maynard Keynes at the centre. The free market protagonists that gathered around, for example, Friedrich von Hayek at the London School of Economics and in the Mont Pèlerin Society were fierce defenders of economic liberalism and even placed it higher than political freedom and democracy, otherwise seen as conditions demanded for a dynamic and competitive economy. At Cambridge University, in contrast, Keynes and his colleagues, pinpointed as the principal enemies of economic freedom by the LSE faculty, tried to synthesize an economic theory fit to practically handle a series of pressing economic and political problems. Both Keynes and Hayek were quite odd figures in their professional field, in particular with regard to the context of today's demand in economics for mathematical formalism and strict deductive reasoning. Hayek was not so keen on equations and formal evidence but wrote, just like his mentor Ludwig von Mises, what are best described as political treatises. Milton Friedman, who otherwise expressed his admiration for Hayek's efforts, was reluctant to even refer to Hayek as an economist in the conventional sense of the term. Still, Hayek's political treatises, regardless of the accuracy of his predictions, helped him gain supporters and admirers in the business world (Philips-Fein, 2009: 52). Keynes, in contrast, was more of a classic intellectual produced by English elite institutions and embodying the interests and virtues of a man of the world, being more of an economist by default than by his very essence (Ahamed, 2009: 109–14). Block and Somers (2014: 24) suggest that Keynes was declared guilty of heresy in the eyes of free market protagonists as he thought the economy was a means to an end, not an end in itself. Concepts such as 'economic freedom', at the very core of the free market advocacy, must have appeared absurd to Keynes. Rather than praising self-interested and risky venturing (yet another core belief in the free market advocacy), Keynes revealed '[a]n abiding suspicion of crass materialism, or money-making, and especially for the "love of money"' (Block and Somers, 2014: 24).

While Hayek and his collaborators were prone to discuss things as how they should *preferably be* in the best of worlds, in a free market protagonist's nirvana, Keynes and his colleagues had less patience with such speculations. They were instead determined to provide policy-makers with maps of the economic territory that could lead political decisions to accomplish solid effects that stabilized the economy and that promoted economic welfare. In brief, 'Keynes now offered the hope of economic engineering' (Adelstein, 1991: 172). In Jones's (2012: 185) account, 'Keynes provided a breath of fresh air for those optimists who wanted economic and political change'. Jones continues: 'Keynes's ideas seemed to arm politicians and public officials with a workable set of tools with which to deliver the reform of capitalism they desired in the wake of its seeming collapse'. In other words, Keynes was not just able to synthesize a number of sub-disciplines within neoclassical economic theory (for example, monetary policy, macroeconomic theory, labour economics and finance theory), but he presented his framework in a way that enabled robust practical accomplishments: 'it was Keynes who put the pieces together by constructing a theory in which the aggregates of income, consumption, and investment were mathematically related to one another and, by simple extension, to government spending and taxation' (Adelstein, 1991: 171). Perhaps even more importantly, as opposed to neoclassical economic theorists, who reasoned deductively on the basis of axiomatic principles based on rational choice theory propositions, assuming that economic men and women were 'rational, well-informed, and prudent' (Schui, 2014: 105), Keynes 'wrote a theory about men and women as they really were: ill-informed, subconsciously aware of their ignorance and always prone to be carried away by irrational fears and hopes', Schui (2014: 105) says. In thinking about economic matters in such terms, Keynes could also escape the deadlock of the individualist methodology prescribed in the rational choice theory framework: '[t]he important change wrought by Keynesianism was thus in establishing that unemployment and poverty are *systemic* rather than individual problems', Konzelmann (2014: 730) argues.

The hostile attitude of free market advocates towards the Keynesian programme was not disarmed when it was received favourably by politicians in first the UK, and thereafter elsewhere in the emerging European and North-American welfare states. Basically seen as the most recent manifestation of the collectivist programme by free market advocates, Keynesianism was laid in the same basket as various forms of socialism, communism and other forms of non-liberal and pseudo-liberal politics that counteracted the restoration of the economic freedom that free marketeers made their objective to restore. This represented an idiosyncratic view as Keynesianism was by and large 'conservative in the broadest sense' (Collins, 1981: 9). 'In essence', Collins (1981: 9) writes, 'Keynes wanted to save free-market capitalism from both the stultifying orthodoxy of laissez faire and the heresy of socialism'. Nevertheless, while the free marketeers understood, for example, unemployment as faulty individual human capital investment decisions (that is, the individual rather than the economic system, 'the market', was to blame: as the market is 'always right' in the pricing of commodities and services, 'blaming the market' is an absurdity in this framework), Keynes thought otherwise, declaring that 'the outstanding faults of the economic society in which we live are its failure to provide for full employment and its arbitrary and inequitable distribution of wealth and income' (Keynes, 1953: 372). Worse still, Keynes even accused proponents of neoclassical economic theory of maintaining a parochial and cloistered attitude, being more prone to point out minor faults and logical inconsistencies in economic policies than to grapple with social and economic problems as they were perceived outside of the narrow community of economists: '[o]ur criticism of the accepted classical theory of economics has consisted not so much in finding logical flaws in its analysis as in pointing out that its tacit assumptions are seldom or never satisfied, with the result that it cannot solve the economic problems of the actual world' (Keynes, 1953: 378). At times, Keynes did not restrain himself from firing off quite harsh accounts of how he regarded economists as being part of secluded communities out of joint with their surrounding times: '[t]he classical theorists resemble Euclidian geometers in a non-Euclidean world who, discovering that in experience straight lines apparently often meet, rebuke the lines for not keeping straight – as the only remedy for the unfortunate collisions which are occurring' (Keynes, 1953: 16).

Born into an upper-middle-class environment and being educated in the most prestigious public schools and universities, Keynes was no revolutionary nor a Marxist, but his thought and work was nevertheless radical in providing the guidelines for how to stabilize the economy and pave the way for the welfare state where economic well-being and stable employment was customary and a guiding principle rather than being an exceptional and/or unintended outcome. Despite the post-World War II expansion, the Keynesian economic theory was always a source of suspicion for neoclassical economic theorists, and as Paul Samuelson, the great authority figure in North-American economics and professor at MIT's prestigious economics department – essentially a Keynesian stronghold in the post-World War II period – remarked, 'Keynesianism was a naughty word politically long after the war' (cited in Fourcade and Khurana, 2013: 134). In conservative and free market circles, Keynesianism was frequently lumped together with communism (Fourcade and Khurana, 2013: 134). Despite his own discipline in part demonstrating some scepticism, Keynesianism was widely embraced in political quarters of all colours (more or less explicitly), but also in the business community, as Keynesian policy ensured the economic and political stability that enables businesses to thrive.

As Keynesians became institutionalized within the Western capitalist economic system as one of its most predominant governance doctrines, the doctrine forked into various paths. Keynes's untimely death in April 1946 prevented him from seeing the full implications of his contributions, but if he had done, he may have observed the separation into a 'social Keynesianism framework' that emphasized public spending and redistributive measures to 'sustain long-term prosperity', and a 'liberal Keynesianism framework' that 'focuses in demand stimulation during economic downturns and favors tax cuts over spending increases' (Pontusson and Raess, 2012: 31). Far from being a totally integrated prescriptive framework for socio-economic engineering, Keynesianism was, and increasingly became, a policy-making framework granting the state a substantial and legitimate part to play in regulating and monitoring the economy. This is also precisely why Keynesianism was so controversial for free market protagonists: they saw in Keynes a figure that justified the violation of the free operation of allegedly efficient and self-regulating markets, ultimately representing little more than yet another thrust of collectivism, now at the very heart of competitive capitalism.

1945–73: Economic Growth and Welfare State Expansion

One of Keynes's most famous *bon mots* was his dismissing of the practical value of predicting long-term consequences of specific economic policies as 'in the long run we're all dead'. For Keynes, economics and economic theory was not only a domain of scholarly debate and critical self-correction, but it was primarily a tool in the hands of politicians and policy-makers, and a pragmatic and experimental method rewarded the innovative and thoughtful economist. In addition, economic theory is not primarily about winning arguments and debates but about engineering an economic system that works and that stabilizes the economy, essentially based on expectations and the assessment of certain economic fundamentals, faulty as they may be. Seeing the Keynesian contribution in such terms makes it an impressive contribution as the post-World War II era was the most significant period of economic growth and increased well-being and economic equality in Western societies. Over the course of the decades of economic expansion on the basis of Keynes's recommendations to stimulate the economy in the downturns of the economic cycle and to 'cool it off' towards the peak of the economic cycle, Keynesianism and the welfare state became intimately associated. Korpi and Palme (2003: 428, original emphasis omitted) define the welfare state as '[p]olicies to affect outcomes of, and conditions for, distributive processes in the sphere of markets so as to decrease inequality and/or poverty'. The welfare state thus no longer only included law enforcement institutions and military defence (what Ferdinand Lassalle dubbed the *Nachtwächterstaat*), but also provided education and training, health care services, child care provisions, social assistance benefits, care for the elderly, and a general protection against poverty and economic hardship through the tax-funded economic transferring systems.

This expansion of the welfare state was not a zero-sum game where the incumbent elites and high-income groups saw their income taxes grow in proportion to redistribute economic resources, but rather provided an environment wherein the working class could benefit from the new economic stability and advance into the growing middle-class strata. In addition, the new economic stability and the assurance of decent living standards promoted entrepreneurialism and risk-taking more broadly, making the welfare state a hotbed for enterprising activities. This was quite the opposite of what conservative critics claimed, portraying the welfare state as what effectively undermined individual responsibility and breeding rampant passivity. Lifting large sections of the poorest population out of the most acute concern for housing and nutrition released time and energy that created novel economic possibilities (for example, on the basis of public education). These more long-term benefits were also complemented by short-term gains, and the mass-production/mass-consumption era of the post-World War II period thus needs to be understood on the basis of economic policies. As, for example, Kristal (2013: 383) points out, between 1948 and 1973, the hourly compensation of a typical US worker 'grew in tandem with productivity, indicating a relatively equal share social distribution of the fruits of economic growth and productivity gains'. This real-wage growth in combination with progressive taxes led to a significant reduction in economic inequality in the period. After the mid-1970s, the situation changed, as a result of both stagnating profit levels in the dominant industries and new policy frameworks no longer favouring economic equality as a key political objective. Between 1972 and 2011, productivity grew 80.4 per cent in the

US economy, but the worker's median hourly compensation 'grew just by 10.7 percent' (Kristal, 2013: 383). After the early 1980s, productivity growth no longer translated into real wage growth in parity with the productivity figures: workers became increasingly more efficient but they did not benefit from their accomplishment. Instead, it was the share-holders who were more successful in advocating their right to the economic value generated. In combination with the tax cuts for primarily high-income groups during the Reagan presidency and the rapid deindus-trialization that left substantial sections of blue-collar worker com-munities jobless (Bluestone and Harrison, 1982), the 1980s was a period of swiftly growing economic inequalities in the US. 'Since 1973', Moss (1996: 175) writes, 'the real wages of production and nonsupervisory workers have exhibited a sustained decline'. He continues: '[a]lthough real per capita GNP and labor productivity have continued to increase, wage earners have had to work longer hours to preserve their share of national income. Never before in American history has an entire gener-ation of workers experienced such a deterioration of earning power' (Moss, 1996: 175). According to the *Los Angeles Times* national political correspondent, Ronald Brownstein (cited in Moss, 1996: 175), 'it is clear that 1973 marked the pivot from the era of secure prosperity to a new era of economic anxiety'. Moss (1996: 175) compares the systemic wage deterioration to the issue of industrial hazards in the progressive era (*c.*1920–40), two factors that create 'a great deal of anxiety' but that nevertheless are a man-made economic externality that can be corrected by legislation, policies, regulatory control and reformed governance practices.

The post-World War II welfare state under the aegis of Keynesian economic policy came to an end by the mid-1970s, partially because the Keynesian economic theory could not explain the combination of eco-nomic stagnation, high inflation and persistent high unemployment (a phenomenon referred to as *stagflation*), but also, and perhaps even primarily, because of the mobilization of a liberal, neoliberal, libertarian and neoconservative community that claimed they offered an alternative to the historically successful Keynesianism, now portrayed on a broad basis as being antiquated and no longer capable of responding to the new economic conditions.

Trust versus Contract: The High Noon of Managerial Capitalism

The New Deal policy-makers were concerned with how to balance market-based economic transactions, in many cases materializing in oligarchies and monopolies, and the policy-makers' interests in a stable economic system. The question of how to combine private enterprise and the benefits of high levels of employment and taxable income and so on, which characterize a functional competitive capitalist economic system, was still haunting theorists, policy-makers and pundits in the 1950s and 1960s. Despite the success of the present system of oligarchic competitive capitalism, giving rise to the divisionalized, multinational corporation (that Williamson, 1981, refers to as the M-form) and its ability to generate economic wealth and employment opportunities, there was a nagging feeling that the new managerial elites populating the executive suites and boardrooms of these gargantuan organizations could not claim a legitimate basis for the seemingly ceaseless expansion of their power and authority in the economic system. While these large-scale corporations and conglomerates provided many economic benefits, there were not only concerns regarding the shareholders' benefits, but also less influential groups such as women and minorities found themselves marginalized or ignored by corporate elites. The new class of corporate mandarins operated organizations dominated by a patriarchal culture and a preference for conformism and conservatism more broadly, and they showed little interest in orchestrating changes or reforms. The 1950s in particular, at the zenith of American economic and cultural dominance, were '[f]amously the high-water mark of managerialism in the U.S. corporate governance, in which boards [were] largely passive instruments of the CEO, chosen by him and strongly disinclined to challenge his decisions or authority', Gordon (2007: 1503) writes. In the 1950s, ideas about shareholder welfare and independent directors checking on self-serving executives were still unheard of, but Adolf Berle's statement regarding the 'the princes of property' was more accurate than ever.

The corporate elites populating the executive suites were in turn not entirely satisfied with the regime of welfare capitalism brought by the New Deal, Jacoby (1997: 232) stresses: in the early 1950s, with McCarthyism looming and left-wing unionism increasingly being marginalized, American employers 'intensified their public relations campaign and began using strident anti-union rhetoric that previously had been outside of the realm of mainstream discourse'. Beneath the surface of corporate well-being and ever-expanding provisions financed on the basis of market growth and economic stability, conservatism and anti-union resentment grew as a subterranean brotherhood:

> As employers grew self-assured, right-wing fringe groups became more visible and influential within the business community. These groups [...] served as shock troops in business's holy war, clearing the way for more centrist organizations like the NAM and the U.S. Chamber of Commerce. Yet

close ties existed between the mainstream and the fringe. Many members of the NAM's executive committee in the late 1940s and 1950s actively supported, and donated heavily to, ultraconservative groups. (Jacoby, 1997: 232)

One approach to marginalizing the influence of unions was, in Jacoby's formulation, to 'routinize charisma by embedding it in daily organizational routines'. Labour relations managers had built their careers around essentially administrative procedures, 'steeped in bureaucratic rationality' (Jacoby, 1997: 244), including collective bargaining processes and grievances handling, all inscribed as esoteric details in labour law and made manifest in labour relation practices. The logic behind this new regime of 'human relations training, attitude surveys, personality tests for managers, communications, programs, and myriad other activities' increasingly used by American employers, was based on entirely different premises such as individualism and 'affective relationships' between employer and employees. Thus, the incumbent generation of labour relation managers found it difficult to accept this scientization of labour relations (Jacoby, 1997: 244). The influence of the new human relations movement is not the least visible in the extensive industrial psychology and industrial sociology literature being published in the 1940s, 1950s and early 1960s. Beginning with the Harvard-based research work led by Elton Mayo (Mayo, 1946; Roethlisberger and Dickson, 1943), financed by the Rockefeller Foundation with the explicit objective to prevent future labour conflicts (O'Connor, 1999), there was a great deal of scholarly output addressing the novel labour relations in the period, including the work of Alvin Gouldner (1954a; 1954b), Reinhart Bendix (1956), Peter Blau (1956; 1963), Everett Hughes (1958), Melville Dalton (1959), and Robert Blauner (1964) in the US, and the studies published by Elliott Jaques (1951) and Tavistock Institute researchers in the UK. Much of this work became staple references in the growing management studies research work located in business schools (Scott, 2004), a relatively recent university innovation that received excruciating criticism from external evaluators regarding their underdeveloped research methods and scholarly standards in the late 1950s and early 1960s (Fourcade and Khurana, 2013; De Rond and Miller, 2005; Whitley, 1986), thus making, for example, industrial sociology a credible and entrusted supplier of studies, theories and methods that would secure scholarly authority. The 1940s and 1950s was thus very much the fine-tuning and modifying of the oligarchic corporate system of competitive capitalism, but with anti-unionism and more malign conservatism at its roots, and dormant but lingering concerns regarding the legitimacy of executive authority.

In the late 1950s and 1960s – a decade characterized by much more social tension and even unrest when various 'minorities' (for example, women, the black community, gays and lesbians) embarked on their own liberation and social equality campaigns – a body of literature addressed how 'the evident disparity of interests between managers and stockholders' (Williamson, 1981: 1559) could be handled. Williamson (1981) refers to this literature as the 'managerial discretion literature', and it included books such as William J. Baumol's *Business Behavior, Value and Growth* (1959) and Robin Marris's *The Economic Theory of 'Managerial' Capitalism* (1964). Again, just as in the New Deal era, the two principal positions pertaining to the issue of managerial discretion were market-based contracting and the legal concept of fiduciary duties operationalized into trust as a central managerial virtue. In the former case, managers were little more than hired professionals, experts in internal operations securing efficient deployment of firm-specific resources. In the latter case, managers were not standard employees but were entrusted with substantial economic resources which they themselves did not own, and therefore the executives' work needed to be understood in entirely different terms than being governed by the formal procedure of contracting. The New Deal legislation, unwilling to unleash an unregulated free market capitalism paving the way for contractual relations, and yet recognizing the value of market-based competition, emphasized that corporations were free-standing legal entities overseen by the board of directors, thus making the CEO and other executives the board's agents. In this legislation and law enforcement, fiduciary duties and trust were key components, also pitted against the 'more pure' market-based contracting model, ultimately, its protagonists argued, representing some kind of primordial economic state where there is no need for fuzzy terms such as trust or legal mumbo-jumbo such as 'fiduciary duties'. Marris (1964), the 'leading managerial economist' in the period (Kaufman et al., 1995: 66), defended corporate law strictures, and made it clear that 'the shareholders are not the legal owners of the assets of the company, nor even, in many countries, of the current profits before distribution' (Marris, 1964: 12). Under this corporate law rule, it is the directors who have the authority to 'determine the dividend' and their discretion grants them the full right to 'withhold considerable proportions of current profits, which then, either as fixed or liquid assets, become the property of the company' (Marris, 1964: 13). That is, Marris (1964: 13) writes, shareholders 'cannot in general directly initiate a capital distribution except by enforcing total liquidation, i.e. by causing the assets to be sold at break-up value'.

Baumol (1959) has little to say about corporate law and corporate governance, but he recognizes the behavioural theory of the firm and stresses that managers are not acting self-interestedly in predictable ways. Instead, managers are concerned about the long-term growth of the firm and its financial stability. This means, Baumol suggests, that managers are not likely to maximize profits but to ensure that the firm can accumulate or attract the finance capital it needs at lowest possible cost. This often means that the growth of the firm, operationalized into maximizing the sales revenues, becomes a key objective for managers: 'profits do not constitute the prime objective of the large modern business enterprise' (Baumol, 1959: 31–2). Instead, Baumol (1959: 43) suggests, '[t]he businessman's desire to increase his profits lends itself to transla- tion into a desire to expand his firm'. This tendency to expand the corporation to be able to secure the access to finance capital leads to the situation of the 1950s and 1960s, where the American economy was best described as oligarchic capitalism, dominated by a few major firms not so much 'competing' as 'coexisting' and catering for their own stock of clients and customers. Unlike many dyed-in-the-wool neoclassicists, prone to thinking of oligopolies as the outcome of systematic procedures to short-circuit the disciplinary effects of market competition, Baumol does not believe that these economic conditions affect the day-to-day work of these firms: 'in day-to-day decision making, oligopolistic dependence plays only a small role' (Baumol, 1959: 27). '[E]ven in fairly crucial decisions, and almost always in routine policy-making, only the most cursory attention is paid to competitive reactions', Baumol (1959: 27) adds. One of the key explanations for this absence of head-on competition between firms is that managers are overseeing immensely complex operations whose intricate details can never be understood in detail. As a consequence, Baumol argues, managers tend to make extensive use of what he refers to as 'rules of thumb', simple yet reasonably effective rules that guide day-to-day decision-making: '[t]hese rules of thumb do not work too badly. They translate hopelessly involved problems into simple, orderly routines. They save executives time and permit a degree of centralized control over the firm's farflung operations' (Baumol, 1959: 28–9). In order to strike a balance between the control of the operations and 'tying itself up to operational details' (Baumol, 1959: 28–9), managers resort to rules of thumb that enable them to maintain the control of the corporation while being able to delegate decision-making authority to lower-level management, professionals and operators located in the production activities. Unfortunately, the cognitive processing of data and information through the reliance on historically justified true beliefs, boiled down to rules of thumb, does not fully exploit the dynamics of market competition: 'rules of thumb tend to reduce competi- tive give and take among oligopolistic enterprises', Baumol (1959: 28–9) says. Therefore, firms reaching a certain size and magnitude are becoming inward-oriented and to some extent cloistered as management can no longer efficiently examine market opportunities, nor take advantage of them, and maintain intraorganizational control. Therefore, Baumol (1959: 50) proposes, managers seek to maintain tolerable levels of dividends to 'keep the shareholders satisfied' at the same time as they contribute adequately to the financing of company growth. More specifically, management will '[b]end its efforts to the augmentation of sales revenues rather than to further increase its profits' (Baumol, 1959: 50).

In comparison to the harsh criticism of managers (and to a lesser extent, directors) articulated in the 1970s and 1980s' agency theory literature, Baumol (1959) recognizes what Herbert Simon (1957) spoke of as the *bounded rationality* of managers and what organizational psychologists such as Amos Tversky and Daniel Kahneman (1981) would address as the *framing of decisions* and *choice situations*, leaving them with the challenge of controlling organizations while at the same time needing to respond to various pressures and demands in the organization's environment, including shareholder interests. Unlike Marris (1964), Baumol (1959) does not draw on corporate law to justify managerial discretion but institutes it on the basis of the managers' ability to balance different objectives and interests.

Arrow (1964: 398), an economist seated at the centre of the neoclassical economic theory tradition, does not say very much about corporate law either, and yet he addresses what he calls 'the problem of organizational control'. This problem is in turn separated into the identification of *operating rules* and *enforcement rules.* Paying allegiance to his theoretical convictions, Arrow (1964: 399) suggests that it is the 'price system' that provides the best solution to the problem of control, that is, it is the *markets* that determine the value of managerial strategies and decision-making (see also Coase, 1960: 40). In his analytical model, Arrow (1964) admits that management plays a key role and recognizes that there is a shortage of information in the top management team. At the same time, Arrow says that management has a role to play as 'the top management of the organization will always have to have some information about the internal workings of the individual activity' (Arrow, 1964: 408). Moreover, Arrow (1964: 408) adds, 'this is far from saying that they have to have complete information'. While the market-based price system ultimately serves as a set of enforcement rules inasmuch as managerial discretion is granted a certain economic value by market actors, Arrow (1964) is concerned about 'moral hazard', being the risk that managers will conduct decisions that benefit themselves without rewarding the shareholders:

[a] manager is not normally held accountable for unfavorable outcomes or credited with favorable ones if they are clearly due to causes not under his control. However, there is a deep problem here which is well known in insurance theory and practice under the name of the 'moral hazard'; it is, in general, almost impossible to separate causes outside the organization from the efficiency of the manager himself. (Arrow, 1964: 407)

In Arrow's account of the corporation, it is not so much the combination of legislation and fiduciary duties that determines the quality of the corporate governance. Instead, it is the pricing system entrenched in the liquid finance markets, assessing the outcome from managerial discretion in the form of the pricing of assets such as stocks and securities, which ultimately determines operating rules and enforcement rules. Arrow's (1964: 398) account still remains riddled by inconsistencies. First, while Arrow explicitly subscribes to a 'rationalistic view', rooted in the 'logic of choice' and the 'mathematics of maximization', he is still concerned about the specific group of managers (but apparently not market-based actors) adhering to other, presumably less noble principles. Hence, the forbidding presence of moral hazard. Second, while Arrow (1964) theoretically subscribes to the virtues of market pricing and the price system, in practice, he does not fail to notice, 'the very existence of large organizations in the commercial world' is a proof of the existence of transaction costs, costs that the pricing system should eliminate through its ability to process available information more efficiently:

When the price system is fully operative, the large organization is equivalent to a large number of separate activities whose connections are the same as those of unrelated firms. Hence, the large organization would *have no differential advantage in economic competition*, and we would not expect to find it so dominant. (Arrow, 1964: 405, emphasis added)

But this is factually not the situation in the American economy of the early 1960s, casting doubt on whether the price system is after all capable of providing these benefits, potentially also undermining the legitimacy of the pricing system argument as an efficient mechanism accommodating the problem of control in organizations. While the pricing system may offer such auxiliary benefits in theory, the actual terrain of managerial capitalism looks vastly different from this theoretical prescription. That is, Arrow's (1964) theory of the firm and the solution to the problem of organizational control leaves the reader with a lingering sense of incompleteness, representing yet another assurance that the market pricing system is capable of ironing out the differences in information access and the variety incentives, thus effectively aligning heterogeneous actors in their supposedly joint efforts to create economic value. The concern for moral hazard remains the ghost in the machinery in an otherwise rationalistic account of the corporate governance of the firm.

Regardless of these concerns, versions of the pricing system argument would be a persistent theme in the corporate governance model that contractarians would advocate over the coming decades. But it took a law school professor well informed about corporate law to provide a more comprehensive and logically consistent argument than a spokesman of the neoclassical economic theory model possibly could have done. Henry Manne (1967), a law school professor, advocated an entirely different understanding of corporate law than Marris (1964). In Manne's view, the key characteristic of the corporate form is not so much its ability to provide a series of socially desirable provisions benefiting many different stakeholders, but to be the legal vehicle for the raising and consolidation of finance capital, thus reducing the internal conflicts between entrepreneurs – Manne (1967) uses the term *promoter* – inasmuch as the corporate form sets certain standards: '[t]he fundamental fact about the development of American corporations in the 19th century is that they came into existence because entrepreneurs, or promoters, needed some device to raise capital from a relatively large number of investors', Manne (1967: 260) writes. Therefore, the corporation is, in essence, a 'capital-raising device' (Manne, 1967: 260). In addition, one of the principal corollaries of the corporate form, that of centralized management, is directly related to this capital-raising activity conducted by the promoter, Manne (1967) argues: 'promoters, in forming a corporation and marketing its shares, perform an entrepreneurial function. But it also implies that the selection of the managerial group is a function of the entrepreneur, and not of the capitalist investor' (Manne, 1967: 260). For this reasons, Manne (1967: 260) forcefully argues, the corporate form is not so much the creation of law and lawyers as it is a bone fide consequence of finance market operations – the process to aggregate finance capital to expand a business venture: '[t]o attribute the success of the modern corporation specifically to law and lawyers is a professional conceit which will not bear scrutiny' (Manne, 1967: 260).

Based on this premise – the corporation is not so much a legal entity as it is a finance market vehicle – Manne further expands the argument that the corporation is to be understood within the mechanism of markets and finance markets more specifically. As a consequence, Manne (1967: 263) says that the liquidity for investment is a 'prime requisite' for the functioning of the corporate system as a capital-raising device. That is, any investor needs to be able to sell off their stocks in the finance market to be able to signal that he or she disapproves of management's decision-making and to eliminate the risks derived from such a perceived inadequate decision. Manne can be cited at length here:

> Another aspect of market liquidity relates not to changes in investment needs but to the investor's freedom to dissociate himself from a particular corporation if for any reason he becomes dissatisfied with its management. There is only one alternative to market liquidity as a way out for corporate investors. That alternative is dissolution of the corporation and the sale of its assets, with subsequent distribution to the shareholders of the proceeds. But the market allows discrete decisions to be made by individual investors, whereas the dissolution alternative requires some level of general agreement among the shareholders before it can be utilized. A system in which a minority shareholder is given the power to force dissolution of a large corporation because of his own dissatisfaction or a change in his own investment needs would not be workable. (Manne, 1967: 264)

As Manne correctly notices, any grievance from the individual investors cannot be handled individually without the entire concept of the business charter being undermined, and therefore the finance market serves a principal function as the arena wherein the investor 'can vote with his or her feet' (that is, sell off their stock) in the case of dissatisfaction with managerial performance. In practice this means, Manne (1967: 264) proposes, that there are three 'markets' that serve to stabilize the corporate system: first, there is the 'the market for investment capital, primarily illustrated by the promoters' search for new funds' (Manne, 1967: 264); second, there is the market for 'the buying and selling of existing securities' – in case the firm needs additional capital when it is up and running – (Manne, 1967: 264); third, there is what Manne (1967) calls 'the market for corporate control', effectively operating on the basis of the investor's ability to sell off stock that for some reason they no longer want to own.

The market for corporate control is in turn based on the idea that individual shares 'carry votes' that can be bought and sold. Based on this mechanism, it is possible to buy the control of the corporation directly (a right sealed at 51 per cent ownership, but practically speaking often entrenched at substantial lower levels of ownership). This 'market for corporate control' serves to discipline managers, Manne (1967: 264) suggests: '[u]nless a publicly traded company is efficiently managed, the price of its shares on the open market will decline, thus lowering the price at which an outsider can take over control of the corporation'. While Manne (1967: 270) recognizes that corporate law does not prescribe that directors (and, a fortiori, the managers they hire to conduct the day-to-day work) owe no specific fiduciary duty to individual shareholders (and thus sides with, for example, Marris, 1964), he insists that the market for corporate control will correct undesirable behaviour and serve to discipline directors and managers so that firms are operating on the basis of sound and widely recognized finance market standard performance measures. More specifically, and of great importance for the debates regarding corporate governance in the succeeding two decades, Manne (1967: 270) proposes that the market for corporate control de facto marginalizes corporate law and therefore questions the efficacy of existing legislation:

> [L]arge corporations function in a largely permissive framework and [...] market forces rather than legal ones have dictated their organization and structure ... One is almost tempted to suggest that the large corporation system could and would function substantially as it does if there were almost no state corporation statutes beyond provisions for incorporation. This may not be so far-fetched, for the effect of most modern amendment programs dealing with basic provisions of the corporation acts has been to modify them in the interest of the close[ly held] corporation. Our general corporation laws seem to be in the process of becoming general close corporation laws with only incidental relevance to large companies. (Manne, 1967: 270)

In summary, Manne (1967) does not emphasize the corporation as a legal entity granted its business charter within the wider interests of the modern sovereign state and the regime of competitive capitalism that the state actively supports but also monitors and regulates. Rather, he changes the perspective and regards the corporation as a vehicle for finance market activities – separated into the early stage finance capital-raising work and the ongoing reliance on, for example, securities markets and the market for corporate control. The liquidity preference in the finance market is in Manne's view a much more effective mechanism in checking managerial opportunism than legislation, and even though directors are *de jure* not the shareholders' agents, under the influence of the market for corporate control they become so de facto as the market pricing of the shares (and also the securities) is the evaluation of managerial decision-making and operative efficiency. Therefore, Manne (1967) suggests and his many followers to come in the 1970s and 1980s would repeat, that corporate law should only provide statutes for provisions for incorporation (that is, the granting of business charters) but little more. In Manne's (1967) view, the 'three markets' that corporations are relying on in their day-to-day operations are more effective in monitoring managerial malfeasance than any court ruling.[6]

The debate over trust versus contracts as the primary source of legitimacy for salaried managers ultimately rested on the fact that in the 1950s and 1960s, competitive capitalism was no longer sharing many features with the primordial free market economy that neoclassical economists regarded as the honourable and desirable state. Instead, managerial capitalism had evolved into a functional but oligarchic economic system more characterized by planning and policy-making than head-on competition in the marketplace. In *The New Industrial State*, John Kenneth Galbraith (1971) captures the prevailing economic conditions in the American economy:

> [W]e have an economic system which, whatever its formal ideological billing, is, in substantial part, a planned economy. The initiative in deciding what is to be produced comes not from the sovereign consumer who, through the market, issues the instructions that bend the productive mechanism to his ultimate will. Rather it comes from the great producing organization which reaches forward to control the markets that it is presumed to serve and, beyond, to bend the consumer to its needs. (Galbraith, 1971: 6)

In the regime of managerial capitalism, Galbraith (1971) argues, the market is 'superseded by what is commonly called vertical integration', that is, corporations could now determine and thus plan what is to be produced and in what amount. Yet, Galbraith (1971) noticed, economists cling on to the entrepreneur as their principal and favoured economic agent regardless of the entrepreneur's diminishing role in the creation of aggregated economic value: '[t]he entrepreneur – individualistic, restless, with vision, guile and courage – has been the economists' only hero. The great business organization arouses no similar admiration', Galbraith (1971: 59) remarks. Charles Wright Mills, a left-leaning sociologist and a careful observer of changes in American society, had already noticed this preference for the entrepreneur, regardless of his or her relevance, in the early 1950s, using the term 'the ideology of utopian capitalism' (Mills, 1951: 34) to denote the free market competition between enterprising economic actors. As Marris (1964) and Galbraith (1971) would repeat more than a decade or two later, Mills (1951) speaks about the entrepreneur as a disappearing figure in the economic landscape of managerial capitalism, yet playing a key ideological role as a form of endangered species in need of protection through policy-making, fiscal reforms and other adequate political initiatives: '[t]he United States has been transformed from a nation of small capitalists into a nation of hired employees; the ideology suitable for the nation of small capitalists persists, as if that small-propertied world were still a going concern' (Mills, 1951: 34). Unfortunately, Mills (1951: 34) continues, 'the logic of the small entrepreneurs is not the logic of our time', being now more accurately portrayed as an economic system characterized by oligarchy and rent-seeking through subsidies and regulations. Precisely because the entrepreneur represents outmoded and archaic values in the age of 'organization men' (Whyte, 1956), he or she is a venerated figure, embodying the ethos of a fading venturesome and enterprising America:

> The principle of the self-made man, and the justification of his superior position by the competitive fire through which he has come, require and in turn support the ideology of free competition. In the abstract political ranges, everyone can believe in competition; in the concrete economic case, few small entrepreneurs can afford to do so. (Mills, 1951: 36)

Therefore, Mills concludes, politicians, policy-makers and business representatives all speak gravely about the fate of the entrepreneur, because, in their rhetoric, 'small business is the last urban representative of free competition and thus of the competitive virtue of the private enterprise system' (Mills, 1951: 44). At the height of managerial capitalism, narratives about an almost mythological golden age of free enterprising sided with and to some extent veiled a functional system of a planned economy dominated by a handful of giant corporations and conglomerates.

The End of an Era: The Decline of Keynesianism

While the 1950s were an era when the modern welfare state emerged primarily in the leading economic, cultural and military power, the United States of America, orchestrating a spectacular change in the way of life for millions of people, the 1960s were more uneasy times. The 1960s were peppered with historical events, including the Cuban missile crisis during the Kennedy presidency, Kennedy's assassination (later followed by the murders of Martin Luther King and Robert Kennedy in 1965 and 1968), social unrest during Vietnam war protests, the civil rights movement, the women's liberation movement, and 'the sexual revolution' propelled by the launching of 'the pill', the first oral contraceptive (Watkins, 2001), and more generally a growing youth culture clearly demonstrating to the older and in many ways more conservative generation that from now on there were new values, norms and ways of life being accepted and even encouraged on a broad front. Centre-left commentators and liberals tended to treat these changes in American society as being indicative of a more deep-seated change in America and gradually accepted the thesis that Americans now by and large were happy to greet the new freedoms granted to certain groups (for example, women, people of colour, younger people, the gay community). When the arch-conservative senator Barry Goldwater from Arizona announced his presidential election candidacy in 1964, he was by and large treated as a conservative crank by the mainstream media and most commentators believed that 'his brand of conservatism was dead' (Philips-Fein, 2011: 725). Goldwater failed to make it into the White House, but when the Californian governor and former Hollywood B-movie actor Ronald Reagan rose as the new star of the increasingly more effectively organized neoconservative movement, the very same liberal commentators underrated how well Reagan and his kind could now exploit beliefs and attitudes that had remained dormant among substantial proportions of the American population: '[f]or many liberal and leftist historians, Ronald Reagan's political popularity seemed an alarming mystery', Philips-Fein (2011: 725) writes. Rather than embracing, accepting, or even tolerating the liberalization of society, large groups in the wealthy suburban communities such as Orange County in southern California (McGirr, 2001) never thought the changes in the 1960s were desirable as they uprooted traditional values and norms and thus threatened 'the American way of life'. This neoconservative community was largely heterogeneous but was united by a few shared themes including 'anticommunism, a laissez-faire approach to economics, opposition to the civil rights movement, and commitment to traditional sexual norms' (Philips-Fein, 2011: 727). For this group, regardless of its own benefits (just as in the case of the New Deal programmes), the Keynesian welfare state was part of the problem as it enabled individuals to participate in all sorts of indulgencies rather that to work hard 'in thy sweat' (as prescribed by Genesis), and there was a perceived causality between the expanding welfare state and all sorts of liberal initiatives and projects. The critique of Keynesianism, the (liberal) welfare state, and the much-despised East-coast liberals in Washington and places like New York and Boston, ultimately rooted in a suspicious cosmopolitanism that did not impress the suburban communities of the American heartland, were again associated with the detrimental effects of collectivism.

As, for example, Mirowski (2005: 86) has noticed, on the basis of all these changes in American society in the 1970s and 1980s, Keynesianism did not lose ground on the basis of stagflation only. No matter if one agrees on a Keynesian economic policy model, the assumption is still that governments and government officials are capable of transcending personal interests and 'work for the greater good', an idea that is simply not tenable for the neoconservative communities. This traditional view was part of the anti-statist critique of Keynesianism, Mirowski (2005) suggests:

> They [neoclassical economists criticizing Keynes] understood that they have
> to come equipped with theories of politics that were more serious than the
> Keynesians had. What is one of the standard complaints about Keynesianism?
> That it looked at the government as if it were totally benevolent and it would
> engage in fiscal and monetary policy for the good of all, with no thought as to
> its own persistence and viability. The neoliberals would retort, 'No, no you
> can't trust them, the government is as self-interested as any of our other
> actors.' (Mirowski, 2005: 88)

The decline in Keynesianism was a relatively quick process. The Republican President Richard M. Nixon had famously declared 'We are all
Keynesians now' (Jones, 2012: 221), but by the time of the Carter
presidency in the second half of the 1970s, the President had already
expressed his concerns regarding the ability of the state to run people's
lives (a mild but still typical critique of welfare state provisions). Carter
announced in a State of the Union address that 'government could no
longer solve people's problems' (cited in Jones, 2012: 254). For Carter's
successor, Ronald Reagan, this critique was not only a declaration of the
limits of the welfare state, but was the very basis for an entire political
agenda and career. Rather than just having its economic and moral
limitations, for Reagan (and also for Prime Minister Margaret Thatcher,
mutatis mutandis, on the other side of the Atlantic) the welfare state
represented a form of totalitarianism, a rampant collectivism poorly
aligned with the favoured American way of life of Reagan's conservative
voters. 'Today', Reagan declared in a speech in 1979, 'there is hardly a
phase of our daily living that doesn't feel the stultifying hand of
government regulation and interference ... This power, under whatever
name or ideology, is the very essence of totalitarianism' (cited in Madrick,
2011: 116). When being elected president in 1980, Reagan embarked on
a pro-business, anti-collectivism political agenda that aimed to restore the
American way of life of the 1950s, the golden age in the American
self-image, the decade of stability, community and economic growth. The
Reagan presidency was the principal decade for the reformulation of the
conditions under which economic value is created and distributed.

Merely conceiving of the pro-business, free market, neoconservative
takeover as a political coup, as some left-leaning commentators may treat
it, is not sufficiently attentive to the details of the process. In the 1970s,
there were reasons for many Americans to be worried. Following the
post-World War II prosperity, the first oil crisis of 1973, caused by
political and military conflicts in the Middle East, was the first major
postwar crisis for US capitalism (Tomaskovic-Devey and Lin, 2011:
542). The consequences of the rising energy costs and the unrelated crisis
in the political system leading to Nixon's impeachment and resignation

created a sense of the US economy and political system being devoid of leaders. Just as after the Wall Street crash of 1929, it was again political leaders and the managers of the major corporations who were criticized for stagnating economic growth, the declining competitiveness of US corporations, high unemployment and the general lack of hope for the future. The consequence was by and large a change of the guard: in the late 1970s and early 1980s, the Keynesians had to make way for the new generation of free marketeers of various kinds, be they neoliberals, libertarians, or simply old-fashioned run-of-the-mill conservatives. '[S]ince the late 1970s, governments around the world have abdicated many of their Keynesian responsibilities concerning social welfare in favor of neoliberal regulatory models', Polillo and Guillén (2005: 1793–4) write.

When the Keynesian model was officially dismissed (more informally, it continued to play a vital role in virtually all advanced economies' policies, not the least for the deficit-spending Reagan administration, pumping tax-money and bond sales income not so much into welfare state activities as into the military–industrial complex), there was now room for new economic ideas to gain a foothold and to be advocated in economic committees and advisory boards. The critics of collectivism could now finally cash in on the credibility of being staunch proponents of free market policy since the earliest days of the New Deal. Now, many of the New Dealers were dead and buried and many of them also forgotten, and figures such as Friedrich von Hayek and Milton Friedman could certainly smell the 'Morning in America' that Reagan used as his campaign slogan. Also on the other side of the Atlantic, where the British economy was encountering entirely different economic difficulties, the free market economic theory and the more recent idea of supply-side economics (a quite broad, imprecise and not so theoretically credible framework for economic stimulation) were regarded as the key to the future of the British economy. As Keynesian economic theory and policy only partially failed (the effects of the oil crisis were in fact substantial and its long-term consequences were hard to predict), the advocators of an entirely different policy regime were very successful in pushing Keynes further to the margins. From now on, free markets were advanced as the solutions to all kinds of economic and social evils.

SUMMARY AND CONCLUSION

Louis Brandeis had already in the pre-World War I period warned of the influence of the 'money trust', representing an early stage of the policy-makers' lasting concern, more pronounced than ever in the New Deal period, regarding the legitimacy of business enterprises in the American economy. Berle and Means (1934) shifted the focus from the trusts and monopolies, and addressed the issue concerning on what basis salaried managers could claim the right to the enormous power they had entrenched as the entrusted decision-makers in oligopolistic competitive capitalism. In addition, Berle and Means (1934) asked pressing questions regarding who this managerial class was accountable to, and to what extent the emerging managerial capitalism regime represented a sustainable economic system. After the Wall Street crash of 1929, the most severe economic crisis at least for American capitalism – for Europeans, the 'Great Depression' occurred in the last decades of the nineteenth century – added to these concerns. In an attempt to restore the American economy, the Roosevelt administration, jump-started by the presence of officials and functionaries who had planned and administrated the thriving American World War I economy (Hawley, 1966), embarked on a series of programmes and reforms. For conservatives, libertarians and the motley crew of pro-business activists, business owners and finance capital investors, the New Deal era represented a thinly veiled collectivist ideology that shared many characteristics with both European welfare state politics and the much-despised planned economy of the communist Soviet Union. Economists and social theorists such as Friedrich von Hayek and his collaborators mobilized what was regarded as a form of counter-intelligentsia to provide a systematic and persistent critique of such 'totalitarian tendencies' on the very soil of the American Republic. Unfortunately, their activism and theoretical work largely failed to be recognized as their concerns regarding the malaise of collectivism were shared by few others at the time. Hayek's writings and predictions had to compete with the economic theory and policy recommendations presented by the brilliant Cambridge economist John Maynard Keynes, and rather than being the pathway to totalitarianism and economic collapse as Hayek had forbiddingly predicted, the post-World War II period was characterized by unprecedented economic growth and prosperity. This was accompanied by the expanding welfare state and its provisions that de facto enabled a larger share of the population to enjoy the fruits of competitive capitalism and their very own hard labour. While this new economic system was far from perfect, being a regime of oligarchic competitive capitalism dominated by divisionalized firms, conglomerates and a growing share of multinational corporations (Galbraith, 1971), the conventional wisdom in the 1945–73 period (when the first oil crisis struck, an event that was preceded by slowly declining profit rates in American industry from the mid-1960s) was to adhere to Keynesian economic policies and to rely on a 'strong state' regulating and moni-toring the economy and its markets.

In the 1970s, the Keynesian economic model increasingly came under assault and much of the previously smoothly operating regime of managerial capitalism lost much of its impetus and credibility. In the period of plummeting economic performance figures and expanding mass-consumption markets, the concerns regarding the legitimacy of managerial authority and privileges could be tolerated, but as soon as the American economy sank into recession, the critique of managerial capitalism resurfaced. In particular, speaking of corporate governance, the legal idea of fiduciary duties of directors and their agents, the managers, was contested by a contractarian view of the firm in the 1970s and 1980s. This made what Manne (1965; 1967) termed the market for managerial control (that is, liquid finance markets) and not court ruling the ultimate check on managerial malfeasance. In the emerging political and business climate of the 1970s and 1980s, much of the post-World War II agreements and conventional wisdom was questioned by a new generation of free market protagonists, in many cases directly funded by pro-business activists such as wealthy capital owners. Using the term *agency theory* to advance their research agenda and the policies derived therefrom, the legalistic view of corporate governance was now fiercely criticized (or, in some cases, just flatly ignored) as economic theories of the firm were brought to the fore to justify new corporate governance policies and practices.

NOTES

1. Between 1880 and 1900, 'nearly 23,000 strikes affected more than 117,000 establishments', Brandes (1976: 1) writes. That figure translates into an average of three new strikes a day for twenty consecutive years. In addition, these strikes were accompanied by violence, and one estimate suggests that state troopers were 'called out to quell strike violence roughly 500 times between 1875 and 1910' (Brandes, 1976: 1). The term *crisis* is thus well founded. During the Great Depression, things turned even more sour: in industrial cities like Toledo and Cleveland in Ohio, unemployment '[r]eached rates of 50 and 80 percent, devastating small shopkeepers and the traditional security of white-collar jobs' (Jenkins and Brents, 1989: 895); by 1937, 1 860 000 employees were on strike (Jenkins and Brents, 1989: 896).
2. When accounting for the first Mont Pèlerin Society meeting, Milton Friedman (cited in Philips-Fein, 2009: 23) said that 'the importance of that meeting was that it showed us that we were not alone', thus supporting Lionel Robbins' concerns.
3. Given the poor predictive capacities of Hayek's work, the status of *The Road to Serfdom* is an interesting case of what sociologists (and in the first instance, theologists) refer to as *consecration*, defined as '[t]he attempt by a group or organization to impose a durable symbolic distinction between these objects and individuals worthy of veneration as exemplars of excellence within a field of cultural production and those that are not' (Allen and Parsons, 2006: 808). In the interwar period, conservative and libertarian activists of the

pro-business community in the US nourished the idea that their movement and advocacy needed 'their own great book' (Philips-Fein, 2009), similar to the economic liberals' praise of Adam Smith's *Wealth of Nations* or left-leaning groups' preference for Karl Marx's *Capital*. Walter Lippmann was interested in neither the agenda of these conservatives and libertarians, nor in being some kind of principal theorist or ideologue for this group, but Hayek, having credentials as a contributor to the widely respected Austrian School of Economics and being a long-standing pro-business advocator, served this role much better. As Lamont (1987: 586) remarks, the consecration of written texts or research findings (that is, a theory) is a specific form of 'intellectual legitimation', which she defines as the process wherein a theory '[b]ecomes recognized as part of a field – as something that cannot be ignored by those who define it themselves, and are defined, as legitimate participants in the construction of a cognitive field' (Lamont, 1987: 586). More importantly, Lamont (1987: 586) continues, this legitimation '[d]oes not proceed from [the] intrinsic value [of a theory] but results from coexisting, highly structured interrelated cultural and institutional systems'. That is, theories or other systematic statements are intellectually legitimized and ultimately consecrated as 'seminal works' not so much on the basis of their intrinsic value but because they are aligned with what Lamont (1987: 586) calls 'specific environmental requirements', which 'permits a fit between the work of specific cultural and institutional features of various markets'. That is, a work or a theory is considered 'great' or 'seminal' because it is functionally aligned with predominant values, beliefs and ideologies. In other words, the consecration of *The Road to Serfdom* is a historically contingent process that arguably says less about the treatise itself than it says about the intellectual climate in the mid-1940s in corporate America.

4. Hayek and his followers' hatred of socialism in all forms (thinly veiled as 'collectivism') did not help them to realize, as historians have pointed out, that much of the postwar economic planners' inspiration did not come from Moscow, but from Rome and Mussolini's fascist state apparatus (or, in the case of France, from Vichy): '[i]t was often fascist, not Communist planning which appealed to the technocrats who took over in the forties', Judt (2015: 25) writes (see also Hawley, 1966: 43–4).

5. This connection between enterprising, competitive capitalism and religious belief runs deep in American society. Kaufman (2008: 404) notices that the early forms of corporate law enacted in New England states such as Massachusetts, Connecticut and Rhode Island, were shaped by the local Puritans' belief in the protestant ethic that predisposed them to not only 'value commerce and the accumulation of capital', but also to see monopolies as 'inimical to the public interest'. This cultural background and historical roots, Kaufman (2008: 404) suggests, buttress 'the uniquely American version of neoliberal capitalism extant today'.

6. As Moore and Rebérioux (2011: 88) remark, while a liquid stock market was perceived as a 'problem' in the post-Berle and Means (1934) managerialist literature, in the doctrine of shareholder primacy based on the market for managerial control, in turn based on a liquid and efficient stock market, the very same market is now the 'solution' to governance problems. But this solution rests on a series of assumptions regarding market efficiency and the ability of market prices to accommodate relevant information. Moore and Rebérioux (2011: 104) doubt the accuracy and empirical evidence of such assumptions and propose that stock markets are '[c]onsiderably limited as a medium for transmitting reliable firm specific information from "insiders" to "outsiders"'. Nor do Moore and Rebérioux (2011: 100) believe that the standard solution in contractarian theory to such informational problems – the role of 'independent directors' – solves the problem, as internal directors contribute with 'firm specific expertise, acquired through direct involvement in the productive process'. Needless to say, contractarians dismiss such assumptions regarding the influence and value of situated and contextual knowledge as an unnecessary theoretical and practical complication that is irrelevant, as market prices always already contain the information needed to effectively execute a final check on managers. This position is closely connected to what Friedman and Kraus (2012: 149) call *price fetishism*, the wide-ranging assumption that '[m]arket prices somehow have the ability to overcome human limitations and accurately predict the future'.

PART II

Rethinking the firm

3. The agency theory model of the firm and its implications

INTRODUCTION

The legal incorporation of a business is not a trivial matter and legal scholars and jurists in service of the state apparatus have always been at pains to balance the benefits of enterprising activities and other societal and economic interests. In the concession tradition of thinking, the incorporated business is a creature of the state wherein the owners of the business are accountable to a variety of objectives and goals in the firm's environment. As Bratton (1989a; 1989b) makes clear, that image of the firm is today outmoded as few legal theorists advocate such a view of the firm. Still, corporate law remains a tool of the state to carefully balance diverse political interests, not only shareholder welfare, and therefore the role of corporate law must not be trivialized but must be understood within the wider socio-economic and political project to support enterprising and entrepreneurial activities.

Taking the strict legal view of corporate law and the firm's wider legal environment, where there is always a practical difference between laws in books and laws in real life, any attempt made by the state to restrict and hem in free market activities is understood as a form of violation of the free market efficiency proposition. As was discussed in Chapter 2, even in the case where the competitive capitalist economic system is at the brink of collapse, as it was in the early 1930s, free market protagonists did not refrain from pursuing their collectivism critique agenda. Even though the Roosevelt administration's NIRA programme helped restore the American economy and the subsequent Keynesian economic programme led to an unprecedented economic growth and welfare, benefiting a larger population of industrialized economies in the post-World War II period, all these robust benefits are still guilty of collectivism, free market protagonists maintain. Friedrich von Hayek claimed that collectivism was the pathway to 'serfdom' in the mid-1940s, but Hayek and his allies rather faced an unprecedented economic prosperity. Despite being unable to present credible predictions of the unfolding events, Hayek's work still managed to mobilize a variety of free market protagonists during the post-World War II period, a community that could do little more than to bide its time in the era of hegemonic Keynesianism. In the 1970s' economic downturn and declining profit levels, Hayek and his collaborators suddenly found themselves to be in what Georges Canguilhem calls '*dans le vrai*' – 'in the truth'. However, the new generation of free market protagonists did not really share Hayek's concern regarding the perils of collectivism including socialism and the influence of trade unions but instead sought to address the virtues of competitive capitalism in new terms:

> The new generation of the free market thinkers – in contrast to Friedrich von Hayek and Ludwig von Mises – wrote far less about communism and the dangers of a planned economy. They were more enamored of specific policies, more ironic about the failures of bureaucracy, in some ways more fixated on particulars and less interested in describing the working of the whole system. The rhetoric was one of hope and optimism instead of danger and foreboding. They lacked the gloomy grandeur of their predecessors, perhaps because they sensed that the world was turning in their favor. (Philips-Fein, 2009: 183–4)

While not being able to contribute in any meaningful way to the stabilization of the economic system during and after the Depression, the free market protagonists could now sense the *Morgenröte* of the new day rising, when they would possibly be given a new role to play in the period of the declining credibility of the Keynesian programme.

In this chapter, the revised critique of collectivism, now centred on the role of executives and directors managing the corporations articulated by agency theorists, will be discussed. This critique abandoned the idea of state administration and the trade unions as the principal agents of a collectivist ethos, and instead turned their attention to the lion's den – the executive suite – to pull out the villains responsible for the declining economic performance. Rather than state administrators and trade unionists being the foremost gravediggers of competitive, free market capitalism – that was conventional wisdom for free marketeers – the present situation was very much an inside job caused by shirking and serf-serving executives and directors who could amass capital for their own benefits to be able to escape the market's fair but unforgiving evaluation of their performance. (For example, agency theorists, addressed shortly, subscribe to the proposition that there is a linear and causal relation between executive performance and stock market pricing.) Taking legal theory and more specifically the concept of contract as their principal theoretical vehicle for articulating this critique of managerialism, while at the same time staying truthful to the methodological individualism of neoclassical economic theory, agency theorists here speak of the firm as a 'nexus of contract'. The theoretical and practical robustness of this proposition will be examined in detail in this chapter.

THE NEW COLLECTIVISM CRITIQUE: SALARIED MANAGERS AND DIRECTORS AS SHIRKERS AND OPPORTUNISTS

Since the mid- to late nineteenth century, American corporate law prescribed that for a business to become incorporated, the state had to pass a law, and the law's charter is seen as the outcome of negotiations between the incorporators and the state government (Hilt, 2014: 8.5). That is, the very juridical form of the corporation is from the outset a bundle of contracts between the incorporators themselves (that is, the entrepreneurs and their financiers) but also between the incorporators and the state. The corporate legal form itself already from the outset assumes a set of responsibilities and rights that cannot be ignored as soon as the corporation is operating in a market and generating its own cash flow. The American corporate law system is thus a solution to corporate governance problems that have been stitched together on the basis of common law, legal innovations and institutional or market-based solutions (Hilt, 2014: 8.17). More importantly, this functional corporate law could never have been accomplished on the basis of free market negotiations alone, as politics has been of critical importance in the evolution of the American corporation (Hilt, 2014: 8.18). Here there is a sharp contrast between what Roy (1997:75) refers to as the *efficiency theory* of corporate law, which assumes that 'private enterprises, disciplined by an unforgiving market, are inherently more efficient than government decision making', and the *institutional theory* perspective, which stresses how corporate law denotes the gradual establishment of legal and regulatory practices to handle governance problems and a variety of interests and to effectively balance time perspectives (see, for example, Dobbin and Dowd, 2000). Therefore, Roy (1997: 174) claims, efficiency theory ignores the historical perspective on corporate law as it declares that efficiency is the sole legitimate performance metric when assessing a corporate law system. Instead, as institutional theorists would argue, the ability to incorporate the business in the first place, long before there were any possibilities for assessing and passing remarks about the efficiency of the corporate law system, rests on political negotiations that enable the creation both of corporations and of the markets wherein they operate (Evans, 1995; Dobbin, 1994). In other words, efficiency theorists ignore how corporate law has emerged in a historical–political process and thus treat it as if it was founded on the very same premises that exist today, effectively being the outcome of the very creation of such a legal–political system. This view is based on the fallacy of treating both the market and the corporation as primordial economic modalities preceding human action and interests.

In the New Deal programme, some of the most elementary legal frameworks guiding the era of managerial capitalism for the coming decades were enacted and implemented. The Glass–Steagall Act of 1933 and The Securities Act of 1934 that instituted the Securities and Exchange Commission (SEC) (Hilt, 2014; Rock, 2013) strongly restricted the finance industry's ability to control corporations and granted executives a central position in the corporate governance system:

> Corporate law always performed a balancing act with management discretion and shareholder power. The balance, however, has always privileged the directors and their appointed managers in business policymaking because they are better informed than the shareholders and thus better positioned to take responsibility for both monitoring and managing the firm and its externalities. (Bratton and Wachter, 2010: 659)

As no corporate law system is perfect, there were certain managerial practices and 'fashions' that dominated and that would be grist for the mill in the agency theory critique of managerial capitalism, articulated from the mid-1970s. In the US, the restrictive enforcement of antitrust laws after the war forced managers to consider acquisitions 'only in unrelated businesses, where the firm's core skills add little economic value' (Kaufman and Englander, 1993: 54). For the legislators, the presence of monopolies in the economy led to greater costs (that is, inefficiencies) than unrelated diversification would, and therefore acquisition of unrelated businesses was encouraged regardless of their economic and financial 'efficiency'. More specifically, it was a specific passage in the Celler–Kefauver Act of 1950 which 'made vertical integration suspect' (Zorn et al., 2005: 283), and therefore the post-World War II executives were instructed to engage in what was known as 'portfolio planning', a managerial practice based on portfolio theory developed in the finance theory branch of economics and where the corporation should preferably hold assets that balanced the cash flow and evened out the stock market value over the economic cycle. Portfolio planning was thus the managerial response to: (1) corporate law prohibiting related diversification; (2) newly developed theoretical models in academic quarters; and (3) the volatility of the competitive capitalist economic system based on stock market evaluations. Providing many benefits, portfolio planning was popular among managers in the period: by the end of the 1970s, '45% of the Fortune 500 [companies] had adopted these portfolio planning techniques' (Zorn et al., 2005: 283).

The free market protagonists had to endure the long march from the 1930s to the early 1970s before their critique of the collectivist and planned economy could be credited. Contrary to what they predicted, government meddling with economic matters seemed to be a very successful formula as it enabled both stability and economic growth. However, when the profit levels started to decline in the US manufacturing industry in the mid-1960s, the global motor of the postwar economic boom, in combination with the first oil crisis of 1973, leading to soaring energy costs and accompanying inflation, there were new opportunities for rehabilitating the critique of collectivism. The first generation of neoliberal intellectuals, active in the 1930s and 1940s, were now ageing (Hayek) or at their very height of influence (Milton Friedman), and a younger generation of free market protagonists were ready to issue their own version of free market thinking, forcefully articulated as a critique of managerial capitalism.

The older generation of free market thinkers had portrayed trade unions and government as being the villains intervening with allegedly efficient (that is, rational) markets. This criticism had received limited attention as the oligarchy-leaning managerial capitalist system based on mass-production and mass-consumption demanded an institutional model wherein both the government and the trade unions could collaborate within the existing system of corporate law. Trade unions were greeted as speaking partners and collaborators of corporations and government agencies, and consequently there were relatively few industry conflicts in the boom years after the war. The new generation of free market theorists thus took an entirely different route and revised the old idea of 'collectivism' as their principal subject of critique and instead targeted salaried managers, the key institutional innovation of managerial capitalism. The fact that government and trade union action distorted naturally efficient markets was conventional wisdom for this generation of theorists, but salaried managers at the helm of increasingly large conglomerates in the post-World War II economy were also guilty of opportunism and malfeasance. In this shift in perspectives, from the traditional enemies of free market protagonists to the very heart of the capitalist system – the executive suites and boardrooms – Berle and Means's (1934) treatise on the dangers of managerial opportunism was dusted off. Agency theorists such as Michael C. Jensen and Eugene F. Fama claimed straightforwardly that the presence of lowly valued conglomerates was not so much the consequence of corporate law and the management fashion of portfolio planning as it was indicative of executives and directors acting self-interestedly to be able to buffer the ups and downs in the economic cycle by storing up capital that rightly belonged to the shareholders (Jensen, 1993; 1986; Fama and Jensen, 1983; Fama, 1980; Jensen and Meckling, 1976; Manne, 1965). In the following, this line of argumentation will be examined.

THE AGENCY THEORY MODEL OF CORPORATE GOVERNANCE

In 1976, there were two seminal publications that both served to render salaried managers subject to intense interest. The first publication was a journal paper published by the economists Michael C. Jensen and William Meckling at Rochester University, generally regarded a Chicago economic theory stronghold, and being sponsored by the neoconservative politician and fundraiser William E. Simon. The second publication was a book by a legal scholar located in California, Melvin A. Eisenberg, which tried to sort out the agency relationships within the firm. While the Jensen and Meckling paper is today widely cited and regarded as a key publication within the agency theory framework, Eisenberg's *The Structure of the Corporation* remains relatively obscure for mainstream researchers. Both are worthy of further attention.

Jensen and Meckling (1976: 308) define an agency relationship as 'a contract under which one or more persons (the principal(s)) engage another person (the agent) to perform some service on their behalf which involves delegating some decision making authority to the agent'. This is today the mainstream agency theory and corporate governance view, and key to this argument is the term *contract*. In orthodox economic theory, market-based activities are normally perceived as transactions that only connect the buyer and the seller temporarily, while the juridical contract presupposes a more long-standing relationship. The differences between these two views of the contract need to be explicated. The efficient market hypothesis, which suggests that markets price assets accurately as they process all available public information, is consistent with this view of market-based pricing and accompanying transactions as a juridical contract. For instance, if the stock market prices a specific share on the basis of available public information, the purchaser of the share pays the price of the asset, set jointly but uncoordinatedly by all the stock traders being active in the market for the time being. This is a case of a straightforward market transaction, terminating the relation between the buyer and the seller when the transaction is completed. However, even though Jensen and Meckling (1976) subscribe to the efficient market hypothesis, they still believe that the *legal concept* of contract is more suitable to define the relation between owners of stock and executives than the regular economics concept of transactions. This model implies that the purchaser of a stock not only buys the stock on the basis of the information available at the point of time when the stock was acquired, but also that this purchase is an agreement or a bet for the future, indicating that executives overseeing firms that issue stocks are operating under the duty to ensure that the stock is not losing substantial shares of its economic value also in the future. Seemingly inconsistent with the otherwise much venerated efficient market hypothesis, free markets cannot operate under such juridical contracts as the future cannot be known *ex ante*. Herein lies the most theoretically fragile element of agency theory: its insistence on both granting the market a series of regulatory benefits and advantages vis-à-vis other control mechanisms (for example, state-controlled regulation), while at the same time relying on a quasi or semi-legal vocabulary to justify shareholder welfare, which is ultimately the foremost policy implication from Jensen and Meckling's (1976) argument, repeated time and again in the agency theory literature. That is, rather than relying on market pricing and transactions (making the juridical term contract obsolete), or adhering to mainstream legal theory (granting the market a less central role in the corporate govern-ance system), Jensen and Meckling (1976) combine two previously separated theoretical models. Still, the tensions between these two theoretical traditions remain unsolved.

In the next stage, Jensen and Meckling (1976: 310, emphasis in the original) further distance themselves from the free market argument and claim that firms are after all '*legal fictions which serve as a nexus for a set of contracting relationships among individuals*'. In the mainstream neoclassical view, the firm per se is mostly ignored as a site for economic production and value creation, but it is still recognized as a 'black box' whose inside operations essentially remain outside the scientific pro-gramme of neoclassical economic theory; what happens inside the firm – by definition a modality of market failure (otherwise, firms would not exist, Coase (1937) had declared) – is of interest for engineers and management scholars. Discrediting the firm as a legitimate site for professional and managerial expertise altogether, Jensen and Meckling (1976) thus say that the firm is a 'legal fiction' – it is a form of inscription of ownership rights into legal documents that in turn can be sold on the market (for example, stock markets). Through this theoretical twist, simultaneously recognizing and ignoring the firm as an economic entity but still rendering the firm a legal construction, Jensen and Meckling (1976) save most of the neoclassical economic theory model, including the efficient market hypothesis, while at the same time accomplishing their real goal: to provide the capital owners (primarily shareholders, but also, but to a much smaller extent, creditors) with a legal argument that would grant shareholders (and nobody else) the right to the variable economic value generated by the firm. In addition, paying homage to their neoclassical convictions and the need to reduce complex social relations to elementary models where individual actors are the vertices and their contractual relations are the edges of the model, the firm disappears entirely in Jensen and Meckling's image of the firm:

> Viewed this way, it makes little or no sense to try to distinguish those things that are 'inside' of the firm (or any other organization) from those things 'outside' of it. There is in a very real sense only a multitude of complex relationships (i.e., contracts) between the legal fiction (the firm) and the owners of labor, material and capital inputs and consumers of output. (Jensen and Meckling, 1976: 311)

Interestingly, at the same time as Jensen and Meckling (1976) erase the firm, making it gradually disappear into market pricing and legal contracts, they and other agency theorists remain intensively concerned with at least one thing that apparently they believe occurs inside the firm: the various forms of alleged managerial opportunistic behaviour and the mismanagement of the economic resources. Before this issue is further discussed, Eisenberg's (1976) argument in favour of a contractual view of the firm is examined.

Unlike Jensen and Meckling, Melvin A. Eisenberg (1976) is a legal scholar and he defines three views of the firm (whereof two will be examined here), including the *shareholder democracy view* and the *managerialist view*. The shareholder democracy view is basically consistent with the agency theory view, suggesting that shareholder welfare is the key objective of the firm, while the managerialist view is more inclined to, as Eisenberg (1976: 25) suggests, 'support managerial discretion in the governance structure'. Within the general 'nexus of contract view' that agency theorists advocate to justify the shareholder welfare governance, Eisenberg's work is interesting for two reasons. First, because he believes the market can ultimately resolve conflicts between organizational stakeholders, including, for example, what agency theorists call principals and agents: 'where conflict arises out of business decisions there is frequently a market which can be used as a standard to measure the decision's fairness', Eisenberg (1976: 30) asserts. This is the familiar free market argument, that, for example, stock market analysts are rewarding or punishing managerial decision-making through their joint but uncoordinated assessment of the economic consequences of the decision. That is, it is market-based actors who determine the efficiency of managerial decision-making. Second, Eisenberg shares with agency theorists the sceptical attitude towards managers – again typical of the mid- to late 1970s where the American economy and industry seemed to be in decline – suggesting that managers are exposed to the temptation to engage in activities that would boost their self-images and/or buffer resources that shelter them from unfavourable market assessments that would reveal faulty decisions and incompetence more broadly:

> Just as desire for power and prestige may lead management to undertake acquisitions, so identification with the enterprise and the desire for security may lead management to oppose corporate contractions, liquidations, or merger into an acquiring corporation, even where such an action would be desirable on economic grounds. (Eisenberg, 1976: 34)

While being a legal scholar, otherwise (it must be assumed) having a fair share of belief in the legal regulation of economic entities, Eisenberg here invokes more social and psychological conditions such as group-think or a shared sense of being morally correct as explanations for why managers are likely to engage in opportunistic behaviour: 'far from perceiving its own conflict of interest, management is likely to perceive its position as morally neutral or morally admirable', Eisenberg (1976: 34) proposes. Here the message is clear: rather than being worthy of being entrusted with the shareholders' capital to create a yield in the form of dividends or rising stock prices, salaried executives should be carefully controlled and monitored. Mistrust in salaried executives is thus a key component of Eisenberg's governance structure. However, it is not evident that Eisenberg shares agency theorists' belief that any actor who operates in a financial market is by definition free from self-interest and opportunistic behaviour, but rather the two groups are cut from the same cloth: 'it remains true that if giant enterprise conflicts with national economic and social goals, it is unlikely that this conflict will be resolved by increasing shareholder power, since it seems fair to assume that most shareholders are at least as interested in profits as is management' (Eisenberg, 1976: 19).

Under all conditions, in the mid- to late 1970s, when many Americans and not the least the business community itself felt that there was a need for a change to reinvigorate the economy and the world of business, executives and directors, the 'princes of property' in Adolf A. Berle's memorable phrase, were now if not the villains of the drama at least something similar to all-too-permissive parents letting their offspring run amok. Therefore, someone had to step forward to discipline managers and stop the economic decline and the squandering of resources. A new breed of politicians and business leaders, better fit to handle the new economic conditions, was claimed to be desperately needed.

This sense of resentment and even betrayal was effectively explored by agency theorists deepening and extending the arguments of Jensen and Meckling (1976) and Eisenberg (1976). Fama and Jensen (1983) argued on the basis of the principal–agent model acquired from Berle and Means's (1934) work that the separation of the ratification and the monitoring of decisions, that is, the whole process from initiation to the implementation of decisions, demands a 'contract structure' (Fama and Jensen, 1983: 302). That is, in the contractual model, the board of directors initiates decisions which the CEO implements, and finally decisions are monitored and assessed by the shareholders who use the stock price to determine the efficacy of the decisions made. To accomplish this work at the lowest possible agency costs (that is, the principal's costs for monitoring agents), the firm is again understood as a nexus of contracts, 'written and unwritten, among owners of factors of production and customers' (Fama and Jensen, 1983: 302). This is by and large the repetition of Jensen and Meckling's (1976) and Eisenberg's (1976) arguments, but Fama and Jensen introduce the key term *residual claimants* as being the shareholders who, Fama and Jensen (1983: 302) assure, have contracted 'for the rights to net cash flow'. The net cash flow is the money that remains when all other costs are covered and when all forward-oriented investments are made (for example, investment in R&D activities). The most important theoretical implication from this argument is that shareholders are not, technically speaking, the *owners* of the firm, but they should be understood as finance market actors *investing* in the firm (that is, the firm is enacted as a finance market venture rather than a production function), and therefore managers are the shareholders' agents, making decisions and enacting policies in the interests of the principals. If failing to execute this agential function effectively, the market for corporate control (that is, the stock market and its pricing mechanism) would punish ineffective managerial action through lower stock prices and thus expose the firm to takeover bids and other disciplinary action undermining managerial discretion. This means that management and the board of directors operating under these contractual relations have neither the legitimate right nor the practical possibility to withhold the residual cash flow from its residual claimants, agency theorists claim. This is a key proposition in the agency theory model.

Unfortunately the proposition is heavily disputed and is substantiated by neither corporate law nor legal theory more broadly. Moreover, the proposed linear and unambiguous relationship between managerial decision-making quality and market pricing, the core of the so-called pricing theory upon which the proposition is based, is yet to be supported by empirical evidence.

Written in a characteristic neoclassical economic theory prose, adding propositions to propositions and advancing the argument through a *modus tollens* line of reasoning ('if A, *but only if* A, then B' and so on), and leaving little room for further explanations or more detailed arguments, Fama and Jensen (1983) largely bypass the legal issues pertaining to their argument, and instead they spend more time discussing the issue of managerial opportunism, addressed as the accumulation of *agency costs*:

> Agency problems arise because contracts are not costlessly written and enforced. Agency costs include the costs of structuring, monitoring, and bonding a set of contracts among agents with conflicting interests. Agency costs also include the value of output lost because the costs of full enforcement of contracts exceed the benefits. (Fama and Jensen, 1983: 304)

This agency cost is particularly complicated when decisions are initiated by individuals who do not themselves benefit or risk losing economic values depending on the decision's outcomes. If such individuals are active in decision-making processes, and there is a lack of detailed control of their activities, Fama and Jensen (1983: 304) warn, 'such decision managers are more likely to take actions that deviate from the interests of residual claimants'. Expressed differently, managers who escape the residual claimants' close surveillance and disciplinary action squander the finance capital that the residual claimants are entitled to according to the contracts they hold in predictable ways. This negative attitude towards salaried managers and managerial capitalism more broadly is the foundation for the agency theory argument. Baker and Smith (1998), for instance, suggest that prior to the increased finance market-based control of managers, brought by shareholder primacy governance, managers were more likely to engage in 'empire-building projects':

> [W]hile managers routinely declared that their actions were based on their fiduciary responsibilities to protect shareholder welfare, they were largely free – more free than ever before – to act independently. Left to their own devices, executive managers of mature businesses acted bureaucratically, tending to favor routine over change, growth over efficiency. Too many managers

overinvested in wasteful projects, acquiring assets simply for the sake of growth. Rather than return surpluses to shareholders, they were prone to invest instead in empire-building projects with little regard for their returns. (Baker and Smith, 1998: 14)

In addition, Baker and Smith (1998: 15) make the commonplace (but also circular) argument that the 'maximization of efficiency' would be 'the best economic outcome for society', and that such outcomes are accomplished *only* if managers 'feel responsible' towards 'their shareholders'. That is, shareholder value creation creates incentives for managers to 'strive for long-term corporate efficiency' and reduce the risk of 'managerial opportunism'. The solution to 'agency problems' (by and large the shareholders' problem, relying on managers' ability to generate economic value also in the future, but not so much a concern for, for example, creditors whose rights are once and for all sealed in the contracts they hold and who primarily need to worry about the firm going bankrupt) is that shareholder value should be maximized. Investment in existing activities, Fama and Jensen (1983) argue, adds less economic value to shareholders in comparison to the economic value potentially generated when shareholders receive the residual cash flow and themselves reinvest the capital in companies and industries with better return-on-investment prospects. The agency theory argument of Fama and Jensen thus rests on two major assumptions: (1) that management induces agency costs in systematic ways and that these costs for monitoring the 'agents' are higher than other comparable costs that the separation of ownership and control (a key precondition for the business ventures' ability to attract sufficient finance capital funds from dispersed owners) would induce; and (2) that the residual claimants (shareholders) are better investors than managers inside the firm.[1] Neither of these assumptions is supported by factual evidence and they both embody a series of practical problems that makes these two propositions virtually impossible to falsify (that is, they are not scientific, testable hypotheses). For instance, it is practically impossible for a board of directors making an investment decision to predict the economic return from the investment *ex ante*, and certainly not in comparison to *all other* possible investments that any individual owner of the stock could make if they received the money in the first place.

In the 1980s and 1990s, Michael C. Jensen continued to advocate the agency theory argument, maintaining that managers tend to induce agency costs and make inadequate investment decisions, especially in large firms in mature industries (that is, the industries by definition generating the largest cash flow): 'managers with unused borrowing power and large free cash flows are more likely to undertake low-benefit or even value-destroying mergers' (Jensen, 1986: 328). As a consequence, the leveraged buyout wave that swept over American industry in the 1980s was instrumental in disciplining managers to return the residual cash flow to the owners of stock, Jensen claims. By and large, there were, Jensen (1986: 329) argues, two types of firm that were targeted: '[f]irms with poor management that have done poorly prior to the merger, and firms that have done exceptionally well and have large free cash flow which they refuse to pay to shareholders'. Unfortunately, Jensen's proposition that it was poorly managed firms that were targeted by tender offers did not stand up well against empirical evidence (Davis and Stout, 1992). Still, his ideas regarding the need to discipline managers through finance market control were well tuned to the pro-business climate of the 1980s and suited the free market advocacy, proposing that finance markets price assets correctly.

While agency theorists display little interest in what happens inside the firm (the judgmental remarks regarding the alleged shirking of managers taken aside), Jensen (1993) is still surprisingly anxious to tell what difficulties firms encounter in their decision-making work. Jensen lists here inadequate internal management control routines and cost–benefit analyses and a limited understanding of the industry as causes of poor investment decisions:

> Firms often do not have good information on their own costs, much less the costs of their competitors; it is therefore sometimes unclear to managers that they are the high-cost firm which should exit the industry. Even when managers do acknowledge the requirement for exit, it is often difficult for them to accept and initiate the shutdown decision. For the managers who must implement these decisions, shutting plants or liquidating the firms causes personal pain, creates uncertainty, and interrupts or sidetracks careers. Rather than confronting the pain, managers generally resist such actions as long as they have the cash flow to subsidize the losing operations. (Jensen, 1993: 848)

As Jensen proposes, not only are internal control systems inefficient – a declaration unsupported by robust evidence – but managers making decisions on the basis of inadequate information are also prone to get stuck in nostalgia and self-serving interests, further complicating the decision-making. No wonder Jensen, fully convinced of the systemic incompetence of professional managers *tout court* (at least vis-à-vis finance market actors), believes in the market as the more effective control mechanism. Still, the reader of Jensen's work may wonder why he so conspicuously ignores the extensive management studies literature in making these assertions outside of his own domain of jurisdiction.

Instead, Jensen (1993: 873) declares, '[w]e have to open up the black box called the firm'. One must here assume that 'we' denotes a narrow group of scholars that share most of Jensen's and other agency theorists' neoclassical economic theory convictions.

Agency Theory's Practical Recommendations and Policies

Reading the work of the first generation of agency theorists is a true test of the management researcher's patience with interdisciplinary scholarship. Much is declared and asserted, but equally much is ignored, mostly for the sake of reaching the destination point, set out prior to the departure, that is, to legitimately claim that: (1) managers are inefficient or even incompetent in overseeing the capital they are entrusted with; (2) that shareholders are the managers' principals and can therefore legitimately claim the residual cash flow; (3) that the finance market control wielded by shareholders not only benefits this constituency but makes the economy overall more efficient. Once these theoretical propositions are announced, there are a number of practical recommendations formulated for how corporate governance work should be organized and how the agency costs should be minimized. First, Eisenberg (1976: 318) says, '[t]he board must be independent of the executives'. More specifically, 'at least 60 percent' of the directors should be independent, that is, they should represent owners, institutions and interests outside of the immediate sphere of the CEO and the firm (on the role of independent directors, see Gordon, 2007; Brudney, 1982). Second, '[t]he body of shareholders and the board must have the capacity for acquiring reliable information on the executives' performance' (Eisenberg, 1976: 318). As will be discussed later, the efficacy of both these recommendations has been complicated to substantiate with empirical evidence and/or has been compromised with new forms of managerial opportunistic behaviour that violates the propositions on which these recommendations rest (that is, the evidence of stock repurchases that both bias the market evaluation of stock and violate the efficient market hypothesis in terms of disqualifying free market finance asset pricing).

Regardless of the lack of empirical support for agency theory propositions, Jensen (1993: 870) declares that agency theory 'has fundamentally changed corporate finance and organization theory' inasmuch as we can no longer 'assume managers automatically act (in opposition to their own best interests) to maximize firm value'. That may be a relevant statement (all assumptions can by definition be disputed), but neither can it be assumed offhand that finance market control curbs managerial opportunism or maximizes firm value. Despite these concerns, agency theory has been, as Jensen (1993) says, enormously influential in shaping the view of the firm and its role in competitive capitalism. It would be fair to say that agency theory became the foremost managerial fashion of the 1980s and has maintained its popularity well beyond the events of 2008–09 (Dobbin and Jung, 2010). Its arguments were forceful and were based on the idea that free market actors (located in finance markets in particular, the liquidity markets *par excellence*) would be better positioned to determine where the free cash would generate higher returns. Unfortunately, the theory ignores the historical roots of US corporate law, that there are many types of principals (including, for example, long-term investors and creditors), and that shareholders cannot, legally speaking, surpass the executive functions of the corporation – the board of directors and the executives the board recruits:

> [a]gency theory's claim as to the alleged superiority of market-based mechanisms for controlling managerial decision-making at the individual firm level can be said to lack empirical and analytical foundations, thus building a negative case for the promotion of nonmarket, law-driven or firm-specific control devices, even on the mainstream corporate governance premise of achieving more effective protection of financial investors. (Moore and Rebérioux, 2011: 92)

While theoretical inconsistencies and historical ignorance apparently can be tolerated under certain conditions, Moore and Rebérioux (2011) also question the accuracy and empirical support for the theory of the market for managerial control, the cornerstone of the contractarian theory:

> Concerning the market for corporate control, meanwhile, the empirical evidence is rather inconclusive: the extensive literature on the effects of takeovers, while pointing to the (positive) short-term implications of takeover bids in terms of market value, suggests that those operations do not have, on average, any positive effect on either market value or operating performance over the long run. Indeed, an extensive series of empirical studies actually suggests that takeover bids have an overall negative impact in the above respects. (Moore and Rebérioux, 2011: 92–3)

Agency theory is thus theoretically inconsistent, empirically unsubstantiated, and ignorant regarding corporate law and legal theory (Farre-Mensa et al., 2014: 17.51; Daily et al., 2003: 372; Davis and Stout, 1992: 627).

In the following, the idea of the firm as being a 'nexus of contracts' (Jensen and Meckling, 1976) will be examined not so much as an empirical condition but as a legal statement in order to see how well this proposition conforms with existing legal theory and legal texts. That is, if the theoretical proposition articulated within the neoclassical economic theory framework is not supported by either legal theory or legal practice, the proposition is more indicative of economists' wish for how the world *could possibly be* rather than being well aligned with predominant legal frameworks. There is, after all, an unfortunate difference between how the world is and how we may wish it were, an undeniable fact also for individuals committed to neoclassical economic theory.

THE CONTRACTARIAN VIEW VS. CORPORATE LAW VIEW

The agency theory model is ultimately based on the idea that the firm is not so much a free-standing and inherently complex and heterogeneous production function that can be more or less effectively managed (in the 1990s, the so-called resource-based view of strategy would enact the firm in such terms) as it is understood as a bundle or a nexus of contracts. In order to save the methodological individualism of rational choice theory being at the very heart of neoclassical economic theory (only individual shareholders own stocks in the public firm) and to bypass all theories and studies of managerial work and managerialism more broadly (which represents a form of collectivist understanding of the firm as a collaborative effort, a site of team production) and still adhere to the principal axiom of neoclassical economic theory, that the market is always the original and primary site for economic transactions, agency theorists make recourse to legal theory. Unfortunately, legal theory is not an unchartered territory and in legal scholarship, equally formalist and methodologically rigorous as neoclassic economic theory, there are many ideas, doctrines and ideologies regarding the nature of corporate governance. Avoiding the work of, for example, management scholars that would have a hard time recognizing, for example, managerial work as being exclusively based on individual contracts with one single group of constituencies, agency theorists instead approach legal scholars whose professional jurisdiction is precisely corporate law and legal theory. As will be demonstrated, the agency theory view and the contractarian theory defining the relationship between principals and agents do not fare well within the legal scholars' jurisdiction.

Kaufman and Zacharias (1992: 528–9) argue persuasively that the contractarian theory is based on the belief that contract law better protects property rights (regardless of whether the agent is propertied or the propertyless, an owner, manager or a worker) than government coercion does. That is, contractarians operate within the intellectual tradition of the American constitution, embodying a deep-seated concern regarding the individual's rights vis-à-vis the sovereign (that is, the state), assuming that market-based contracting provides a more robust property rights protection than corporate law does. The neoclassical economic theory view, rendering the market the ultimate information processor and superior price-setting mechanism, is thus pitted against a more political process of corporate legislation rendering the sovereign a central actor. As the literature advocating the idea that firms are no more than a nexus of contracts does little to justify that theoretical position – a few references to allegedly seminal works such as Ronald Coase's (1937) article about the transaction costs (advancing a theoretical rather than a legal claim) is regarded as a sufficient demonstration of the accuracy of the claim – it is more intriguing to examine the responses to this proposition. 'The word "firm" is simply a shorthand description of a way to organize activities under contractual arrangements that differ from those of ordinary product markets', Cheung (1983: 3) states. Baysinger and Butler (1985: 180) suggest that standardized legal contracts may include fiduciary duties, and yet the firm is understood as a bundle of contracts: '[t]hrough the law of fiduciary duties, which proscribe theft and specified standards of care and loyalty, corporate law serves as a standard form contract that substitutes for costly, fully contingent agency contracts'.[2]

Cheung (1983) and Baysinger and Butler (1985) are economists with limited interest in legal theory, but their advocacy of contractual theory can be complemented by legal scholarship in the Chicago law and economics school tradition, a theoretical framework based on so-called price theory and the central proposition regarding the influence of transaction costs in economic activities (further discussed in Chapter 4). Easterbrook and Fischel (1993), two legal scholars, address the costs induced by the monitoring of managers and the legal theory solution to introduce the concept of fiduciary duties – that is, a non-economic concept treated as an unnecessary theoretical complication by contractual theorists and free market advocators – by simply conflating fiduciary duties and agency:

> During the last two centuries, courts have been adapting this duty of loyalty and its remedy to other agency relations, under the title 'fiduciary' duty. That is adaptation, not extension. The many agency relations that fall under the 'fiduciary' banner are so diverse that a single rule could not cover all without wreaking havoc. (Easterbrook and Fischel, 1993: 425)

In the contractual theory that Easterbrook and Fischel (1993: 427) advocate, contracts are a 'fiduciary relation' characterized by '[u]nusually high costs of specification and monitoring'. Therefore, they (1993: 431) continue, '[l]egislatures, courts, and commissions treating fiduciary duties as presumptive contractual terms, promoting the parties' welfare in the absence of express contracts, is all but inevitable. Anything else is self-defeating.' That is, in a world characterized by the difficulty to specify detailed contracts *ex ante* that can be monitored by both agents and the legal system at a reasonable cost, the legal theory concept of fiduciary duty rests on little more than the fallacy that economic relations can be established on the basis of non-economic terms, Easterbrook and Fischel (1993: 438) claim: '[s]cholars of non- or anti economic bent have had trouble coming up with a unifying approach to fiduciary duties because they are looking for the wrong things. They are looking for something special about fiduciary relations. There is nothing special to find' (Easterbrook and Fischel, 1993: 438). Expressing their firm belief in the robustness of the price theory underlying the contractual theory of the Chicago law and economics school, Easterbrook and Fischel (1993: 446) simply discredit legal theory and the concept of fiduciary duties: '[c]ontract and fiduciary duty lie on a continuum best understood as using a single, although singularly complex, algorithm' (Easterbrook and Fischel, 1993: 446).

The Strategic Choice of Level of 'Firmness'

One of the corollaries of the contractual view of the firm is, as Baysinger and Butler (1985: 180) remark, that firms operating in the US can choose in what state they want to incorporate their business. This choice provides promoters, directors and executives with an active choice regarding how much 'legal freedom' they want in their operation: '[m]arkets lead managers to adopt the optimal mix of legal and market governance structures for their firms. The optimal mix reflects *the preferences of the firm's residual claimants*' (Baysinger and Butler, 1985: 182–3, emphasis added). The idea is that a preferred combination of legal and market governance can be chosen if executives and directors listen carefully to the principals' wishes and thereafter move the entire corporation, lock, stock and barrel, to the state that provides the 'optimal governance mix'. Baysinger and Butler (1985: 191) repeat the contractualists' proposition that corporate law is instituted to maximize shareholder value, and therefore, the success of individual corporations depends on the freedom of directors to 'choose a legal environment consistent with the firm's ownership structure'.

Lamoreaux (1998: 66) follows this rationalist view of the incorporation of the business and speaks about such choices in terms of determining the degree of 'firmness' of the corporation: 'businesspeople could choose from a range of contractual forms that offered varying degrees of firmness, that is, that differed in the extent to which they protected contractual parties against holdup'.[3] By implication, when speaking about degrees of firmness, the line of demarcation between key neoclassical economic theory concepts such as markets and hierarchies becomes less useful, Lamoreaux (1998: 70) says. Instead, Lamoreaux (1998) suggests that the terminology should recognize how different 'contractual arrangements' are arrayed according to their 'degree of "firmness"': '[s]ome contracts offered parties relatively little protection against holdup; that is, they had relatively little of that attribute I am calling "firmness". Others with more "firmness" offered stronger protection' (Lamoreaux, 1998: 70).

The Contractual Theory of the Firm Becoming Conventional Wisdom

By the early 1990s, Kaufman and Zacharias (1992: 559) write, 'a consensus has emerged that state fiduciary incorporation charters should be understood in contractual terms'. That is, the contractual theory of the firm was now the new conventional wisdom. From this proposition, a series of declarations regarding the nature of the firm and its preferred governance can be deduced. First, Kaufman and Zacharias (1992: 559) say, the firm is understood as 'a self-regulating contractual arrangement among independent bargaining groups'. This means, which is of key importance in the agency theory framework, that 'managers have no semi-public responsibility to the firm's underrepresented stakeholders or to liberal values that distinguish between private and public pursuits'. In other words, managers cannot claim any wider role than being contracting agents '[w]hose mediating services are evaluated by the firm's internal monitoring devices and by the market in corporate control' (Kaufman and Zacharias, 1992: 559). This means that the contractarian view of the firm is entirely different from the managerialist notion of the firm as a collaborative undertaking, being a site for team production and with wider social responsibilities beyond the mere contractual relations.[4] Advocators of the managerialist model of the firm stress that the firm has an 'organizational reality' – that is, the firm is more than legal fiction – and that team production implies the consideration of stakeholder interests along with product market competition (Kaufman and Zacharias, 1992: 560). Based on these premises, advocators of the managerialist model call for managerial discretion.

Second, contractual theory regards the shareholders not so much as the 'owners' of the firm as they are understood as 'finance market investors' with legitimate claims on the firm's residual cash flow (Kaufman and Zacharias, 1992: 554).

> The rejection of the concept of ownership, as applied to the business firm, is a standard assumption of this contractarian approach in law and economics ... By definition, one cannot possess a contract (or contracts) as one can possess a standard asset. Shareholders are therefore not depicted as owners, but rather as 'principals'. The implications, as far as corporate governance is concerned, are basically the same: managers and directors, who are the 'agents', should be accountable solely to shareholders. (Moore and Rebérioux, 2011: 87)

This shift in vocabulary may seem insignificant but in fact it denotes a stronger emphasis on the contractual relation between shareholders and managers, as traditional ownership implies the need to recognize a wider set of stakeholder interests derived from the business charter. Third, and finally, the contractual theory understands the firm as a legal fiction and thus ignores the transaction costs that justify the existence of corporations. Being entirely set within the limits of the market, this legal fiction does not, *ex hypothesi*, induce any transaction costs, and therefore, Kaufman and Zacharias (1992: 557) say, '[i]n a transaction-costless world, economic efficiency will occur regardless of legal rules'. As some legal scholars have remarked (to be discussed below), the neoclassical economic theory model of the contract-based firm not only undermines the role of the state as the legitimate sovereign granting the business charter, it also renders the legislative process irrelevant and a source of unnecessary costs burdening the contracting parties: '[t]he contractarians ... argue that the courts should apply market rules, derived from modern economics, when considering the claims of disgruntled shareholders, especially in tender-offer controversies. If adopted, these rules would end the courts' excessive reliance on the business judgment rule, which has granted management wide discretion' (Kaufman and Zacharias, 1992: 559).

Ultimately, the contractual theory makes legislation a complication that adds little to what market-based contracting and accompanying control functions are capable of accomplishing. Therefore, corporate law is little more than a reminiscence of collectivist and statist politics characteristic of the post-World War II era, being the prolongation of the New Deal programme that undermines what conservatives and libertarians refer to as economic freedom.

Under all conditions, the contractual theory, based on economic theories such as price theory (in the case of the Chicago law and economics school), and agency theory were advanced on a broad front in the 1980s and 1990s. While corporate law previously served to enable sustainable market creation and thoughtful enterprising beneficial for the economy and society as a whole, corporate law was now understood either as what supported the interests of shareholders (that is, the finance capital investors) or, as suggested by Easterbrook and Fischel (1993), as being a specialized version of contractual relations anyway, wherein agency and fiduciary duties are substitutive terms denoting essentially the same responsibilities. Legal scholars did not receive this new view of corporate law very favourably. In the following, some of the responses to this proto-legal enactment of the firm are examined.

THE LEGAL THEORY VIEW OF THE CONTRACTUAL THEORY OF THE FIRM

The critique articulated by neoclassical economic theorists regarding the corporate governance structure derived from the extant corporate legislation has been carefully responded to by legal scholars. The response can be claimed to include three types of critique of the contractual theory: (1) the analysis of the inconsistencies between the nexus of contracts view and legal theory; (2) the practical difficulties derived from the theory; and (3) the wider ideological aspects of the contractual theory.

Contractual Theory Inconsistencies

Masten (1988: 185) argues that '[e]conomists have either downplayed or rejected outright the role of law in defining the firm', and suggests that economists tend to confuse ownership and governance: '[o]wnership itself is a condition sustained by legal rules and remedies. But a change in legal status obviously does not physically transform an asset' (Masten, 1988: 195). This disregard of and tendency to take legal theory lightly is a shared theme in the following sections. For legal scholars, the concept of *contract* is not just a metaphorical term that can be used to portray a social relation in 'general terms' but is a juridical device situated within legal theory and legislative traditions (DeMott, 1988). Brudney (1985: 1406) argues that the use of the concept of contract in the agency theory model of corporate governance stretches the term quite far as it includes 'both the simple cross-market buy–sell agreements (implicit and explicit) and the mechanism for relating investors to the selection and retention of executives in the large firm'. As such situations are different from both legal and practical viewpoints, the concept of contract is not correctly used in the advocacy of the term (Brudney, 1985: 1406). Brudney emphasizes that the contractual theory is primarily used to denote the relation between the shareholder and the corporation's executives and directors, and therefore the term 'contract' is used in an unorthodox way:

> An essential component of the nexus-of-contracts vision of the corporation is the conception that when a corporation (or its owner) initially sells stock to public investors (and possibly whenever investors buy its stock on the market), the investor 'contracts' with the owner (or the managers) about the terms of relationship between the investor and management. (Brudney, 1985: 1411)

Implicit in this view is that the shareholders are in the position to negotiate their relation with executives and directors, but that is factually not the case, Brudney says. As a consequence, the very idea of the shareholders being in a contractual relation in the legal sense of the term is far-fetched and thus irrelevant:

> [The contract theory of the firm] stretches the concept of contract beyond recognition to use it to describe either the process of bargaining or the arrangement between investors of publicly held corporations and either theoretical owners first going public or corporate management. Scattered stockholders cannot, and do not, negotiate with owners who go public (or with management – either executives or directors) over hiring managers, over the terms of their employment, or over their retention. (Brudney, 1985: 1411)

This point is also stressed by Eisenberg (1989):

> The characterization of the corporation as a nexus of contracts is ... inaccurate. A corporation is a profit-seeking enterprise of persons and assets organized by rules. Some of these rules are determined by contract or other forms of agreements, but some are determined by law, and most are determined by the unilateral action of corporate organs or officials. (Eisenberg, 1989: 1487)

Therefore, the new idea emerging in the early 1980s, that the firm is 'a legal fiction that serves as a nexus of contractual relationships among individual factors of production' (Bratton, 1989a: 1471), is an inadequate image of the relation between shareholders and the executive functions of the firm.

DeMott (1988: 882) adds that contractarians (for example, Easterbrook and Fischel, 1993) misinterpret and trivialize the legal term 'fiduciary duty': '[t]he fiduciary's duties go beyond mere fairness and honesty; they oblige him to act to further the beneficiary's best interests. The fiduciary must avoid acts that put his interests in conflict with the beneficiary's.' In the case of corporate law, one case where the term applies, the directors are bestowed with such fiduciary duties:

A corporation's directors occupy a trustee-like position: unlike trustees, directors do not themselves have legal ownership interests in transferable property beneficially owned by others, but, like trustees, directors are entrusted with powers to use in the interest of others. Invested by corporation statutes with discretionary authority to manage or supervise the management of the corporation's business, directors are bound by fiduciary principles. (DeMott, 1988: 880–82)

When leaving the scholarly understanding of legal terms and opening up for practical issues, the concept of fiduciary duties is still conducive to higher efficiency when controlling managers, Brudney (1997) says. If the proposition that executives are in fact at risk to act opportunistically is worthy of empirical testing – an idea that few legal scholars object to as being illegitimate or irrelevant – and that the legal structure of the firm is part of this difficulty to discipline managers and directors, then the legal vehicle of the contract is *less effective* than so-called fiduciary law, Brudney (1997) argues (see also Lan and Heracleous, 2010: 303). The very idea of shareholders and executives and directors being in the position to freely choose to contract with one another is problematic, as that model ignores the role of the state as a legitimate actor that in the first place instituted the legal framework to actively promote economic venturing and market creation:

> [T]he notion of contracts as a private management rests upon the exercise of the state's power and the rules it promulgates to enforce or limit the arrangement ... The suggestion is that parties are as free to 'contract' with one another as they would be in a pre-state world with no such socially-imposed restrictions. That basic structural assumption is problematic. (Brudney, 1997: 597)

As contractarians explicitly state that the role of the contract is to ensure that value is maximized for the benefit of shareholders (Brudney, 1997: 622), the very idea of a contract outside of the realm of the state's interest is incompatible with legal theory and mainstream corporate governance. Also Eisenberg (1989: 1480) stresses how the contractual theory fails to distinguish between different types of rules and that the fiduciary rules being at the core of corporate law are mandatory: '[t]he principle that governs publicly held corporations is the same as the principle that governs closely held corporations: fiduciary rules should be mandatory at the core'. Thus, the market-based control that the contractarians propose is after all a *weaker form* of control than the mandatory rules of existing corporate law: '[m]any of the most important rules of corporation law – such as those dealing with unfair self-dealing, insider trading, proxy voting, and disclosure – are largely mandatory, at least for publicly held corporations' (Eisenberg, 1989: 1486). Therefore, being of greater relevance for the practical work of executives and directors, the contract vehicle in fact justifies some opportunistic behaviour on the part of the contractors, and therefore the contract device provides less protection from managerial malfeasance than contractarians suggest, Brudney (1997) argues. Instead, it is the notion of fiduciary duties and fiduciary law that would prohibit opportunistic behaviour. This is a non-trivial legal theory argument, so Brudney is cited at length. Brudney remarks that fiduciary duty is considered to be an obstacle against shareholder welfare proposed by contractarians:

> The classic fiduciary duty is considered to be a significant obstacle to that maximizing goal particularly as prophylactically precludes transactions that might maximize – or at least make – gains for the enterprise. The classic fiduciary duty is also said to dampen the incentives of decision-makers by denying them the rewards from self-aggrandizing behavior that they think necessary, in addition to the rewards for which they expressly contract. Hence, the policy aspiration of contractarians is to reduce, if not to eliminate, state-imposed fiduciary restrictions on the power of corporate managers and controllers to engage in conflict of interest transactions or otherwise to serve themselves collaterally at the possible expense of public stockholders. (Brudney, 1997: 622–3)

The contractual theory is mistaken from a legal theory view as the traditional fiduciary concept, Brudney (1997: 622–5) argues, would by definition forbid or substantially curtail opportunistic behaviour by management or controllers that the contract notion permits. Brudney (1997: 622–635) continues: 'traditional fiduciary loyalty strictures more rigorously protect common stockholders against opportunistic behavior by managers or controllers than does classic contract doctrine'. In other words, the idea of the shareholder and the executives and directors jointly contracting to ensure that agency costs are minimized provides a weaker legal vehicle to accomplish such objectives than the traditional fiduciary duty law would.[5] On the other hand, the latter alternative would recognize the state as a legitimate actor but that is precisely what contractarians want to avoid. In seeking to preserve the methodological individualism and to bypass the theoretically complicated question of what a firm is in a market-based economy, contractarians, agency theorists and others choose what they regard as the most theoretically elegant solution – to enact the firm as a bundle or nexus of contracts. Unfortunately, Brudney (1997) suggests, when doing so, they (1) misunderstand or violate the legal theory view of the contract and under what conditions this legal device applies, and (2) ignore the distinction between contracts and fiduciary duty, leading to the confusion of the two legal concepts.

Howard (1991) takes an entirely different route in his advocacy of fiduciary duties and points not so much to the inconsistencies in the application of and limited understanding of the legal term as such. Instead, Howard (1991) scrutinizes the assumptions made in contractual theory. Howard (1991: 5) argues that contractarians assume that 'the statutory corporate governance rules now prescribed by statute are oppressive in the sense they permit heavy-handed interference in the affairs of the corporation by government administrators, the courts or both'. Howard disputes this assumption; in fact, 'nothing could be further from reality', he says (1991: 5). Still, based on this foundational principle, contractual theory is developed on the basis of a syllogistic operation where theoretical propositions (that is, regarding the market efficiency hypothesis and the efficacy of market pricing) are added to expressed preferences (that is, the virtues of efficiency, decontextualized and separated from time and space) in order to formulate new propositions:

> The basic hypothesis of the contractarians appears to be syllogistic: the regulation of any market function by government tends to inefficiency; business corporations are regulated; therefore business corporations should be replaced by largely unregulated contracts (a 'nexus of contracts') that will incrementally adjust to equilibrium in accordance with atomistic investor decisions as to value, taking into account all factors that relate to a specific corporation (including, in the extreme argument, even the probability of management fraud and breach of fiduciary duty). (Howard, 1991: 11)

Howard (1991: 11) agrees that contractarians have a 'sympathetic objective', greater efficiency – who would object to greater efficiency if it came with no additional costs? – but the contractual theory quickly ends up in as a convoluted argument based on 'implied excessive government regulation, agency relationships, organizational theory and the capital market efficiency hypothesis' (Howard, 1991: 11). To all this, Howard (1991: 11) says, 'some obvious common sense' about the '[f]iction of shareholders maintaining effective control over management' is added to seal the argument. However, even though Howard (1991) does not share the belief in the robustness of these syllogistic operations, his *coup de grâce* has little to do with the preference for 'reasoning-on-basis-of-theoretical-propositions-and-fictive-examples' among contractarians but targets their foundational assumption that companies are strictly economic entities – 'market commodities' – separated from wider social and cultural interests and traditions, an idea that Howard believes is mistaken and deceiving (see, for example, Westphal et al., 2012; Westphal and Khanna, 2003; Davis, 1991, for an empirical illustration and extended argument):

> If one can reify a public business corporation and thus trade it as one more market commodity, the contractarian efficiency model is attractive. If, however, you conceive a corporation as a living, complicated, dynamic social and economic institution – as I do – the contractarian argument is meaningless, a convoluted, oblique attack on political decision-making in the name of 'efficiency', a result no one could ever prove. (Howard, 1991: 13)

DeMott (1988) also highlights and equally rejects the proposition that companies are ultimately nothing but commodities. Expressed in a somewhat opaque legal theory vocabulary, DeMott (1988: 923) suggests that the work to determine 'whether fiduciary obligation applies in a particular context' demands 'situation-specificity', that is, a detailed understanding of the context and actual case being considered. If enacting the company as nothing but a market commodity, the contractarian argument is seductive as it is both simple and elegant, Howard (1991: 5) says. But this elegance is deceptive as it is sustained only on the basis of the assumptions that sweep away all the difficult issues that corporate law deals with, and because contractual theory is founded on the ability of its proponents to set up straw men that they can knock down with 'seemingly irrefutable logic' (Howard, 1991: 5). As a consequence, the contractual theory cannot in any meaningful way substitute the existing corporate legislation and court ruling, as the additional costs for this transition cannot be justified on the basis of higher efficiency in the legal and governance system or otherwise, Howard (1991: 18) contends: '[n]either the logic of economic efficiency nor case law nor business experience justifies such dilution of a legal standard that is well understood and that appears to work effectively to constrain potentially abusive exercise by directors and officers of their sweeping discretion'. 'Shortcuts in legal reasoning through metaphoric and unanalytic appeals to contract law serve only to muddle the analysis', DeMott (1988: 923–4) adds.

In summary, the contractual theory of the firm that justifies shareholder welfare is far from theoretically consistent from a legal theory perspective. As legal theory is underlying legal practice, the neoclassical economic theory use of legal concepts is problematic. Worse still, the contractual theory also imposes practical difficulties. If the contractual theory is theoretically incredible from the legal theory view, how is it to be implemented in actual day-to-day corporate governance activities?

Practical Difficulties with the Nexus of Contract View

To start with, Bratton (1989b: 410) points out that the nexus of contract view of the firm is not a scientific theory (in the Popperian sense of the term as what lends itself to empirical testing and corroboration), as there is no robust way to test the model: '[u]nlike some economic theory, but like much legal theory, the nexus of contracts (and much of the theory built on it) resists empirical verification. As with legal theory, verification depends on the tester's characterization of real world institutions and relationships'. In this view, the contractual theory is more of a metaphor or heuristic conjuring an image of the firm as an economic entity that can be sliced into a set of contracts being owned by various free-standing agents. This view is also advanced as a normative and political assertion regarding legal rights and claims of efficiency, but these claims, Bratton (1989b: 411) says, are advocated 'in the guise of ontological statements'. The neoclassical economic theory style of reasoning, based on deductive reasoning, tends to obscure that many claims made within the contract-arian literature are both theoretically, legally and empirically unsubstantiated or at least ambiguous in terms of the legitimacy of the claims made. Such more scientific concerns may be of more limited interest for the day-to-day governance of firms, but legal scholars repeat Brudney's (1985) argument that shareholders do not generally negotiate with executives and directors. Even in the case of what Eisenberg (1989: 1472) calls *positional conflicts*, divergences in the interests of principals and agents (being typical cases in court ruling), there are few such possibilities for negotiations. Shareholders do not simply access the contract and agreement that guide executives' and directors' work, and therefore they cannot serve the role as active negotiators that the contractual view implies: '[i]nsofar as managers' duties and entitlements are expressly defined by agreement, those agreements are rarely, if ever, exhibited to public stockholders, let alone negotiated with stockholder participation' (Brudney, 1985: 1414). This argument is repeated in the corporate law literature:

- 'Stockholders do not direct management's activities. Indeed, stockholders are explicitly denied power to interfere in management's activities. That they may not, or rationally should not, wish to do so does not detract from the distortion in characterizing management as their agent' (Brudney, 1985: 1425).
- 'Under these conditions [dispersed ownership], bargaining among the shareholders, or between managers and the shareholders as a body, is virtually impossible. Accordingly, most of the constitutive

rules of such corporations are determined not by contract, but by law or by private bureaucratic rulemaking – for example, by managerial orders, by board or committee resolutions, by board-adopted by-laws, or by board determination of governance terms of preferred stock, stock rights, or debt instruments' (Eisenberg, 1989: 1471).

- 'The stockholder's ability to monitor the behavior of their officers, while formally greater than the ability of trust beneficiaries to monitor the trustees, is nearly as ineffective in practice' (Brudney and Clark, 1981: 1023),

For these reasons, Clark (1989: 1706) argues, 'practically minded judges and legislators' have been known to dismiss general contractual theory arguments 'out of hand'. The reason for this refusal to accept the contractual view as a legitimate argument derives from practical considerations, Clark (1989: 1706–7) says: '[t]o many [judges and legislators] who have had experience in the corporate world, it seems obvious that if a corporation adopts a charter amendment opting out of the fiduciary duty of loyalty, the net effects will be clearly bad for investors'.

More specifically, even if shareholders had access to such documents, the contractual view assumes that there is a functional 'market for executives' in place where poorly performing managers can be dumped and more skilled managers are recruited. That image or theory of the market for executive work is 'limited in several aspects', Brudney (1985: 1417) suggests. The ability to assess whether executives and directors do a good job (that is, to determine whether they are 'efficient') is based on the idea that there are universally accepted standards for the commensuration of executive performance. In the contractual theory model, it is the stock market that provides such benefits, and therefore there is a strong assumption regarding a straightforward and unambiguous relationship between executive performance and stock evaluation (Manne, 1965). This model is riddled with two theoretical and practical inconsistencies. First, as Brudney (1985: 1425) notices, even if markets were efficient, as prescribed by the efficient market hypothesis (EMH), that condition per se would not in any way ensure that managers were not acting opportunistically: '[t]he "efficiency" of the stock markets does not of its own force drive management to compete in limiting its rewards or its power to divert assets, or even to be more efficient managers'. Eisenberg (1989) shares Brudney's (1985) concern regarding the ability of market pricing to effectively substitute for the mandatory and fiduciary rules of corporate law. In fact, Eisenberg (1989: 1492) refers to the idea that '[m]andatory rules are unnecessary because *on average* the interests of managers and shareholders are adequately aligned by market forces' as a fallacy. This fallacy includes two parts, whereof the first concerns how corporations are assembling unique capacities and resources that in turn generate economic value, and that corporations therefore can contain and neutralize a substantial share of incompetent decision-making and opportunistic behaviour before any market pricing mechanisms would be able to punish such behaviour:

> Although a highly competitive market may have [a controlling] effect, an imperfectly competitive market will not quickly convert unfair self-dealing or inefficiency into insolvency. Most publicly held corporations have sufficient resources and market power to absorb substantial losses resulting from inefficiency, gross miscalculations, or unfair self-dealing. (Eisenberg, 1989: 1489)

Second, in a more theoretical perspective, while free market protagonists have put their faith in the abstract notion of efficient markets, few others share the belief in the auxiliary benefits of the pricing mechanism being at the heart of the agency theory and shareholder welfare argument. At least Eisenberg (1989: 1515) does not: 'the pricing argument is largely hypothetical, because most of the core fiduciary and structural legal rules that govern publicly held corporations are not in fact subject to substantive variation'. Expressed in less opaque terms: 'the pricing argument applies to just those cases in which the constitutive rules of a corporation do *not* adequately align the interests of top managers and shareholders and address the problem of managerial inefficiency' (Eisenberg, 1989: 1515). Again, the mandatory and fiduciary rules of corporate law provide a better protection against managerial self-dealing than any market-based pricing of the stock. Furthermore, as an empirical fact, stock prices are much more volatile than in many cases illiquid corporate resources and activities would suggest, and speculation and future expectations are always of necessity part of finance markets, leaving contractarians with an assessment method being most loosely coupled with executive performance. Moreover, practically speaking, managerial competence and moral standards are unlikely to be as volatile as market indices, thus separating the pricing mechanism from governance practices. As the claim that the contractarian view is better exploiting the market for executives rings rather hollow, one can question the accuracy of the contractarian view altogether.

In addition to the practical difficulties (and the underlying theoretical inconsistencies) involved in implementing a finance market pricing mechanism as a governance principle for individual firms, actual corporate governance activities in the market such as the leveraged buyout

(LBOs) in the mid-1980s are quite revealing of what the contractarian view means in practice. Bratton (1989a) argues that the wave of LBOs did not so much aim to reinforce shareholders' control over corporations, nor to discipline opportunistic executives and directors, but to accomplish a less strongly emphasized objective in the contractarians' theoretical model – to extract economic value from the firm being subject to tender offers: '[u]nlike the conglomerate-building managers of the earlier periods, they did not use the devices of the corporate control market [for example, buyout bids] to enhance operational power positions. They simply sought to force large payments to equity holders' (Bratton, 1989a: 1517). This argument is consistent with the findings of Davis and Stout (1992), who found that, contrary to the agency theory argument, it was the most well-functioning firms with the lowest amount of debt that were targeted by hostile takeover bids. In contrast, the agency theory model predicts that only poorly functioning executives who induce excessive agency costs and manage companies that therefore become incapable of competing in unforgiving markets are the primary subjects of LBOs, thus being a mechanism to discipline such behaviour.

In addition, while contractarians argue that their favoured model serves to curb managerial malfeasance, it does in fact accomplish little to overturn the hierarchical structure of the corporation: '[r]estructuring takeovers do not threaten the hierarchy; they only replace one set of managers with another' (Bratton, 1989a: 1525). More importantly, as Eisenberg (1989: 1499) points out, US courts have generally approved defences against takeover bids, indicating that such managerial responses to threats to their discretion are not seen as a violation of the legislator's intentions. That is, takeover bids are not, contrary to the agency theory view, treated by the courts as efficiency-enhancing operations that benefit the economy at large. Leaving the executive hierarchy essentially intact, it does still accomplish another thing: to render the finance market investor the new king of the hill and to reduce the executive function to a support function determined by finance industry interests, ultimately being assessed and rewarded on the basis of finance market performance indicators: '[t]oday's popular conception of the powerful business figure is not the managerialist chief executive officer but the capitalist deal maker – the financial entrepreneur of the investment banker. Character-ized in the vocabulary of the new economic theory, these figures acquire power as transaction cost engineers' (Bratton, 1989a: 1523–4).

In addition to the economic and governance arguments speaking against the practical efficacy of the contractarian view, there are behav-ioural aspects of managerial work to consider, Eisenberg (1989) adds.

First of all, Eisenberg regards the proposition that managers act opportunistically in systematic and predictable ways both theoretically unsatisfying and empirically counterintuitive because most managers, especially those who have qualified for executive positions, have internalized certain moral beliefs and a work ethic that in most cases prevents them from such undesirable behaviour: '[m]ost top managers will probably refrain from shirking simply because their self-esteem is tied to hard work and accomplishments. Most top managers will probably refrain from unfair self-dealing simply because they have internalized the rules of social morality' (Eisenberg, 1989: 1473; see also Westphal and Khanna, 2003; Useem and Karabel, 1986; Useem, 1979). Second, if managers did violate such moral beliefs and work ethic, it is not self-evident that managers or shareholders would be fully aware of the positional conflicts being at play as there are numerous behavioural aspects that inhibit such self-reflexivity, especially 'in the fog of war' and the turmoil of everyday working life:

> managers may fail to even recognize that positional conflicts exist. Inefficient top managers are unlikely to believe themselves to be inefficient. Top managers to enhance their position through corporate growth, diversification, or the like, usually believe (often, but not always, correctly) that their actions are in the interest of the shareholders. (Eisenberg, 1989: 1473)

Unfortunately, such a behavioural view of managerial work is not included in the agency theory model as rational choice theorists avoid such 'unnecessary complications' and instead rely on market forces to serve as both the assessor of managerial performance and the mechanisms that alert shareholders when there may be evidence of opportunistic behaviour in the executive suites. Eisenberg's (1989) governance problems derived from behavioural conditions are thus overlooked by agency theorists – at best, they are anomalies but most likely yet more evidence of the shortage of skilled executives.

In addition to this seismic shift in perspective of the corporation, replacing the executive with the finance market trader at the top of the pyramid (see Blair and Stout, 1999), the contractual view is also based on an ideology that actively discredits the role of the state as a legitimate actor in economic affairs. If markets are after all the most efficient mechanism to structure economic transactions, the state and the government are at best support functions whose roles should be marginalized to the highest possible extent.

The Ideology of the Nexus of Contract View: Anti-Statism and Anti-Collectivism

Unlike neoclassical economic theorists, legal scholars do not regard the state as what, by definition, intervenes in self-regulating markets and economic affairs. Instead, for legal scholars, the state is an indispensable actor that serves as the warrant for a functional legal system and as the lender of last resort for, for example, the finance industry. Theoretically speaking, legal scholars and economists thus inhabit different ends on the continuum, taking entirely different views of the state. Again, the question regarding economic stability versus economic efficiency becomes a key issue to consider. Economists believe short-term value extraction and market efficiency are two principal 'political' objectives, while legal scholars, at least when representing the state's interests, believe a balanced and stable growth is more beneficial for a wider set of social actors. Brudney (1985) is quite explicit regarding the ideological underpinning of the nexus of contract view of the firm:

> Apart from the debatable normative consequences generated by the rhetoric of contract in the corporate context, it may be noted that the rhetoric serves an ideological purpose. The evolution of the legal theory of the corporation in the United States, although uneven and complex, proceeds from the vision of a 'concession' granted by the state as a special privilege, often to do public good, to that of a contractual arrangement between private parties. That development was part of the process of legitimating corporate freedom of action in the burgeoning industrial capitalism. The notion of private contract implicated lessened public concern with the impact of new entrepreneurial giants on consumers, employees, suppliers, and public generally. (Brudney, 1985: 1409)

Brudney (1985) continues:

> The effect of the notion of contract was to disconnect the enterprise and its 'owners' (whether the corporation was managed by persons who were substantial owners or by managers for more or less dispersed stockholders) from dependence upon state authority for their power, and therefore from subjection to state regulation of that power in the interest of consumers, employees, suppliers, and the public. (Brudney, 1985: 1409)

This is another case of neoclassical economics theory ignoring or downplaying the history of corporate law, suggesting that once the ladder has been climbed, it can be kicked away without any ground being lost. Corporate law and the entire legal framework developed by the state to secure market opportunities and to discount risks to enable economic growth and enterprising activities were major accomplishments of the state in the eighteenth, nineteenth and twentieth centuries. But as neoclassical economic theory regards the market as a naturally occurring phenomenon (Harcourt, 2011), economists subscribe to a doctrine that renders them blind to historical conditions and past achievements. As soon as a functional market is in place, all the institutions and mechanisms that serve to create such benefits are ungratefully treated as unnecessary and costly government activities. For free market advocators, history is irrelevant as only the future matters, and being unable to take a historical view renders many previous accomplishments beside the point or even unintelligible. 'Today's contractualists', Bratton (1989a: 1515) writes, 'limit their critique to the largest hierarchical institution, the government. To bolster opposition, they legitimize nongovernmental institutions with a diluted version of the atomistic social ideal.' Guided by anti-statist and pro-market ideologies, 'the new economic theorists have misstated materially the political issues underlying corporate law' Bratton (1989b: 432) contends.

Roe's (2000) article on the differences between American corporate governance and that of various European countries during periods of social democratic government is one exemplary case of anti-statist and anti-collectivist reasoning. Early on in his article, Roe (2000: 541) declares that social democratic policy undermines the market for managerial control by protecting managers from external control and the pressure to make efficient use of resources: 'I argue here that the shareholders' core problems in the public firm cannot be readily resolved in a strong social democracy. Social democracies weaken the ties between managers and dispersed shareholders'. Social democratic policy is not committed to 'private property', Roe (2000: 543) claims, and therefore such policy benefits managers' natural agenda and demeans shareholders' natural agenda. This leads to a situation wherein the conflict of interest between managers and shareholders remains unsolved as the 'tools that would induce managers to work in favor of invested capital' such as 'high incentive compensation, hostile takeovers, transparent accounting, and acculturation to shareholder-wealth maximization norms' are weak, Roe (2000: 543) proposes. Roe adds that social democratic policy does not of necessity favour managerial welfare, but the tendency is to side with the interests of the employees, that is, in practical terms, with labour unions, and the policy overlooks or downplays agency costs. As Roe (2000: 542) correctly notices, 'most corporate governance analyses ignore employees', in itself indicative of the strong American dominance in the corporate governance literature, in turn embedded in the American 'antigovernment bias' (Roe, 2000: 577) and the interrelated fact that American corporate law is essentially 'made in contexts (such as in Delaware's legislature and courts) where labor's influence is indirect and weak' (Roe, 2000: 560). However, Roe continues, in Europe the situation is different, and the persistent tension between invested capital and current employees is not muted. Employees share their risk-aversion with managers as their human capital is 'tied up in the firm and they are not fully diversified' (Roe, 2000: 546) – and attitude and position per se fully consistent with rational choice theory – and therefore managers and labour unions join forces with social democratic and other left-wing political parties to marginalize shareholders. This means in practice that social democracies 'favor incumbent employees', which leads to soaring agency costs as government policy '[w]edges open the gap between managers and employees on one side and shareholders on the other' (Roe, 2000: 551). Roe thus takes a public choice theory view of political alliances and collaborations to accomplish specific objectives (see, for example, Buchanan, 1954) and treats political voting as a specific form of economic decision-making derived from idiosyncratic combinations of preferences, incentives and choice alternatives: 'one could see social democracies as labor's crude but successful rent-seeking, whereby they gain at the expense of others in the political arena' (Roe, 2000: 577).

In Roe's (2000) account, social democratic governments raise the pressure on managers to abandon their shareholders and side with their employees, which, in turn, theoretically speaking, induces agency costs. As Roe (2000: 546) remarks, the same tendency is observed in the US, despite the scepticism towards federal government interventions and the weak labour movement, as '[l]ess-monitored managers in [American] states where anti-takeover laws are strong conceding higher salaries to employees than similar managers in states where anti-takeover laws are weak'. Curiously enough, in this view, the higher compensation of labour vis-à-vis other states is here not, as it is otherwise understood in neoclassical economic theory, the outcome from the production market pricing of resources but is instead understood as the outcome from allegedly faulty legislation[6]: if labour is paid better, it is *not* because the skills of blue-collar workers are valued more highly on the market, but because of weak legal protection of shareholder interests. In Roe's (2000) and other free market protagonists' view, the alleged 'rent-seeking' of social democratic and left-wing party voters is problematic because they assume that efficient corporate governance (that is, practices adhering to shareholders' agendas) is socially beneficial:

Society wins if governance works. When it works, boards evaluate managers' reactions to problems before product market competition seriously hurts the firm. Although shareholders profit first from good governance, their profits are not the 'bottom line' for public policy here: poor management imposes costs on the firm's employees, its suppliers, its customers, and its communities. (Roe, 1994: ix)[7]

The same argument is advanced by Easterbrook and Fischel (1996) using the standard free market theory and agency theory argument that managers must not be confused with multiple objectives that would undermine their possibilities for maximizing economic wealth:

[a] manager told to serve two masters (a little for the equity holders, a little for the community) has been freed of both and is answerable to neither. Faced with a demand from either group, the manager can appeal to the interest of the other. Agency costs rise and social wealth falls. (Easterbrook and Fischel, 1996: 38)[8]

More specifically, shareholder welfare is justified on the basis of the proposition – generously lending itself to empirical investigation, fortunately – that what is good for the shareholders and finance capital investors is good for the whole of society:

maximizing profits for equity investors assists other 'constituencies' automatically. The participants in the venture play complementary rather than antagonistic roles, a successful firm provides jobs for workers and goods and services for consumers. The more appealing the goods to consumers, the more profits (and jobs). Prosperity for stockholders, workers, and communities goes hand in glove with better products for consumers. (Easterbrook and Fischel, 1996: 38)

This firm belief in the reason and sturdiness of shareholder welfare – not a bit susceptible to the Panglossian claim that 'profits and social welfare are perfectly aligned' (Easterbrook and Fischel, 1996: 39) – is in turn rooted in the belief in agency costs being one of the principal and most influential social costs imposed on society in the regime of competitive capitalism. That is, in comparison to, for example, the consequences of economic inequalities derived from unfair compensation for labour (which, it must be remembered, is non-existent in neoclassical economic theory and in human capital theory more specifically as naturally occurring and unbiased markets always by definition price commodities and other resources, including labour, correctly), the agency cost is a much more worrying factor, having detrimental consequences for the whole economy. Needless to say, this foundational principle regarding the devastating economic and social consequences of agency costs generating so much attention in the governance literature is debatable. Nevertheless, Roe's dismissing of any kind of political action on the part of salaried employees, be it in terms of labour movement activism or voting in their own best interests (two activities consistent with rational choice theory and the very idea of rent-seeking as a 'natural propensity' of all actors), is evidence of economically uninformed choices and therefore, by implication, a morally questionable preference for stability over maximized economic efficiency.[9] Roe summarizes this core proposition of the contractual model he subscribes to (see Roe, 1994: 23):

> Why maximize shareholders' wealth, when shareholders make up such a small and already-favored part of society? One answer is that this is the distributional 'price' for getting good capital allocation. Another is that shareholder wealth roughly proxies for total wealth and no other norm is, right now, plausible to implement in diffusely-owned firms. (Roe, 2000: 553)

For Roe (2000) and his contractarian allies, shareholder value is not primarily a vehicle for the redistribution of wealth from managers, employees and other constituencies (even though this is the foremost economic consequence and social implication, as ample evidence shows) but a legitimate and even morally justified mechanism for maximizing economic efficiency. 'Maximizing the stock price serves two normative ends: promoting the interests of shareholders and making use of the information impounded by the market to allocate capital efficiently', Gordon (2007: 1472) writes. This core proposition, that agency costs are at such a persistently high level that it undermines the efficiency of the entire economy, remains disputed (Rock, 2013: 1916; Dobbin and Jung, 2010: 32; Bratton and Wachter, 2010: 660; Bratton, 1989b: 417–18). In addition, there is much evidence that other corporate governance systems than the American one based on shareholder welfare are capable of producing substantial economic wealth and supporting economic growth (Fligstein and Choo, 2005: 66–7): 'on average, between 1979 and 2006, economic growth per capita was essentially the same in the fifteen core nations of Europe as it was in the United States', Hacker and Pierson (2010: 26) write.[10]

AN ALTERNATIVE LEGAL VIEW I: ELITE RULING

As opposed to this neoclassical and anti-statist view of the corporate system, Clark (1989) advocates what he refers to as a corporate system rooted in *paternalistic elitism* – a non-pejorative term in this legal theory

context – that justifies the mandatory rules of existing corporate legislation (see also Gordon, 1989). First of all, Clark (1989) addresses the
utilitarian argument for 'contractual rule making' as being both simple
and powerful: '[i]f A and B both agree to a rule governing their
relationship, both must think they will be better off, or at least not worse
off, because of the rule; otherwise they would not have agreed to it'
(Clark, 1989: 1714). Expressed in neoclassical economic theory terms,
contractually created rules will be Pareto-efficient rules, that is, they are
located on the optimum curve with '[o]ne or both parties better off, and
neither party worse off' (Clark, 1989: 1714). While this may be a
theoretically intriguing proposition, of relevance for the construction of
economic theorems, it is a high impractical starting point for, for
example, a business venture. In addition, the argument is conspicuously
ignorant of the underlying assumptions of the utilitarian model upon
which it rests, assuming that the world is riddled by opportunistic
behaviour and that humans 'naturally' strive to maximize pleasure (or
'utility' more generally) and avoid pain. For this reason, Clark (1989)
proposes, elite ruling is a more beneficial system for the subject
motivated by utilitarian interests, an essentially Hobbesian position where
elites granted certain decision-making privileges by the sovereign state
on the basis of formal education, credentials and previous accomplishments set the rule to balance interests. This is a non-trivial argument, and
Clark (1989) offers precise step-wise arguments to justify his position.

Contrary to the standing neoclassic economic theory argument that the
market is a superior processor of information, Clark (1989: 1718) claims
that elite rule is based on better access to information vis-à-vis contracting subjects, and therefore elite rule would better promote '[t]he welfare
of the subjects of a rule than the subjects themselves do'. Clark here lists
the role of a number of regulatory bodies including the Food and Drug
Administration (FDA) and the Securities and Exchange Commission
(SEC), being two cases where elite rule and monitoring benefit the
efficiency of the corporate system: '[a]rguably, for example, the staff of
the Securities and Exchange Commission may have a better based belief
than do most individual shareholders about whether charter amendments
to create dual class common stock are often in the best interests of
shareholders' (Clark, 1989: 1718). In contrast to this benign view of
legislators and regulators, free market protagonists (of the Chicago
school type) would strongly object and regard such legislative and
regulatory practices as being a form of totalitarian repression of the
individual's economic freedom, prescribing operative rules a priori that
essentially harm the interests of economic agents and that grant elites
such privileges without them having to take any risks (see, for example,

Nik-Khah, 2014). Clark is not insensitive to such arguments and recognizes some parts of the argument, but does not recognize the idea that only governmental and regulatory agency subjects are susceptible to biased assessments and opportunistic behaviour, while, for example, finance market-based actors are not (see, for example, Chong and Tuckett, 2015; Pixley, 2012; Tuckett, 2011; Lo et al., 2005; Froot et al., 1992): 'one could argue (implausibly, in my view) that consumers would be better off if the Food and Drug Administration (the "FDA") had no power to keep drugs off the market or prescribe appropriate and inappropriate uses for them, and consumers relied more completely on their physicians' expert judgments as to what medicines should be taken' (Clark, 1989: 1718, footnote 39).[11] This argument is thus ignorant of the conditions in what Clark calls 'real-world contexts', that is, the intricacies of the practical problems that contracting parties encounter:

> [S]ome antipaternalists follow the odd strategy of arguing against paternalistic regulation on the ground that it is unlikely that regulators know better than the regulated what is in their interests. This is an odd strategy because the reason given for resisting paternalism – no information asymmetry exists – is desperately implausible in many real-world contexts, and because much better reasons for resisting paternalism can be offered. (Clark, 1989: 1718–19)

In addition, Clark (1989: 1720) argues, many people do in fact demonstrate both trust in and a preference for the rule of 'a competent bureaucrat' who promulgates 'welfare-enhancing rules simply because it is his job to do so' in comparison to some 'charismatic leader' who is 'endowed with a consuming altruistic vocation'. In fact, this trust in the elite is one of the key mechanisms explaining economic performance in advanced economies (Algan and Cahuc, 2013), an argument that contractarians would not ignore, even if they would possibly use other explanatory models for such achievements. Clark does not believe that elite rule is a flawless, impeccable governance system – the elitism and fiduciary relationships generate agency costs and agency costs 'are not trivial', (Clark, 1989: 1724) writes – but in comparison to the competing contractual theory, 'elite rule making may have net benefits for rule subjects' (Clark, 1989: 1720). That is, paternalistic elitism has 'decisive relative advantages over contractual rule-making in a wide variety of contexts', Clark (1989: 1726) contends. More specifically, a good society depends on both autonomy and heteronomy, 'each present in large measure' (Clark, 1989: 1726), and therefore policy-makers, legislators and theorists need to prescribe principles, laws and regulations that secure that 'a good society' can be upheld on the basis of autonomous venturing and heteronomous collaboration. Clark's (1989) argument in favour of paternalistic elitism – a term that few free market protagonists would embrace or even recognize – represents a competitor for the contractual theory, neither ignoring nor trivializing the principal arguments of the contractual governance model, and yet providing a set of principles justifying the mandatory rules of existing corporate law.

In summary, the contractual view does not fare well in the legal scholar's view. It misunderstands the concept of contract, confuses contract and fiduciary duty legislation, and fails to prescribe adequate and robust mechanisms (unless one believes finance market prices are capable of accommodating all available information) for how the contractual view should operate in practice. Finally, the ideologically embedded attempt to separate corporate governance and the objective of shareholder welfare from the state and the corporate law framework further emphasize that the nexus of contract model of the firm is more of a conceptual model than a robust and legally anchored operative model of the firm. Given the brittle nature of this theoretical and practical model of the firm, it is hard to believe in the theoretical propositions and claims derived from this model. The contractual model of the firm is simply too riddled with theoretical and practical inconsistencies to be credible outside the free market framework.

AN ALTERNATIVE LEGAL VIEW II: THE TEAM PRODUCTION THEORY OF THE FIRM

A fair argument in favour of the agency theory shareholder primacy would be to emphasize its pragmatic effects in terms of providing a practically useful guideline for what managers should do and why. While agency theory is not logically consistent, violates corporate law and legal theory and remains unsubstantiated by empirical studies, it can still claim a practical usefulness unless there are other alternative models being proposed. Blair and Stout (1999) propose a similarly practically useful corporate governance model, consistent with corporate law and legal theory and lending itself to empirical investigation. Unlike agency theory, drawing on the efficient market hypothesis and the proposition that markets have the capacity to correctly price assets and, *eo ipso*, have the capacity to discipline managers in ways that reduce agency costs, Blair and Stout's argument is explicitly based on information economics theory (Greenwald and Stiglitz, 1986; Stiglitz and Weiss, 1981; Grossman and Stiglitz, 1980; Akerlof, 1970). This suggests that information is both costly to acquire (and not immediately accommodated in market prices) and has a market value inasmuch as the access to valuable information enables certain actors to perform better than others. That is, a superior capacity to collect and use information and data has a market value per se (see, for example, Chong and Tuckett, 2015; Zaloom, 2003; 2006). Information, operationalized as skill, competence, knowledge and so on, is in turn costly to coordinate and control, making leadership and corporate governance an attractive resource or skill for an organization and the members of the organization: '[t]he duties of the top executives of a public corporation normally require full-time application of their managerial talents and energies and leave no room for active participation in the development or operation of other businesses', Brudney and Clark (1981: 1003) write. Based on these assumptions, what Blair and Stout (1999) call *team production theory* will be outlined.

If information is costly to acquire and thus needs to be controlled and protected, there is always a free-rider problem in all coordinated activities that, curiously enough, agency theory overlooks, otherwise being preoccupied with opportunistic behaviour as one of its central theoretical tenets, Blair and Stout (1999: 266) argue. This leads to the difficulty of designing a contract or agreement of how to divide the joint efforts and the economic value generated by an organization:

> If the team members [individuals contributing to the work] agree in advance to allocate any profits according to some fixed sharing rule, obvious free-rider problems arise: Each team member will have an incentive to shirk, since he will get the same share of the total whether or not he works hard. On the other hand, if the team members have no fixed sharing rule but simply agree to allocate resources after the fact, when the time comes to divvy up the surplus all have incentives to indulge in wasteful rent-seeking, squandering time and effort haggling and trying to grab a larger share of the total output. The result in either case is suboptimal. (Blair and Stout, 1999: 266)

If the share received from the joint work is defined *ex ante*, there are incentives to shirk; if the share received is defined *ex post*, a considerable amount of effort will be dedicated to negotiate benefits after the fact. In either case, resources are consumed in ways that benefit neither part. Agency theory, Blair and Stout (1999: 271) say, recognizes the problems of 'collusion, side agreements, and rent-seeking' but only in terms of the harm they cause for principals (and shareholders in particular). But such costs are undesirable for *all* stakeholders and actors participating in the team production, and therefore coordinated team production under the influence of information costs and protection costs leads to a Hobbesian situation where individuals may in fact benefit from surrendering some of their autonomy for the benefit of stability and predictable rules that maximize the output from the joint work.

[W]hen the potential for shirking and rent-seeking is especially pronounced team members as a group might prefer to relinquish control over both the team's assets and output to a third party – a 'mediating hierarch' – whose primary function is to exercise that control in a fashion that maximizes the *joint welfare of the team as a whole*. (Blair and Stout, 1999: 271, emphasis in the original)

Therefore, individuals that in various ways contribute to the corporation are only willing to do so if there are conditions in place that on a legal, regulatory, institutional and managerial level secure that their interests are not subject to rent-seeking on the part of any employee or stakeholder, including not the least the shareholders. '[B]y forming a corporation, the original team members *all agree to give up control right over the output from the enterprise and over their firm-specific inputs'*, Blair and Stout (1999: 277, emphasis in the original) argue. That is, the economic surplus generated in the team production should not be squandered through bargaining after the fact, and therefore the costs/disadvantages of submitting to the leadership of a board of directors and the executive team the directors employ is lower than the gains/benefits that accrue to team members: '*In other words, team members submit to hierarchy not for hierarchy's benefit, but for their own'*, Blair and Stout (1999: 274, emphasis in the original) contend.[12]

The team production theory neither abandons the idea of self-interests, nor does it reject coordination costs or information costs, and is therefore compatible with neoclassical economic theory. Moreover, the theory does not assume the proposition that it is solely the shareholders who are entitled to the surplus economic value generated, nor does it assume that markets are better at assessing investment options than the board of directors (both corporate law and court ruling grant the directors discretion).[13] In contrast to the view that shareholders are located 'outside and above' the board of directors, the shareholders are instead part of the team production, being suppliers of capital and thus granted the right to be considered by the board of directors as one participant in the team production efforts. The theoretical implications of the team production model are significant and of great relevance for the agency theory model. For instance, the public corporation, whose stock can be acquired by any investor on the stock exchange, is in reality '[n]ot so much a "nexus of contracts" (explicit or implicit) as a "nexus of firm-specific investments", in which several different groups contribute unique and essential resources to the corporate enterprise, and who each find it difficult to protect their contributions through explicit contracts', Blair and Stout (1999: 275) argue. In addition, which is an important deviation from the agency theory model, the directors are not 'agents' but are trustees for the corporation itself, having fiduciary duties and being located within a hierarchy and assigned the work to 'balance team members' competing interests in a fashion that keeps everyone happy enough that the productive coalition stays together' (Blair and Stout, 1999: 280–81). 'In the eyes of the law', Blair and Stout (1999: 291) say, 'corporate directors are a unique form of fiduciaries who, to the extent they resemble any other form, perhaps most closely resemble trustees'. Speaking in terms of the now obsolete agency theory, the 'agency costs' – the principals' costs to monitor their agents – are substantially lower than the costs that would accumulate in the case of no 'mediating hierarchy' being in place, serving to reduce shirking and rent-seeking during and after the team production. The team production model thus provides a robust theoretical model that takes into account not only one of the team members' interests (that is, shareholders), but seeks to explain, on the basis of both legal theory and neoclassical economic theory, how incorporated businesses are much more efficient and capable of balancing various interests than the agency model recognizes. In contrast, the team production theory of corporate governance includes shareholders in the team and grants directors the role of trustees who help make sense out of how corporate law is enacted and practised in the US. When abandoning the agency theory prescription, corporate law is consistent and practically useful.

CONSEQUENCES OF THE CONTRACTUAL VIEW

Academic theories and scholarly debates are one thing; the *vita activa* is something different. While agency theory and the contractual view were never theoretically credible outside of neoclassical economic theory, nor practically supported by empirical evidence, it still suited the pro-business climate of the late 1970s and early 1980s when the winds of change swept over the corporate landscape and the wider society. The most significant change in the American context in the 1980s was the deregulation and accompanying growth of the finance industry and the deconstruction of managerial discretion through the use of leverage buyout activities (at times referred to as 'hostile takeover bids') that serve to erode the regime of managerial capitalism and to install the new regime of investor capitalism (for an extended argument, see Styhre, 2015). In the following, this practical application of the nexus of contract view of the firm will be examined.

Leveraged Buyouts and Corporate Restructurings

To repeat, the new generation of free market protagonists turned their gaze inward to the corporation itself and branded the executives (and no longer government officials or trade unionists) as being the villains in the drama about the decline of the American economy in the 1970s. Just as in the classic Sherlock Holmes story, the new generation of free market protagonists, usually labelling themselves agency theorists to underline the finance theory grounding of their argument, asked themselves why the dog did *not* bark. They claimed that the reason was that the withholding of the free cash flow was a violation of free market principles committed by insiders, operating inside the corporate executive function. The prescribed solution to reduce agency costs generated by alleged managerial malfeasance was to emphasize shareholder value creation, to recruit CEOs that shared a commitment to finance market control, and to engage external directors monitoring the implementation of the shareholder value policy. Expressed differently, the primary mechanism for managerial control was now the finance market, providing the skills and competence to calculate the stock value of firms, the ultimate measure of managerial competence in the agency theory model and free market advocacy.

Once the symptoms were diagnosed, there was suddenly room for finance market activities previously unseen in the American economy at this scale. When a new generation of finance market entrepreneurs such as the 'junk bond king' Michael Milken revolutionized the use of below-investment grade bonds (Bratton and Levitin, 2013; Polillo, 2011) and started to collaborate with firms such as Kohlberg Kravis Roberts & Co. to finance leverage buyout activities in the late 1970s and 1980s (Kaufman and Englander, 1993: 53–4), some commentators regarded this as a most abject form of predator capitalism (Schneper and Guillén, 2004: 263: Lipton, 1987). In contrast, agency theorists (for example, Jensen, 1993: 832) generally saw these activities as the restoration of free market pricing and thus welcomed such activities. The finance market engineering and hostile takeover manoeuvres coincided with the Federal Reserve's high-interest policy to curb inflation in the 1980s, which in turn led to an overrated dollar as overseas savings from surplus trade economies flooded the US economy (Stearns and Allan, 1996). In this milieu of pro-business activism and political agendas in combination with a steady supply of capital, the new form of financial engineering including leveraged buyouts (LBO) became fashionable, leading to both short-term and long-term consequences for the American and the global (and increasingly *globalizing*) economy.

The epic heroes (or villains, depending on perspective and preferences) were the finance company Drexel Burnham Lambert (mostly just known as Drexel) and their brilliant junk bond trader Michael Milken, located in sun-kissed Los Angeles, and the New York-based private equity firm Kohlberg Kravis Roberts & Co. (KKR). The work of these two firms, separated by a continent but sharing the ambition to revolutionize the American industry from within and on the basis of the new less strict finance market control regulations of the Reagan era, was indicative of how the firm is now being released from its institutional foundations and was now to be treated as precisely a bundle of contracts subject to finance engineering.

Michal Milken was a Berkeley graduate raised in Los Angeles who more or less singlehandedly created the 1980s' junk bond market, realizing that also below-investment grade financial assets such as bonds (hence the condescending term 'junk bonds') could be a useful vehicle for corporate financing. While Milken has been commonly portrayed as some kind of destructive force released in the seasoned American business community, he is now ultimately resurrected as a philanthropist and better understood as a classic entrepreneurial figure, seeing a business opportunity where few others would care to even look. In fact, Milken's image of himself as a benefactor of cash-starved entrepreneurs who faced limited interests from the mainstream banking community was not unsubstantiated. Polillo (2011: 374) speaks of Milken as a 'populist innovator' in finance, and a review paper in *The Economist* (2010) suggests that Milken served to 'democratize finance': '[j]unk-bond issues … offered a new way for many small but growing firms, which had been starved of capital by stodgy, commercial banks and sniffy investment banks, to finance themselves'. Milken himself took pride in serving such a heroic role, possibly an attitude embraced in California in the late 1960s: '[u]nlike other crusaders from Berkeley, I have chosen Wall Street as my battleground for improving society', Michael Milken declared (cited by Polillo, 2011: 374). In Milken's view, low credit rating of certain bonds represented a form of 'discrimination' (Polillo, 2011: 374). This 'discrimination' occurred when specific bond-issuers had their bonds systematically undervalued by rating agencies, preventing these businesses from acquiring the finance capital they needed to expand their operations. Recognizing at some point in the 1970s that 'junk bonds' were far from worthless or inefficient in raising money (and ultimately based on inaccurate credit rating practices), Milken developed a business on the basis of underwriting junk bonds at Drexel. The costs for junk bond financing were higher than for investment-grade bond issuers as Drexel demanded around 4 per cent in fees in comparison to the standard

1 per cent fee that was customary for investment-grade bonds (*The Economist*, 2010), but as other financing opportunities were exhausted, junk bond issuers turned to Milken to take advantage of the money machinery he developed at Drexel. As *The Economist* article suggests, the key to the loyalty of these clients was Milken's 'commitment to buy or sell on demand the bonds that Drexel had underwritten: he thus offered them a liquid market and a way out of investments they no longer wanted'. Milken and Drexel were no altruists but were instrumental in exploiting the inadequate credit rating practices and helped finance less attractive (from a finance industry perspective) clients' businesses at the same time as Drexel and the junk bond market grew in large proportions in the mid-1980s. By 1986, Drexel was Wall Street's most profitable firm, and junk bonds, once despised and treated with contempt, had now become mainstream. Junk bonds consequently outlived Milken's activities in Drexel: in the 1990s, the outstanding stock of junk bonds was about $1590 billion in the US; in 2010, it stood at $1 trillion.

Despite his remarkable success, the Milken narrative has an Icarus ending as Milken flew too close to the sun and enraged the mainstream business community. This narrative also includes the private equity firm Kohlberg Kravis Roberts & Co (KKR in the following). KKR was founded in 1976 by three former Bear Stearns co-workers (Kaufman and Englander, 1993: 67–8) and specialized in designing investor-controlled governance structures in family businesses that underwent a succession and therefore wanted to ensure that the ownership remained in the family (Kaufman and Englander, 1993: 55). As policy-makers and legislators in the US have voiced political support for management-controlled firms rather than investor-controlled firms, and have repeatedly passed legislation that 'either prohibited or inhibited financial institutions from holding ownership blocks in American major corporations' (Kaufman and Englander, 1993: 54), the predominant legislation favoured managerialism over investor-dominated governance. KKR revolutionized the 'contractual rewriting of the rights and responsibilities of the firm's constituent stakeholders – principally those between investor and management – that qualitatively reorganized these businesses from managerial to investor-controlled undertakings' (Kaufman and Englander, 1993: 53–4). In the 1980s, the leveraged buyout procedure acted as an advanced form of legal-financial engineering which enabled capital owners to take control of the corporation. This restructuring of firms' corporate governance structures had benefits for large institutional investors (for example, mutual funds, pension funds, and insurance companies holding large shares of stock) as this operation provided a partial solution to the perplexing problem of how to discipline managers.

Baker and Smith (1998: 2) correctly notice that financial entrepreneurs are 'rarely held in esteem by Americans', and portray the leveraged buyout as a 'classic entrepreneurial coup': '[i]ts economic impact was great; its practitioners were accordingly respected and feared' (Baker and Smith, 1998: 2–3). As in so many previous cases, this economic innovation was also developed outside of the economic mainstream, in what Baker and Smith (1998: 2–3) call 'the peripheries of high finance'. Essentially addressing KKR in favourable terms, Baker and Smith (1998: 29) argue that buyers of undervalued companies did not simply 'acquire, strip, and sell assets', but 'fostered improvements in the long-run values of the assets they controlled'. Not everybody was equally impressed with the LBO wave that swept over American business in the mid-1980s. The journalist Susan Faludi (1990) published a cover story in the *Wall Street Journal* examining the consequences of the Safeway grocery store chain buyout that carefully accounted for all the economic and social costs of this financial engineering, including job losses, hardship, depression and even suicide. The article secured a Pulitzer Prize for Faludi.

In contrast, Baker and Smith (1998) are less concerned about such stories but focus on the more straightforward economic consequences of the corporate restructuring of the grocery chain and not least the finance capital generated on the basis of these operations:

> Overall, by August 1988 Safeway had divested 11 major operations, including 1,000 stores. Meanwhile the company's workforce had dropped from 185,000 to 107,000 employees. Safeway cut its headquarters staff by 300 people, or 20 percent, which alone saved $15 million annually. During the asset sales Safeway aggressively renegotiated most of its 1,300 labor contracts. (Baker and Smith, 1998: 109–10)

Baker and Smith (1998) continue:

> At the end of 1994, Safeway's stock, for which KKR had paid $2 per share, was valued at $31,875 ... As for KKR, by the end of 1997 [the deal] had accumulated a total cash value of $4.97 billion on an original $130 million equity investment, for an annual compounded rate of return of 42.7 percent. (Baker and Smith, 1998: 113)

Based on such accomplishments, Baker and Smith (1998: 89) make clear that KKR and its financiers and business partners enabled a 'major innovation' in the financing and management of corporate organizations. More than that, the legacy of KKR is that it '[b]reathed new life into a moribund system of financial capitalism, which in turn stimulated a new era of sustained economic growth, vibrant securities markets, and at this writing, nearly full level of unemployment' (Baker and Smith, 1998: 206). They continue:

> Once scorned as a dangerous form of paper capitalism, [LBOs/'Management buyout'] demonstrated the beneficial effects of linking managerial and capital interest in the common pursuit of value. It showed how creative financial strategies could impel and assist corporate reform and how varied, rather than formulaic, were the paths to value creation ... As both prod to action and example, the management buyout has helped restore American business to its vital promise. (Baker and Smith, 1998: 206)[14]

By the late 1970s, KKR were putting together funds primarily on the basis of wealthy individuals' private capital, but around 1982, KKR started to approach commercial banks, which previously had participated in LBO activities only in the role of creditors (Kaufman and Englander, 1993: 71). Commercial banks agreed to participate in KKR's work, and LBO activities expanded to the next level, no longer being a concern only for smaller family-owned businesses or of interest to a relatively limited group of capital owners, but becoming a more widespread phenomenon in the US economy. In this take-off phase, Drexel Burnham Lambert and Michael Milken became a trusted partner of KKR (Kaufman and Englander, 1993: 75): 'Drexel's unmatched ability to sell high-yield securities, or "junk bonds", enabled KKR to develop more elaborate debt structures for ever-larger buyouts', Baker and Smith (1998: 25) write. In 1989, Drexel financed KKR's buyout of RJR Nabisco, a cigarette and biscuit company, but this spectacular takeover led to massive criticism from mainstream business America. Rather than being some marginal phenomenon, the finance market and legal entrepreneurs now threatened the very core of American business. As *The Economist* writes, Drexel had suddenly 'plenty of enemies who welcomed its downfall': '[t]he firm's ability swiftly to raise vast sums for LBOs struck fear into the heart of corporate America. The job losses that often followed a junk-financed buy-out, as hitherto inefficient firms were sweated for cash, created a lot of political fury' (*The Economist*, 2010).

While Milken was charged with relatively small tax-legislation violations and was sent to prison for 22 months in 1990, KKR survived this flush of animosity and is still in business to this date. In contrast, Drexel Burnham Lambert filed for bankruptcy in the period of Milken's trial and disappeared from the finance industry in its present form. Regardless of this unhappy ending, the two firms were eminent representatives of the new generation of finance market entrepreneurs who took advantage of the more lenient regulation of the finance industry and the new possibilities emerging on the basis of the managerial capitalism legislation and its practices (for example, to engage in unrelated diversification as prescribed by the portfolio theories that were fashionable in the 1960s and 1970s). In Kaufman and Englander's (1993: 75) generous account, KKR were actively 'revitalizing' American industry in ways that the government failed to do: 'Kohlberg Kravis Roberts & Co. most success-fully took advantage of this environment – particularly the federal government's ideological refusal to develop a coherent program to revitalize U.S. industry, instead leaving it to the private capital markets to fund new investments' (Kaufman and Englander, 1993: 75).

Some commentators take a less benign view of the new arbitrageur and financial entrepreneurs. Lipton (1987: 4) notices that the existence of 'large pools of capital' generated by the swiftly expanding junk bond market served to both justify and finance 'a wave of highly leveraged takeovers'. This wave of takeover bids, in turn, Lipton (1987: 4–5) continues, 'threatens a variety of constituencies, including shareholders, employees, customers, suppliers, and communities, as well as the economy as a whole'. While finance theorists, agency theorists and contractarians saw these takeover activities as being indicative of a well-functioning and essentially healthy economy, now finally unfettered by regulatory control and partisan politics, Lipton (1987) and others regarded the 1980s takeover wave as being propelled by '[s]peculative, financial considerations rather than by intrinsic business considerations'. Above all, the tendency to maximize short-term performance at the expense of a wider set of corporate objectives, including the long-term investment in production capital and human resources, illiquid as they are, were thought to endanger a variety of constituencies, including not least bondholders and other creditors.[15] Lipton's (1987) position on the matter is clearly stated:

> institutional investors are driven to maximize profits in the short term. They have become enamored with options, futures, junk bonds, computer program trading, and a host of other speculative devices designed to enhance short-term performance. Their desire for quick profits has contributed to the current wave of highly leveraged takeovers to the detriment of both undervalued companies and individual shareholders with a long-term investment motive. (Lipton, 1987: 7–8)

This in turn, the finance market sceptics claimed, called for political and legislative action.

Despite this wave of criticism and political outrage, Milken, Drexel and KKR were iconic players of the new pro-business, pro-finance landscape of corporate America, regardless of whether the broader public approved or benefited from these activities. Their new ways of thinking about and enacting the firm would last long after they themselves disappeared from the limelight, now making way for a new generation of finance theory-minded actors. Milken et al. ploughed the earth so that harvests would be reaped for the decades to come.

Managerial Responses to LBOs

Gordon (2007: 1521) refers to the 1980s as the 'Deal Decade' as takeover bids were made in large numbers in the period (see also Useem, 1990): '[d]ebt-financed buyouts increased enormously in the 1980s. In 1979, there were 75 buyouts valued at $1.3 billion: by 1988 there were 214 transactions, exceeding 477 billion', Kaufman et al. (1995: 76) write. Of the major US corporations, nearly a quarter 'received an unwanted bid' (Gordon, 2007: 1521). As Useem (1993: 3) remarks, 'as with home purchases and delayed airplane flights, almost everybody had a personal story to offer'. In addition, Useem (1993: 3) says, 'the accounts frequently centered on the extraordinary human stress and personal costs involved'.

Despite their intensity and magnitude, the executives and directors managing public corporations were not totally defenceless against the new finance market activities. As the fear of hostile takeover bids spread throughout the executive community in corporate America, there were new tools being developed. First of all, so-called 'poison pills' (based on the metaphor that if an animal is already poisonous, no predator being aware of this peril would care to kill and eat it), a corporate governance practice that included contracts that made it less attractive for presumptive takeover bidders to submit tender offers, were developed in the early 1980s (Rhee and Fiss, 2014: 1735; Davis, 1991). Such protective devices were controversial as they were widely understood as what preserved managerial welfare and privileges: '[a] company that uses a pill would ... raise agency costs by shielding managers from many takeovers', Roe (2000: 592) says. As a consequence, poison pills need the board of directors' and top management's justification when being announced (Rhee and Fiss, 2014: 1736).

A body of literature examines whether the use of poison pills and other protective devices support either what Walkling and Long (1984: 59) call the *shareholder welfare hypothesis*, suggesting that management has exclusive fiduciary responsibilities vis-à-vis shareholders and therefore they should accept tender offers, or the *managerial welfare hypothesis*, suggesting that management's fiduciary responsibilities vis-à-vis shareholders are secondary or should be weighed against other interests, including a wider set of stakeholders and not least the managers themselves. Based on the analysis of a sample of 95 tender offers in the

US, Walkling and Long (1984: 59) provide empirical support for the thesis that actions that maximize the welfare of executives will not of necessity maximize the welfare of the majority of shareholders, that is, there is a significant risk of managerial malfeasance from a shareholder welfare perspective. 'These results lend credence to the "convenient excuse" hypothesis. Management seems to oppose nonconglomerate and foreign offers when it is in their own best interest to do so', Walkling and Long (1984: 64) summarize. Walkling and Long (1984: 67) thus support the *managerial welfare hypothesis* and provide 'substantial evidence' that the decision to contest a tender offer is '[c]onditioned on personal wealth changes' (Walkling and Long, 1984: 67). In the light of such research findings, it is little wonder that poison pills are controversial as they insulate managers and directors from finance market control (Rhee and Fiss, 2014). Needless to say, agency theorists, who were already taking a hostile view of managers and their ability to create economic value, regard poison pills with few exceptions as yet another manoeuvre to withhold residual cash flow from the owners of stock and to insulate managerial interests and privileges. Yet again, agency theorists' argumentation had little support in legislative practices, granting management discretion on a broad basis: '[b]etween 1968 and 1980, at least thirty-five states passed tender-offer legislation, most of which set up legal hurdles against hostile bids', Kaufman and Zacharias (1992: 570) write.

Executives managing large conglomerates that were also priced low on the stock market after the 1970s' bear markets, were naturally concerned about losing their jobs if being approached by tender offers from the new and aggressive finance industry actors. In addition to the widespread use of poison pills, yet another procedure, this time protecting the interests of these executives themselves, was widespread in the 1980s: the 'golden parachute'. In the event of being taken over by new owners, the executives knew they would get fired and therefore they ensured that the present board of directors would grant them the right to generous compensation in the unfortunate event of losing their job, including both salary compensation and pension fund packages:

> A typical 'chute' provided for a severance of approximately three times salary plus the average bonus of prior years ... The chute could be seen as compensation for the depreciation in the terminated CEO's human capital, in respect of the termination decision. This was a significant consolation prize for the terminated CEO, which presumably reduced resistance, and also made it easier for the board to attract a replacement CEO under similarly unforgiving performance expectations. (Gordon, 2007: 1533–4)

In the eyes of both agency theorists and the wider public, the use of golden parachutes was illegitimate as the companies were – at least in theory, if not so much in practice, it would prove (Davis and Stout, 1992) – approached with tender offers exactly because they had been poorly and irresponsibly managed.[16] Paying these executives additional compensation and rewards for inadequate performance naturally stirred a lot of debate. Golden parachutes were thus again more evidence of managerial welfare unwarranted by extraordinary performance or accomplishments:

> In the broader court of public opinion ... golden parachutes continued to be widely viewed as inappropriate payoffs for an abdication of stewardship. Rather than viewing golden parachutes as incentives that lubricate value-maximizing change in ownership, an alternative sphere and segment of society conceptualizes golden parachutes as seven- and eight-figure payoffs given to executives for standing aside to let their companies be acquired and, in some cases, broken up in ways that meant thousands of workers lost their jobs. (Fiss et al., 2012: 1080)

Regardless of such critiques, the uses of such compensation contracts spread in the 1980s: by 1981, 15 per cent of the 250 largest US corporations had golden parachute packages for their executives; in 1986, 33 per cent did (Fiss et al., 2012: 1078). The interesting thing is that once the LBO wave vanished by the end of the 1980s, and the regulatory control of, for example, the junk bond market was restored, the genie was already out of the bottle. No longer enduring the constant pressure to evade tender offers, executives were still making sure they could contract these golden parachutes, increasingly more generous and disconnected from both actual performance and other hard-end economic data (for example, size, turnover) previously determining the levels of compensation. 'Golden parachutes, golden handcuffs, and the whole panoply of mechanisms for lavishly rewarding CEOs without regard to performance – all of which were unheard of before the age of investor capitalism – became standard features of CEO pay packages', Khurana (2002: 191) notes. The long-term consequence is an unprecedented growth in executive compensation that per se could be interpreted as the advancement and reinforcement of the management welfare that, for example, agency theorists criticized (Kim et al., 2015; Lord and Siato, 2010; DiPrete et al., 2010; Bebchuk and Fried, 2004). In other words, seemingly paradoxically, agency theorists were worried about managerial malfeasance (at least to the extent that it was used as the principal argument in favour of shareholder welfare), but one of the foremost consequences was to push executive compensation and benefits to unprecedented levels. Apparently the finance market control did not serve to discipline managers in the way that it was once claimed to be able to do.

SUMMARY AND CONCLUSION

If collectivism was a general term used in the critique of the movement away from free market liberalism in the 1930s and in the post-World War II period, in the 1970s a new enactment of the firm as a nexus of contracts rendered the wide-sweeping term 'collectivism' obsolete. With this new image of the firm, it is not so much the government and the unions that intervene in free market activities and thus bias competition and reduce efficiency, but the managers at the very heart of competitive capitalism – in the executive suites and boardrooms. Managers are made suspicious of withholding residual cash funds from shareholders to benefit their own interests. In order to neutralize this corporate govern- ance structure, neoclassical economic theorists needed to walk the tightrope and recognize the firm as a legitimate economic entity while still ignoring it as being of key importance in the production of economic value and thus worthy of more detailed analysis (that is, to recognize organization theory and management studies, in many cases subscribing to a behavioural theory of the firm in the Herbert Simon tradition, rather than following the methodological individualism of rational choice theory). The escape out of this theoretical dilemma was to enact the firm as a legal fiction, being a bundle of contracts where individual share- holders pay for the right to the residual cash flow generated by the firm. To avoid behavioural theories of the firm, tolerant of all sorts of all-too-human inadequacies on the part of managers, agency theorists instead have recourse to legal theory but here they encounter another scholarship maintaining its own intellectual standards and traditions. As have been discussed, the contractual view is by and large ignorant of legal theory and turns a blind eye to the historical development of corporate law. Moreover, the contractual view seeks to bypass the state as a legitimate and active agent in corporate governance and corporate law and law enforcement, thus representing an ideological shift towards a free market advocacy that is alien to the legal tradition of the US.

The world is not run on rational and scientific reasoning alone, but emotions, wishful thinking, and inspiring images of desirable futures that guide practical action are also part of its functioning, and regardless of its theoretical robustness, the contractual view was well tuned to the emerging pro-business climate of the late 1970s and 1980s. As overseas savings were invested in the American economy in the 1980s, propelled by the Federal Reserve's high-interest rate policy and an overrated dollar in combination with a less strict monitoring of the finance industry, finance capital raised through junk bond underwriting could be used to gain control over large-scale American conglomerates. In this new regime of investor capitalism, management welfare (formally defined as agency costs by agency theorists) was originally the target for such operations, but through strange ways and twists and turns, executives would still come out as the real winners in terms of personal benefits by the end of the 1990s. The finance market was now treated as an effective 'market for management control' as stock price evaluations were proposed as a reliable measure of managerial performance. The investor capitalism of the 1990s and the new millennium were thus in many ways simultaneously different from and similar to the post-World War II managerial capitalism. But when all was said and done, the winners of the shift in corporate governance were the shareholders and the executives and directors of large-scale corporations. That is, capital owners and 'the working rich' benefited the most from the decline of managerial capitalism. Who the losers were will be discussed shortly.

NOTES

1. It is noteworthy that Fama and Jensen's (1983) view of managers and directors is neither of necessity accepted, nor endorsed by all schools of neoclassical economic theory. Demsetz (1983) represents a more moderate position than Fama and Jensen (1983), saying that he does not believe that 'resorting to agency relationships reduces the value of the firm to its owners'. In addition, Demsetz (1983) is sceptical regarding the agency cost proposition: 'I do not believe that on-the-job consumption is necessarily, or even probably, greater with professional management than with management by the owners. The cost of agency, I believe, is borne by the firm, not by its agents' (Demsetz, 1983: 376, footnote 3). More explicitly, Demsetz (1983) remarks that it is a fallacy to mistake the map for the territory and thus to believe that what is theoretically consistent and thus appealing for the theorist's mind accurately depicts actual everyday work in corporations: '[i]t is a mistake to confuse the firm of economic theory with its real-world namesake. The chief mission of neoclassical economics is to understand how the price system coordinates the use of resources, not to understand the inner workings of the real firm' (Demsetz, 1983: 377). This is a key critique of the theoretical realism of the agency theory proposal.

    In addition, the transaction cost theory model represented by Williamson (1975; 1979) recognizes the firm as an actual entity whose internal practices and resources are worthy of detailed analysis. Williamson (1975: 22–3) recognizes the bounded rationality of human actors, and thus moves beyond the reductionist rational choice view of the firm. Williamson's work includes many declarations that sharply contrast with the agency theory model inasmuch as the corporation is understood as the site where specific skills are developed, skills that are not easily acquired in the market and/or at low cost. First, corporations 'economize the cost of negotiating and concluding' (Williamson, 1975: 4). Second, the shirking argument of, for example, Jensen (1986), derived from the factual evidence of the growth of conglomerates in the post-World War II economy, is not understood as an indication of managerial malfeasance but as a matter of 'failures in the capital market' (Williamson, 1975: 156). This is a key statement in Williamson's work, having substantial implications. Third, the agency theory argument that managers over-invest in, for example, R&D to protect managerial interests is rejected as Williamson suggests that 'rivalry generally favors R&D' (Williamson, 1975: 177), which implies that large organizations in an oligopolistic position have less incentive to invest in R&D. Rather than being indicative of indolent rent-seeking on the part of managers, investment in R&D is driven by market competition. If market competition is reduced, we can deduce from Williamson's second point above, it is the failure of capital markets that is to blame, not the managers. Fourth, as opposed to the free market advocacy of agency theory, treating markets and their pricing mechanism as the ultimate disciplinary mechanism in the economy, Williamson grants hierarchies a legitimate role in the economy: '[m]arkets and hierarchies are regarded as alternative contracting modes' (Williamson, 1975: 248). Fifth, instead of making opportunistic behaviour a cornerstone of his theoretical argument and defining agency costs or monitoring costs as the single most important costs generated by corporations, Williamson adheres to a bounded rationality view of the corporation: '[o]pportunism is more than simple self-interest seeking. It is self-interest seeking with guile; agents who are skilled at dissembling realize transactional advantages' (Williamson, 1975: 255). In other words, both other agency theorists (Demsetz) and transaction costs theorists (Williamson) reject many of the key propositions of agency theory advanced by Jensen et al., thus portraying the orthodox version of agency theory as a far-fetched form of free market advocacy, granting shareholders virtually unlimited privileges and assuming a priori that shareholders would have an interest in allocating their finance capital in ways that are beneficial for the wider society.

2.   The term 'fiduciary' derives from the Latin *fiducia*, or trust, and the 'fiduciary is expected to act in good faith and honesty for the beneficiary's interest' (Lan and Heracleous, 2010: 302). Fiduciary duty law is therefore based on the idea that social norms shape the behaviours of actors. In contrast, contractual relationships generally include the threat of liability, in many cases written into the formal contract.

3.   By 'holdup', Lamoreaux (1998) means how well the business charter protects the firm against one or more business partners' or shareholders' claim to the firm's funds and other firm-specific resources, ultimately being the degree of protection against divestiture in the face of emerging business opportunities. Protection against holdup is crucial for the business partners and other actors' willingness to invest in the firm and helps to bring together producers and investors in ways that foster joint collaboration and enable efficient use of firm-specific resources. Therefore, the question of degree of firmness is then to determine 'how much protection is optimal under different circumstances' (Lamoreaux, 1998: 70).

4.   It is noteworthy that a non-contractarian position does not of necessity imply a recognition of expanded social responsibilities. Lipton (1987: 41), for instance, otherwise being sceptical of corporate governance practices promoting shareholder welfare, argues persuasively that managers are 'ill-equipped to deal with questions of general public interest', and that imposing additional objectives on managers would put the corporations at risk as they would no longer be able to compete on an equal basis in product or service markets. In addition to the economic argument, widely endorsed by free market communities, Lipton (1987: 41) highlights political and ethical concerns that complicate the possibilities for such expanded corporate responsibilities: '[e]ncouraging corporations, a powerful group not directly accountable to or representative of our society, to take positions on the controversial social, moral, and political issues of the day also has dangerous anti-democratic implications'. If there are concerns that corporations misbehave or otherwise violate their business charters, Lipton (1987: 41–2) contends, the adequate response would be increased regulation or even legislation rather than to advocate additional social responsibilities.

5.   When Hawley and Williams (1997) reintroduce the concept of fiduciary duties but now within the otherwise overtly contractual model of investor or money manager capitalism, the distinction between contractual and trust-based (for example, mainstream corporate

law) theories of the firm and their specific corporate governance practices gets even more muddled. 'In fulfilling their role, [financial] institutions are legally required to act as a "fiduciary". That is, they are legally required to take any actions a "prudent person" would take to further the best interest of the beneficiary', Hawley and Williams (1997: 206) argue. Are institutional investors now suddenly expected not only to execute the managerial control function as prescribed by, for example, Manne (1967), but to take on wider socio-economic responsibilities, even making capitalism more 'democratic' (see also Seth, 2001)? And if so, for whom, beside the obvious case of the investors in the funds these money managers monitor, are they the agents? If investment fund managers are no longer strictly the agents of the investors in the funds (in turn being their principals), as the straightforward contractual theory would suggest, what corporate governance benefits (if this term applies to investments funds) would the unexpected reintroduction of the legal theory term fiduciary duties provide? Hawley and Williams's (1997) argument leaves many questions to be answered.

6. This remark regarding factual conditions raises questions about the consistency of the theory of market pricing – derived from the fact that *all* states do have legislation for business charters – as such pricing apparently occurs in free markets in some cases, while in other cases it does not, with few distinguishing practical features between the two situations. Why certain firms incorporated in states with labour law providing stronger protection for the employees would not value their employers higher than elsewhere is not explained by Roe (2000), claiming that it is the legislation that determines employee compensation, thus sidelining the regular neoclassical price system mechanism explanation for the level of labour compensation. As a consequence, the theory of market pricing of labour is either situated and conditional (that is, it does not apply universally as is generally claimed by neoclassicists) or it must accommodate a wider set of non-economic conditions including, for example, legislation, 'political rent-seeking' (using Roe's own term) and so on. That is, the theory abandons its strict claim to be exclusively based on market conditions.

7. The question regarding the democratic benefits of governance based on the market for corporate control is worth taking seriously, both because it is a cornerstone in the free market advocacy and the shareholder primacy model of corporate governance and because it is a field that has received substantial attention from scholars from different disciplinary camps. The literature on the political power of corporations (for an overview, see Walker and Rea, 2014) addresses issues such as political campaign contributions (Claessens et al., 2008; Salt, 1989), the funding of research work and think-tanks (Akard, 1992; Vogel, 1983), lobbying activities (Choi et al., 2015), the funding of politicians and political bodies during political decision-making (Mian et al., 2010; Jacobs, 1988), and how directors' political connections affect firm performance (Goldman et al., 2009). In sociology (Mills, 1956) and economic theory (Pareto, 1901), there has been a long-standing belief that elites are in the position to execute substantial political power on the basis of its access to and control over financial capital (see, for example, Maclean et al., 2014; Faux, 2012; Burris, 2001; Jenkins and Eckert, 2000; Useem and Karabel, 1986; Useem, 1979). Neoclassical economic theory does not deny the presence of elites but assumes that the access to financial capital, which in turn engenders political influence, derives from rational choices in terms of, for example, individual human capital investments with higher economic compensation accruing to the actor whose market value is priced at a certain level. That is, *ex hypothesi*, there are no structural inefficiencies regarding economic and political power derived from (efficient) market pricing. Jacobs (1988) refers to this assumption, based on a political theory that is commonly not made explicit in economic theory, as economists' unstated preference for 'a pluralist world-view'. This pluralist worldview, based on meritocratic market valuation, removes the questions of social class and class interest and instead speaks of 'interest groups', Jacobs (1988: 856) suggests. In contrast to this view, economic and political sociologists provide ample evidence of the influence of '[a]n inner group of large corporations that work together to ensure that public policies will not depart from their core interests' (Jacobs, 1988: 857). Jacobs' own empirical study of how fiscal

policy is influenced by the interests of corporations demonstrates that '[t]he huge economic resources of the great corporations can be translated into political influence, at least when taxation is at issue' (Jacobs, 1988: 877). The most important theoretical implication from this research finding is that 'the core pluralist supposition about the equal representation of interests' in political policy-making cannot hold (Jacobs, 1988: 867). That is, the political theory of mainstream neoclassical economists, treating policy-making and other political decision-making as 'pluralistic contests between rough equals' (Jacobs, 1988: 876), is empirically unsubstantiated and theoretically incredible: '[w]hen there is a strong relationship between the economic resources of the great firms and important political outcomes, public decisions will not be of equivalent benefit to citizens who do not have access to these resources. This result does not support the pluralist inclination to disregard the economic sources of political power', Jacobs (1988: 876) contends.

For mainstream agency theorists, Jacobs' (1988) findings would easily be dismissed as evidence of managerial opportunism, being yet another piece of evidence of the accuracy of and moral justification for corporate governance practices embedded in the market for corporate control. However, Roe's (1994) argument that shareholder value creation is socially beneficial is based on the political theory of a pluralist world characterized by competition between equals. In addition, this agency theory response to Jacobs' (1988) empirical findings does not explain why capital owners – not very likely to be 'imbued with a professional spirit of public service', in Dodd's (1932: 1153) memorable formulation – should be less concerned with corporate interests than managers at large. In other words, the claim that shareholder primacy governance is socially beneficial needs to stand up to empirical testing. As will be discussed in Chapter 4, the socio-economic consequences of shareholder governance poorly support a pluralist theory assuming auxiliary benefits derived from shareholder welfare.

8. Hillman and Keim's (2001: 134) empirical study measuring market value added in Fortune 1000 companies for the years 1994, 1995 and 1996 suggests otherwise, showing that 'shareholder wealth creation indicate[s] a positive relationship with stakeholder management,' a result that Hillman and Keim (2001) believe casts doubt on the accuracy of the shareholder welfare model: 'shareholder value creation today should not be construed as coming at the expense of the interests of other primary stakeholders' (Hillman and Keim, 2001: 136).

9. Roe (2000) here touches on one thorny question in free market advocacy, which is how the alleged benefits of free market economies (for example, 'economic freedom', superior efficiency, supposedly meritocratic career possibilities anchored in market assessment and pricing and so on) can appear appealing for the majority when it is apparently not the case that the majority would not be the primary beneficiaries of such free market policies. One way to handle this is to follow Friedrich von Hayek and to shun democracy altogether on the basis that people are not yet ready to make decisions that are in their own best interest (Grocott, 2015). Such a reactionary position is not very well received outside of free market zealotry. The other approach is to reinterpret the state and politics more widely as representing a specific form of economic action (as Roe, 2000, does), to '[b]end the state to a market logic, pretending one can replace "citizens" with "customers"' (Mirowski, 2013: 56). Such state apparatus is preferably monitored by the same mechanisms and procedures as any corporation submitting to the market for managerial control (that is, the finance market), including numerous audit devices and forms of 'new public management'. In the best of worlds, the state provisions are delivered on a contractual basis, rendering the entire state apparatus (with only few exceptions, for example, the juridical system and potentially the police force) a new market for governmental services and yet another arena for venturing. Under all conditions, the anti-democratic sentiment tangential to free market advocacy, always already overtly concerned about letting individuals who are ignorant and uninformed about economic issues (representing a not so veiled elitism), prefers to keep the state and the government (and hence democracy as a political system per se) '[r]elatively impotent, so that citizen initiatives rarely are able to change much of anything' (Mirowski, 2013: 56).

10. These comparable economic growth figures in Europe and the US should be comple-mented by labour statistics regarding hours worked. Between 1970 and 2002, household work hours rose around 20 per cent in the USA, while in the European Union, household work hours fell by 12 per cent (Wisman, 2013: 936). Between 1979 and 2006, the share of the population being part of the workforce grew more quickly in Europe than in the United States, but the number of individual hours worked declined in Europe. In contrast, in the US, overall work hours rose substantially (Hacker and Pierson, 2010: 27). This tendency to work harder and longer hours appears to be primarily an American phenomenon, subject to scholarly attention (for example, Perlow, 1999; Hochschild, 1997; Schor, 1993), unfortunately coinciding with increased economic inequality and raising levels of debt in the US.

11. In fact, the Chicago economist Sam Peltzman advances precisely this argument, using the term 'information' as the key analytical category in his analysis, and thereafter advocating the elimination of regulatory control in the pharmaceutical industry. That is, in Peltzman's free market view, 'the marketplace was best able to generate information about new drugs' (Nik-Khah, 2014: 494). As Nik-Khah (2014: 494) remarks, this theoretical proposition about drugs *already being in the market* is relatively inadequate when it comes to the most complex, knowledge-intensive, and convoluted process of *developing new drugs*, making Peltzman's anti-FDA campaign quixotic and by and large ignorant of a long series of aspects of the pharmaceutical industry and its regulatory control (for an introduction, see Brody, 2007; Petryna et al., 2006, Gassman et al., 2004; Hara, 2003; Jungmittag et al., 2000). Ultimately, Peltzman squandered most of his credibility outside of the circle of free market zealotry when he declared in a BBC interview that the thalidomide scandal in the 1960s was something that should be tolerated, even welcomed, by the public as the alleged costs for curbing free market contracting were higher than the costs of such events: '[i]t turns out that the cost [of the 1962 pharmaceutical industry regulations] is far in excess of the costs of having a thalidomide tragedy ... I will have to say, how very shockingly it might seem, that we don't have enough thalidomide tragedies in the United States today' (Sam Peltzman in an interview with the BBC, cited in Nik-Khah, 2014: 495). This kind of cloistered worldview, devoid of empathy and reason in its applications of utilitarian arguments, is likely to appeal to only a small subset of belligerent free market protagonists. For the wider public, such arguments are heartless and deranged and arguably undermine much of the free market advocacy and implied utilitarian principles.

12. The idea of team production is not new but has Greco-Roman roots (Lopez, 1976). The so-called Rhodian sea law (derived from the Greek island of Rhodos) and the basis of the *column* contract used in Italo-Byzantine seaports in the medieval period listed all contributions of capital and labour by those who travelled on a ship – including the captain, sailors and merchants – in a column of the ship log. Thus, risks and profits were shared according to 'the value ascribed to each contribution' (Lopez, 1976: 75).

13. 'Corporate law only permits shareholders to bring successful derivative claims against directors in circumstances where bringing such claims benefits not only shareholders, but other stakeholders as well', Blair and Stout (1999: 298, original emphasis omitted) write. Making explicit reference to one Delaware Chancery Court decision, Blair and Stout (1999) demonstrate how Delaware corporate law (being popular among incorporators as roughly all publicly traded companies in the United States and *c.*64 per cent of the Fortune 500 companies are registered in Delaware; see State of Delaware, 2015) regard directors as trustees with wider responsibilities than to enrich shareholders: '[the Board] had an obligation to the community of interests that sustained the corporation, to exercise judgment in an informed, good faith effort to maximize the corporation's long-term wealth creating capacity' (Delaware Chancery Court statement, cited in Blair and Stout, 1999: 296).

14. Tillman (2012) is less sure about the social and economic benefits of the type of financial engineering and economic value extraction that Baker and Smith (1998) celebrate. Private equity funds, not functionally different from Milken's junk bond funds, served to create substantial pools of inexpensive capital and provided the means through which banks

could 'hide infirmities from regulators' (Tillman, 2012: 1605). In serving this role, private equity funds lowered the cost of finance capital speculation and encouraged excessive risk-taking that ultimately led to the collapse of the entire finance industry. In other words, the combination of an increased supply of cheap capital and active financial engineering is not of necessity improving the performance of the economy, nor does it provide additional benefits. Instead, the costs of excessive and systemic risks are pushed onto the sovereign state and ultimately its taxpayers, as was the case in the 2008–09 finance industry meltdown.

15. Corporate leverage, that is, the increase of the level of debt, the very mechanism that makes the access to the pool of junk bond-financed capital useful and takeover bids financially attractive (but only if the supply of finance capital is substantial, that is, the cost of capital is low), increases the risks for bondholders but without the economic benefits that accrue to the takeover bidders. This makes outstanding bonds a more risky investment and thus less valuable. The result is therefore a transfer of wealth from bondholders to stockholders that is not, Lipton (1987: 27) argues, justified by existing corporate legislation.

16. Interestingly, as Gordon (2007: 1504) notes, boards with a higher representation of independent directors were *more*, not *less*, likely to make golden parachute decisions. Agency theorists advocate a higher degree of independent directors to ensure director independence from the CEO, in turn leading to reduced agency costs and lower risks of decision-making benefiting managers. Gordon's data therefore fails to support the agency theory proposition.

4. Investor capitalism and the nexus of contract view of the firm: assessing the consequences

INTRODUCTION

By the early 1990s, after roughly fifteen years of mobilization of the business community and free market advocacy and reform, the new theory of the firm was conventional wisdom. It consisted basically of two principal ideas, both rooted in the combination of theoretical perspectives, derived from the same propositions and methodological assumptions, mutually reinforcing one another and yet representing their own specific interests including price theory (in economics), contractual theory (in legal studies), and agency theory (in corporate governance and management theory): (1) the firm was understood as a nexus of contracts, a 'legal fiction', that granted owners of stock the right to claim their proportional share of the residual cash flow generated by the firm; and (2) corporate governance practices were strongly oriented towards shareholder welfare at other principals' and stakeholders' expense. Gordon (2007: 1535) summarizes the essence of the new conventional wisdom as '[t]he 1950s tendency was to believe that firms could create and manage markets. By contrast, as evidenced by the growth of disaggregated, networked firms, the 1990s tendency was to use market signals to manage the firm'. In this new milieu, it was asserted, shareholders claimed their share of the residual cash flow but also provided the auxiliary benefit to reduce agency costs and better allocated the stock of finance capital to industries and niches in the economy with a better growth potential than mature or stagnating industries. To act in accordance with these prescriptions, executives were incentivized to fully commit to cost-cutting to maintain and hopefully boost the stock price (Brockman et al., 2007; Budros, 1997). The strong orientation towards finance markets in companies and industries, until recently dominated and managed by industrialists and engineers, therefore not only reallocated the stock of finance capital from a wider set of constituencies (including, for example, salaried blue-collar and white-collar workers) to the owners of stock, but was in a broader sense part of a restructuring of the corporate system and competitive capitalism (Tabb, 2012; Dencker, 2009; Useem, 1990). The managerial capitalism was the primary target for the new generation of free market advocators, no longer so much concerned about trade unions and their political project to ensure decent working conditions and reasonable economic compensation for work, now instead making the executives and directors the key actors inducing costs and creating inefficiencies (Jensen, 1986: 328). This criticism regarding managerial malfeasance, not as an exceptional case of derailment but as a systemic feature of competitive capitalism, was never credible as the economic system of managerial capitalism had to date produced an unprecedented economic growth and welfare previously unseen in any human society (Galbraith, 1958). That is, the agency theory argument that agency costs are excessively high (not a credible proposition as that would undermine the competitiveness of the firm) and that the only way to reduce such costs is to hand over the money to the owners of stock, needed an enemy within the system of managerial capitalism. Claiming that, for example, trade unions or the government generate additional costs by intervening in supposedly self-regulating free markets, as had been repeated time and again since the early 1930s by conservatives, pro-business activists, neoliberals and libertarians, proved to be an inefficient strategy beset by significant political difficulties. The staunch anti-unionism of free market advocators such as Friedrich von Hayek was certainly appreciated in conservative communities (Philips-Fein, 2009; Vogel, 1996), but the oligarchic nature of the predominant system of managerial capitalism demanded a specific institutional framework wherein trade unions played their role to support the interests of salaried workers (Jacobs and Myers, 2014; Brady et al., 2013; Rueda and Pontusson, 2000). In addition, outside of populist demagoguery, few believed in a total withdrawal of the state and government from the regulation of the economic system.

The new generation of free market advocators therefore abandoned this old tune of trade union and government bashing and instead constructed a theoretical argument (agency theory and the idea of agency costs, residual cash flow and the virtues of finance market control and so on) and a recipe (shareholder welfare) for how to transfer the finance capital to the shareholders while at the same time portraying this transfer as not just being in the interest of a small elite but being for the greater good (Roe, 2000: 553; Easterbrook and Fischel, 1993: 445). In the best of possible worlds, which all Panglossian thinkers reckon that we do in fact inhabit, the agency theory argument stipulates that more capital is released from mature industries to better serve the entrepreneurial function of the economy, thus benefiting the entrepreneurs and creators upon whom the capital-owning class is after all dependent and must entrust with their capital (Beckert, 2013: 331–2; Kalecki, 1943: 328), thus justifying the agency theory framework as a viable economic policy. Unfortunately, there is scant evidence of such a massive transfer of capital from mature industries to novel industries. Instead of fuelling the next generation of capitalist enterprises (the first, it should be recalled, was essentially grounded in state-financed initiatives, attracting private capital only *after* much of the early risks were discounted and/or if risks could be externalized and carried by a third party; see Roy, 1997), the shareholder welfare-centred governance led to the hollowing out of existing industries as there were few incentives to reinvest in new productive capital (Stockhammer, 2004; Hall, 1993; 1994). This was because economists and pundits declared that mature industries could now be shipped off to low-cost countries as they were anyway bound to disappear from the Western advanced economies sooner or later (Milberg and Winkler, 2010; Milberg, 2008). The shareholder welfare model also coincides with an endemic lack of venture capital that little benefited entrepreneurial activities. That is, capital owners did not, as agency theorists hoped (or at least claimed capital owners would do to justify their arguments), pipe their residual cash flow into emerging industries. In, for example, Silicon Valley, the ventures started were not financed by the East-coast finance institutions but the new generation of digital media entrepreneurs had to rely on the money generated within the industry (Ferrary, 2003; Saxenian, 1994). Only when the computer industry cluster had already generated substantial wealth, did regular venture capital firms enter the cluster (Ferrary and Granovetter, 2009). In the life sciences, it was again the state and the government that had to take the lead in terms of financing university-based start-ups in biotechnology and pharmaceuticals (Mazzucato, 2013; Sunder Rajan, 2012: 2–3; Mowery, 2009: 30). The success of Michael Milken's new junk bond business in the mid-1980s was partially explained by the difficulties experienced by entrepreneurs in financing their activities. In the end, owners of finance capital did not put their money at risk unless absolutely necessary, especially as there are less risky and more liquid investment opportunities provided by the finance industry and its quickly expanding number of financial innovations. Therefore much of the political argument in favour of shareholder welfare – that, when all is said and done, it is good for the dynamics of competitive capitalism, maximizes social wealth, and minimizes agency costs, and is therefore 'good for everybody' – falls flat.

Yet the agency theory model was hugely successful in the regime of shareholder welfare, as the principal corporate governance objective.

Daily et al. (2003: 371) suggest that 'the overwhelming emphasis in governance research has been on the efficacy of the various mechanisms available to protect shareholders from self-interested whims of executives'. 'Agency theory has colored the air we breathe', Dobbin and Jung (2010: 32) add. That is, Rock (2013: 1910) argues, since the early 1980s, the US economy has moved from being a 'management-centric system' to a 'shareholder-centric system'; today, Rock (2013) says, 'there is substantial reason to believe that managers and directors today largely "think like shareholders"'. Rock (2013: 1923) emphasizes the institution of the business school as the vehicle for the establishment of the central idea of shareholder primacy: '[i]f business school were a church, shareholder value maximization would be its religion'. As a consequence of shareholder primacy, substantial amounts of money were transferred from industry to capital owners: between 1982 and 1997, the Dow Jones Industrial Index 'increased eight-fold', while salaries were by and large stagnant in the US (Blair and Stout, 1999: 325). The question is then where all the money went if it was not reinvested in existing industry or in the entrepreneurial function of competitive capitalism. This intriguing question will be discussed in this chapter, looking at the changes of competitive capitalism from being an oligarchic managerial capitalism, dominated by a few major multinational manufacturing companies, to an oligarchic investor capitalism, dominated by a few major finance institutions (Eichengreen, 2015; Blinder, 2013; Mandis, 2013; Tabb, 2012; Cohan, 2011). That is, the money generated in industry and transferred to the owners of stock, either as dividends or raised stock prices (in some cases through announced or actual stock repurchases; see, for example, Lazonick and Mazzucato, 2013; Kahle, 2002; Grullon and Ikenberry, 2000), was returned to the finance industry itself. This led in turn to a remarkable and, some say today, as being part of the post-2008 debate, unsustainable growth of the finance industry after 1980. In terms of capital accumulation in the finance industry and the sharp growth of economic compensation of finance industry workers, the term *investor capitalism* is an adequate label for the new regime of economic accumulation in Western capitalism.

To repay the business community that financed the community work, research programmes, academic research positions, political activist groups, think-tanks and other activities that were part of the neoliberal and neoconservative movement of the 1970s, agency theorists in particular found the most efficient way to break the seal of collectivism that had worried neoliberals and conservatives since the Depression era. Like no previous theoretical framework or analytical model put forth by the pro-business community, agency theorists, themselves combining many different elements of the neoclassical economic theory framework (for example, the theory of the firm literature, price theory, and the efficient market hypothesis presented by finance theorists) and contractual theory from legal scholarship, finally managed to present a convenient little theory that possibly once and for all undermined the legitimacy of any claims to the right to the finance capital generated in industry by anyone but shareholders, the capital owners of competitive capitalism.

Seen in this view, agency theorists such as Michael C. Jensen, building a career within academic institutions directly or indirectly funded by industrialists being part of the pro-business community (Chabrak, 2012; Philips-Fein, 2009; Cockett, 1994; Himmelstein, 1992), were instrumental in undermining managerial capitalism. But just like any other belligerent reformers, agency theorists managed above all to create a sense of fragmentation of what was once seemingly unified. Competitive capitalism was no longer an economic system that should unquestionably benefit all of its participants and all citizens of the welfare state who hosted and supported the economic activities. Such conspicuous and morally questionable forms of collectivism could no longer be tolerated as agency costs allegedly soared in poorly managed corporations, it was declared. From now on, the fruits of the labour ploughed down in corporations were preached *ex cathedra* to belong exclusively to one group, the capital owners who had unselfishly put their savings and capital at stake when investing it in companies managed by executives with strong incentives to shirk and to squander the capital in systematic and predictable ways. Repeating this argument *ad nauseam*, agency theorists, contractarians and followers of price theory accomplished what the older generation of free market advocates assembling in Paris and Mont Pèlerin in the 1930s could only dream of. They overturned the allegedly collectivist economic system of managerial capitalism and paved the way for the finance market-based regime of investor capitalism that today is occasionally referred to as the financialized economy (Carruthers, 2015; Davis and Kim, 2015; Van der Zwan, 2014; Palley, 2013; Krippner, 2005; Epstein, 2005).

THE SHAREHOLDER PRIMACY IN THE NEW MILLENNIUM

By the turn of the millennium, the agency theory view of corporate governance and its proposed shareholder welfare model was widely recognized and embraced by a variety of market actors and policymakers that recognized how this normative model could help them accomplish one or more objectives. At the same time, at this zenith of free market advocacy and policy-making, there was still a standing critique from legal scholars regarding the cursory analysis of corporate law in the shareholder welfare literature. As was pointed out in the 1980s, legal theory and legal practice does not primarily favour market efficiency at the expense of other interests and socio-economic benefits but rather seeks to create a legal system that takes into account the interests of a wider set of constituencies. As a consequence, much of the agency theory argument becomes irrelevant in terms of being the basis for a solid theoretical framework guiding corporate governance practices. What remains though, is a number of normative declarations regarding how agency theorists believe corporate law *should* be structured to better fit with the shareholder welfare ideology. Unfortunately, starting to draw the map and only thereafter recognizing that the territory does look different from how one wished it to look cannot justify and legitimate a radical restructuring of the land to secure the usefulness of the map. Still, at the beginning of the new millennium, such claims were made, also by legal scholars, that the normative model would justify legal changes, indeed to serve as a guideline for pervasive legal reform. In this section, this debate between shareholder primacy protagonists and their critics will be discussed to indicate how the ignorance of existing corporate law and legal theory was again subsumed under generalized economic arguments regarding the 'efficiency' of shareholder welfare.

SHAREHOLDER WELFARE AT THE END OF HISTORY

In 2000, the legal scholars Henry Hansmann and Reinier Kraakman published an article entitled *The End of History for Corporate Law*, a tract that purportedly once and for all declared the triumph of shareholder welfare governance. Gordon (2007: 1535) suggests that the downfall of the communist regimes by the early 1990s had the important consequence that one potential political competitor for the allegiance of workers was now finally eliminated, leading to the new self-assured attitude among liberal, libertarian and conservative theorists and pundits that they had been right all the time about the true nature of collectivism in all forms. Influenced by the triumphalism of, for example, Francis Fukuyama speaking about Western societies finally making liberalism, competitive capitalism and representative democracy the only legitimate and viable political system, not so much as an eschatological treatise as being an affirmative statement regarding the virtues of the liberal market economy, Hansmann and Kraakman (2000) did not spare their readers any self-asserted claims regarding the efficiency and normative and moral qualifications of the shareholder welfare model, now immodestly referred to as the 'standard model of corporate governance'. 'The basic law of corporate governance – indeed most of corporate law – has achieved a high degree of uniformity across developed market jurisdictions, and continuing convergence toward a single, standard model is likely', Hansmann and Kraakman (2000: 439) write. In making the argument in favour of shareholder welfare, Hansmann and Kraakman (2000) list the standard agency theory arguments: the decline of the conglomerate form is indicative of the capital owners' impatience with managers' systemic incompetence and shirking; the managers are the shareholders' agents and the shareholders can legitimately claim the economic value generated by the firm; other alternative models taking into account the interests of a wider group of stakeholders represent little more than a naive and unsustainable governance idea that few qualified commentators seriously consider as being of relevance:

> The collapse of the conglomerate movement in the 1970s and 1980s ... largely destroyed the normative appeal of the managerialist model. It is now the conventional wisdom that, when managers are given great discretion over corporate investment policies, they tend to serve disproportionally their own interests, however well-intentional managers may be ... The price paid in inefficiency of operations and excessive investment in low-value projects is now considered too great. (Hansmann and Kraakman, 2000: 444)

The idea that managers expressed a preference for the conglomerate form needs to be weighed against the consequences of antitrust legislation and policy that banned related diversification in the post-World War II period. In addition, the claim that conglomerates disappeared on the basis of sheer managerial incompetence should be contrasted against the literature that shows that it was propelled by policy-making deregulating finance markets. However, few of these more elaborate and complex arguments explaining the dominance and subsequent disappearance of the conglomerate form fit into Hansmann and Kraakman's (2000) narrative. Next, stakeholder theories are dismissed on the very same basis as the managerial discretion model, declared to be unable to provide managers with straightforward instructions regarding decision-making and firm priorities:

> Stakeholder models of the fiduciary type are in effect just reformulations of the manager-oriented model, and they suffer the same weaknesses. While untethered managers may better serve the interest of some classes of

> stakeholders, such as the firm's existing employees and creditors, the managers' own interests will often come to have disproportionate salience in their decision making, with cost to some interests groups – such as shareholders, customers, and potential new employees and creditors – that outweigh any gains to the stakeholders who are benefited. (Hansmann and Kraakman, 2000: 448)

So far Hansmann and Kraakman (2000) present the conventional agency theory set of arguments, but they add what may be called an organization theory argument and an efficiency argument, both equally complicated to justify. First, Hansmann and Kraakman (2000: 449) propose that the triumph of shareholder primacy is manifested in a wide number of market actors now subscribing to shareholder primacy governance:

> The persuasive power of the standard model has been amplified through the acceptance by a worldwide network of corporate intermediaries, including international law firms, the big five accounting firms, and the principal investment banks and consulting firms – a network whose rapidly expanding scale and scope give it exceptional influence in diffusing the standard model of shareholder-centered corporate governance. (Hansmann and Kraakman, 2000: 449)

The fact that firms and institutions (for example, credit rating agencies and audit firms) appreciate a 'theoretical' description that both justifies their own role and purpose and benefits their own interests cannot be taken as a legitimate argument (similar to high-income groups justifying tax cuts on the basis of the argument that it is beneficial for the economy – a standard argument in tax reform policy-making), but must be understood within Hansmann and Kraakman's (2000) wider horizon of meaning. Moreover, beyond the fact that certain groups may benefit from shareholder welfare governance, Hansmann and Kraakman (2000) speak in general terms, just like previous shareholder welfare protagonists, about the 'efficiency' of the standard model: '[a] simple comparison across countries adhering to different models – at least in very recent years – lends credence to the view that adherence to the standard model promotes better economic outcomes' (Hansmann and Kraakman, 2000: 450). Unfortunately, there is little evidence to support this claim, and it is for instance unclear whether this statement relates, for example, to the economic performance of certain American states (all with their own corporate legislation) or if it calls for international comparisons across different countries and regions representing different governance regimes. Under all conditions, as will be demonstrated in this chapter, shareholder welfare governance does not correlate with greater economic efficiency overall, and there is no robust evidence of any particular regional or national governance system being 'more efficient' than any other (Flig-stein and Choo, 2005). Regardless of the absence of more convincing evidence regarding shareholder primacy governance, Hansmann and Kraakman (2000: 454) '[m]ake the claim that no important competitors to the standard model of corporate governance remain persuasive today'.

On the basis of this line of argument ('theoretical' arguments discred-iting managerialism, complemented by 'preferences' – some market actors approve shareholder welfare – and 'efficiency' arguments), Hans-mann and Kraakman (2000) reach the point where they make the declarative statement that corporate law should now, in the absence of 'important competitors' to the standard model, be modified to better fit with this allegedly widely recognized prescription: '[w]e expect that reform of corporate governance practices will generally precede the reform of corporate law, for the simple reason that governance practice is largely a matter of private ordering that does not require legislative action' (Hansmann and Kraakman, 2000: 455).[1] Therefore, Hansmann and Kraakman (2000: 455) expect shareholder pressures and 'the power of shareholder-oriented ideology' to make legislators move in the direc-tion of an 'Anglo-American corporate and securities law'. In making this declaration, that the standard model is the only credible and practically useful corporate governance model, Hansmann and Kraakman (2000: 463) pepper their argument with quasi-revolutionary arguments, where it is after all (or at least not only) the 'efficiency argument' that matters in shareholder primacy advocacy, but there is also a concern 'for the little guy' being thrown into the story (for this populist trope, see, for example, Frank, 2012):

> [T]he increasing salience of the standard model makes empire-building and domination suspect, and the extraction of private value at the expense of minority shareholders illegitimate ... Viewed through the lens of the new ideology, the old practices are not only inefficient but also unjust, since they deprive ordinary citizens, including pensioners and small investors, of a fair return on their investments. (Hansmann and Kraakman, 2000: 463)

Large industrial oligarchies are supposedly not operating in the interest of the average taxpayers, Hansmann and Kraakman (2000) say, while in fact the large-scale, divisionalized corporation was precisely the vehicle for post-World War II welfare, including stable employment and rising real wages for, for example, the blue-collar community (Davis, 2010). In fact, the decline of the conglomerate firm, the anathema of shareholder welfare protagonists, coincides with the deindustrialization of the US economy. Hansmann and Kraakman (2000) still insist that the same people who justified the deindustrialization of the American industry under the aegis of market efficiency are now in the best position to ensure that at least pension funds can optimize their results. Such argumentation unflatteringly reveals the triumphalism of Hansmann and Kraakman's (2000) declaration that the standard model is now 'a second nature' and that soon enough, also 'legal academics' will regard the ideological and competitive attractions of the standard model 'indisputable' (Hansmann and Kraakman, 2000: 468).

AN EXAMPLE: STUDIES OF CONSEQUENCES OF STATE-LEVEL ANTI-TAKEOVER LEGISLATION

Bertrand and Mullainathan's (2003) study of anti-takeover legislation in the US is exemplary of how the new dogma of the efficiency criteria and the shareholder welfare preference – two normative propositions never addressed in such terms – are innate to corporate governance research at the beginning of the new millennium. They open with the standard argument that managers, left unchecked and not operating under 'takeover threats', the monitoring of 'large shareholders', or reporting to 'effective boards', 'pursue their own goals rather than maximize shareholder wealth' (Bertrand and Mullainathan, 2003: 1044); this in turn, constitutes a 'moral hazard', Bertrand and Mullainathan (2003: 1044) declare. Studying the enactment of anti-takeover law and its consequences, in Bertrand and Mullainathan's (2003) view directly benefiting managerial welfare, three distinct findings are reported: (1) '[p]roduction workers' wages rise by about 1 percent in the protected plants and white-collar wages rise by about 4 percent' (Bertrand and Mullainathan, 2003: 1046); (2) a decline in 'plant creation and destruction' (that is, fewer existing plants were closed and fewer were opened); (3) a null result in terms of capital expenditures' (Bertrand and Mullainathan, 2003: 1046). These results are accompanied by an overall productivity decline (measured in terms of return on capital) 'by nearly 1 percent' (Bertrand and Mullainathan, 2003: 1046). On the basis of these quite unspectacular findings, arguably by and large what the legislators intended to accomplish, Bertrand and Mullainathan (2003) make a number of statements regarding the managers' preferences and skills, more rooted in inherited doctrines than in a more substantial understanding of the role of anti-takeover legislation and the managerial practices that engendered these outcomes.

To start with the question of rising wages, Bertrand and Mullainathan (2003: 1052) admit that one of the main difficulties with the results is the 'extreme noisiness of the Compustat wage data'. Still, the finding that wages rise by 1 per cent for blue-collar workers and up to 4 per cent for white-collar workers is explained by a line of reasoning assuring that 'managers appear to care more about workers, especially white-collar workers, than shareholders do' (Bertrand and Mullainathan, 2003: 1046). This care for the workers is not without benefits for managers, Bertrand and Mullainathan (2003) claim, as it helps to buy them what they refer to as a 'quite life', that is, managerial discretion that does not translate into efficiency gains benefiting shareholders:

> There are several reasons to believe that managers may prefer to pay higher wages than profit-maximizing shareholders do. For example, empire-building managers might care more than owners about the prestige of being surrounded by high-quality workers. High wages can also make a manager's job easier by reducing turnover, reducing the need for bargaining effort in a union context, or simply buying 'peace' from the workers. (Bertrand and Mullainathan, 2003: 1058)

This is therefore, Bertrand and Mullainathan (2003: 1058) argue, clear evidence of moral hazard and more generally 'bad management'. Raising wages for the employees, regardless of industry context and labour market conditions, is thus normatively portrayed as a morally questionable decision bordering on sheer incompetence. However, as Bertrand and Mullainathan (2003: 1058) make clear in the same section, 'popular accounts of raiders raiding firms support this idea, suggesting that some of the gains of a takeover come from reducing the high wages produced by the previously bad management'. In addition, they reference the study of Rosett (1990), who calculated that a substantial share of the shareholders' win is the wage earners' loss in successful hostile takeover bids: '[a] substantial portion of the gains from a takeover can be attributed to a reduction in wages' (Bertrand and Mullainathan, 2003: 1058). In other words, what Bertrand and Mullainathan (2003) normatively describe as a moral hazard and incompetent management is exactly to be unwilling to participate in the transfer of economic wealth from a variety of stakeholders to the specific group of shareholders. Anti-takeover legislation is enacted on a state level, and it is reasonable to assume that such legislative effort is made exactly because it is in the interest of the state to keep well-paid salaried work, the basis for income taxation, within the state rather than to promote shareholder welfare governance that apparently serves to reduce wages and cut jobs to enrich shareholders, who may pay capital gain taxes elsewhere. Bertrand and Mullainathan (2003) thus suggest that managers operating in accordance with novel legislation and the legislator's intentions are either exposed to moral hazard risks and/or act incompetently. Anti-takeover law is therefore discredited on the basis of the normative belief that shareholders are entitled to a larger share of the economic value generated. There is no theoretical or empirical support for this normative assumption made.

In terms of the 'plant death and birth' data, Bertrand and Mullainathan (2003) find little evidence of increased activity. At the same time, they calculate the probability of a 'plant death in a given year' to be about 9 per cent, and the probability of 'a plant birth' to be about 6.5 per cent (Bertrand and Mullainathan, 2003: 1054). That is, there is a relatively high risk of, for example, plant closure in any given year, and yet Bertrand and Mullainathan (2003: 1047) interpret this lack of closure as being evidence of managers' preferences for what they refer to as a 'quiet life'. But there is no evidence whatsoever regarding how much work and effort it would take in any given year to keep a plant running and what kind of intramural activities are required to uphold and maintain existing production activities. Instead, the lack of increased activity in plant death and birth is interpreted along with the rising workers' wages as an indication of managers being lazy, incompetent and not interested in enriching the shareholders. Finally, while Bertrand and Mullainathan (2003: 1047) do not find any empirical support for the standard agency theory argument that managers, left unchecked, 'build empires' to protect themselves from undesirable consequences of market evaluations – which de facto falsifies one of the most widespread arguments put forth to justify shareholder enrichment – they again interpret this to the disfavour of managers as a form of passivity and preference for avoiding 'cognitively difficult activities' (Bertrand and Mullainathan, 2003: 1067). Managers are thus, *ex hypothesi*, put in a double bind: as soon as they engage in decisions that do not directly enrich shareholders they are either acting self-servingly or they are merely demonstrating a preference for doing basically as little as practically possible.

On the basis of this study, a series of observations regarding the shareholder welfare governance literature at the beginning of the new millennium can be formulated. First, the act of legislation, a prerogative of states in turn competing over the incorporation of public companies and job opportunities generating tax income, is by and large discredited as the intentions of the legislators (for example, to distribute economic value between a larger group of stakeholders) are claimed to fabricate moral hazard and promote 'bad management' in predictable ways. Second, when managers follow existing legislation, they are dismissed as being either incompetent and/or being poorly motivated to add economic value. Third, praised qualities such as 'efficiency' and 'productivity' thus by default denote the transfer of economic value from various stakeholders to shareholders and nothing else; this in turn suggests that certain seemingly neutral and technical terms are given specific meanings that they normally do not have in everyday language: they become part of an idiosyncratic economics vocabulary peppered with euphemisms (for example, 'rationalization', 'efficiency', 'moral hazard'). Fourth, the normative stance that shareholders are entitled to, if not all, at least most of the economic value generated (explicitly translated into a decline of wages and job opportunities) is not in any way justified or explained but is simply assumed to be part of the conventional wisdom. Fifth, far-fetched declarations are made regarding managers' preferences unaccompanied by contextual data and empirical details. In short, by 2003, proponents of shareholder welfare governance such as Bertrand and Mullainathan (2003) could legitimately make a series of statements and declarations to pursue their goal to further entrench shareholder welfare and to downplay and discredit legislative practice whenever it counteracts or complicates this stated objective.

RESPONSES TO THE SHAREHOLDER WELFARE ARGUMENTS

Lynn Stout (2002; 2012) is a foremost example of the 'legal academics' who do not yet share Hansmann and Kraakman's (2000) unbridled enthusiasm for 'the standard model'. In fact, Stout undoes[2] the key propositions of the shareholder primacy. She claims that the two main 'theoretical' arguments in favour of shareholder primacy are (1) that shareholders 'own' the firm (in the sense of being the firm's principal and the managers and directors their agents), and (2) that shareholders can legitimately claim the economic value (that is, they are the 'residual claimants' of the corporation). Both these central pillars of the agency theory argument are incorrect and therefore its more practically oriented prescriptions cannot be justified or inform corporate governance practices. However, even *if* the two propositions were correct, Stout says that shareholder welfare is still unrealistic and undesirable, not only for other constituencies and but also for the shareholders themselves.

'From a legal and an economic perspective, the claim that shareholders own the public corporation simply is empirically incorrect', Stout (2002: 1192) writes. Corporations are free-standing, legal entities that 'own themselves', and are not granted the right to delegate the ownership to, for example, shareholders under current corporate legal strictures. This legal condition can also be complemented by economic theory, derived from within the same neoclassical economic theory as agency theory and sharing the underlying assumption that only markets are capable of efficiently pricing assets, suggesting that the firm not only has principals who are owners of stock but also principals who are creditors, again being more or less ignored in the agency theory literature. Stout (2002) references option pricing theory (see, for example, Black and Scholes, 1973), taking into account the role of debt when pricing an option that in turn related to an underlying stock:

> Options theory teaches us that once a firm has issued debt (as almost all firms do), it makes just as much sense to say that the debtholders 'own' the right to the corporation's cash flow but have sold a call option to the shareholder, as it does to say that the shareholder 'owns' the right to the corporation's cash flow but has bought a put option from the debtholders. Put differently, option theory demonstrates that bondholders and equity holders each share contingent control and bear residual risk in firms. (Stout, 2002: 1192)

Indicative of the neglect of the creditors, neither agency theorists, nor legal scholars including Stout make the claim that creditors (debtholders) 'own' the corporation as firms are legal entities in their own right.

Second, the argument that shareholders are the legitimate residual claimants is not true outside of the specific case of bankruptcy law, and this specific case (again also recognizing the creditors' rights) cannot serve as a standard argument in favour of shareholder welfare because managers, shareholders and other stakeholders do not regard bankruptcy as an attractive alternative as it represents – legally, economically and socially – the ultimate failure of the business charter. Instead, in the charter of the incorporated firm, it is the board of directors that is entitled to make the decision as to whether the shareholders should receive dividends (or, indirectly, for example, benefit through stock repurchases): '[a]s a legal matter, shareholders of a public corporation are entitled to receive nothing from the firm *unless and until the board of directors decides that they should receive it*' (Stout, 2002: 1194, emphasis in the original). 'Under existing corporate statutes', Bebchuk (2007: 681) writes, 'shareholders cannot adopt decisions to amend the corporate charter, merge, reincorporate, or dissolve the company; such decisions must be initiated by the board'. Lan and Heracleous (2010: 302) further substantiate the claim regarding board discretion by referencing existing court ruling:

> In a multitude of legal cases, judges have refused to allow shareholders to overrule board decisions on management matters, and common law courts have from early on in the life of the modern corporation supported centralization of power within the board. The legal system and legal precedent thus point to the doctrinal inefficiency of shareholder primacy (under the law, directors are expected to use their independent judgment to make decisions that are in the interest of the corporation, even if this is contrary to

shareholders' interests), as well as its practical inefficacy (the courts have consistently upheld the high levels of autonomy of directors). (Lan and Heracleous, 2010: 302)

In other words, when agency theorists advocate shareholder welfare governance or when Hansmann and Kraakman (2000) take the argument one step further, claiming that corporate law *should* prescribe and justify shareholder welfare, they make statements regarding how things *should be* on the basis of how they believe things *would be* in the best of the possible worlds of unlimited shareholder authority: 'the argument for shareholder primacy becomes a tautology: corporate law *ought* to incorporate shareholder primacy (or so the argument goes) because shareholders *ought* to be the firm's sole residual claimants' (Stout, 2002: 1195). Also in practical terms, the authority of shareholders is more of a desired state for some commentators than a factual condition, Bebchuk (2007: 732) says: '[t]he shareholder franchise is a myth. Shareholders commonly do not have a viable power to replace the directors of public companies. Electoral challenges are rare, and the risk of replacement via a proxy contest is extremely low'.

In addition to the undoing of the legal basis of shareholder welfare governance, Stout (2002) turns to the actual financial and economic practices to further undermine the practical legitimacy and usefulness of shareholder welfare. One case where the attractiveness of the shareholder primacy model can be demonstrated is in Initial Public Offerings (IPOs) programmes where, for example, start-up firms or firms previously held in private equity issue stocks to raise finance capital. In the IPO contracts, it is possible to manifest the shareholders' rights and privileges, Stout (2002: 1207) says, but the crux is that such charters are apparently unattractive as there are virtually no companies that adhere to the 'standard model': '[i]f shareholders really valued shareholder primacy rules, one would think at least a few promoters might have thought of inserting such provisions in the corporate charter at the IPO stage' (Stout, 2002: 1207). In a more recent publication, Stout (2012) suggests that many firms, in some cases remarkably successful firms such as Google and LinkedIn, choose to 'go public' with 'dual-class voting structures that disenfranchise public shareholders almost entirely' (Stout, 2012: 8–9). In addition, as a response to Hansmann and Kraakman's (2000) argument in favour of a 'standard model', Stout (2012: 8) says that there is evidence that American states demonstrate (1) a significant variety of the charters for the incorporation of businesses, and (2) that states with corporate law that 'offer directors strong protection against hostile takeovers, seem more successful in attracting new incorporations and in retaining existing firms, than states whose laws are more "shareholder friendly"' (Stout, 2012: 8). That is, there is no 'standard model' – not even in the more restricted case of the US – and the 'shareholder friendliness' of such a charter appears to be unattractive for firms raising capital in finance markets.

On the basis of Stout's (2002; 2012) argumentation, there is good reason to question the accuracy of the agency theory model underlying shareholder welfare governance on both theoretical and empirical grounds. Agency theory, Weinstein (2013: 46) suggests, must be regarded as a 'performative theory' rather than 'a positive one', that is, the role of agency theory is not so much about capturing the inner essence of an efficient and fair social or economic governance system but to serve as a vehicle for the very *transformation* of corporate governance per se. Its value resides not so much in accuracy and logical coherence as in its vigorous and engaging narrative regarding firms, management, governance and the creation and distribution of economic value under the influence of the preference for 'efficiency' – the foundational and unquestioned principle of price theory, contractarian theory and agency theory – over other social and economic objectives. And yet such an analysis generates the puzzling question as to why and how 'the standard model' became so influential. Perhaps the neoclassical economic theory concepts of rent-seeking and opportunistic behaviour apply?

To start with, Weinstein (2013) proposes, agency theory and its shareholder welfare programme was part of the advancement of finance theory in the 1970s as being a new branch in the neoclassical economic theory framework being able to provide logically consistent and practically useful models that helped finance market actors make sense of their professional work (Mackenzie, 2006: 265); agency theory thus advances a 'quasi-financial conception of the corporation' (Weinstein, 2013: 53). In this enactment of the firm, the concept of 'efficiency' was advanced as a term that denotes specific and virtuous qualities that now compete with other economic parameters such as *stability*, the leitmotif of managerial capitalism. In addition, Stout (2012) and many other commentators have remarked, the agency theory model not only provided a simplified and seemingly coherent theoretical framework, understandable for virtually anyone, but it also fitted nicely into the institutional model of the pro-business mobilization of the 1970s and 1980s, where capital owners generously financed think-tanks, lobbyists, learned societies and academic communities to re-examine the nature of economic systems and corporate capitalism. These financiers understood that not all battles could be won through head-on offensives, but sponsored free market advocacy to gain benefits in a medium to long-term perspective. And yet the agency theory model – in a way a 'vending machine theory' typical of the new pro-business and private capital-backed institutions – justified the interest of capital owners as it discredited other constituencies' claims to, for example, the economic value generated. Says Stout:

> To the popular press and business media, shareholder primacy offered an easy-to-explain sound-bite description of what corporations are and what they are supposed to do. To businesspeople and reformers seeking a way to distinguish between good and bad governance practices, the shareholder-centric view promised a single, easily-read measure of corporate performance in the form of share price. (Stout, 2012: 3)

As a consequence, which Hansmann and Kraakman (2000: 454) make clear, there were 'no important competitors to the standard model of corporate governance'. Those who thought otherwise were not taken very seriously:

> Some commentators continued to argue valiantly for a more stakeholder-friendly view of the public corporation, but they were increasingly dismissed as sentimental, sandals-wearing leftists whose hearts outweighed their heads. Shareholder primacy became widely viewed as the only intellectually respectable theory of corporate purpose, and 'maximize shareholder value' the only proper goal of boards of directors. (Stout, 2012: 3)

So, 'at the end of history' (Hansmann and Kraakman, 2000), executives and directors are equipped with a theoretico-practical framework that has acquired a hegemonic status, effectively pushing all the critique to the margins by its sheer weight and influence, but that at the same time fails to live up to even the most elementary qualities of a theoretical proposition. Moreover, if Stout (2002; 2012) is right, shareholder welfare is by and large not chosen by the business people themselves when they do have a choice when they issue stock or choose the state wherein to incorporate their businesses. The end of history (here dated to 2001), instead of being the beginning of a long and harmonious Golden Age, just as in Francis Fukuyama's argument, proved to be something entirely different; that is, as Fligstein (2005) suggests, the last and most accelerated phase of the regime of investor capitalism.

A MANAGEMENT THEORY REVISION OF CORPORATE GOVERNANCE

Management scholars have always had a quite inharmonious relationship with neoclassical descriptions of governance practices, basically because management theory by and large rests on a behavioural theory of the firm (Simon, 1976; 1957; Cyert and March, 1963) rather than rational choice theory and utilitarian principles. In the field of corporate governance, the neoclassical agency theory model has been hugely influential, but over the last decades there has been a growing impatience with its theoretical inconsistency and its inability to make predictions and, practically speaking, to create a more robust corporate governance system.[3] The legal theory critique articulated by Lynn Stout, William Bratton, Melvin Eisenberg and many other legal scholars is thus a welcome contribution to the revision of corporate governance theory. Lubatkin (2005: 213) argues that agency theory is 'a theory which only an orthodox, micro-economist could love', as it is based on deductive reasoning on the basis of the axiomatic first principle of self-interest being at the very heart of the reductionist methodology of rational choice theory. When adhering to this description, the management studies fieldworker is likely to encounter something entirely different from what they might expect, Lubatkin argues: '[t]hose of us who have attempted to use the Jensen and Meckling principal–agent model to explain organizational phenomena have unwittingly borrowed a theory that describes a "bizarro" worldview, one entirely different from that which we, as organizational scholars, should reasonably hold as self-evident' (Lubatkin, 2005: 213).

In particular, Lubatkin (2005: 215) is concerned, like many other empirically oriented corporate governance researchers, with the idea of the presence of consistent managerial shirking in corporations: 'you don't have to be an organizational scholar to understand that managers and principals learn from past interactions; they are not the kind of social dopes that the Jensen and Meckling (1976) model would have us believe'. While Lubatkin (2005) is critical of the Jensen and Meckling (1976) model on the basis of empirical research work and experience, Lan and Heracleous (2010) more closely follow the legal theory critique of agency theory, the nexus of contract view of the firm, and the shareholder welfare governance derived from the two first theoretical frameworks, and seek to revise agency theory to better respond to empirical observations. Their synthesis of agency theory and legal theory includes three major propositions, closely following the mainstream legal theory view:

1. The shareholder is not the 'principal' but the corporation is the legal entity that owns itself (Lan and Heracleous, 2010: 295).
2. The board is not an agent (and especially not the shareholders' agent) but is an 'autonomous fiduciary', that is, 'someone who is entrusted with the power to act on behalf of and for the benefit of a

beneficiary' (Lan and Heracleous, 2010: 295). In this view, directors enjoy decision-making jurisdiction beyond the interests of shareholders.

3.   As a consequence of (2), the board is not an instrument to maximize the pricing of the corporation's publicly held stocks but serves as a 'mediating hierarch'. In this role, the board '[b]alances the often competing claims and interest of the groups that contributes to the team production process, makes decisions on the allocation of team surpluses, and is legally ultimately in control of a corporation's assets and key strategic decisions' (Lan and Heracleous, 2010: 295).

Lan and Heracleous' (2010) revision of corporate governance theory in the light of the critique of the existing 'standard model' is thus a fairly unspectacular management theory adaptation of the mainstream legal theory criticism. What is particularly noteworthy is that the board of directors should work in the interest of a wider set of constituencies, and thus should potentially be in the position to avoid the undersocialized view (Granovetter, 1985) of corporate governance that Lubatkin (2005) sees as one of the most conspicuous weaknesses of 'the standard model'; 'governance entails a complex set of dynamics that does not lend itself to reductionist and undersocialized theorizing' Lubatkin (2005: 215). 'Agency theory neglects to consider what general obligations, moral or otherwise, principals might have either to their agents or to other groups inside or outside the firm', Donaldson (2012: 264) adds.

In summary, 'the standard model' is far from taken for granted, and as it becomes subject to systematic scholarly criticism, its legitimacy erodes to the point at which it can no longer sustain its authority. In its place, a revised and less theoretically purified yet empirically relevant theory of corporate governance is presented, wherein shareholder value creation may still be a legitimate and widely recognized corporate governance principle, but no longer on the basis of the premises advocated by agency theorists including contractual rights, alleged efficiency benefits, and supposedly reduced agency costs.

As Weinstein (2013: 49) remarks, the shareholder primacy governance needs to be understood in a wider socio-economic change where 'financial capitalism' is advanced as the new dominant economic regime. In the following sections, the concept of 'shareholder value ideology' (Weinstein, 2013: 49) will be examined as being an integral component of the movement towards increased financialization of the economy in the era of investor capitalism – the new regime of competitive capitalism.

THE ADVANCEMENT OF INVESTOR CAPITALISM AND THE GROWTH OF THE FINANCE SECTOR: MONEY MANAGEMENT CAPITALISM AND OVERBANKING

Conard (1988) introduced the term *investor capitalism* at the end of the 1980s, a decade of straightforward free market deregulation on the basis of economic ideas advocated by neoliberal, libertarian and conservative advisors, think-tankers and lobbyists, and leading to a finance industry expansion. In Conard's (1988) view, the preceding regime of managerial capitalism (see Marris, 1964) offered some advantages, including the ability to make enterprises grow to 'enormous dimensions', a condition that Conard (1988) says was propelled by the number of shareholders participating effectively in the governance of the firm through the central mechanisms of executives and the board of directors. *Investor capitalism*, in turn, would '[r]ecapture the essential genius of capitalism by restoring primacy to the interest of the suppliers of capital' (Conard, 1988: 135). The essence of investor capitalism is therefore to restore the authority of capital owners at the executives' and managers' expense. Only by balancing the interest of principals and agents can capitalist accumulation be more effective, and during the post-World War II period, Conard (1988) suggests, executives and managers have gained the upper hand as they have been able to construct large-scale corporations and conglomerates around them to protect their own rather than capital investors' interest.

Finance Industry Growth

There is an abundance of statistics that reveal the recovery of the finance industry as the dominant economic actor in contemporary competitive capitalism. The literature indicates two features of the finance industry: its growth in size and in proportion and its concentration into a smaller number of finance market institutions. First of all, the finance industry has grown remarkably after 1980: '[a]t its peak in 2006, the financial services sector contributed 8.3 percent to US GDP, compared to 4.9 percent in 1980 and 2.8 percent in 1950' (Greenwood and Scharfstein, 2013: 3). This growth of the finance industry in turn accounted for 'more than a quarter of the growth of the services sector as a whole' in the US (Greenwood and Scharfstein, 2013: 3). In terms of the growth of the economic value of the finance industry, the industry has basically doubled after 1980: 'the value of total financial assets was approximately five times US GDP in 1980; by 2007, this ratio had doubled' (Greenwood and Scharfstein, 2013: 4). Philippon and Reshef (2013) demonstrate that this growth of the finance industry in the advanced Western capitalist economies after 1980 is a return to the 1870–1910 period of finance industry growth:

> Until 1910 financial output [measured as bank loans/GDP in relation to log real GDP per capita] and income grow together: ... Income continues to grow, while finance contracts. In the postwar period, after 1950, financial output grows with income. But after 1980 the relationship changes; the proportional change (elasticity) of financial output with respect to income is much higher after 1980 relative to 1951–1980. (Philippon and Reshef, 2013: 77–8)

The so-called FIRE sector (Finance, Insurance and Real Estates) is growing in proportion vis-à-vis other industries. Deutschmann (2011: 353) reports data from Europe and the 27 member states of the European Union showing that the so-called FIRE sector contributed with no less than 28.8 per cent of GDP in 2010. In comparison, industry added 18.5 per cent and even in countries with a strong and export-oriented manufacturing industry such as Germany, the FIRE sector represented 30.4 per cent and manufacturing industry 23.4 per cent of GDP.

The growth of the finance industry, an industry endowed with the charter to produce money (Cassidy, 2009), can partially be explained by the unprecedented growth of new financial assets such as derivatives and securities, finance assets developed to make illiquid assets (for example, home mortgages) liquid through the 'dicing and slicing' of such long-term contracts into derivate instruments traded on global finance markets. By 2007, the total estimated value of derivatives was US$600 trillion according to the United Nations, a figure responding to 964 per cent of world GDP (Levitt, 2013: 166). That is, the finance industry today creates synthetic economic values that outnumber actual economic value by a factor of ten. Greenwood and Scharfstein (2013: 5) argue that the more or less doubling of the finance industry after 1980 in the US can be explained on the basis of two related activities: '[a]sset management and the provision of household credit'. To start with, household debt approximately doubled between 1980, when it stood at 48 per cent of GDP, and 2007, when this figure had reached 99 per cent of GDP (Greenwood and Scharfstein, 2013: 5; see also Zinman, 2015: 254). As mortgage lending was 'liberalized' (widely interpreted by market actors and, more importantly, regulators as being indicative of increasing market efficiency, in turn being the fruits of the deregulation of the finance markets), household debt rose to unprecedented levels in the US economy (Zinman, 2015; Peñaloza and Barnhart, 2011; Hyman, 2011; Montgomerie,

2009; Barba and Pickett, 2009). This in turn created a new market for securities as illiquid mortgages were repackaged as mortgage-backed securities (MBS) (Mian and Sufi, 2014; McConnell and Buser, 2011). Between 1980 and 2007, the 'securities industry' quadrupled from 0.4 per cent of GDP to 1.7 per cent of GDP (Greenwood and Scharfstein, 2013: 7). Milberg (2008: 428) shows that the money supply, defined as 'the sum of currency outside banks, demand deposits other than those of the central government, and the time, savings and foreign currency deposits of resident sectors other than the central government', has grown sharply between the mid-1990s and 2006; in the period, the average inflation has been around 2 per cent, while during the same period of time, 'money supply growth rose by over 7 per cent per annum' (Milberg, 2008: 428).

One of the consequences of the growth of the finance industry after 1980 is the increase in economic compensation in the FIRE sector, in turn leading to a growing inflow of talents in finance, previously embarking on other types of careers in, for example, the sciences and engineering. In 1980, a 'financial services employee' earned about the same as his or her counterpart in other industries, while by 2007, the finance industry employee earned on average 70 per cent more than their counterpart (Greenwood and Scharfstein, 2013: 4–5). Checking for the factors of technological development and higher skill levels in the industry, Philippon and Reshef (2013: 94) found that this change in economic compensation policy is robust, not explained by any changes in economic fundamentals. As a consequence, the finance industry was able to attract talent (operationalized by Greenwood and Scharfstein, 2013, as the proportion of Harvard graduates being recruited to the finance industry): in the 1969–73 period, 6 per cent of Harvard graduates went into financial services; in 2008, 28 per cent did so (Greenwood and Scharfstein, 2013: 5).

Not only has the finance industry grown in absolute and relative size, it is also able to collect an increasingly large share of the aggregated profits in advanced economies. In the case of the US, this figure has increased significantly after 1980:

> Financial sector profits as a proportion of all profits in the economy grew slowly between 1848 and 1970, dropped across the 1970s, and increased dramatically after 1980 ... This trend peaked in 2002 when 45 percent of all taxable profits in the private sector were absorbed by finance sector firms. (Tomaskovic-Devey and Lin, 2011: 539–40)

The question is then to what extent the economic system of competitive capitalism benefits from this finance industry expansion. Philippon and

Reshef (2013: 93) argue it is '[d]ifficult to believe that the growth of finance has not come with some benefits'[4] – either in the form of credit being more widely available and cheaper to acquire (that is, credit is 'democratized') or leading to an increase in the 'quality of services' – Philippon and Reshef (2013) still cannot provide any straightforward conclusion regarding the economic benefits of a sizeable finance industry, especially not in economies like America's, with large and growing finance industries. On the contrary, empirical data reveals that '[t]here is a small negative correlation after 1950 between financial output and GDP growth per capita' (Philippon and Reshef, 2013: 79):

> there is no particular correlation between the size of the financial sector and economic growth in time series data ... While there is a positive relationship between credit and income in the period after 1950, this relationship changes considerably after 1980 when income grows more slowly relative to credit. (Philippon and Reshef, 2013: 94)

As the post-World War II period until 1980 – a key year in both Philippon and Reshef's (2013) and Greenwood and Scharfstein's (2013) analyses[5] – was characterized by a slower rate of finance industry growth, the reduction of economic inequality and the expansion of the welfare state, income spent on financial services correlates negatively with economic growth: '[o]verall, we see that most of the rise in living standards after 1870 was obtained with less income spent on finance and less financial output than what is observed after 1980; and the relationship between financial output and income has changed after 1980' (Philippon and Reshef, 2013: 79).

The economic benefits of a sizeable finance industry can thus be debated both in terms of its direct consequences (that is, its factual correlation with economic growth and other key economic fundamentals) and indirect consequences (that is, how talented younger people increasingly engage in money management rather than embarking on, for example, scientific careers, thus reducing, at least in theory, the innovative capacity of an economy in a long-term perspective).

What further complicates the image is that there is strong evidence of market concentration (oligopolistic tendencies), not the least after the 2008 finance market collapse which led to a restructuring of the US finance sector including bankruptcies, mergers and consolidations (Blinder, 2013). Even prior to these events, the concentration of economic wealth in a limited number of finance market institutions has been accounted for: '[i]n 1990 the ten largest US financial institutions held only 10% of financial assets – now it is 50%; the top twenty institutions hold 70% (compared with only 12% in 1990)' (Wray, 2009: 818). The concentration of finance capital has led to a situation where individual finance market institutions control more economic wealth than many national states in which they are registered and from which they have acquired their charter to operate. In, for example, the Eurozone, this condition is an acute political concern in the case of finance market downturns as countries can no longer afford to bail out its banks. One such case was Iceland, a small Northern welfare state republic hosting no less than three major international banks, unable to take over the bank's liabilities when they failed as part of the global finance market collapse of 2008. Blyth (2013: 6) offers more empirical evidence of this condition, saying that by 2008, France's three biggest banks '[h]ave assets worth nearly two and a half times French GDP'. Blyth (2013) continues:

> [In 2008] [t]he top two German banks had assets equal to 114 percent of German GDP ... Deutsche Bank had an asset footprint of over 80 percent of German GDP and runs an operational leverage of around 40 to 1 ... One bank, ING in Holland, has an asset footprint that is 211 percent of its sovereign's GDP. The top four British banks have a combined asset footprint of 394 percent of UK GDP. The top three Italian banks constitute a mere 115 percent of GDP, and yet Britain seems to get a free pass by the bond markets in comparison to Italy. (Blyth, 2013: 83; see also Dodd, 2014: 114)

When banks and other finance market institutions outgrow the national economies in which they are incorporated, a 'too big to fail' scenario crystallizes, where the allegedly 'real economy' will tumble down when finance institutions collapse, which in turn institutes moral hazard that neither politicians nor finance markets are eager to recognize, nor to handle practically. That is, the last decades of policy-making and finance industry regulation, based on the frisky assertion that 'rational markets can take care of themselves' (in Alan Greenspan's much-cited adage, cited in Palma, 2009: 831), led to little self-correcting behaviour as risk-taking was rewarded rather than punished by markets. The long-term consequence was that the state had to use tax money to save the banks and to restore the economic system of competitive capitalism in a programme that free market protagonists would certainly have branded 'collectivism' or 'socialism' if it had benefited stakeholders other than finance market oligarchies. The unprecedented growth of the finance industry was thus not primarily explained on the basis of the virtues of realized free market efficiencies and increasingly professional finance theory know-how and expertise, as the proponents of finance market deregulation had persistently argued, but because finance market actors were given carte blanche to increase the risk-taking (operationalized as leveraged capitalization) while not having to worry about the downside risks that could be pushed onto taxpayers and state agencies. As stated by, for example, former Fed chairman Ben Bernanke, these moral hazards, more actual than merely theoretical, appear to be endemic in this finance market governance model (Cassidy, 2009: 320).

The Drivers of Finance Market Expansion: Capital Inflow and Deregulation

The finance industry expansion is a widely documented phenomenon, being a central component in the regime of investor capitalism. 'There is little question that the U.S. economy has experienced a remarkable turn towards financial activities in recent years', Krippner (2011: 3) states. The question is then how the finance industry could be transformed from being a support function within the economic system of competitive system to become its *primus motor*.

In the 1970s, when the profit levels of American industry declined and unemployment rose, there was still the puzzling presence of inflation, primarily derived from the rising energy costs caused by the unwilling-ness of the OPEC countries to export oil to countries that politically supported Israel during the 1973 war in the Middle East. According to the conventional wisdom of economic theory, unemployment would push down compensation claims, leading to lower inflation in the economy, but such theoretical models were incapable of explaining the new situation. President Jimmy Carter hired Paul Volcker as the chairman of the Federal Reserve in 1979 and assigned him the explicit goal of bringing down the inflation figures as soon as possible (Stein, 2011). Volcker embarked on a high-interest policy that failed to reduce inflation but instead and somewhat unexpectedly served to make the American bond market attractive for overseas savers. Krippner (2010: 157) accounts for the capital inflow in the American economy in the Reagan era: '$85 billion in 1983, $103 billion in 1984, $129 billion in 1985, and a staggering $221 billion in 1986'. As a consequence, overseas savings poured into the US economy, further inflating the value of the US dollar, which in turn undermined the competitiveness of the American manufac-turing industry, already being criticized for its inability to uphold its productivity growth and profit levels:

> The high interest rates yielded a high dollar, which priced U.S. manufacturing out of the world markets. Instead of fingering the dollar, pundits questioned U.S. industry's ability to compete with foreign companies. But unlike government and the service sectors, productivity in manufacturing increased

over 3 percent in 1984 and 1985. The expensive dollar aborted an industrial renaissance. The dollar's overall value rose 63 percent from 1980 to March 1985 – the equivalent of taxing U.S. exports by 63 percent and providing U.S. import with an equivalent subsidy. (Stein, 2011: 269)

At the same time, what seriously harmed the export-oriented manufacturing industry, providing the bulk of blue-collar jobs in the US economy, was highly beneficial for the emerging finance industry, the new favourite industry for free market protagonists as it was the most 'pure' of industries in its reliance on market transactions and calculative practices to price its commodities, and therefore being closer to the armchair economist's image of the efficient and self-regulating market. As opposed to, for example, the oligarchic manufacturing industry, bound up with trade union activism, close-knit ties with Washington politicians and policy-making bodies, and above all being the foremost representative of the managerial capitalism regime including supposedly ineffective and slow-to-adopt executives, the finance industry was in a way (in theory) the rational choice theorist's nirvana: individual actors who operated on a highly liquid market on the basis of their own calculations and essentially being unrestrained by wider socio-economic interest and concerns. Unburdened by industry traditions, for economists and finance theorists, the finance market actor was in a way representing the image of the free-floating calculating brain, strictly operating on the basis of self-interest, which, as Adam Smith long ago asserted, was favouring everybody's long-term interest through its tendency to punish and marginalize ineffective decision-making and unskilled venturing.

In the early 1980s, the significant capital inflow in the US economy further reinforced economic ideas regarding the virtues of the finance market and the qualifications of its actors. The new finance market growth was also supported by political reform, part of the Reagan administration's new 'pro-business agenda', where think-tankers and lobbyists recruited from industry and business-backed institutions served as officers and advisors in the new administration: '[t]he U.S. economy made the transition from being a system in which the flows were subject to state controls internally and externally to one in which all such constraints had been removed' (Krippner, 2010: 165). These finance market reforms also benefited domestic savings, and, for example, the savings and loan associations (eventually subject to the first major finance crisis of the 1980s) reported a sharp growth in their holdings:

> As the capital market institutionalized, S&L [Savings and Loan Associations] underwent deregulation, and mutual funds expanded, new sources of capital became available to merger activities ... In 1978, foreign funds, S&Ls, and

mutual funds held \$103.2 billion (10 percent) of all corporate liabilities. By 1983, the holdings of these three groups increased threefold (to \$301.8 billion, or 19 percent). (Stearns and Allan, 1996: 704–5)

While the American economy was quickly deindustrialized (Bluestone and Harrison, 1982), the 1980s were the heydays of Wall Street, the beginning of what Krippner (2011) refers to as *la belle époque* of finance, ending abruptly in 2008 (but thereafter more or less continuing its operations is if nothing ever happened, a few institutions disappearing taken aside). In the 1990s, the pro-finance market policy reforms continued more or less without disruption, and during the Clinton administration (1993–2000) the number of laws pertaining to finance passed by Congress increased from around 5 per cent to 25 per cent of all new legislation (Martin, 2002: 28). The pro-finance market policy culminated with the repeal of the New Deal era Glass–Steagall Act when the Financial Services Modernization Act (often referred to as the Gramm–Leach–Bliley Act) was enacted in 1999 and the Commodity Futures Modernization Act of 2000 followed suit, two political decisions which 'created opportunities for management to transfer much of the risk to unsuspecting investors by using complex financial instruments in unregulated equity markets' (Prechel and Morris, 2010: 350). For critics such as Suárez and Kolodny (2011: 76), the Financial Services Modernization Act facilitated a '[c]hange in the institutional landscape of the financial industry but without creating a corresponding regulatory structure to oversee it'. When the global economy entered the new millennium, the global finance industry was no longer the maid of competitive capitalism: it was its master.

As demonstrated by, for example, Fligstein and Habinek (2014), as part of the post-2008 analysis and the various grievances issued regarding the finance market instabilities that few saw (or cared to worry about), there is strong evidence of the exportation of finance market deregulation policy to other parts of the global economy through the issuing and transfer of, for example, new complex finance instruments such as MBS and CDO (LiPuma and Lee, 2004). The transfer of such assets served to both spread the risks from the issuer of the instrument but also to 'infect' the whole global economy with overcapitalization and excessive risk-taking, leading to the systemic failure that Posner (2009) and a handful of other free market advocators were alarmed about. '[B]etween 2001 and 2007, banks from mostly Western European countries dramatically increased their holdings of US MBS and CDO', Fligstein and Habinek (2014: 639) report. The globalization of such financial assets was accentuated in the 2002–05 period, when the sub-prime market quickly expanded in the US: '[f]rom 2002 to 2005, private-label securitization soared. As a percentage of all MBS issued, it increased from less than 20 to over 50 percent from 2002 to 2006, before collapsing entirely in 2007' (Mian and Sufi, 2014: 97).

Money Management Capitalism and the Liquidity Preference of Finance Market Actors

In a society where the finance industry grows in proportion to the rest of the economy, there is pressure to make illiquid assets more liquid and to make them amenable for finance market engineering. Hyman Minsky (1980) stresses that the 'essential liquidity preference' in any capitalist economy is what unifies 'bankers and businessmen', and this preference strongly affects how the finance industry values economic assets. Unfortunately, Minsky adds, any economic system based on a high degree of liquidity also encourages speculation, leading to an endemic instability of the finance-based capitalist economic system: '[t]he financial processes of a capitalist economy introduce instability by making a tranquil state unstable in an upward direction and set flexible limits to this upward expansion', Minsky (1980: 518) suggests. This means that theories about 'general equilibrium' in the economy, widely recognized in neoclassical economic theory (Fazzari and Minsky, 1984), are not very helpful as soon as actual economic conditions are examined, Minsky (1980) says:

> Once we shift from an abstract economy and turn to analyzing the behavior of a capitalist economy with expensive capital assets and a sophisticated financial system, the equilibrium, equilibrating, and stability properties derived in standard economic theory are not relevant. Such a capitalist economy is unstable due to endogenous forces which reflect financing processes. These processes transform a tranquil and relatively stable system into one in which a continued accelerating expansion of debts, investment, profits, and prices is necessary to prevent a deep depression. (Minsky, 1980: 519)

What Minsky called *money manager capitalism* is an economic system where liquidity is favoured over illiquidity (Whalen, 2002; 1997; Chick, 1997; Dymski, 1997), and, as a consequence, it represents the triumph of 'speculation over enterprise' (Wray, 2009: 810). Investing in production capital means to build a stock of tangible resources, dependent on a variety of skills and professional expertise, and only after some time and within a relatively complex system of production activities, price setting, market interactions and negotiations, and transactions can the illiquid capital generate liquid finance capital. One additional consequence of money manager capitalism is, Bryan and Rafferty (2014) remark, that unlike in previous regimes of competitive capitalism, 'people's subordination to capital comes not just from the extraction of a surplus in the workplace', but now, when they *own* illiquid assets (for example, homes and mortgage loans) and *hold debt*, they become subordinated to the interest of finance market actors in two ways. First, by transforming the illiquid assets they hold into liquid financial, tradable assets (for example, mortgage-backed securities), and thereafter, the very same homeowners functionally serve as 'systemic "shock absorbers" in global financial markets' (Bryan and Rafferty, 2014: 891).

As Beckert (2013) notes, being willing to be indebted is a key mechanism in capitalist economies, but such 'bets on the future' cannot be taken for granted:

> On the side of the debtors, the expansion of credit relations presupposes the willingness to become indebted in order to increase monetary wealth in the future. This can also not be taken for granted: borrowing money for investment has a social precondition in a life plan of individuals that is directed towards upward social mobility and entails the willingness to engage in risks and speculation to increase one's wealth. (Beckert, 2013: 332)

Bryan and Rafferty (2014: 891) thus suggest that the 'substantial meaning of financialization' is not only that the finance industry grows in proportion in terms of standard measures such as turnover and profit levels, but that it gradually penetrates non-financial industries and the everyday life of human beings as the 'financial ways of calculating are becoming more pervasive socially'. Today, as Davis (2009) makes clear, virtually nothing is spared in the attempt to transform illiquid assets into liquid finance assets through calculative practices and contracting in finance markets; any asset can be financialized.

Within the neoclassical economic theory framework, price volatility is explained on the basis of shifts in supply and demand, but as supply is reasonably stable in a short-term perspective (if conflicts such as strikes can be avoided, cutting down on supply more or less immediately), the demand may vary over time. Price volatility can also derive from market manipulation if, for example, producers and traders hoard commodities to push up prices. In addition, and of relevance in this setting, price volatility in an economic system dominated by the finance capital preference for liquid assets may primarily derive from speculation, and especially if policy-makers believe that such speculation is part of the regular market procedure to price assets such as commodities and therefore permit finance market interventions into commodities markets

(Wray, 2009: 822; for an extended argument, see Sockin and Xiong, 2015; Henderson et al., 2014; Singleton, 2014; Tang and Xiong, 2012). Cheng and Xiong (2014: 419) examine how the global oil market suffered from finance capital investors' escape from the previously lucrative home mortgage market in 2007, when the sub-prime market finally proved to be unsustainable, and capital investments were brought elsewhere. While many economic fundamentals indicated a slow-down in the world economy, likely to be accompanied by a lower oil price, the index for Brent oil on the contrary continued to soar in the spring of 2008:

> The S&P 500, the FTSE 100, DAX, and Nikkei equity indices had peaked by October 2007; with the collapse of Bear Stearns in March 2008, and the world financial system was facing imminent trouble ... With the benefit of hindsight, it is difficult to argue that the growth of emerging economies, themselves slowing, was strong enough to more than offset the weakness in the developed economies to push up oil prices by over 40% over the first half of 2008. (Cheng and Xiong, 2014: 419)

Cheng and Xiong (2014) show that this seemingly contradictory evidence, one based on an 'actual' downturn in the economic cycle, and one based on oil price speculation, was interpreted by policy-makers and regulators in ways that performatively produced a rise in interest rates, which in turn further cooled off an already declining economy:

> In fact, the large commodity prices increases even motivated the ECB to increase its key interest rate in early July 2008, just before the bust in oil prices. Thus, the large increases in commodity prices in early 2008, a portion of which may be attributable to investment inflows into commodity markets coming from the declining real estate market ... may have temporarily influenced people's expectations of global economic strength and thus commodity demand by distorting price signals. (Cheng and Xiong, 2014: 419)

The stock of liquid capital released from the waning US sub-prime market was thus piped into oil market price speculation, and the subsequent rise in oil prices was interpreted in ways that further prevented the recovery of a faltering economy. Cheng and Xiong's (2014) case is thus one first-hand account of the presence of speculation in money manager capitalism, but also indicating how the preference for liquid assets in fact raises the costs for investment in production capital. For Minskyans (Hyman Minsky passed away in 1996), the current economic recession is a convincing case of the failure of a policy regime based on 'deregulation, reduced oversight, privatization, and consolidation of market power' (Wray, 2009: 826). Such statements have engendered much debate regarding the sustainability of the existing capitalist economic system, dominated by finance industry interests. Tabb (2013: 527) doubts that is the case, saying that 'when the financial sector moves beyond lubricating the wheels of commerce to dominate the real economy, problems develop'.

The Sustainability of Investor and Money Management Capitalism

Müller (2014) makes the point that financialization, being both the driver and the foremost consequence of the new enactment of the firm (that is, these two changes are co-produced), is not a consequence of the finance industry meddling with the 'real economy' but rather the *distancing* between the finance industry and non-financial industries, the 'dissolution' of their historical bonds: '[f]inancialization does not entail close institutional interconnections between banks and industry, but rather their dissolution and a widening of the distance between them' (Müller, 2014: 548). He continues:

> Financialized capitalism is marked less by direct institutional ties and more by anonymous structural imperatives. It is, therefore, not a contradiction to state that the intermediate influence of the financial sector has shrunk, but that the finance *logic* – which ultimately boils down to the logic of money capital – has gained influence through the tighter coupling of listed companies to capital markets. (Müller, 2014: 548)

For instance, in the regime of managerial capitalism, banks were not primarily interested in maximizing their profits but in having their loans repaid, and therefore they engaged in long-term relationships with their clients. This in turn led to the delegation of the responsibility to manage the corporations to, for example, engineers and accountants, two groups that favoured long-term growth and economic stability over a short-term distribution of profits. As a consequence, profits were reinvested in production capital, a decision that agency theorists systematically treat as the squandering of the shareholders' capital. In contrast, Müller (2014: 548) contends, 'financialization implies a strengthening of financial discipline in spite of much loosened institutional ties between finance and industry'. The institutional relations between finance industry actors and non-financial industries that dominated in the era of managerial capitalism have now been deinstitutionalized in the regime of investor capitalism and its most advanced form of money manager capitalism. Phenomena being discussed under 'the rubric of financialization' can be traced back to the dominance of the circuit of money capital, Müller (2014: 548) concludes. The consequences of this deinstitutionalization of managerial capitalism under the aegis of market efficiency are yet to be determined, and it is far from too early to oversee all the consequences of radical ideas such as the shareholder primacy, but there is no lack of commentators who express their deep concerns regarding the new situation:

> In the twenty-first century, financialization has achieved new highs of dizziness, far beyond anything ... imagined. With the invention of derivatives, and their metastasization, the commodification of money has floated so free of the materiality of social life as to take on a life of its own. Untethered from reality and out of control, securitization has unleashed a tsunami of insecurity, nearly crushing the world economy, bringing down governments, mortgages and destroying the jobs and the livelihood of billions of people. (Fraser, 2014: 553)

Next, the consequences of investor capitalism and money manager capitalism on the firm level – what Krier (2005) refers to as *speculative management* – will be examined in greater detail. Did the agency theory prescription, aimed at reducing agency costs – the most important and sizeable cost generated by the corporate system based on business charters, agency theorists claim – lead to a more efficient economy, higher profit levels, lower level of unemployment, or improvements in any other economic fundamentals as suggested by the free market protagonists? In short, is investor capitalism a better economic system than managerial capitalism in terms of firm efficiency?

CORPORATE GOVERNANCE SCHOLARSHIP AFTER THE 2008 FINANCE INDUSTRY COLLAPSE

The 2008 finance industry meltdown was a major event in the history of competitive capitalism, revealing several misconceptions and faulty ideas regarding the resilience and self-regulatory capacities of the market economy. The events of 2008 would therefore be a plausible turning point for how corporate governance is theorized, researched, debated and not the least practised in corporate boardrooms and executives suites and, in relevant cases, in the courtroom. Unfortunately, there is limited evidence of any major shifts after 2008: the same discussions regarding shareholders' influence in decision-making and the relationships between directors and managers prevail (Bebchuk and Weisbach, 2010). The basic framework developed in the 1970s and 1980s, with shareholders as the primary benefactor of the corporate value creation and with managers as their agents stands fast. Debates between, for example, Bebchuk (2005; 2006) and Bainbridge (2006) are therefore primarily evolving around the fine-tuning of a corporate governance system by and large designed to benefit shareholders while still legally granting directors decision-making authority and managers operative discretion. Some scholars are still sceptical regarding government regulation and regard the market for corporate control as a more efficient mechanism for reducing agency costs (Macey, 2008). Other scholars (for a review, see below) argue that contractarians and others putting their faith in market-based control of corporations fail to account for, for example, information asymmetries in the marketplace and for overstating the differences in interests between shareholders, directors and managers.

Despite the lack of novel thinking, there is a lingering concern regarding the quality of the governance in the US economy. Beginning with the failure of Enron, once the seventh largest public corporation in America and followed by several similar cases (Coffee, 2009: 2), the Sarbanes–Oxley Act (SOX) of 2002, the principal political response to these issues, was 'the most comprehensive federal regulation of corporate governance ever' (Fisch, 2010: 925). The enactment of SOX indicated, five years before the next systemic crisis, that the market for corporate control and the regulatory framework did not of necessity operate in ways that benefited economic growth and wider social interests. As Fisch (2010: 923) remarks, once the finance industry collapse had begun, there were numerous cases of substandard and poor governance reported in companies such as Bear Stearns, Lehman Brothers, Citigroup, the US auto industry, and AIG. Such failure to properly govern the largest and some of the most widely respected American corporations, Fisch (2010: 923) argues, 'wreaked unprecedented turmoil in the capital markets and a widespread crisis of confidence in the quality of operational decision making at US corporations'. In Bear Stearns ('Bear'), for instance, Fisch (2010: 923) accounts, the first major finance industry institution to default, '[the] board of directors met just six times a year, leaving primary oversight of the company to Bear's all-insider executive committee. Bear did not create a finance and risk committee until January 2007, just a year before its failure'.

Despite the widespread evidence of remarkably lax standards for corporate governance and other mechanisms (most notably the deteriorating credit-rating discipline, Coffee, 2009), the 2008 events led to less political and regulatory action than the Enron bankruptcy. If turning to the underlying theories and propositions that justified Federal Reserve and SEC's light-handed (some would say permissive) regulation of the finance market and the sanguine views of, for example, soaring real estate prices taken by the two FED chairmen in the new millennium, they did not fare so well when the levee broke. Klausner (2013: 1329) examines the claims made by contractarian corporate governance theorists: '[o]n the whole, the empirical literature over the past three decades has provided little support for the contractarian theory. Key pillars of the theory do not match the empirical facts'. First of all, contractarians' firm belief in price theory and market efficiency misled them to underrate the role of transaction costs and other market imperfections:

> The contractarians assumed that the relevant transaction costs were drafting costs, which could not be high enough to undermine the theory in any significant way, and that there were no other market imperfections. But instead, market imperfections are more complex and more important than the contractarians realized. In defining the rights and obligations of the shareholder–manager relationship, general standards are often more suitable than specific rules. Fiduciary duties in various contexts are an example. (Klausner, 2013: 1330)

In addition, being fully convinced of the efficacy of their theoretical framework, contractarians 'paid little attention to actual corporate contracts' (Klausner, 2013: 1330–31). If they would have been more interested in examining how corporate charters are written, such an analysis would have revealed that 'the real-world facts differed in important ways from what the contractarian theory implied' (Klausner, 2013: 1331). For instance, empirical studies of IPOs, which contractarian theory assumes is a process characterized by a high degree of innovation regarding tailored governance mechanisms, reveal on the contrary that this is factually not the case: '[c]orporate charters are "plain vanilla" with statutory takeover defences commonly added, and nothing more', Klausner (2013: 1338–9) contends. Second, based on the belief in heterogeneity in corporate governance mechanisms and practice, the contractarian theory regards different American states as a market for business charters, an idea popular in the 1970s (see, for example, Cary, 1974) that assumed that states are competing to attract incorporations by customizing corporate laws that are appealing to directors (who are *de jure* entitled to make the decision in what state to seek business charters). But empirical studies do not show any evidence of such a market for business charters; while contractarians had '[a]ssumed that all fifty states compete with one another in a national market ... studies found that no such market exists' (Klausner, 2013: 1343). Instead, the Delaware corporate legislation – by far the most 'popular' – does not operate in 'a competitive environment' (Klausner,

2013: 1345). The value of the Delaware corporate legislation – a study of Delaware corporations in the 1981–96 period revealed that these companies had a higher Tobin's Q (a measure of market value) than did non-Delaware corporations (Bainbridge, 2006: 1743) – does not derive from, Klausner (2013: 1345) claims, the legislation being modified to promote shareholder welfare (or any other governance mechanisms valued by business promoters) in the face of fierce competition over business charters. It is more likely from 'lawyers' familiarity with Delaware law and the ease with which they can provide reliable legal advice' (see also Sandefur, 2015):

> Widespread Delaware incorporation, therefore, is weak support for the contractarian theory regarding value maximization at the IPO stage. Moreover, the fact that a substantial minority of firms incorporate in their home states, apparently without regard to the content of state law, suggests that market pressure to maximize firm value, if it exists, is not strong. (Klausner, 2013: 1345)

Regarding the question of takeover protection such as poison pills, a mechanism to secure managerial welfare in the contractarian's theory (see, for example, Easterbrook and Fischel, 1981), rooted in the empirical evidence demonstrating that 'target shareholders reap substantial gains from hostile acquisitions' (Klausner, 2013: 1349; see also Andrade et al., 2001), the presence of poison pills does not affect the market valuation of a focal firm – in fact, firms with poison pills were valued more highly than firms with no such mechanism. This in turn suggests that the substantial literature debating the role of poison pills and golden parachutes does not really address how economic value is created; expressed differently, the question of takeover protection does not correlate with economic value creation. Taken together, Klausner (2013: 1369–70) says, contractarian theory fails to provide a robust and credible model of how corporate governance mechanisms and practices optimize firm value (including the minimization of agency costs): as a corollary, contractarians' claim that extant corporate legislation and regulatory control should be adjusted to comply with the theoretical propositions they endorse is illegitimate:

> [T]here is room to argue for changes in corporate default rules or for corporate law to offer menus of standardized governance choices. Contractarians cannot reasonably argue, as they frequently have, that if a governance arrangement is not present in IPO charters then there is no basis for a court, legislature, or the SEC to adopt it. (Klausner, 2013: 1369–70)

Moreover, the assumption made in contractarian theory that market-based pricing of corporate stocks and bonds is the only efficient mechanism for disciplining managers is questioned as being unrealistic and naive. Based on empirical evidence that markets are in fact not efficient and that the literature on price formation (that is, price theory) and market efficiency does not incorporate the role of the 'intermediaries' (that is, credit rating agencies) in its models, Fisch (2010: 956) argues that shareholder interests and long-term interests do not converge:

> Inconsistency threatens the standard economic story, in which shareholder primacy maximizes firm value because the interests of the shareholders are most closely aligned with the long-term interests of the corporation. Most importantly, investors who are evaluated on the basis of relative returns or market benchmarks may be insufficiently sensitive to systemic risk. This in turn precludes the market from imposing adequate discipline on firm managers who engage in excessive risk-taking. (Fisch, 2010: 956)

In order to counteract these informational imbalances and the tendency of market-based actors to exploit them for their own benefit (see, for example, Froot et al., 1992), there is a need for legislation and law enforcement that establish what Fisch (2010: 956) calls 'meaningful accountability for disclosure violations' to secure efficient capital markets. However, Fisch (2010: 956) continues, 'under the current system, corporations and corporate officials face only limited accountability for incomplete and inaccurate disclosures'. This in turn undermines the strictly calculative logic of practice that contractarian theory assumes structures markets' behaviour and thus justifies the belief in the efficacy of the market for corporate control. If individual actors are not only operating on the basis of their numerical calculations but also draw on, say, emotions and preferences, and are rewarded on the basis of this not so strictly economic behaviour, much of the efficient market argument becomes irrelevant. A recent authoritative review of the corporate governance literature thus opens up not only for 'norms', but also '[t]he complex set of relationships that exists among these three sources [contracts, law, and norms] of corporate governance' (Macey, 2008: 15). That is, the calculative practice that contractarians assume is the only practice being rewarded by efficient markets remains important but is complemented (as demonstrated by a substantial empirical literature on finance trading, previously discussed in this volume) by other human faculties and skills, indicative of the modest market information efficiency.

Finally, the claims made in the agency theory literature, that agency costs are minimized if independent directors are recruited to the board, is yet another doctrine of the 1970s and 1980s that has been abandoned in the recent corporate governance literature. '[d]irectors chosen for their independence alone often know little if anything about the actual operations or strategic challenges that face companies on whose boards they serve', Macey, (2008: 15) argues. Therefore, he continues, shareholders may be 'better-off abandoning the myth of independent directors and moving back to boards of directors with several insiders on the board'. Bebchuk and Weisbach (2010: 945) reject the independent director argument on the basis of the heterogeneity of outside directors: '[f]inancial economists should not generally assume that independent directors seek to maximize shareholder value; rather, the decisions of independent directors, like those of other economic agents, might well be influenced by their incentives, which in turn are a product of various features of the environment in which they operate' (Bebchuk and Weisbach, 2010).

More specifically, the inability of contractual theory, agency theory and price theory (being all entangled in various ways) to recognize elementary behavioural science know-how (Avgouleas, 2009) in its hardnosed attitude to grant any scholarly authority to any group outside of the economic theory orthodoxy[6] made unrealistic expectations regarding individual independent directors' integrity become part of the normative statements provided by agency theory:

> To date, the entire infrastructure of board conduct is based on the idea that the board is a collegial decision-making body. It would be possible, of course, to imagine replacing the current highly collegial norms of board behavior with an adversarial model. Human nature being what it is, it is not plausible to imagine directors simultaneously being collegial and adversarial, or shifting seamlessly between these two patterns of interaction with management. To do so would require unrealistic assumptions about human behavior.[7] (Macey, 2008: 68)

Demanding a capacity to participate in board work oscillating between its collegial and adversarial end-points, independent directors were simply burdened with too much on their shoulders. Consequently, they have not been proven to curb managerial self-dealing projects and reduce agency costs in systematic ways, something that is glaringly evident when, for example, the recent soaring executive compensation figures are scrutinized.

The corporate governance literature still demonstrates some interest in opening up for a more political and politicized view of corporate legislation and law enforcement, a tendency that indicates that economic theory (for example, the Chicago law and economics tradition) is perhaps losing some of its authority in the field (see, for example, Macey, 2008). Bebchuk and Neeman (2010: 1090) address the perennial issue of how public firms' corporate insiders, 'who seek to extract rent from the capital under their control', and outside investors, 'who provided them with capital' are capable of regulating their relations through the use of lobbyism. In this view, lobbying on investor protection is important because it is ultimately the corporate law and court rulings (and not theoretical propositions, yet to be empirically substantiated) that determine what the lawful corporate governance practices are. Bebchuk and Neeman (2010: 1090) thus stress that corporate legislation can be informed by 'organized interest groups', an idea entirely alien to the orthodox economic theory that made market prices the only reliable mechanism in corporate governance. Even more noteworthy, Bebchuk and Neeman (2010: 1093) suggest a 'reverse causality' (in comparison to orthodox economic theorists, refusing to recognize the presence and even relevance of any political interest out of hand) regarding the drivers of investment protection, with economic wealth and capital accumulation and concentration coming first and investment protection being its primary consequence:

> [a] high level of investor protection may be, at least partly, the product – rather than the cause – of high economic growth, a developed stock market, or an advanced-stage economy. This effect might be partially responsible for the observed correlation between investor protection and economic and capital markets growth. (Bebchuk and Neeman, 2010: 1093)

'A high level of investor protection may be', Bebchuk and Weisbach (2010: 954) add, 'at least partly, the product – rather than the cause – of high economic growth, a developed stock market, or an advanced-stage economy'. An increased theoretical and methodological sophistication, including both behavioural science and political science theory, and perhaps also management theory, holds the promise of making corporate governance an important field of scholarly inquiry in the future, in a society and an economy characterized by growing economic inequality and an uneven distribution of resources. When orthodox economic theory has conspicuously failed to explain and predict corporate governance practices, and not the least to present normative advice on how to institute sustainable corporate governance mechanisms and practices, other social and economic theories may be added to the scholarship on corporate governance.

AT THE FIRM LEVEL: THE CONSEQUENCES OF SHAREHOLDER WELFARE AND INVESTOR CAPITALISM

Shareholder welfare arguably simultaneously served to institute the investor capitalism regime and was one of its foremost accomplishments, anchored in the widely shared idea that free markets and finance capital markets, grounded in mathematical modelling and calculative practices, price commodities efficiently as such pricing procedures accommodate available information, no matter how vague or seemingly incomprehensive it is. Taking all the theoretical insistencies aside and recognizing the performative nature of agency theory and its practical prescriptions, agency theory has been applied on a broad basis to justify shareholder welfare. In practice, this often means that managers, now responding to finance market control, have focused on short-term cost-cutting to maintain or even raise stock prices. This is a perfectly understandable response to the incentives that were provided by the compensation packages that were designed on the basis of the agency theory proposition that managers are the shareholders' agents. The question is thus what the long-term consequences are of the change from investment in illiquid but value-generating production capital to the 'liquidification' of existing resources such as human capital ('downsizing' was after all the primary managerial response to the new shareholder value objective; see, for example, Goldstein, 2012; Budros, 1997; Gordon, 1996). Lazonick and O'Sullivan (2000: 17) propose that firms today operate in accordance with a 'downsize and distribute' model, and if that is true across industries, production capital is gradually hollowed out as further investment in illiquid capital is assessed unfavourably by finance markets that do not fully recognize medium to long-term investment decisions.[8] Such questions fortunately lend themselves to empirical investigations.

In addition, if Lazonick and O'Sullivan (2000) are correct in their assessment, it would also imply that there is a substantial supply of venture capital benefiting the entrepreneurial function of competitive capitalism, as finance capital is now increasingly transferred as dividends or increased stock prices to the capital owners, who in turn, *ex hypothesi*, are in a better position than managers to reinvest their capital in high-rent industries. But as we have already seen, the finance industry has today outgrown virtually any other industry, and therefore a meaningful proposition would be whether rent-seeking capital owners are perhaps not so interested in potential high-rent industries unless the capital remains liquid. That is, investment in, for example, start-up ventures in emerging industries would still be unattractive for capital owners because an investment in, for example, a life science start-up is both uncertain and lasts, in its standard contract, over ten years. If that is the case, it can be deduced on the one hand that there is an abundance of finance capital in society seeking high-rent (but also highly liquid) investment options, while on the other hand, there are many entrepreneurs and start-up firm executives looking for venture capital. As such ventures are beset by uncertainty (that is, non-calculable risk), they may still be starved of cash despite the abundance of capital. This new economic landscape is characterized by substantial paradoxes: an oversupply of capital leads to speculation in, for example, oil prices (Cheng and Xiong, 2014), while at the same time entrepreneurs in highly sophisticated emerging industries cannot finance their activities because, as neoclassicists would say, 'the risk-aversion function has shifted'. In this section, some of these contradictions derived from and co-produced with the re-enactment of the firm will be discussed.

Downsize and Distribute: Falling R&D Investment

In the 2001–10 period, Lazonick (2013: 497) writes, S&P 500 companies, accounting for about 75 per cent of the market capitalization of all US publicly listed corporations, spent about three trillion US dollars on stock buybacks, a figure representing 'in excess of 50 percent of their net income'. In addition, these companies distributed dividends equal to 'about 40 percent of net income over the decade, bringing a total payout ratio (buybacks plus dividends) to well over 90 percent' (Lazonick, 2013: 497). That is, shareholders benefited either directly through increased stock prices or through dividends to the extent that more than 90 per cent of the accountable profits were returned to the shareholders.[9]

Another way to express the dominance of shareholder primacy governance is to examine the investment in R&D, the investment in illiquid production capital within only a long-term planning horizon, in fact the opposite of stock repurchases, being the most straightforward way to boost stock prices. Orhangazi (2008: 883) examines investment in R&D for the 1973–2003 period and reports '[a] negative relationship between financialization and capital accumulation, especially for large firms'. These results thus 'support the view that financialization has negative implications for firm investment behavior' (Orhangazi, 2008: 883). Hall (1993) studied the R&D investment in American industry after 1985, when hostile takeover threats made executives and directors acutely aware of the need for maintaining a stock price that discouraged takeover bidders. Hall (1993) finds a significant reduction of R&D investment after 1985: '[a]lthough intangible R&D assets from 1973 through about 1983–1984 were about equally valued with tangible capital, this relationship broke down completely during the mid-1980's, with the R&D stock coefficient falling by a factor of 3 or 4' (Hall, 1993: 259). The R&D stock coefficient was in the range of 1.0–0.6 until 1983–84, but after 1985, it started to shrink and in 1989–90 the coefficient was 0.2 (Hall, 1993: 263).

Hall (1993) speculates about the shift in investment behaviour and suggests that the explanation that the expected profitability rate of R&D investment would suddenly have fallen in the mid-1980s is unlikely. Second, the hypothesis that R&D capital depreciation rates accelerated after 1985 also seems untenable. That is, R&D investments were as likely to produce long-term benefits in, say, 1983 as in 1989. Hall (1993) thus discusses how institutional and attitudinal changes in the US economy were the driver of the new investment behaviour: '[a] third possibility is that the stock market has become more myopic and is discounting the cash flows from R&D capital at a very high rate, treating them as if they were highly uncertain' (Hall, 1993: 263). In other words, finance traders were less patient with investment in illiquid production capital after 1985 when they learned from, for example, agency theorists that distributing the residual cash flow would be beneficial not only for themselves but for *all of the economy*. That is, the liquidity preference that Minsky (1980) treats as the very core axiom of investor capitalism was now not just a preference but became a form of dictate. Fourth and finally, Hall (1993: 263) lists the related phenomenon of a 'wave of mergers and leveraged buyouts during the 1980s' as an explanation for the shift in the utility function among directors and executives regarding R&D investment.

One additional explanation for the new preference for short-term liquidity over long-term production capital investment may be found in the expansion of finance markets and the finance industry more broadly, making finance industry actors a more powerful factor to consider for directors and executives, as we have seen, *de jure* protected by the corporate law from such influences. What finance theorists refer to as 'capital lock in' or 'asset shielding' (Stout, 2012: 13) is an important condition in finance markets where there is either a shortage of investment opportunities or each finance capital investor controls so large a share of stock that they cannot easily sell off their shares without affecting the finance market's stock price evaluation:

[E]quity investors in a corporation, unlike investors in a partnership or proprietorship, cannot unilaterally withdraw their capital from the firm. If they want their money back, they cannot simply demand the company to return it. Their only hope is to find another investor willing to buy their shares in the secondary market. (Stout, 2012: 13)

In the case where finance actors cannot 'vote with their feet' (that is, sell the stock as an exit option) if they are not satisfied with the performance, they can only choose to use 'voice' to address their concerns (Hirschman, 1970). The conventional wisdom *c*.1980, Dobbin and Zorn (2005: 188) say, was that '[i]f an investor did not like the way a firm was managed, she could vote with her feet, moving her money elsewhere'. But as funds grew in size, institutional investors '[c]ame to believe that it made more sense to reform management than to sell off stock' (Dobbin and Zorn, 2005: 188). When the exit options were exhausted, the 'intentions' of corporate law, granting managers and directors discretion, suddenly had to be compromised by institutional investors' newly awakened interest in managerial decision-making. In the 1970s and 1980s, large stocks of finance capital accumulated in, for example, pension funds, from now on being a key factor in finance markets:

> [In the 1990s] pensions became a critical pillar of US finance. In 1955 pension funds owned only 2.3 percent of total equity holdings, and insurance companies 3.2 percent. By 1997 pension funds held 24 percent, and insurance companies 5.7 percent of total US holdings. Households held 93 percent of all US equity in 1945; this proportion dropped to 42.7 percent in 1997. (McCarthy, 2014: 461)

By 2005, Davis (2009: 33) writes, 'nearly three-quarters of the average Fortune 1000 corporation's shares were owned by institutional investors' (see also Orhangazi, 2008: 869).[10] As the fund managers handling the pension funds and mutual funds were rewarded essentially on the basis of their ability to compete with or even beat the stock index, this new generation of finance market actors expressed a strong preference for liquid assets over more uncertain and long-term reinvestment decisions. '[I]nvestment in new productive capital became less attractive and financial investment became more attractive ... Institutional investors encouraged corporate CEOs to adopt the aspects of agency theory they preferred, focusing on short-term stock market value goals and tying executive compensation to stock prices' (Tomaskovic-Devey and Lin, 2011: 546; see also Cobb, 2015; Connelly et al., 2010).

This so-called 'short-termism' (Orhangazi, 2008: 869) fitted nicely into the agency theory-motivated shareholder welfare governance model, and fund managers became early supporters of the agency theory model as it sounded logically reasonable, encouraged liquidity over long-term commitment, and not least was aligned with the incentive systems that have been implemented to motivate fund managers to increase their performance. This convergence of a variety of theories, policies and practices were not coincidental but were all part of the same movement to disqualify and discredit the institutions and practices of managerial capitalism. Central to that project was to enact the firm as no longer being a site where economic value is generated on the basis of advanced engineering and management expertise, but as being more or less 'market transactions continued by other means', that is, contracts. One of the foremost long-term consequences was that the agents of competitive capitalism became myopic in their unwillingness to discount R&D investment at the previous rate and increasingly favoured more short-term-oriented payout policies.

SUMMARY OF KEY ARGUMENTS WITH REGARD TO CORPORATE GOVERNANCE THEORY AND PRACTICE

Below, the main arguments advanced throughout Chapters 1 to 4 are summarized:

- Corporate law serves a social function to provide business ventures with the charter to operate and to eliminate risks emerging from both inside and outside the firm.
- Corporate law was based on the idea that business ventures should provide opportunities for attracting and securing the finance capital needed to operate and expand their activities but also on the idea that business ventures should generate socially beneficial effects. Corporate law was thus primarily concerned with supporting economic enterprise and creating markets, further reinforcing and encouraging enterprise. Questions regarding the 'efficiency' of the newly instituted corporate system could only be articulated after the fact and on the basis of the efficacy of the corporate system and its legal statutes.
- In the critique of collectivism during the New Deal era and in the post-World War II period, corporate law was initially not a source of critique for free market protagonists and conservatives as the state administration and trade unions were targeted as key entities of the allegedly collectivist governance of the economy that threatened so-called economic freedom.
- By the 1970s, executives and (to a minor extent) directors were criticized for decreasing productivity growth and economic performance, leading to a more broad-sweeping critique of the

regime of managerial capitalism as promoting managerial welfare at the shareholders' expense and, allegedly, to the detriment of the efficiency of the economy at large.

- In the critique of managerial capitalism, the theory of the firm was redefined in economic terms as being a nexus of contracts wherein shareholders were not so much owners as regular finance market investors entitled to claim what agency theorists call residual cash flow. This new contractarian model of the firm justified shareholder welfare governance.

- Unfortunately, the shareholder welfare governance and the agency theory model of the firm are poorly aligned with existing corporate law, legal theory and state-level court ruling. The contractual view of the firm remains a theoretical image rooted in formalist neo-classical economic theory and the preferences for efficiency over stability and other desirable economic outcomes.

- Despite its theoretical inconsistencies, ignorance of corporate law, and weak empirical support, the agency theory emphasis on shareholder welfare governance has come to dominate firms and corporations since the mid-1980s. The dominance of finance market control of managerial malfeasance is still separated from existing corporate law.

- Taken together, the history of the development of corporate law and the forceful advancement of shareholder welfare governance and complemented by theoretically puzzling phenomena such as soaring executive compensation (agency theory's primary target was the agency costs), are exemplary of how economic ideas can be successfully advanced and advocated regardless of the ignorance of existing legislation and court ruling, the absence of supportive robust empirical data, and the inability to stand up to scientific standards regarding logically consistent theoretical propositions. This ultimately renders corporate governance a matter of preferences and ideologies rather than being rooted in substantiated empirical evidence.

- For this reason, corporate governance should be subject to additional scholarly attention, specifically exploring the basis for the claims made by agency theorist and free market protagonists more broadly.

CONCLUDING REMARKS

'[T]he rentier aspect of capitalism [is] a transitional phase which will disappear when it has done its work', Keynes (1953: 376) announced in his magnum opus, *The General Theory of Employment, Interest and Money*. This statement is still today prophetic as rentier capitalism seems to be very much alive and exerting a greater influence than ever in the economic system of competitive capitalism. Today, the disdainful term 'rentier' can be associated with the shareholder welfare that has been advocated and has served to transform the view of the firm from being a site for joint economic value creation to a legal fiction and a bundle of contracts that for neoclassicists is little more than the market continued by other means. In the present period of time, the firm has been re-enacted as what is no longer seated within the socio-economic and legal system, instituted through and by corporate law and the regulatory control of the market. In contrast, the firm is now being seen as a primary vehicle for shareholder welfare, and several commentators have emphasized the return to a *rentier capitalism* being a characteristic feature of the pre-World War I and interwar periods. This ultimately leaves us with an economic system where the finance industry no longer serves as a support function of, for example, the manufacturing industry, but where it is the few remaining oligarchies of the finance industry (Goldman Sachs, et al.) that set the rules and determined the game. In the economic regime of investor capitalism, there is no evidence of rentier interests being on the way out: on the contrary, the century-long advocacy of free market capitalism in combination with the critique of 'collectivism' in any form or shape as an illegitimate violation of the virtues of free market capital accumulation – the 'economic freedom' of Hayek and his collaborators – has not only led to the comprehensive shift from the managerial capitalism system that dominated in the 1930–70 period to investor capitalism, but has also served to undermine the firm as a meaningful theoretical construct and object of scholarly study. Both legal theory and management theory, able to explain how the corporation was from the outset instituted by the state as a legal entity that provided several opportunities and benefits while preventing certain undesirable behaviour, and capable of demonstrating how economic value is created 'on the shop floor', have been ignored and marginalized in neoclassical economic theory.

The shift from managerial capitalism and the enactment of the firm as a site of professional skills and competencies being combined and managed in unique and hard-to-imitate ways, to investor capitalism and shareholder welfare governance is based on the idea that the firm is a strictly financial phenomenon, neither responding to the allegedly collectivist tradition of legislation and regulation, nor understood in any meaningful way as a site where managers and their subordinates actually add value to the operations they oversee. Both law and managerial practices are thus 'unnecessary complications' in the new conventional wisdom, but not only did free market protagonists throw out the baby (corporate law and management theory) with the bathwater; the entire social system that embeds markets and renders them efficient sites for economic transactions was thrown out too. What legitimately remains in this model is little more than finance industry oligarchies, more anxiously looking for new markets and industries where they can reinvest their surplus finance capital, now when the American mortgage market is defunct and, for example, many national states are indebted to the level where they can no longer maintain or restore a sustainable prosperity. If this is the economic freedom that Friedrich von Hayek dreamt of, then we should all now enjoy the fruits of their and many others' hard work to deconstruct the collectivism of managerial capitalism and its accompanying and co-produced welfare state and embrace the 'economic freedom' in the new millennium. Unless we firmly believe in the virtues of this economic freedom, rooted in the unrestrained right to use our own calculation of benefits and economic outcomes to benefit individual interests, we may share some of the worries of the French economist Jacques Attali (cited in Harriss-White, 1996: 41), suggesting that 'conflict is more likely now that the Cold War has ended and the market has triumphed ... for inequality will cleave the new world order as surely as the Berlin Wall once divided East and West'.

Pierre Bourdieu (2000: 71) proposes the term 'epistemocratic sociodicy', the intellectuals' incorrect assumption that if something is '[s]hown to be logically or scientifically unacceptable, it will be superseded by new forms of social practice' (Fowler, 2003: 473). In contemporary times, this is a helpful term, as Martin (2014: 217) says, 'history is replete with records of the extraordinary resilience of intellectual orthodoxies'. That is, just because one specific economic idea or system has failed in ways that make it reasonable beyond doubt that it is inaccurate or inoperable, it will not of necessity vanish into thin air on the basis of the will of some mysterious divine bringer of justice. Escaping the epistemocratic fallacy that easily blindfolds the critics of what Harriss-White (1996: 41) calls 'market romanticism', demands novel ways of challenging and sidelining ideas, ideologies and theories that undermine the long-term viability of competitive capitalism. Free market protagonists and conservatives have built and enforced their argumentation and policy-making around a set of principal economic ideas including rational choice theory, the axiom of self-interest, and price theory and the market efficiency hypothesis. As, for example, the American author David Foster Wallace (2006: 113) has remarked, liberals and 'leftists' have been uncomfortable using the very term *self-interest* (and its derivative terms) as they have fashioned more noble roles and narratives for themselves. Unfortunately, Wallace (2006: 113) claims, this has granted conservatives the monopoly to define the rules in the world of practical matters, and has enabled them '[t]o depict progressives as pie-in-the-sky idealists and themselves as real-world back-pocket pragmatists'. The fallacy here is not so much the Hegelian belief in the superior rationality of the world as we perceive it, inherent to the epistemocratic fallacy, as it is a self-flattering attitude inviting liberals to ascribe for themselves the role to act as legitimate moralists, wagging the index-finger when telling, for example, free market protagonists and conservatives that there are other virtues in life than not-so-admirable self-interest. This has unfortunately served conservatives' interests perfectly well as it has helped them to further reinforce the image of liberals and social democrats as smug moralists, all too ready to tell others what to think and what to do: 'leftists' big mistake is not conceptual or ideological but spiritual and rhetorical – their narcissistic attachment to assumptions that maximize their own appearance of virtue tends to cost them both the theater and the war' (Wallace, 2006: 114).

In other words, free market advocacy cannot be met by moral storytelling about either factual conditions, or moral obligations as the virtues of such stories are probably not shared by conservatives, neoliberals and libertarians treating economic freedom as an objective per se and not a means to other, more virtuous ends. Expressed differently, the grandiose fiasco of the 2008 finance market collapse was not, as some liberal and left-leaning commentators would have it, the Titanic disaster of investor capitalism; instead, the finance industry actors quickly dusted off their suits and continued their work as if the music had in fact never stopped. No change will come on its own (as the epistemocratic fallacy assumes), but change will only come if there are new and better economic ideas being advanced, able to compete with the well-entrenched gospel of free market efficiency. Therefore, a detailed analysis of the underlying theoretical arguments supporting free market advocacy is acutely needed.

NOTES

1. The argument that corporate law should be adjusted to theoretically derived economic efficiency criteria is based on work of the Chicago law and economics school and its critique of antitrust legislation, Davies (2010) shows. The antitrust legislation developed in the US since the enactment of the Sherman Act in 1890 had been used to pursue various political and moral goals, from '[d]efence of small businesses, to ensuring public accountability of cartels and monopolies, to redistributing wealth, to attacking organized

crime' (Davies, 2010: 65). As opposed to this diverse, legal view of antitrust legislation, Chicago economists such as Ronald H. Coase and Aaron Director developed what they called 'price theory' to advocate the proposition that law should serve to reinforce and shape incentives (see, for example, Coase, 1960). The objective was thus to develop a 'positive theory of legislation' on the basis of economic theory, in contrast to 'the normative approach of welfare economics' (Becker and Stigler, 1974: 1). Such incentives in turn rested on economic grounds and more specifically the core assumption that, faced with a range of comparable options, individuals will '[r]ationally select the one that pays them the greatest utility, over and above its cost' (Davies, 2010: 66). In pursuing this universal model, based on the coupling of what Davies (2010: 68) refers to as methodological dogmatism and ontological agnosticism – price theory does not distinguish between 'the economy' and 'society' as they are both structured on the basis of the same universal and utilitarian rationality, thus treating, for example, 'a family' as being no different from 'a corporation', that is, price theory is advanced in strict methodological terms – the Chicago law and economics school is an eminent example of the intellectual colonialism of neoclassical economic theory. This enforcement of economic theory (that is, price theory) and its methodological dogmatism in particular in novel policy domains was 'a hallmark of the Chicago School' (Davies, 2010: 66). Aaron Director, the leading scholar in establishing the new perspective on law at the law school of the University of Chicago, followed Hayek in his scepticism about democracy. Just as Hayek and his collaborators argued in the mid-1930s, Director argued that 'the spirit of equality' was a potential threat to economic freedom, which for him was 'a greater political virtue' than the political freedom to vote (Van Horn and Emmett, 2015: 1447). Ebenstein (2015: 18) here speaks about the 'neoanarchist' position of Hayek and Friedman to denote their uncompromising denial of society *tout court*. Therefore, Director distrusted democratic discussion and '[s]aw majority voting as a necessary evil to be used in those rare instances where the competitive order did not suffice' (Van Horn and Emmett, 2015: 1453). Director criticized leading intellectuals and policy-makers and argued that 'they neglected to appreciate that only under a system of voluntary exchange would freedom be maximised' (Van Horn and Emmett, 2015: 1451). For Director, freedom was 'ultimately the freedom of choice, expressed most completely in a market economy' (Van Horn and Emmett, 2015: 1453). Based on these premises, the priority of economic freedom at all costs and the firm belief in market pricing (that is, relying on Coasean price theory), the law and economics school aimed to reform law to 'improve the incentives' and reduce 'costs' in law enforcement (Becker and Stigler, 1974: 1). The ground-breaking achievement of the Chicago law and economics school was to convince judges and lawyers (for example, the legal theorist and judge Richard Posner, 1973; 1979), other economists, and not least policy-makers (such as President Ronald Reagan in the 1980s), that (1) economic policy and legislation should be '[e]xclusively concerned with the goal of maximizing efficiency' (Davies, 2010: 65), and (2) existing legislation is filled with 'nonsense' and assumptions regarding the incentives and behaviours of actors. Rather than being a free-standing tool in the hand of democratically elected policy-makers to balance a number of interests advocated by a variety of constituencies, the champions of price theory advocated that antitrust law (and law in general, including corporate law) should obey the efficiency criteria defined by economists committed to price theory. Coase and his followers thus claimed to renounce '[a]ll ontological or a priori claims about individuals, economy and society' (Davies, 2010: 68), and replaced it with the doctrine of rational utility-maximizing choice, making efficiency, by implication, Davies (2010: 68) argues, little more than an empirical term for 'freedom', the familiar catchphrase of the 1930s' anti-New Deal and anti-Keynesianism community. In this law and economics programme, merging freedom and efficiency on the basis of methodological dogmatism (see e.g., Landes and Posner, 1978), successfully rolled out in the 1970s and implemented in the 1980s, law loses its authority to define legal entities and their relations and becomes a specialized branch of price theory or is even relegated to the role as its support function.

2. 'There are two ways in which to criticize a proposal, doctrine, or dogma. One is to argue that it is false. Another is to argue that it is not even a candidate for truth or falsehood. Call the former *denial*, the latter *undoing*', Hacking (2002: 55) writes. For educative purposes, as will be demonstrated, Stout's undoing of shareholder primacy governance is an eminent illustrative case of this term proposed by Hacking (2002).

3. Agency theory prescribes that independent directors execute a central control function to minimize managerial malfeasance and to maximize shareholder wealth. Brudney (1982) dismisses the argument that independent directors are capable of monitoring shareholder wealth maximization as counterintuitive and illogical for a variety of reasons, including the following. (1) Independent directors are recruited from the same pool of individuals as inside directors, with 'common business and professional backgrounds' and living in 'the same social and economic milieu', thus failing to bring new know-how and expertise to the table (Brudney, 1982: 613). (2) Independent directors principally provide 'expert advice' and 'consultation' from 'a less involved point of view' than inside directors (Brudney, 1982: 632), that is, they are poorly equipped and positioned to be able to curb self-dealing and/or maximize wealth. (3) Independent directors are 'relieved' of the 'obligation to be diligent' by corporate law and its business judgement rule (Brudney, 1982: 638), that is, they are not expected to obey any corporate legislation different from that of inside directors (Brudney, 1982: 638). Therefore, Brudney (1982: 638) argues, 'the received learning is that, in fact, outside directors cannot and do not diligently police management's wealth-maximizing function'. 'Logic and experience', Brudney (1982: 631) continues, suggests that independent directors can serve as '[a]n admonisher of proper behavior rather than a marketline judge or an immunizer of self-dealing'.

    In addition, empirical studies reveal that there is no support for the proposition that independent directors are conducive to better performance (Daily et al., 2003; Dalton et al., 1999): in fact, there is a slight *negative* correlation (that is, contrary to the theoretical prescription) between independent directors and firm performance (Bhagat and Black, 2002: 263). Spectacular and much-debated corporate failures such as the Enron bankruptcy have also proved to be an 'embarrassment' (Gordon, 2003: 1241) for the proponents of the idea of the disciplinary role of independent directors as Enron could display 'a splendid board on paper', including fourteen members and 'only two insiders' (Gordon, 2003: 1241; see also Krasna, 2006). In addition, agency theory suggests that the market for corporate control serves to discipline managers, but an extensive empirical literature on credit rating (White, 2013; 2010; Bolton et al., 2012; Hunt, 2009; Rom, 2009; Frost, 2007; Partnoy, 1999) shows that this proposition is unsubstantiated and grounded in wishful thinking regarding the efficacy of market pricing and, *eo ipso*, finance market-based regulatory control. These are worrying findings as credit rating remains the principal means for executing finance market-based control (in addition to a variety of accounting and auditing procedures, unfortunately also ineffective in curbing managerial malfeasance; see Erb and Pelger, 2015; Sikka, 2009; Kedia and Philippon, 2009; Robson et al., 2007; Knechel, 2007; Roberts et al., 2006). Also studies of how corporate governance rating has been subject to measurement reveal limited efficacy of such practices (Bebchuk et al., 2009; Bhagat et al., 2008). A host of studies of finance traders' practical work reveal that finance markets do not solely work on calculative practices, but also extensively rely on a variety of social, cultural and even emotional resources and competencies (Chong and Tuckett, 2015; Zuckerman, 2012; 1999; Pixley, 2012; Lépinay, 2011; Tuckett, 2011; Beunza and Garud, 2007; Zaloom, 2006; 2003; Abolafia, 2001). This empirical material challenges the strictly rationalist and calculative image of finance markets that neoclassicists are anxious to maintain, as the calculability of prices is a central tenet within their advocacy of a finance market control of managers. Finally, while agency theory excludes the entire social embedding of corporate governance practices for the perceived benefit of a sleeker and more parsimonious theoretical and methodological framework, a substantial body of research indicates that a certain amount of practical work in executive suites and boards is committed to circumventing and evading the alleged disciplinary control of independent directors (Rhee and Fiss, 2014; Westphal and Graebner, 2010; Westphal and Clement,

2008; Westphal and Bednar, 2005; Westphal and Khanna, 2003; Davis, 1991). These studies render agency theory little more than a normative prescription of an economy and a corporate system where only shareholders should benefit from the team production work organized within the firm.

4. The literature on finance industry growth provides some mixed evidence but generally stresses that an expanding finance industry depresses the economy and slows down economic growth. Tomaskovic-Devey et al. (2015: 538), using a sample of economic data over the 38-year period 1970–2008, show that 'the financialization of the non-finance sector of the economy depressed non-finance sector value added by 3.9%, roughly the equivalent of 3 years of lost economic growth'. Aizenman et al.'s (2013: 20) study shows that 'disruptions in financial sector', today a widespread phenomenon (see, for example, Eichengreen, 2015; Calomiris and Haber, 2014), especially in economies with a liberalized finance industry regulation, are associated with a '[l]arge decline in the value added of key real sectors, with the construction sector affected the most'. Unfortunately, such 'economic shocks' are highly stressful for individuals and households and lead to a persistent sense of economic insecurity, defined as 'the psychologically mediated experience of inadequate protection against hardship-causing economic risks' (Hacker et al., 2013: 25). This economic insecurity translates into increased support for government action to buffer the effects of economic decline (Hacker et al., 2013: 40). In addition, periods of 'financial expansions' do not seem to have 'much of an effect' on economic growth. Cetorelli and Gambera (2001: 619) report similar results, suggesting that 'bank concentration has an average depressive effect on industry growth', affecting all sectors indiscriminately. However, firms and industries demanding external finance to expand their operations benefit from the facilitation of credit access to, for example, young firms (Cetorelli and Gambera, 2001: 618). Bekaert et al. (2005: 18) examined data from 95 countries and found that on average, an equity market liberalization induced a statistically significant 1.20 per cent real per capita growth rate in GDP. 'Liberalization' here denotes at least three types of reform, including 'macro-reforms, financial reforms, legal reforms' (Bekaert et al., 2005: 29). They also found, *pace* Aizenman et al. (2013), that the benefits of equity market liberalization were higher if there was an advanced banking system already in place in the economy. More specifically, this advanced banking system needs to be seated within an elaborate institutional structure: the positive effects from equity market liberalization were almost three times higher in countries with 'higher than median level of the quality of institutions index (1.29% versus 0.45%)' (Bekaert et al., 2005: 39). Using data from 80 countries from the 1960–89 period, including both developed and developing economies, King and Levine (1993: 719) suggest that 'the predetermined component of financial development is a good predictor for long-run growth over the next 10 to 30 years'. In addition, King and Levine (1993) continue, higher levels of financial development are '[s]trongly associated with future rates of capital accumulation and future improvements in the efficiency with which economies employ capital'. In other words, King and Levine (1993: 731) assert, finance does not only 'follow growth', but seems '[i]mportantly to lead economic growth'. Substantial evidence falsifies this proposition (Tomaskovic-Devey et al., 2015; Aizenman et al., 2013; Cetorelli and Gambera, 2001).

In addition, Kus (2012) reports data from a sample of 20 OECD countries over the 13-year period 1995–2007, and demonstrates a significant positive association between an expanding finance industry and increased income inequality. These are unsurprising results given Tomaskovic-Devey et al.'s (2015: 535) finding that financialization was most significant in manufacturing, the primary provider of blue-collar worker jobs, in turn reducing total labour income 'by as much as 60% over the 38-year observation period' (corresponding to a 1.5 per cent consecutive annual loss of labour income in the period). One of the key drivers of this reduction of total labour income is the new preference for shareholder welfare governance, Tomaskovic-Devey et al. (2015) suggest:

> The shareholder value movement encouraged firms to replace equity with debt and to reduce employment. Reductions in employment were taken as signals of managerial seriousness and rewarded with surges in stock prices. By replacing equity with debt to

finance production and to purchase outstanding stocks, firms immediately boosted their return on equity, the prime indicator stock analysts follow in evaluating firm performance. Thus the shareholder value movement produced a perverse set of incentives to reduce total production and perhaps in the long-run total profit, while boosting stock prices and dividend payments on the remaining equity. (Tomaskovic-Devey et al., 2015: 542)

Given this empirical evidence, establishing an inverted relationship between economic growth and finance industry expansion, Tomaskovic-Devey et al. (2015: 541) suggest '[i]t is safe to say that for the vast majority of the US population financialization has led to lower standards of living as well as weaker state investment capacity for both the population and infrastructure than what would have been possible under a more production-focused regime'.

5. 'Something seems to have changed in the early 1980s', Greenwood and Scharfstein (2013: 4) write, apropos the shift in market regulation policy and finance industry growth occurring in the 1980s.

6. The ignorance of economists somewhat surprisingly also includes law scholars, a category of analysts favouring a formalist mode of thinking not entirely different from orthodox economic theory. Klausner (2013: 1368) retells a joke that captures this attitude: '[i]n the law and economics field, there is a saying: "[i]f a law professor wants to write a paper that is economically sophisticated, he or she needs an economist as a coauthor; if an economist wants to write a paper that is legally sophisticated, he or she needs to take a lawyer to lunch"'. 'More lunches with lawyers are needed', Klausner (2013: 1368) adds crisply.

7. Another case of advocacy making 'unrealistic assumptions about human behavior' is Easterbrook and Fischel's (1981: 1201) argument in favour of 'managerial passivity' in the face of tender offers. Despite the fact that it was conventional wisdom that managers were released from their assignments after successful takeovers – Easterbrook and Fischel's (1981: 1190) whole argumentation in favour of takeovers as being 'socially beneficial and desirable' is based on the assumption of excessive agency costs induced by shirking and/or incompetent managers – Easterbrook and Fischel (1981: 1201) mandate managers to endorse a self-sacrificing ethos and patiently await their own layoff. They say 'management should not propose antitakeover charter or bylaw amendments, file suits against the offeror, acquire a competitor of the offeror in order to create an antitrust obstacle to the tender offer, buy or sell shares in order to make the offer more costly, give away to some potential "white knight" valuable corporate information that might call forth a competing bid, or initiate any other defensive tactic to defeat a tender offer' (Easterbrook and Fischel, 1981: 1201). Why deeply distrusted managers, who *ex hypothesi* squander shareholders' wealth in predictable ways, should suddenly demonstrate such a benign and compassionate attitude remains unexplained. Somewhat perplexingly for the reader, for Easterbrook and Fischel (1981), managers are first sinners but suddenly appear as saints, submitting to the allegedly greater good of the pursuit of shareholder welfare.

8. Political scientists like Paul Pierson (1996, 1998) suggest that despite all the neoconservative and neoliberal campaigning to discredit the welfare state, there is still strong political support for welfare provisions financed by tax income. The contemporary welfare state operates in a distinctively new environment including a shift from industrial production to services, leading to lower productivity increases, and an ageing and more vital population living longer than ever before (Pierson, 1998: 551), which puts a strain on the welfare state and makes it operate under 'permanent austerity' (Pierson, 1998: 554). Still, the welfare state continues to function. In comparison, the corporate welfare system that was built up in the US as a form of market-based patriarchal welfare model being part of the managerial capitalism regime has decomposed over time (for a literature review, see Bidwell et al., 2013; Hacker, 2006); 'U.S. corporations have largely abandoned their role as a primary risk bearer', Cobb (2015: 1332) argues. In terms of health insurance benefits, the share of workers who receive health benefits from their employers 'fell from almost 42% to just over 26% between 1979 and 1998', Hacker (2004: 253) writes. This decline is even more salient for part-time employees: data reported in the 2006 CPS [Current

Population Survey], published by the US Bureau of Labor Statistics show that across US industries, 'only 18.6 percent of part-time hourly workers were covered by health insurance through their employer' (Lambert, 2008: 1206). Also what Hacker (2004: 253) calls 'retirement security' has been affected by the new doctrine to primarily benefit shareholders at other stakeholders' expense, leading to 'a basic decline in employers' support for retirement benefits': '[b]etween the early 1980s and the mid-1990s, the value of pension benefits to current workers dropped in every income group, but by far most rapidly among the lowest paid workers, who already had the lowest coverage levels' (Hacker, 2004: 255). Worse still for these disfavoured groups, 'tax breaks for private pensions and other retirement savings options heavily favor better-paid employees: two-thirds of the nearly $100 billion in federal tax breaks for subsidized retirement savings options accrue to the top 20% of the population' (Hacker, 2004: 255). This policy and corporate decision-making has systemic implications as risks are essentially 'privatized' but without an accompanying safety net, offering large groups including not only the unemployed and 'the working poor' (Brady et al., 2013: 873) but also for growing segments of the middle class little else than 'debt-fare' – the expansion of private debt to pay for basic needs such as medication; '[r]oughly half of all personal bankruptcies are due in part to medical problems', Montgomerie (2009: 17) reports. Furthermore, studies of finance markets providing these loans to the already poor and disenfranchised demonstrate a relatively low degree of 'rationality' in how consumers handle their debt: consumers are '[f]ar more efficient at minimizing costs among loans they already have than they are at choosing debt contracts in the marketplace' (Zinman, 2015: 253). That is, Zinman (2015: 260) continues, '[m]any millions of mortgagers pay hundreds or even thousands of dollars in markups they could avoid with a seemingly modest amount of additional shopping effort or sophistication at origination'. In addition to increased household debt, poor families eke out an existence on the basis of whatever means they access: 'the number of pawn shops has grown 50% since the start of the Great Recession, with over 10,000 outlets in the United States currently', Zinman (2015: 258) concludes. It is against this evidence that statements such as, 'maximizing profits for equity investors assists other "constituencies" automatically' (Easterbrook and Fischel, 1996: 38) need to be assessed.

9. In 2007, the last year before the Great Recession, US public firms '[p]aid out more than $767 billion in dividends and purchases' (Farre-Mensa et al., 2014: 17.2). This divest and distribute policy was justified on the basis of agency theory reasoning, seeing dividends and repurchase as a method to reduce overinvestment: '[t]he accumulated evidence on payout and agency indicates that firms use payouts to reduce potential overinvestment by management. Firms increase their payouts as they mature; and markets "appreciates" more dividends and repurchases paid by firms with more free cash flow' (Farre-Mensa et al., 2014: 17.3). Agency theorists have thus been hugely successful in their advocacy of shareholder welfare. 'In 2012, industrial public US firms paid more than $258 billion in dividends, whereas in the early 1970s aggregate dividends were approximately $70 billion of real 2012 dollars', Farre-Mensa et al. (2014: 17.7) notice, reporting evidence that supports Lazonick's (2013) proposition.

What is yet to explain is the shift in preferences from dividends to repurchases as the primary vehicle for the transfer of the residual cash flow. '[D]ividends fell from 66.5% in 1978 to 20.8% in 1999', Farre-Mensa et al. (2014: 17.5) write. Agency theorists and neoclassicists tend to either blame the tax system for the increase of payout, or argue that repurchases is a way for executives and the board of directors to 'signal' to the market actors that they believe the stock is undervalued (leaving aside for the moment the fact that such a statement would violate the Efficient Market Hypothesis that is the foundation for agency theory in the first place). Farre-Mensa et al. (2014: 17.52) suggest that such theoretical explanations fall short when it comes to explaining factual evidence: '[taxes] do not seem to be a first-order explanation for the observed variation in payout, especially at the aggregate level' (Farre-Mensa et al., 2014: 17.3). They continue: 'significant evidence has been accumulated to prove that the market reactions to repurchase announcements are not semi-strong form efficient, which casts some doubt on traditional signaling explanations for payouts' (Farre-Mensa et al., 2014: 17.3). Instead, Farre-Mensa et al. (2014: 17.52) point to the design of the executive compensation packages as the primary driver of this evidence: '[e]xecutive compensation is often based (explicitly or implicitly) on EPS [Equity-per-share]', and executives are thus incentivized to boost stock price as it immediately benefits their own economic compensation. Expressed differently, the shift from dividends to repurchases and repurchase announcements (in many cases being enough to raise the stock assessment as market actors are given the information that the executives and directors regard the stock as being valued too conservatively) does not rest on the analysis of any sound economic evidence or can it be explained on the basis of the role of regulation or taxation, but is instead an immediate effect of the agency theory prescription favouring shareholder welfare.

Kliman and Williams (2014: 76) add to the argument that productive investments have *not* been reduced (as claimed by Lazonick, 2013) but have been financed by 'borrowed funds'. In the periods where stock repurchases in the US have exceeded 10 per cent of net operating surplus, in the three periods of 1984–90, 1998–2000 and 2004–07 (Kliman and Williams, 2014: 75), there was also a 'very strong positive association between net productive investment and "borrowing" – the proportion of net investment and dividends not funded out of after-tax profit – as shares of after-tax profits' (Kliman and Williams, 2014: 78). Still, if firms increasingly rely on credit markets for investment and thus reach historically high levels of debt at the same time as they buy back their own stock, this does not violate Lazonick's (2013) 'divest and distribute' argument as this shareholder welfare governance increases the level of debt. This leads to (1) stronger ties to the capital markets, reducing the possibilities for executives and directors to make autonomous future investment decisions, and (2) weakens the creditors' position qua principal, as they are less interested in, for example, stock buyback activities in comparison to securing long-term growth and economic value creation. '[C]redit markets have been an increasing important source of funding [for corporations]', Kliman and Williams (2014: 89) conclude. That is, Kliman and Williams (2014) highlight an interesting phenomenon – US corporations simultaneously increase their level of debt and their payout, indicating a new conventional wisdom in corporate governance – but the data does not justify or in any way support the shareholder welfare governance advocated by agency theorists inasmuch as this debt-driven investment combined with historically high payout levels counteracts the creditors' and long-term-oriented shareholders' interests.

10. A related phenomenon, also rooted in the expansion of the finance industry and its deregulation, is the decline of the public company and the increasing importance of closely held private equity firms (Appelbaum and Batt, 2012). These are firms that are owned by investors who raise money from, for example, pension funds and mutual funds and therefore are heavily indebted, yet capable of keeping the firm in private equity, that is, the firms do not have distributed ownership. As the access to cheap finance capital has flooded, for example, the American economy, new ways to finance companies have been developed. Appelbaum and Batt (2012: 43) emphasize that the private equity model of the firm needs to be understood in entirely different terms from the stock company, and that 'private equity funds buy businesses the way individuals purchase houses – with a down payment or deposit supported by mortgage finance'. The concern is that the supply of finance capital and the rise of the private equity-based firm have altered the way corporations are managed, not so much focusing on Return On Investment (ROI) as on Return On Equity (ROE). This means, Mazzucato and Shipman (2014: 1078) suggest, that also managers in listed companies feel obliged to pay dividends (or make stock repurchases, another channel to distribute cash flow to shareholders) and defend share prices that do not expose private equity-based investors to comparably higher risks than debt holders. In practice, this means that '[t]he growing convergence of equity and debt reduces management's scope to put shareholders' capital at risk through product or process innovation' (Mazzucato and Shipman, 2014: 1078). The consequence is that publicly listed companies find themselves under pressure to restore and uphold ROE by reducing the

shareholder's equity through moving assets off the balance sheet and buying back shares. This has at times included violations of standard accounting practices but has also led to firms 'running down their reserves' and failing to justify investments in production capital with medium to long-term payback times (Mazzucato and Shipman, 2014: 1078). Expressed differently, the growth of private equity has further entrenched the finance industry view of the firm as a bundle of contracts that de facto are understood as a bundle of financial assets to extract economic value.

Epilogue: neoclassical economic theory and ideology

COMPETITIVE CAPITALISM AS IDEOLOGY AND UTOPIA

In Karl Mannheim's *Ideology and Utopia* (1936), a seminal work in the field of the sociology of knowledge (see, for example, Merton, 1957), Mannheim reserves the term *ideology* for ideas that support the interests of privileged social groups and strata. *Utopian ideas*, in contrast, support underprivileged classes, and for the proponents of ideological ideas, utopian ideas are of necessity unattainable scenarios that violate the key propositions of ideological ideas, and therefore utopian ideas need to be marginalized and disarmed. In addition, Mannheim's (1936) sociological theory of ideological and utopian ideas underlines the constitutive nature of such ideas and how they create a shared sense of community and joint understanding, which is what Ludwik Fleck once referred to as a *thought collective*:

> We belong to a group not only because we are born into it, not merely because we profess to belong to it, nor finally because we give it our loyalty and allegiance, but primarily *because we see the world and certain things in the world* the way it does (i.e., in terms of the meanings of the group in question). (Mannheim, 1936: 19, emphasis added)

'An economist by training think of himself as a guardian of rationality, the ascriber of rationality to others, and the prescriber of rationality to the social world', the renowned economist Kenneth Arrow (1974: 16) admits.[1] This declaration is revealing as it indicates how economists tend to think of themselves as defenders not of specific ideological ideas but of reason pure and simple, allegedly unburdened by political ideologies and preferences. Unfortunately, that very claim of transcending the all-too-human realm of political ideologies and preferences is, per se, a key ideological statement. 'Scratch an economist and you find a deeply committed rationalist', Oliver Williamson (1975: 256) writes, stressing Arrow's (1974) point but with a more disconcerting implication in mind.

In the following, looking at how economists came to declare themselves as 'the ascribers of rationality to others' in contemporary society, a claim to authority of relevance for the previous analysis in this volume, shows that some of the most influential economic theories rooted in neoclassical synthesis, agency theory, are riddled with serious flaws. Preaching the gospel of neoclassical economic theory and teaching policy-makers the virtues of, for example, market efficiency is in short not to legitimately claim the position as the interpreter and spokesperson of rationality raw to the bone, but to advocate ideological beliefs in Mannheim's (1936) sense of the term.

COMPONENTS OF ECONOMIC REASONING

Reay (2012; 2007) examines how economists regard their own profession, and suggests that what economists above all perceive as 'proper' economic theory is not so much dependent on political convictions regarding, for example, free markets, as it is a form of systematic reasoning on the basis of a set of theories and mathematical models drawing on empirical data:

> What distinguishes the core from other worldviews [in economics] is not an overwhelming focus on market efficiency, but more generally a use of quantitative data and modeling techniques, concern for comparing costs and benefits, ideas about people responding to incentives, and the treatment of major economic phenomena as being systematically interconnected. (Reay, 2012: 76)

Hirschman and Berman (2014) identify two basic elements in what they refer to as the 'cognitive infrastructure' of economics: (1) a particular 'style of reasoning' (Hirschman and Berman, 2014: 794); and (2) the use of 'economic policy devices' (Hirschman and Berman, 2014: 796). The style of reasoning provides what Hirschman and Berman (2014) call 'devices for seeing' – the theories, models and tools that constitute the professional vision of the economist. Economic policy devices are in turn 'devices for choosing' from the alternatives that crystallize through the analysis of, for example, empirical data. Economists thus operate a theoretico-methodological apparatus that produces statements regarding economic conditions but also lends itself to policy-making. One of the consequences of this well-entrenched cognitive infrastructure is that economists, Reay (2007: 113) says, are relatively liberal regarding the line of demarcation between scholarly economics and mere punditry as long as the same economics theory and research methods were used to substantiate, for example, policy advocacy: '[o]verall, in fact, the general impression from most interviews was that boundaries between genuine economists and mere pundits were both vague and relatively unimportant'.

At the same time as economic reasoning is based on theories and empirical data, Reay (2012) notes that what distinguishes economics from other social sciences is that it more or less ignores factors and conditions outside of its own conceptual and theoretical domain, being satisfied with its own disciplinary foundation as a sufficient source for economic reasoning:

> Its narrow definition of what counts as 'economic' can be applied without questioning wider cultural and institutional contexts, and this again distinguishes it from most work in the other social sciences, making it an ideal resource for encouraging the impression that current norms of production, employment, and consumption are natural and inevitable. (Reay, 2012: 76)

This reliance on narrow analytical constructs is a distinct feature of the scholarly and professional discipline of economics (Kogut and Macpherson, 2011). In the case of economic reasoning, the critique of the core of the discipline commonly revolves around the mathematical modelling as a *sine qua non* for economic reasoning and policy advocacy. Also economists, including, for example, Velupillai (2014: 1336), are concerned about the dominance of mathematical formalism in the discipline: '[i]t is necessary to demystify the mathematical formalism in which current orthodoxy frames its economic theory to give it an air of objectivity that it does not deserve – and, moreover, cannot carry in the foundations of the mathematics its uses'.

Despite their historic success in shaping policy and politics more widely in the twentieth century (Fourcade, 2006; 2009), also economists encounter the tension between the production of economic theory in the 'republican' setting of academia and policy work in the 'unforgiving policy world' (Reay, 2012: 72–3), wherein uncertainty, negotiations and personal contacts matter equally as much as the capacity to be able to present robust theories and supportive empirical evidence (see, for example, Chwieroth, 2010; Conti, 2010; Chorev and Babb, 2009). This makes economics a field of expertise that on the one hand relies on strict formalism, theoretical development on the basis of empirical analysis, and a set of core principles (for example, rational choice theory and data collection methods derived therefrom), while on the other hand, it is brought into a world that is beset by complexities and a multitude of social activities and cultural beliefs that economists have for the most part mindfully ignored in order to present themselves as a rational and, if not a fully unified discipline, at least as one discipline anchored in certain shared premises.

As will be examined below, these shared premises did not emerge on the basis of free, unregulated scholarly research in the university setting, but were actively initiated, funded and sponsored by American institutes and think-tanks affiliated with military organizations. More specifically, the rational choice theory, today being the bedrock of neoclassical economic theory and its *Weltanschauung*, was one of the foremost and lasting consequences of the Cold War mobilization to defend the open, liberal society and economic freedom against totalitarian contestants, that is, communist planned economies.

RATIONAL CHOICE THEORY AND THE FREE SOCIETY

In Amadae's (2003: 4) account, the rational choice theory that constitutes the foundation of mainstream neoclassical economic theory needs to be understood as a Cold War-era technology, developed to defeat Soviet communism, Marxism and other competing collectivist ideologies, and to secure the '[i]nevitable linkage between free-market economics and democratic politics'. Amadae (2003) thus sheds light on the military roots of economic theory, where theory is war pursued by other means. 'Rational choice scholars simultaneously rebuilt the theoretical foundation of American capitalist democracy and defeated idealist, collectivist, and authoritarian social theories', Amadae (2003: 13) argues. In the new millennium, the degree to which rational choice theory has come to pervade popular discourse 'cannot be overestimated' (Amadae, 2003: 5).

Rational choice theory is simultaneously deeply entangled with and the foremost product of what Erickson et al. (2013) refer to as 'Cold War rationality'. The Cold War rationality that bred rational choice theory rested on a distinct set of defining characteristics: ideal rationality should be 'formal, and therefore largely independent of personality and context' (Erickson et al., 2013: 3); it frequently took the form of algorithms – 'rigid rules that determine unique solutions' – which were moreover supposed to provide 'optimal solutions to given problems, or delineate the most efficient means toward certain given goals' (Erickson et al., 2013: 3). Finally, to discover and lay bare this Holy Grail of *real* rationality, a redefinition of reason in a more narrow, instrumentalist meaning of the term, formalist and reductionist methodologies were developed and applied: 'complex tasks were analysed into simple, sequential steps; the peculiarities of context, whether historical or cultural, gave way to across-the-board generalizations; analysis took precedent over synthesis. And finally, at least ideally, advocates hoped that the rules could be applied mechanically: computers might reason better than human minds' (Erickson et al., 2013: 3–4).

This interest in computation and the mechanization of rationality – the dual and essentially recursive movement to make humans act as machines (or machine-like, on the basis of algorithms) and to devise machines making decisions like (idealized) humans – is thus a form of rediscovery and reformulation of eighteenth-century mechanics (*c.*1730–90). This was an epistemology and a scientific ideology, Riskin (2003: 99) argues, that both regarded 'living creatures as machines' and aimed to 'vivify machinery' and that ultimately sought to 'collapse the gap between animate and artificial machinery' (Riskin, 2003: 101).

Truthful to this overarching research programme, rational choice theory 'presupposes that rational agents have a consistent set of preferences and act to obtain that which they most prefer' (Amadae, 2003: 5), a proposition applying to *all* decision situations. Therefore rational choice theorists value consistency more highly than any other analytical parameter. As a consequence, human behaviour is widely understood as being '[s]elf-interested in a narrowly constructed, self-oriented manner' (Amadae, 2003: 5). At the same time, this preference for and firm belief in consistency contains and breeds the tragedy of rational choice theory and the rationality it preaches as it offers a far more contrived image of rationality than previous and competing theories do:

> Rational choice theory supersedes the theoretical principles defining 'efficiency' in engineering, in scientific management, and in economics as constrained maximization. It is an unprecedented system, informing human practices and governing them by an internal rationale built on basic logical principles. The most rudimentary of these principles – that individuals' preferences obey transitive orderings – has only a tenuous relationship with the means–end rationality characterizing the older concept of efficiency that requires [a] well-specified criterion for maximization such as psychic pleasure. (Amadae, 2003: 292–3)

The historian of science Lorraine Daston (2015) presents an argument regarding the economic theory's colonialization of the term *rationality* and, by implication, as we will see, renders *prediction* (that is, correlation, and in some cases even causality) more important than *theory* (in the conventional use of the term as what enables understanding and explanation). In Daston's (2015) account, economists have surrendered the scientific ambition to explain and understand to be able to construct a fully integrated and seemingly watertight analytical framework. When economists like Eugene Fama contend that markets are always rational – even when 'markets go mad', like in the many bubbles and collapses that, for example, Deringer (2015), Baker (2013), Levitin and Wachter (2012) account for – they are, Daston (2015: 672) suggests, '[b]oth flirting with tautology (markets *define* what is rational) and shifting the burden of being rational from individual actors (who may be addled or confused or deluded) to the market itself, which allegedly never errs'. In other words, in order to make their analytical models consistent and to maintain their jurisdictional authority as the privileged spokespersons of such analytical models, '[e]conomists prefer the blind logic (sometimes known as the invisible hand) of the market to the intelligent design of individual actors and governments' (Daston, 2015: 673). Through this operation, the term *rationality* is colonialized by economic reason, and the term *rationality* becomes 'almost synonymous' with *economic rationality* (Daston, 2015: 675).[2] 'Deliberative reason is a luxury that the parsimonious efficiency of rationality cannot afford', Daston (2015: 673) summarizes.

As the economist Thomas Schelling proposes (cited in Daston, 2015: 675), it would be more adequate to speak of an 'economic theory of rationality' carefully separated from the use of the term *rationality* in other disciplines and discourses; instead, Daston (2015: 675) contends, 'economic rationality (of several sorts) simply swallowed up rationality'. Using the famous example of Ulysses and the Sirens (where Ulysses had himself tied to the mast of his ship by his crew – the crew having their ears plugged, in turn – in order to escape the Sirens, and yet gain the benefit of hearing their otherworldly beautiful song), one of the most widespread cases of instrumental rationality in the social science litera- ture, Daston (2015) suggests that economic theory based on a tautologi- cal or circular definition of rationality fails to explain and understand Ulysses' behaviour as his reason remains concealed beneath the surface of instrumental rationality:

> [Ulysses] wants to hear the Sirens, to know their song, though he does not trust himself to resist its lure … It was obviously rational to want to evade the Sirens' deadly trap for seafarers; was it also rational to want to hear their song? Economic rationality is mute on this topic: individual utility functions accommodate all manner of desires, no matter how strange, so long as preferences are consistently ordered. (Daston, 2015: 676)

This preference for analytical models that reduce rationality to consist- ency and the defenestration of the scientific virtue of explanation and understanding with allegedly murky concepts such as beliefs and norms (which mainstream economists cannot accommodate in their models at low costs and/or regard as being deceptive *tout court*), is also a concern for the economists themselves. Bear and Orr (1967) criticize Milton Friedman's 'positive economics program' for dismissing theory as a means for understanding economic affairs and making predictions the principal virtue of economics: 'Friedman proposed that a theory is strictly an instrument for generating predictions, and it should be evaluated by the empirical examination of its predictions, not by empirical or introspective appraisal of its "assumptions"' (Bear and Orr, 1967: 188). In Bear and Orr's (1967) view, this is an unacceptable position, simply because, they continue (1967: 191), 'a scientist is concerned with how things happen, not only with what happens, and the Friedman methodology makes it impossible effectively to pursue that concern'. In Bear and Orr's (1967) account, the sheer difficulty of developing a comprehensive and logically consistent economic theory entices proponents of 'positive economics' to surrender such scientific objectives altogether:

> Dismay over the state of theory is held to a minimum if theories are regarded as mere predictive instruments. However, the distinctness of the alternative hypotheses, and the lack of generality of either taken alone, rule out any claim of explaining the empirical phenomenon in its full range – the prediction statements of neither theory are congruent with all the empirical observations. (Bear and Orr, 1967: 192)

Using (by today's standards) a relatively trivial example, that of Galileo's measurement of the acceleration of falling bodies (see Koyré, 1968), Bear and Orr (1967) argue that just because certain simplifications are made in the experimental situation, it does not follow that such simplifications should not be accommodated by the analytical models being developed on the basis of the empirical evidence, even in cases where certain predictions are correct (which they may be under certain conditions). If that were the case, the analytical model, despite its ability to make accurate predictions, would fail to help the experimenting researcher understand and explain the phenomenon observed in scientific terms:

> To predict that a falling body will accelerate at a rate of thirty-two feet/second is to assume that air resistance is unimportant ... In every case, the cost of incorporating air resistance is probably high; and, in many cases, the resulting greater accuracy of prediction is small compared to error of measurement, and the return from greater accuracy is trivial. This return, by the way, will always depend on the purposes and needs of the investigator. Thus, judgment concerning the effect of air resistance must be exercised in each new

situation; a theory based on zero air resistance sometimes succeeds, sometimes fails. But note *how peculiar it would be to assert that air resistance
should be omitted from predictions about falling bodies as a matter of course,
even if it could be included at zero cost!* (Bear and Orr, 1967: 195, emphasis
added)

Expressed differently, Bear and Orr (1967: 195) contend, '[i]n the
development of theory, feasibility may temporarily override logic, but it
cannot permanently supplant logic'. In Daston's (2015: 673) view,
orthodox economic theory's definition of rationality inscribed a priori
into market evaluation is a puzzling concern as it is in conflict with
'many of the most fundamental aims of science', namely to 'understand
the causes of things as comprehensively and coherently as possible'.

The Tragic Failure of Rational Choice Theory

Discussing the well-known conundrum of the prisoner's dilemma,
Amadae (2003: 294) demonstrates how rational choice theory cannot
transcend its own conceptual rigour imposed by its consistency criteria,
making 'loyalty, trust, and commitment between individuals' an aporia
for the proposed analytical model and its standards for rationality. These
persistent human faculties present the greatest challenge to game
theorists (game theory is an application of rational choice theory)
because, in the rational choice theory view, 'the ever-present incentive
for individuals to cheat on each other renders cooperation an unstable
equilibrium' (Amadae, 2003: 294). As a consequence, ratifying the
consistency criteria, rational choice theorists mandate agents to act
self-interestedly under *all*, nor *specific* conditions (*ex hypothesi*, the idea
of 'specific choice situations' is an illegitimate and unnecessary theoretical complication):

> In the world of rational choice theory, betrayal in the Prisoner's dilemma,
> which is thought to characterize many aspects of human relationships, is not
> just commonplace, but a rationally sanctioned norm … [F]or rational choice
> theorists, the litmus test for a rational choice liberal is one who defects when
> confronted by a Prisoner's dilemma, and cheats in collective action scenarios
> unless it is clearly in his interest to do otherwise. (Amadae, 2003: 295)

The presence of such normative prescriptions within what rational choice
theorists understand as a universal and logically consistent model for
rationality is yet another concern. Rational choice theory purports to
'accept people as they are without censure' (the rational choice theory
literature is peppered with references to 'human nature'), and yet it

'proposes specific standards of rational behaviour' – two apparently irreconcilable positions (Amadae, 2003: 296). Thus, Amadae (2003: 296) continues, 'while presenting itself as nonnormative, rational choice theory both proposes logical tenets of rationality and assumes the presence in society of individual pursuit of self-interest. Both of these theoretical stances are normative.' The ultimate consequence of the sacrificing of all human faculties, not capable of obeying unreasonably strict rationality criteria for the benefit of alleged theoretical consistency and practical consistency on the part of supposedly rational agents, is that much human behaviour is debarred from reason *tout court*:

> To insist that human behaviour be understood, even predicted, in terms of a well-ordered set of transitive preferences combined with strategic calculations of how to maximize expected utility is to nullify modes of existence not structured around payoffs; love, sympathy, respect, duty, and valor fall by the wayside. Transitivity, completeness, and the axioms of expected utility become the defining characteristics of rationality whereas the dictum of treating individuals as ends in themselves has no basis in reason. (Amadae, 2003: 296)

Therefore, rational choice theory, grown from Cold War rationality and its militarism culture and the fear and hatred of Soviet communism (and in some cases, of any political and social system deviating from the democratic system contained by competitive capitalism) was favoured by a small but highly influential group of social actors. Rational choice theory would soon serve to further spread economic theory to, for example, include also political choice under the label *public choice theory* (see, for example, Buchanan, 1954), based on the proposition that political interests and political freedom are subordinate to economic interest and economic freedom (Amadae and Bueno de Mesquita, 1999) But that is another story, not further explored in this setting.

THE THEORETICAL REALISM OF NEOCLASSICAL ECONOMICS

Ultimately, Bennett and Friedman (2008: 199) suggest, rational choice theory misleads economists to overstate the virtues of formalist and mathematized reasoning, a tendency that undermines their ability to explain and understand the world:

> economics is not necessarily a science that confers expertise *about reality*, as natural sciences do. The opinions of those who hold economics Ph.D.s do not

stem from the results of controlled experimentation … Unlike mathematical axioms, the assumptions taught to economists are supposed to describe the real world, and we think that they often do. But without empirical testing of a type that is usually unavailable in social science – controlled experimentation – they cannot merely be assumed to do so, *a priori*. In principle, economists' opinions *per se* have no better grip on reality than did the opinions that were taught to theologians at the University of Paris 700 years ago. (Bennett and Friedman, 2008: 202)

Block and Somers (2014: 231) speak about 'theoretical realism' as the primary epistemological position of neoclassical economic theory, an ideological idea that '[i]t is not empirical observations but logical deduction that is the source of their foundational tenets'. As theory always trumps empirical observations in this theoretical realism, a thorny question is why only a limited group of 'ascribers of rationality' are capable of realizing what few others can see (especially if economic phenomena are portrayed as being 'naturally occurring'), and on what basis this favoured group can maintain the authority to articulate and prescribe remedies for existing economic problems:

> Common sense … demands an answer to the question of how any generally accepted knowledge can be achieved if truth is hidden from all but the anointed knowers … Reality becomes a matter of deductive reasoning, which builds from arbitrary assumptions that can never be democratically adjudicated … This type of economic reasoning relies on the special capacities of the few, those who are the priests of philosophical logic rather than of empirical observation. (Block and Somers, 2014: 234).

Ultimately, Block and Somers (2014) remark, the preference for formalism and mathematical modelling inherent in rational choice theory, effectively marginalizes the role of critical self-correction: '[a]s a group [economists] mistook beauty, clad in impressive-looking mathematics, for truth … The central cause for the profession's failure was the desire for an all-encompassing, intellectually elegant approach that also gave economists a chance to show off their mathematical prowess' (Paul Krugman, cited in Block and Somers, 2014: 232).

What Bourdieu (2005: 13) referred to as the *morbus mathematicus* of economic theory – its 'mathematical sickness' – thus became more of a blindfold than an instrument for economists eager to advance their ideas on the basis of mathematical modelling. In the current use of the term (mathematized) rationality, its foremost purpose is to accomplish things in this world, 'not to understand it', Daston (2015: 673) suggests. Even more to the point, this capacity to act – that is, to make more or less accurate predictions and to issue statements regarding economic conditions and affairs – comes at the price of abandoning the understanding of the economy as a proper object matter. Thus economists deliberately fashion an ontology and an epistemology for themselves that provide them with little opportunity than to speak 'the economic language of efficiency rather than insight, of correlations rather than causes' (Daston, 2015: 673). When choosing between the authority to speak on behalf of an analytical system and to develop scientific theories conducive to understanding and explanation, proponents of market-based rationality opt for the former. Thus economic theory endorses, like some other 'big data' scientific fields (say, systems biology; see Burbeck and Jordan, 2006; Fujimura, 2005; Walkenhauer, 2001), a 'theory-free science' (Daston, 2015: 676), a scientific pursuit that renders rational scientific virtues such as understanding and explanation secondary to other interests.

For instance, the axiomatic principle of market efficiency, by no means endorsed by all economists and yet still being at the very core of the neoclassical economic theory framework, has time and again been disqualified as a credible proposition: '[m]arket failure isn't an intellectual curiosity. In many areas of the economy, such as health care, high technology, and finance, it is endemic', Cassidy (2009: 9) writes. Black's (2005) study of the US savings and loans industry crisis of the 1980s, one of the first financial crises in the new era of finance industry deregulation, proposes that economists are paying the price for their ignorance of other disciplines (in this case legal theory and behavioural science) when markets no longer operate as prescribed:

> Economists know almost nothing about fraud. The dominant law-and-economics theory is that there is no serious control fraud, so it is not worth studying ... prominent U.S. economists generally believe that regulation is the problem and deregulation is the solution. The deregulation ideology was the initial problem, but the fact that their policies led to disaster also brought acute embarrassment. They had the normal human wish to avoid taking responsibility for their mistakes. Their embarrassment was particularly acute because they consider themselves the only true social scientists and believe that theory and facts, not ideology, drive their ideas ... Economists missed the problem because of social class and self-interest. Few economists are prepared to see business people, particularly patrons, as criminals. Many of the top financial economists worked for the control frauds, and the collapse created such embarrassment that they felt compelled to deny that their employers were frauds ... Economists developed a conventional wisdom about the debacle and have not reexamined it ... All aspects of the conventional wisdom proved false upon examination. (Black, 2005: 12–13)

Unfortunately, the owl of Minerva only flies at dusk. Ben Bernanke, the chairman of the Federal Reserve during the 2008 finance industry collapse, who assured only a few years before the system-wide breakdown of the economic system that, for example, the remarkable rise of prices in the housing market was sound and ultimately a beneficial effect of free market reform,[3] now agrees that markets may after all fail and that there is evidence of moral hazard: "'I think we did the right thing to try to preserve financial stability", [Ben Bernanke] said of the Bear [Stearns] interventions. "That's our job. Yes, it's moral-hazard-inducing, but the right way to address this question is not to let institutions fail and have a financial meltdown'" (Ben Bernanke, cited from an interview with Cassidy, 2009: 320).

Knowing in advance and knowing in hindsight are two quite different things, and taking pride in being a predictive science in the Newtonian tradition sides poorly with the failure to predict even the most pervasive, spectacular and systemic collapse of the capitalist economic system since the Great Depression in the 1930s. It is thus no wonder that the Great Recession has spawned a massive and still growing body of literature where economists, social scientists and pundits seek to make sense of this divergence between the alleged 'sophistication' of the neoclassical economic theory framework and the macroeconomic and finance market causes and consequences of the 2008 events (see, for example, Blinder, 2013; Wolfson and Epstein, 2013; Friedman and Kraus, 2012; Stiglitz, 2010; Griffith-Jones et al., 2010; Sinn, 2010; Sorkin, 2009). When being interrogated about the 2008 events, the free market theorist Eugene F. Fama, a major authority figure for free marketeers, argued that his theories 'fared quite well' during the events (Cassidy, 2009: 356). In 2013, Fama was awarded the Bank of Sweden's Nobel Memorial Prize in Economic Sciences, but the jury's motivation did not mention the efficient market hypothesis that brought fame to Fama, but instead spoke of his studies of finance markets more broadly. For Davis and Kim (2015), though, there is little doubt why Fama could claim this prestigious prize. For scholars that do not share this belief in the efficiency of free markets, this was a curious statement omitting Fama's most widely renowned and influential contribution to economic theory and economic policy-making: it almost appeared as if the prize committee was embarrassed to highlight what is likely to be Fama's lasting legacy, given the 2008 events. For Eugene F. Fama, granted the highest credential of his scholarly discipline, it is still the midday of market efficiency and the sun shines brightly over the world fashioned on the basis of neoclassical economic theories.

CORPORATE GOVERNANCE IN INVESTOR CAPITALISM: THE ARGUMENT REVISITED

In his performance *Dress to Kill* (1998), the celebrated stand-up come-dian Eddie Izzard spins a joke around the role of importance of accessing proper flags in the British colonialist project. When the British 'built empires' – or 'stole countries', as Izzard puts it – the 'cunning use of flags' was one of the key strategies of the British officers. These officials could just 'sail around the world' and 'stick a flag' into the ground to declare that the territory was now officially British whenever they wished to. When indigenous people, for example, in India, objected and denied the legitimacy of such declarations – 'You can't claim us, we live here!, they go' – the British officers would laconically retort, 'Do you have a flag?' When the frustration derived from this interrogation grew on the part of the now formally colonialized people, the British officers could neatly defend their authority on the basis of their ability to stick flags in the ground: 'No flag, no country!' Then they would add, 'That's the rules that have been just made up!', bringing the discussion to an end. Those with the flag could righteously make the claim that they were now the lords of the territory, regardless of who inhabited the land upon their arrival. The new rules did not recognize that specific condition or anything else for that matter. Colonial authority is here strictly under-stood as a matter of the relation between the flag, the territory and the ownership-claim allegedly legitimized by performing the procedure of sticking a flag in the ground.

It is tempting to claim that economists have followed a similar strategy, but with 'a cunning use of theory'. Economists entered the discussion regarding corporate law and governance equipped with (in order of appearance) an ideology of economic freedom, a stated preference for efficiency (vis-à-vis other social and economic objectives), price theory (grounded in carefully selected parts of neoclassical economic theory) expressed as the efficient market hypothesis, and the belief in the autonomous, calculating subject separated from all meaningful social relations – a methodological orthodoxy that they argued could be meaningfully applied to all cases. As this package of ideologies, theoret-ical propositions and methodological preferences could not rationalize away corporate law (as it did with all 'social and behavioural theories' about corporate governance and other economic activities), law was now to be understood in 'economic terms' (the Chicago law and economics school position). In cases where law could not be subsumed under the price theory/efficient market hypothesis framework, it was declared to be either obsolete (that is, inducing unnecessary 'law enforcement costs') or more head-on violating the principle of 'economic freedom', commonly clad in the language of efficiency (no further justification needed, apparently, within this circulatory, recursive line of reasoning), a term that was widely advocated as being desirable for society as a whole – per se a bold claim. The claim that economic theory has served within a programme of 'theoretical imperialism' has long been a cliché, a widespread and popular statement among both economists and non-economists not sharing the commitment to prescribed theoretical frameworks and methodological prescriptions. Still, in the case of the advancement of the entangled set of propositions and assumptions in price theory, agency theory and contractual theory in the field of corporate governance, few other terms more aptly capture how maps (theories) have been used to define the territory (legislation, economic practices, and their consequences and outcomes). The 'free market theory' (in fact, a blend of various ideologies, theoretical propositions and methodological prescriptions) that brought agency theory and contractual theory and served to redefine corporate governance as the pursuit of shareholder happiness was very much the corporate governance counterpart of the flag that helped Izzard's colonialists make their claim that they were now the lords of the territory. Economists who pledged their allegiance to economic freedom and the efficacy of free market pricing 'just made up the rules' that managers induced agency costs that were higher than any other comparable costs derived from the separation of ownership and management (an institutional innovation indisputably at the core of competitive capitalism, whose economic benefits most plausibly dwarf the aggregated agency costs in comparison) and that 'the market for managerial control' would effectively minimize these allegedly towering agency costs. In practice this meant – and this would be the precise moment when the economists 'stick the flag into the ground' – that shareholders should be given if not all, at least most of the residual cash generated by the corporation. 'No theory, no corporate governance policy guidelines', economists would then boldly announce.

A related question is whether the entire 'economic freedom theory and policy framework' was ever at all intended to present an accurate theoretical model of effective corporate governance; perhaps all this was just a charade to justify the unbridled authority of capital owners that the shareholder welfare model has performatively imposed in the era of investor capitalism. Perhaps the shareholder welfare advocacy 'worked backwards', not really starting with microeconomic propositions regarding individual preferences and utility functions, but instead growing from the fear of collectivism and policies aimed at creating economic and political equality in the New Deal era and thereafter. Perhaps this is a moot question, a form of academic hair-splitting that introduces 'unnecessary complications' such as questions regarding causality and intentions in the model (as mainstream economists could object) as the outcomes have been exactly the same regardless of the trajectory. Using allegedly 'scientific arguments' or simply adhering to preferred ideologies matters little when the long-term consequences diverge very little and, that is, a significant growth of economic inequality on the basis of a combination of theoretical elaborations, policy-making footwork, and ideological storytelling. Once the flag is stuck in the ground and the controversies are at least temporarily reconciled, the flag per se, Eddie Izzard reminds us, is easily forgotten as the material object that initially was invoked as an obtrusive symbol of authority and sovereignty. Enforcing policies and winning in the political field is rarely only a matter of 'winning debates' and 'being right' (in the conventional sense of the term) and certainly not, as some academics may think, derived from the presentation of the most accurate and sophisticated theory, but to organize collaborations between heterogeneous but influential actors and to demonstrate a persistence in the arguments presented over time. When that work is successfully accomplished, inconsistent theories and erroneous assumptions suddenly no longer matter and policies and legislation can be influenced regardless of the robustness of underlying propositions and the logical consistency of truth claims. Such is the world we live in, hemmed by bounded rationality in conceivable ways. Truth is a thing of this world, and making the claim to speak the truth over time may be rewarded in the end, regardless of what is actually being said.

In summary, economics is undoubtedly a science that strongly influences the governance and regulation of the economy and society, and as the economy and society are after all human accomplishments rather than being (in the former case) a naturally occurring phenomenon embedded in market transactions, it would be helpful if economists committed to the mapping of economic systems would pay attention to a wider set of conditions and theories, including not least economic sociology and management studies. 'Few theorists', Posner (2009: 259) says, 'spend their time poring over or digging behind banks' balance sheets'. In fact, that is precisely what, for example, accounting researchers do. Perhaps, then, they should be interrogated next time some neoclassicist sits down to formulate a grand but parsimonious theoretical framework, carefully designed to majestically hover over all this all-too-human world of business including all its complexities and 'ifs' and 'thens', so perplexingly manifold for the theorists valuing purity, formalism and elegance over accuracy and usefulness.

In the aftermath of the events of 2008, economists have done the best they could to protect their jurisdictional discretion but no matter how well they fight to uphold inherited and entrenched authority and privileges, the events of 2008 were too large and substantial and violated too many central propositions of the free market doctrine to simply let themselves be swept under the epistemological carpet. The capitalist economic system remains the most efficient system to produce the highest possible output, but such benefits are not exclusively derived from free market contracting and transactions but have emerged on the basis of a variety of innovations in legislation, political and regulatory oversight, managerial skills and practices, engineering competence, and not least a sheer sense of ethical responsibility and moral standards. Reducing the merits of the economic system of competitive capitalism and its corporate system to a matter of the virtues of market efficiency grounded in 'economic rationality' (that is, rational choice theory) may be an issue that can entertain seminarists participating in economic theory discussions in cloistered communities, but it is a fragile basis for a viable economic system and meaningful policies.

NOTES

1. When the term *economists* is invoked in this epilogue, the term does not denote the entire economist profession (being a most heterogeneous professional community) but economists who put their faith in the efficient market hypothesis and endorse price theory to justify and advocate, among many other things, shareholder welfare governance, contractual theories and minimal market regulation.

2. More specifically, this 'economic rationality' is, as demonstrated in Buturovic and Tasic's (2015) brilliant dissection of Daniel Kahneman's experimental studies of decision-making (see, for example, Kahneman, 2011), a very specific, contrived and overtly statistics-induced kind of rationality that has little to do with everyday decision-making and certainly not when it comes to non-trivial decisions. Presenting the experimental subject with a series of puzzles that purport to test the subject's ability to make statistically correct inferences, Kahneman and his colleagues overlook that the experimental subject may interpret the experimental situation and the experimenter's intentions differently than the experimenter, thus (1) making the highly artificial experimental situation very loosely coupled to actual, real-life decisions, and (2) ignoring the rationality of the subject's response to the experimenter's inquiries when he or she interprets the broader social situation wherein he or she is located (see also Cohen, 1980). '[P]eople may not recognize that they are answering a trick question that is likely to lead them to the wrong answer. Designed with only literal interpretation and formal probability theory in mind, such experiments can lead to the interpretation of subjects' rational interpretations of the entire context in which the questions are asked as "irrational"', Buturovic and Tasic (2015: 137) say. Regardless of fallacious research experiment design, the experimenters still make the normative assumption that the capacity to make logically correct statistical inferences is 'more rational' than 'good heuristics' (Buturovic and Tasic, 2015: 133). Making the argument that people by and large have a problem with intuitively applying elementary statistical methods when making decisions is one thing, but to speak of such shortcomings as evidence of 'irrationality' more

broadly is to stretch research findings beyond what is scientifically credible; amusing experimentally derived anecdotes do not justify bold claims regarding human behaviour.

Moreover, even if people demonstrate fallacious behaviour, such findings are insignificant and matter little in everyday life, Buturovic and Tasic (2015: 141) argue persuasively. Stubbornly to think strictly in terms of statistical knowledge and statistical inferences would be widely interpreted as mere foolishness because the capacity to think creatively and imaginatively is today 'a staple in business, clinical, and educational contexts, to the point where phrases like "thinking outside the box" have become clichés' (Buturovic and Tasic, 2015: 141): 'It is in the discovery of options and possibilities where most of the challenge of decision making lies, not in precisely comparing predefined and given options' (Buturovic and Tasic, 2015: 141; see, for example, Huang and Pearce, 2015). Finally, as real-world problems that actually engage individuals and are likely to mobilize their entire capacity to make 'rational decisions' are complicated to study (in many cases simply because there are no widely agreed-upon standards for what 'rational behaviour' is under such conditions, thus rendering such research projects 'undoable'), experimental situations are widely but disputably treated as a proxy for 'real-life rationality' (Buturovic and Tasic, 2015: 140). Buturovic and Tasic (2015) strongly question the legitimacy of making universal claims on the basis of data generated in experimental situations, even in the case where methodological problems are eliminated.

In summary, if there is one thing that can be learned from Buturovic and Tasic's (2015) analysis, it is that behavioural economics researchers are irrationally deducing what they regard as universally and practically relevant theories about humans' alleged systematic irrationality (or, perhaps better, 'sub-rationality', that is, 'bounded' rationality) on the basis of data extracted in highly artificial settings riddled with theoretical and methodological problems and inconsistencies. This is accompanied by unwarranted normative assumptions regarding how decisions *should* be made (for example, be consistent and based on statistical inference), at the same time as decisions of practical relevance are simply overlooked on the basis of methodological challenges. This literature, presented by the champions of rationality, ultimately 'tell[s] us very little about how people think', Buturovic and Tasic (2015: 141) say: '[a]rtificially induced quirks of human cognition are examined in excruciating detail while everyday decision making of great individual and social consequence are ignored'.

3. 'Housing prices have risen by nearly 25 percent over the past two years. Although speculative activity has increased in some areas, at a national level these price increases largely reflect strong economic fundamentals' (Ben Bernanke, Chairman of Council of Economic Advisers, speech before Congress, October 2005, cited in Mian and Sufi, 2014: 78).

Bibliography

Abdelal, Rawi (2007), *Capital rules: the construction of the global finance*, Cambridge: Harvard University Press.

Abolafia, Michael (2001), *Making markets: opportunism and restraint on Wall Street*, Cambridge: Harvard University Press.

Abraham, John and Sheppard, Julie (1999), Complacent and conflicting scientific expertise in British and American drug regulation: clinical risk assessment of Triozolam, *Social Studies of Science*, 29(6): 804–43.

Adelstein, Richard P. (1991), 'The nation as an economic unit': Keynes, Roosevelt, and the managerial ideal, *Journal of American History*, 78(1): 160–87.

Ahamed, Liaquat (2009), *Lords of finance: bankers who broke the world*, London: Penguin.

Aizenman, Joshua, Pinto, Brian and Sushko, Vladyslav (2013), Financial sector ups and downs and the real sector in the open economy: up by the stairs, down by the parachute, *Emerging Markets Review*, 16(1): 1–30.

Akard, Patrick J. (1992), Corporate mobilization and political power: the transformation of U.S. economic policy in the 1970s, *American Sociological Review*, 57(5): 597–615.

Akerlof, George (1970), The market for 'lemons': quality uncertainty and the market mechanism, *Quarterly Journal of Economics*, 84(3): 488–500.

Alchian, Armen and Demsetz, Harold (1972), Production, information costs and economic organization, *American Economic Review*, 62(5): 777–95.

Algan, Yann and Cahuc, Pierre (2013), Trust and growth, *Annual Review of Economics*, 5: 521–49.

Allen, Matthew (2004), The varieties of capitalism paradigm: not enough variety?, *Socio-Economic Review*, 2(1): 87–108.

Allen, Michael Patrick and Parsons, Nicholas L. (2006). The institutionalization of fame: achievement, recognition, and cultural consecration in baseball, *American Sociological Review*, 71(5): 808–25.

Almandoz, Juan (2014), Founding teams as carriers of competing logics: when institutional forces predict banks' risk exposure, *Administrative Science Quarterly*, 59(3): 442–73.

Amadae, Sonya Michelle (2003), *Rationalizing capitalist democracy: the Cold War origins of rational choice liberalism*, Chicago and London: The University of Chicago Press.

Amadae, Sonya Michelle and Bueno de Mesquita, Bruce (1999), The Rochester school: the origins of positive political theory, *Annual Review of Political Science*, 2: 269–95.

Andrade, Gregor, Mitchell, Mark and Stafford, Erik (2001), New evidence and perspectives on mergers, *Journal of Economic Perspectives*, 15(2): 103–20.

Andrews, Edmund L. (2009), *Busted: life inside the great mortgage meltdown*, New York: W.W. Norton.

Appelbaum, Eileen and Batt, Rosemary (2012), *Private equity at work: when Wall Street manages Main Street*, New York: Russell Sage Foundation.

Arrow, Kenneth J. (1964), Control in large organizations, *Management Science*, 10(3): 397–408.

Arrow, Kenneth J. (1974), *The limits of organization*, New York: W.W. Norton.

Ashford, Nicholas, Ayers, Christine and Stone, Robert (1985), Using regulation to change the market for innovation, *Harvard Environment Law Review*, 9(2): 419–66.

Avgouleas, Emilios (2009), The global financial crisis, behavioural finance and financial regulation: in search of a new orthodoxy, *Journal of Corporate Law Studies*, 9(1): 23–59.

Babb, Sarah (2013), The Washington Consensus as transnational policy paradigm: its origins, trajectory and likely successor, *Review of International Political Economy*, 20(2): 268–97.

Bainbridge, Stephen M. (2006), Director primacy and shareholder disempowerment, *Harvard Law Review*, 119(6): 1735–58.

Baker, Dean (2013), Speculation and asset bubbles, in Wolfson, Martin H. and Epstein, Gerald A. (eds), *Handbook of the political economy of financial crises*, New York and Oxford: Oxford University Press, pp. 47–60.

Baker, George P. and Smith, George David (1998), *The new financial capitalists: Kohlberg, Kravis and Roberts and the creation of corporate value*, Cambridge: Cambridge University Press.

Barba, Aldo and Pivetti, Massimo (2009), Rising household debt: its causes and macroeconomic implications – a long-period analysis, *Cambridge Journal of Economics*, 33(1): 113–37.

Baron, James N., Dobbin, Frank R. and Jennings, P. Devereaux (1986), War and peace: the evolution of modern personnel administration in U.S. industry, *American Journal of Sociology*, 92(2): 350–83.

Baumol, William J. (1959), *Business behavior, value and growth*, New York: Macmillan.

Baysinger, Barry D. and Butler, Henry N. (1985), The role of corporate law in the theory of the firm, *Journal of Law and Economics*, 28(1): 179–91.

Bear, D.V.T. and Orr, Daniel (1967), Logic and expediency in economic theorizing, *Journal of Political Economy*, 75(2): 188–96.

Bebchuk, Lucian A. (2005), The case for increasing shareholder power, *Harvard Law Review*, 118(3): 835–914.

Bebchuk, Lucian A. (2006), Reply: letting shareholders set the rules, *Harvard Law Review*, 119(6): 1784–813.

Bebchuk, Lucian A. (2007), The myth of the shareholder franchise, *Virginia Law Review*, 93(3): 675–732.

Bebchuk, Lucian A. and Fried, J. (2004), *Pay without performance: the unfulfilled promise of executive compensation*, Cambridge: Harvard University Press.

Bebchuk, Lucian A. and Neeman, Zvika (2010), Investor protection and interest group politics, *Review of Financial Studies*, 23(3): 1089–119.

Bebchuk, Lucian A. and Weisbach, Michael S. (2010), The state of corporate governance research, *Review of Financial Studies*, 23(3): 939–61.

Bebchuk, Lucian A., Cohen, Alma and Ferrell, Allen (2009), What matters in corporate governance?, *The Review of Financial Studies*, 22(2): 783–827.

Becker, Gary S. and Stigler, George J. (1974), Law enforcement, malfeasance, and compensation of enforcers, *Journal of Legal Studies*, 3(1): 1–18.

Beckert, Jens (2013), Capitalism as a system of expectations: toward a sociological microfoundation of political economy, *Politics and Society*, 41(3): 323–50.

Bekaert, Geert, Harvey, Campbell R. and Lundblad, Christian (2005), Does financial liberalization spur growth?, *Journal of Financial Economics*, 77(1): 3–55.

Bellow, Saul (2015), *There is simply too much to think about*, Collected nonfiction, ed. Benjamin Taylor, New York: Viking.

Bendix, Reinhart (1956), *Work and authority in industry*, New York: Wiley.

Bennett, Stephen Earl and Friedman, Jeffrey (2008), The irrelevance of economic theory to understanding economic ignorance, *Critical Review*, 20(3): 195–258.

Berkowitz, Edward and McQuaid, Kim (1978), Businessman and bureaucrat: the evolution of the American social welfare system, 1900–1940, *Journal of Economic History*, 38(1): 120–42.

Berle, Adolf A. and Means, Gardiner C. (1934 [1991]), *The modern corporation & private property*, New Brunswick: Transaction Publishers.

Berman, Elizabeth Popp and Pagnucco, Nicholas (2010), Economic ideas and the political process: debating tax cuts in the U.S. House of Representatives, 1962–1981, *Politics and Society*, 38(3): 347–72.

Bertrand, Marianne and Mullainathan, Sendhil (2003), Enjoying the quiet life? Corporate governance and managerial preferences, *Journal of Political Economy*, 111(5): 1043–75.

Beunza, Daniel and Garud, Raghu (2007), Calculators, lemmings or frame-makers? The intermediary roles of securities analysts, *Sociological Review*, 55(2): 13–39.

Beunza, Daniel and Stark, David (2004), Tools of the trade: the socio-technology of arbitrage in a Wall Street trading room, *Industrial and Corporate Change*, 13(2): 369–400.

Bhagat, Sanjai and Black, Bernard (2002), The non-correlation between board independence and long-term firm performance, *Journal of Corporation Law*, 27: 231–74.

Bhagat, Sanjai, Bolton, Brian and Romano, Roberta (2008), The promise and peril of corporate governance indices, *Columbia Law Review*, 108(8): 1803–82.

Bidwell, Matthew, Briscoe, Forrest, Fernandez-Mateo, Isabel and Sterling, Adina (2013), The employment relationship and inequality: how and why changes in employment practices are reshaping rewards in organizations, *Academy of Management Annals*, 7: 61–121.

Black, Fisher and Scholes, Myron (1973), The pricing of options and corporate liabilities, *Journal of Political Economy*, 81(3): 637–54.

Black, William K. (2005), *The best way to rob a bank is to own one: how corporate executives and politicians looted the S&L industry*, Austin: The University of Texas Press.

Blair, Margaret M. (2003), Locking in capital: what corporate law achieved for business organizers in the nineteenth century, *UCLA Law Review*, 51(2): 387–455.

Blair, Margaret M. and Stout, Lynn A. (1999), A team production theory of corporate law, *Virginia Law Review*, 85(2): 247–328.

Blau, Peter M. (1956), *Bureaucracy in modern society*, New York: Random House.

Blau, Peter M. (1963), *The dynamics of bureaucracy: a study of interpersonal relations in two government agencies*, 2nd edn, Chicago: The University of Chicago Press.

Blauner, Robert (1964), *Alienation and freedom: the factory worker and his industry*, Chicago: Chicago University Press.

Blinder, Alan S. (2013), *When the music stopped: the financial crisis, the response, and the work ahead*, New York: Penguin.

Bloch, Marc (1962), *Feudal society, Vol II: social classes and political organization*, trans. L.A. Manyon, London: Routledge & Kegan Paul.

Block, Fred and Somers, Margaret R. (2014), *The power of market fundamentalism: Karl Polanyi's critique*, Cambridge and London: Harvard University Press.

Bluestone, Harry and Harrison, Bennett (1982), *Deindustrialization of America: plant closings, community abandonment, and the dismantling of basic industry*, New York: Basic Books.

Blyth, Mark (2002), *Great transformations: economic ideas and institutional change in the twentieth century*, New York: Cambridge University Press.

Blyth, Mark (2013), *Austerity: the history of a dangerous idea*, Oxford and New York: Oxford University Press.

Bolton, Patrick, Freixas, Xavier and Shapiro, Joel (2012), The credit ratings game, *Journal of Finance*, 67(1): 85–112.

Bourdieu, Pierre (2000), *Pascalian meditations*, Cambridge: Polity Press.

Bourdieu, Pierre (2005), *The economic structures of society*, Cambridge: Polity Press.

Bowen, Howard (1953), *Social responsibilities of the businessman*, New York: Harper & Brothers.

Bozanic, Zahn, Dirsmith, Mark W. and Huddart, Steven (2012), The social constitution of regulation: the endogenization of insider trading laws, *Accounting, Organizations and Society*, 37(7): 461–81.

Brady, David, Baker, Regina S. and Finnigan, Ryan (2013), When unionization disappears: state-level unionization and working poverty in the United States, *American Sociological Review*, 78(5): 872–96.

Brandeis, Louis D. (1914 [1967]), *Other people's money and how the bankers use it*, New York: Harper Torchbooks.

Brandes, Stuart D. (1976), *American welfare capitalism, 1880–1940*, Chicago and London: The University of Chicago Press.

Bratton, William W., Jr (1989a), The new economic theory of the firm: critical perspectives from history, *Stanford Law Review*, 41(6): 1471–527.

Bratton, William W., Jr (1989b), The 'nexus of contracts' corporation: a critical appraisal, *Cornell Law Review*, 74: 407–65.

Bratton, William W. and Levitin, Adam J. (2013), Transactional genealogy of scandal: from Michael Milken to Enron to Goldman Sachs, *Southern California Law Review*, 86: 783–921.

Bratton, William W. and Wachter, Michael L. (2008), Shareholder primacy's corporatist origins: Adolf Berle and the modern corporation, *Journal of Corporate Law*, 34: 99–152.

Bratton, William W. and Wachter, Michael L. (2010), The case against shareholder empowerment, *Pennsylvania Law Review*, 160(1): 653–728.

Braudel, Fernand (1977), *Afterthoughts on material civilization and capitalism*, trans. Patricia M. Ranum, Baltimore: Johns Hopkins University Press.

Brockman, Jeffrey, Chang, Saeyoung and Rennie, Craig (2007), CEO cash and stock-based compensation changes, layoff decisions, and shareholder value, *Financial Review*, 42: 99–119.

Brody, Howard (2007), *Hooked: ethics, the medical profession, and the pharmaceutical industry*, Lanham: Rowman & Littlefield.

Brudney, Victor (1982), The independent director: heavenly city or Potemkin village?, *Harvard Law Review*, 95(3): 597–659.

Brudney, Victor (1985), Corporate governance, agency costs, and the rhetoric of contract, *Columbia Law Review*, 85: 1403–44.

Brudney, Victor (1997), Contract and fiduciary duty in corporate law, *Boston College Law Review*, 38(4): 595–666.

Brudney, Victor and Clark, Robert C. (1981), A new look at corporate opportunities, *Harvard Law Review*, 94(5): 997–1062.

Bryan, Dick and Rafferty, Michael (2014), Financial derivatives as social policy beyond crisis, *Sociology*, 48(5): 887–903.

Bryer, Robert A. (1997), The mercantile laws commission of 1854 and the political economy of limited liability, *Economic History Review*, 50(1): 37–56.

Buchanan, James M. (1954), Individual choice in voting and in the market, *Journal of Political Economy*, 62(4): 334–43.

Budros, Art (1997), The new capitalism and organizational rationalities: the adoption of downsizing programs, 1979–1994, *Social Forces*, 76(1): 229–49.

Burbeck, S. and Jordan, K.E. (2006), An assessment of the role of computing in systems biology, *IBM Journal of Research & Development*, 50(6): 529–43.

Burgin, Angus (2012), *The great persuasion: reinventing free markets since the Depression*, Cambridge: Harvard University Press.

Burris, Val (2001), The two faces of capital: corporations and individual capitalists as political actors, *American Sociological Review*, 66(3): 361–81.

Buturovic, Zeljka and Tasic, Slavisa (2015), Kahneman's failed revolution against economic orthodoxy, *Critical Review*, 27(2): 127–45.

Calomiris, Charles W. and Haber, Stephen H. (2014), *Fragile by design: the political origins of banking crises and scarce credit*, Princeton and Oxford: Princeton University Press.

Campbell, John L. (2002), Ideas, politics, and public policy, *Annual Review of Sociology*, 28: 21–38.

Campbell, John L. (2010), Neoliberalism in crisis: regulatory roots of the U.S. financial meltdown, *Research in the Sociology of Organizations*, 30B: 65–101.

Campbell, John L. and Lindberg, Leon N. (1990), Property rights and the organization of economic activity by the state, *American Sociological Review*, 55(5): 634–47.

Canguilhem, George (1989), *A vital rationalist: selected writings from George Canguilhem*, New York: Zone Books.

Carosso, Vincent (1970), Washington and Wall Street: the New Deal and investment bankers, 1933–1940, *Business History Review*, 44(4): 425–45.

Carruthers, Bruce G. (2015), Financialization and the institutional foundations of the new capitalism, *Socio-Economic Review*, 13(2): 379–98.

Cary, William L. (1974), Federalism and corporate law: reflections upon Delaware, *Yale Law Journal*, 83(4): 663–705.

Cassidy, John (2009), *How markets fail: the logic of economic calamities*, New York: Picador.

Cetorelli, Nicola and Gambera, Michele (2001), Banking market structure, financial dependence and growth: international evidence from industry data, *Journal of Finance*, 56(2): 617–48.

Chabrak, Nihel (2012), Money talks: the language of the Rochester School, *Accounting, Auditing & Accountability Journal*, 25(3): 452–85.

Chandler, Alfred (1984), The emergence of managerial capitalism, *Business History Review*, 58: 473–503.

Chandler, Alfred D. (1977), *The visible hand: the managerial revolution in American business*, Cambridge: Harvard University Press.

Chatterjee, Arijit and Hambrick, Donald C. (2007), It's all about me: narcissistic chief executive officers and their effects on company strategy and performance, *Administrative Science Quarterly*, 52(3): 351–86.

Cheng, Ing-Haw and Xiong, Wei (2014), Financialization of commodity markets, *Annual Review in Financial Economics*, 6: 419–41.

Cheung, Steven N.S. (1983), The contractual nature of the firm, *Journal of Law and Economics*, 26(1): 1–21.

Chick, Victoria (1997), Some reflections on financial fragility in banking and finance, *Journal of Economic Issues*, 31(2): 535–41.

Choi, Seong-Jin, Jia, Nan and Lu, Jiangyong (2015), The structure of political institutions and effectiveness of corporate political lobbying, *Organization Science*, 26(1): 158–79.

Chong, Kimberly and Tuckett, David (2015), Constructing conviction through action and narrative: how money managers manage uncertainty and the consequence for financial market functioning, *Socio-Economic Review*, 13(2): 309–30.

Chorev, Nitsan and Babb, Sarah (2009), The crisis of neoliberalism and the future of international institutions: a comparison of the IMF and the WTO, *Theory and Society*, 38: 459–84.

Chwieroth, Jeffrey M. (2010), *Capital ideas: the IMF and the rise of financial liberalization*, Princeton and Oxford: Princeton University Press.

Claessens, Stijn, Feijen, Erik and Laeven, Luc (2008), Political connections and preferential access to finance: the role of campaign contributions, *Journal of Financial Economics*, 88(3): 554–80.

Clark, Cynthia E. and Newell, Sue (2013), Institutional work and complicit decoupling across the U.S. capital markets: the work of rating agencies, *Business Ethics Quarterly*, 23(1): 1–30.

Clark, Robert C. (1989), Contracts, elites, and traditions in the making of corporate law, *Columbia Law Review*, 89(7): 1703–47.

Coase, Ronald H. ([1937] 1991), The nature of the firm, in Williamson, Oliver E. and Winter, Sidney G. (eds) (1991), *The nature of the firm: origin, evolution, and development*, New York and Oxford: Oxford University Press.

Coase, Ronald H. (1960), The problem of social cost, *Journal of Law & Economics*, 3(1): 1–44.

Cobb, J. Adam (2015), Risky business: the decline of defined benefit pensions and firms' shifting of risk, *Organization Science*, 26(5): 1332–50.

Cockett, Richard (1994), *Thinking the unthinkable: think-tanks and the economic counter-revolution 1931–1983*, London: HarperCollins.

Coffee, John C., Jr (2009), What went wrong? An initial inquiry into the causes of the 2008 financial crisis, *Journal of Corporate Law Studies*, 9(1): 1–22.

Cohan, William D. (2011), *Money and power: how Goldman Sachs came to rule the world*, London: Allen Lane and New York: Anchor Books.

Cohen, L. Jonathan (1980), Whose is the fallacy? A rejoinder to Daniel Kahneman and Amos Tversky, *Cognition*, 8: 89–92.

Cole, Rebel A. and White, Lawrence J. (2012), Déjà vu all over again: the causes of U.S. commercial bank failures this time around, *Journal of Financial Services Research*, 42: 5–29.

Collins, Robert M. (1981), *The business response to Keynes*, New York: Columbia University Press.

Commons, John R. (1924), *Legal foundations of capitalism*, New York: Macmillan.

Conard, Alfred F. (1988), Beyond managerialism: investor capitalism?, *The University of Michigan Journal of Law Reform*, 22: 117–78.

Connelly, Brian L., Tihanyi, Laszlo, Certo, S. Trevis and Hitt, Michael A. (2010), Marching to the beat of different drummers: the influence of institutional investors on competitive actions, *Academy of Management Journal*, 53(4): 723–42.

Conti, Joseph A. (2010), Producing legitimacy at the World Trade Organization: the role of expertise and legal capacity, *Socio-Economic Review*, 8(1): 131–55.

Craig, R.J. and Amernic, J.H. (2004), Enron discourse: the rhetoric of a resilient capitalism, *Critical Perspectives on Accounting*, 15(6–7): 813–51.

Culpepper, Pepper D. and Reinke, Raphael (2014), Structural power and bank bailouts in the United Kingdom and the United States, *Politics and Society*, 42(4): 427–54.

Cyert, Richard M. and March, James G. (1963), *A behavioral theory of the firm*, Englewood Cliffs: Prentice Hall.

Daily, Catherine M., Dalton, Dan R. and Cannella, Albert A., Jr (2003), Corporate governance: decades of dialogue and data, *The Academy of Management Review*, 28(3): 371–82.

Dalton, Dan R., Daily, Catherine M., Johnson, Jonathan L. and Ellstrand, Alan E. (1999), Number of directors and financial performance: a meta-analysis, *Academy of Management Journal*, 42(6): 674–86.

Dalton, Melville (1959), *Men who manage: fusion of feeling and theory in administration*, New York: Wiley.

Daston, Lorraine (2015), Simon and the Sirens: a commentary, *Isis*, 106(3): 669–76.

Davies, William (2010), Economics and the 'nonsense' of law: the case of the Chicago antitrust revolution, *Economy and Society*, 39(1): 64–83.

Davis, Gerald F. (1991), Agents without principles? The spread of the poison pill through the intercorporate network, *Administrative Science Quarterly*, 36(4): 583–613.

Davis, Gerald F. (2009), *Managed by the markets: how finance reshaped America*, Oxford: Oxford University Press.

Davis, Gerald F. (2010), After the ownership society: another world is possible, *Research in the Sociology of Organizations*, 30B: 331–56.

Davis, Gerald F. (2013), After the corporation, *Politics and Society*, 41(2): 283–308.

Davis, Gerald F. and Kim, Suntae (2015), Financialization of the economy, *Annual Review of Sociology*, 41: 203–21.

Davis, Gerald F. and Stout, Suzanne K. (1992), Organization theory and the market for corporate control: a dynamic analysis of the characteristics of large takeover targets, 1980–1990, *Administrative Science Quarterly*, 37(4): 605–63.

DeMott, Deborah A. (1988), Beyond metaphor: an analysis of fiduciary obligation, *Duke Law Journal*, 1988(5): 879–924.

Demsetz, Harold (1983), The structure of ownership and the theory of the firm, *Journal of Law and Economics*, 26: 375–90.

Demsetz, Harold (1988), The theory of the firm revisited, *Journal of Law, Economics and Organization*, 4(1): 141–61.

Dencker, John C. (2009), Relative bargaining power, corporate restructuring, and managerial incentives, *Administrative Science Quarterly*, 54(3): 453–85.

Deringer, William (2015), For what it's worth: historical financial bubbles and the boundaries of economic rationality, *Isis*, 106(3): 646–56.

De Rond, Mark and Miller, Alan N. (2005), Publish or perish: bane or boon of academic life?, *Journal of Management Inquiry*, 14(4): 321–29.

Deutschmann, Christoph (2011), Limits of financialization: sociological analyses of the financial crisis, *European Journal of Sociology*, 52(3): 347–89.

DiMaggio, Paul and Powell, Walter W. (1983), The iron cage revisited: institutional isomorphism and collective rationality in organizational fields, *American Sociological Review*, 48(2): 147–60.

DiPrete, Thomas A., Eirich, Gregory M. and Pittinsky, Matthew (2010), Compensation benchmarking, leapfrogs, and the surge in executive pay, *American Journal of Sociology*, 115(6): 1671–712.

Djelic, Marie-Laure (2013), When limited liability was (still) an issue: mobilization and politics of signification in 19th-century England, *Organization Studies*, 34(5–6): 595–621.

Djelic, Marie-Laure and Bothello, Joel (2013), Limited liability and its moral hazard implications: the systemic inscription of instability in contemporary capitalism, *Theory and Society*, 42(6): 589–615.

Dobbin, Frank (1994), *Forging industrial policy*, Cambridge: Cambridge University Press.

Dobbin, Frank and Dowd, Timothy J. (2000), The market that antitrust built: public policy, private coercion, and railroad acquisitions, 1825 to 1922, *American Sociological Review*, 65(5): 631–57.

Dobbin, Frank and Jung, Jiwook (2010), The misapplication of Mr. Michael Jensen: how agency theory brought down the economy and why it might again, *Research in the Sociology of Organizations*, 30B: 29–64.

Dobbin, Frank and Kelly, Erin L. (2007), How to stop harassment: professional construction of legal compliance in organizations, *American Journal of Sociology*, 112(4): 1203–43.

Dobbin, Frank and Zorn, Dirk (2005), Corporate malfeasance and the myth of shareholder value, *Political Power and Social Theory*, 17: 179–98.

Dodd, E. Merrick, Jr (1932), For whom are corporate managers trustees?, *Harvard Law Review*, 45(7): 1145–63.

Dodd, Nigel (2014), *The social life of money*, Princeton and London: Princeton University Press.

Donaldson, Thomas (2012), Epistemological fault lines in corporate governance, *Academy of Management Review*, 37(2): 256–71.

Dore, Ronald, Lazonick, William and O'Sullivan, Mary (1999), Varieties of capitalism in the twentieth century, *Oxford Review of Economic Policy*, 15(4): 102–20.

Downer, John (2007), When the chick hits the fan: representativeness and reproducibility in technological tests, *Social Studies of Science*, 37(1): 7–26.

Downer, John (2011), '737-Cabriolet': the limits of knowledge and the sociology of inevitable failure, *American Journal of Sociology*, 117(3): 725–62.

Dymski, Gary A. (1997), Deciphering Minsky's Wall Street paradigm, *Journal of Economic Issues*, 31(2): 501–8.

Dymski, Gary A. (2013), Bank lending and the subprime crisis, in Wolfson, Martin H. and Epstein, Gerald A. (eds), *Handbook of the political economy of financial crises*, New York and Oxford: Oxford University Press, pp. 411–29.

Easterbrook, Frank H. and Fischel, Daniel R. (1981), The proper role of a target's management in responding to a tender offer, *Harvard Law Review*, 94(6): 1161–204.

Easterbrook, Frank H. and Fischel, Daniel R. (1993), Contract and fiduciary duty, *Journal of Law and Economics*, 36(1): 425–46.

Easterbrook, Frank H. and Fischel, Daniel R. (1996), *The economic structure of corporate law*, Cambridge: Harvard University Press.

Ebenstein, Lanny (2015), *Chicagonomics: the evolution of Chicago free market economics*, London: St Martin's Press.

Economist, The (2010), Drexel Burnham Lambert's legacy: stars of the junkyard, 21 October, accessed 6 March 2015 at http://www. economist.com/node/17306419.

Edelman, Lauren B. (1990), Legal environments and organizational governance: the expansion of due process in the American workplace, *American Journal of Sociology*, 95(6): 1401–40.

Edelman, Lauren B. and Suchman, Mark C. (1997), The legal environ-ment of organizations, *Annual Review of Sociology*, 23: 479–515.

Edelman, Lauren B., Fuller, Sally Riggs and Mara-Drita, Iona (2001), Diversity rhetoric and the managerialization of law, *American Journal of Sociology*, 106(6): 1589–641.

Edelman, Lauren B., Krieger, Linda H., Eliason, Scott R., Albiston Catherine R. and Mellema, Virginia (2011), When organizations rule: judicial deference to institutionalized employment structures, *American Journal of Sociology*, 117(3): 888–954.

Eichengreen, Barry (2015), *Hall of mirrors: the Great Depression, the Great Recession, and the uses – and misuses – of history*, New York and Oxford: Oxford University Press.

Eisenberg, Melvin A. (1976), *The structure of the corporation*, Boston: Little, Brown and Company.

Eisenberg, Melvin A. (1989), The structures of corporate law, *Columbia Law Review*, 89: 1461–526.

Ellul, Andrew (2015), The role of risk management in corporate govern-ance, *Annual Review of Financial Economics*, 7: 279–99.

Engel, Kathleen C. and McCoy, Patricia A. (2007), Turning a blind eye: Wall Street finance of predatory lending, *Fordham Law Review*, 75(4): 2039–103.

Epstein, Gerald A. (ed.) (2005), *The financialization of the world economy*, Cheltenham, UK and Northampton, MA, USA: Edward Elgar Publishing.

Erb, Carsten and Pelger, Christoph (2015), 'Twisting words'? A study of the construction and reconstruction of reliability in financial reporting standard-setting, *Accounting, Organizations and Society*, 40(2): 13–40.

Erickson, Paul, Klein, Judy L., Daston, Lorraine, Lemov, Rebecca, Sturm, Thomas and Gordin, Michael D. (2013), *How reason almost lost its mind: the strange career of Cold War rationality*, Chicago and London: The University of Chicago Press.

Evans, Peter (1995), *Embedded autonomy*, Princeton and London: Princeton University Press.

Fahlenbrach, Rüdiger and Stulz, René M. (2011), Bank CEO incentives and the credit crisis, *Journal of Financial Economics*, 99(1): 11–26.

Faludi, Susan (1990), The reckoning: Safeway LBO yields vast profits but exacts a heavy human toll, *Wall Street Journal*, 16, A1.

Fama, Eugene F. (1980), Agency problems and the theory of the firm, *Journal of Political Economy*, 88: 288–305.

Fama, Eugene F. and Jensen, Michael (1983), Separation of ownership and control, *Journal of Law and Economics*, 26(2): 301–25.

Farre-Mensa, Joan, Michaely, Roni and Schmalz, Martin (2014), Payout policy, *Annual Review of Financial Economics*, 6: 17.1–17.60.

Faulkner, Alex (2009), Regulatory policy as innovation: constructing rules of engagement for a technological zone of tissue engineering in the European Union, *Research Policy*, 38: 637–46.

Faux, Jeff (2012), *The servant economy: where America's elite is sending the middle class*, Hoboken: Wiley.

Fazzari, Steve and Minsky, Hyman P. (1984), Domestic monetary policy: if not monetarism, what?, *Journal of Economic Issues*, 18: 101–16.

Feldman, Martha S. and Pentland, Brian T. (2003), Reconceptualizing organization routines as a source of flexibility and change, *Administrative Science Quarterly*, 48: 94–118.

Fernández-Albertos, José (2015), The politics of central bank independence, *Annual Review of Political Science*, 18: 217–37.

Ferraro, Fabrizio, Pfeffer, Jeffrey and Sutton, Robert I. (2005), Economics language and assumptions: how theories can become self-fulfilling, *Academy of Management Review*, 30(1): 8–24.

Ferrary, Michel (2003), The gift exchange in the social networks of Silicon Valley, *California Management Review*, 45(4): 120–38.

Ferrary, Michel and Granovetter, Mark (2009), The role of venture capital firms in Silicon Valley's complex innovation network, *Economy and Society*, 38(2): 326–59.

Fichtenbaum, Rudy (2011), Do unions affect labor's share of income: evidence using panel data, *American Journal of Economics and Sociology*, 70(3): 784–810.

Fine, Sidney (1969), *Sit-down: the General Motors strike of 1936–1937*, Ann Arbor: University of Michigan Press.

Fisch, Jill E. (2010), The overstated promise of corporate governance, *The University of Chicago Law Review*, 77(3): 923–58.

Fiss, Peer, Kennedy, Mark T. and Davis, Gerald F. (2012), How golden parachutes unfolded: diffusion and variation of a controversial practice, *Organization Science*, 23(4): 1077–99.

Fleck, Ludwik (1979), *Genesis and development of a scientific fact*, Chicago and London: Chicago University Press.

Fligstein, Neil (2005), The end of (shareholder value) ideology, *Political Power and Social Theory*, 17: 223–8.

Fligstein, Neil and Choo, Jennifer (2005), Law and corporate governance, *Annual Review of Law and Social Science*, 1: 61–84.

Fligstein, Neil and Habinek, Jacob (2014), Sucker punched by the invisible hand: the world financial markets and the globalization of the US mortgage crisis, *Socio-Economic Review*, 12(4): 637–65.

Foss, Nicolai J. (1996), Knowledge-based approaches to the theory of the firm: some critical remarks, *Organization Science*, 7(5): 470–76.

Foss, Nicolai J. and Klein, Peter G. (2012), *Organizing entrepreneurial judgment: a new approach to the firm*, Cambridge: Cambridge University Press.

Fourcade, Marion (2006), The construction of a global profession: the transnationalization of economics, *American Journal of Sociology*, 112: 145–94.

Fourcade, Marion (2009), *Economists and societies: discipline and profession in the United States, Britain, and France, 1890s to 1990s*, Princeton and London: Princeton University Press.

Fourcade, Marion and Healy, Kieran (2013), Classification situations: life-chances in the neoliberal era, *Accounting, Organizations and Society*, 38(8): 559–72.

Fourcade, Marion and Khurana, Rakesh (2013), From social control to financial economics: the linked ecologies of economics and business in twentieth-century America, *Theory and Society*, 42(2): 121–59.

Fowler, Bridget (2003), Reading Pierre Bourdieu's masculine domination: notes towards an intersectional analysis of gender, culture, and class, *Cultural Studies*, 17(3–4): 468–94.

Frame, W. Scott and White, Lawrence J. (2004), Empirical studies of financial innovation: lots of talk, little action?, *Journal of Economic Literature*, 42(1): 116–44.

Frank, Thomas (2012), *Pity the billionaire: the hard times swindle and the unlikely comeback of the Right*, New York: Metropolitan Books/ Henry Holt.

Fraser, Nancy (2014), Can society be commodities all the way down? Post-Polanyian reflections on capitalist crisis, *Economy and Society*, 43(4): 541–58.

French, E.A. (1990), The origin of general limited liability in the United Kingdom, *Accounting and Business Research*, 21(81): 15–34.

Friedman, Jeffrey and Kraus, Wladimir (2012), *Engineering the financial crisis: systemic risk and the failure of regulation*, Philadelphia: University of Pennsylvania Press.

Froot, Kenneth A., Scharfstein, David S. and Stein, Jeremy C. (1992), Herd on the street: informational inefficiencies in a market with short-term speculation, *The Journal of Finance*, 47(4): 1461–84.

Frost, Carol Ann (2007), Credit rating agencies in capital markets: a review of research evidence on selected criticisms of the agencies, *Journal of Accounting, Auditing & Finance*, 22(3): 469–92.

Froud, Julie, Johal, Sukhdev, Papazian, Viken and Williams, Karel (2004), The temptation of Houston: a case study of financialisation, *Critical Perspectives on Accounting*, 15(6–7): 885–909.

Fujimura, Joan H. (2005), Postgenomic futures: translating across the machine–nature border in systems biology, *New Genetics and Society*, 24(2): 195–225.

Funk, Russell J. and Hirschman, Daniel (2014), Derivatives and deregulation: financial innovation and the demise of Glass–Steagall, *Administrative Science Quarterly*, 59(4): 669–704.

Galbraith, John Kenneth (1958), *The affluent society*, Boston: Houghton Mifflin.

Galbraith, John Kenneth ([1967] 1971), *The new industrial state*, 2nd edn, Boston: Houghton-Mifflin.

Gassman, O., Reepmeyer, G. and Von Zedtwitz, M. (2004), *Leading pharmaceutical innovations: trends and drivers for growth in the pharmaceutical industry*, London: Springer.

Gay, Peter (2001), *Schnitzler's century: the making of middle-class culture, 1815–1914*, London: Allen Lane.

Gillespie, Michael Allen (2008), *The theological origins of modernity*, Chicago and London: The University of Chicago Press.

Goldman, Eitan, Rocholl, Jörg and So, Jongil (2009), Do politically connected boards affect firm value?, *Review of Financial Studies*, 22(6): 2231–60.

Goldstein, Adam (2012), Revenge of the managers: labor cost-cutting and the paradoxical resurgence of managerialism in the shareholder value era, 1984 to 2001, *American Sociological Review*, 77(2): 268–94.

Gordon, David (1996), *Fat and mean: the corporate squeeze of working Americans and the myth of managerial downsizing*, New York: Free Press.

Gordon, Jeffrey N. (1989), The mandatory structure of corporate law, *Columbia Law Review*, 89(7): 1549–98.

Gordon, Jeffrey N. (2003), What Enron means for the management and control of the modern business corporation: some initial reflections, *The University of Chicago Law Review*, 69: 1233–50.

Gordon, Jeffrey N. (2007), The rise of independent directors in the United States, 1950–2005: of shareholder value and stock market prices, *Stanford Law Review*, 59(6): 1465–568.

Gouldner, Alvin W. (1954a), *Patterns of industrial bureaucracy*, Glencoe: The Free Press.

Gouldner, Alvin W. (1954b), *Wildcat strike*, New York, Evanston and London: Harper Torchbooks.

Graebner, William (1987), *The engineering of consent: democracy and authority in twentieth-century America*, Madison: University of Wisconsin Press.

Grandin, Greg (2009), *Fordlandia: the rise and fall of Henry Ford's forgotten jungle city*, New York: Picador.

Granovetter, M. (1985), Economic action and social structure, *American Journal of Sociology*, 91(3): 481–510.

Greenwald, Bruce C. and Stiglitz, Joseph E. (1986), Externalities in economies with imperfect information and incomplete markets, *Quarterly Journal of Economics*, 90: 229–64.

Greenwood, Robin and Scharfstein, David (2013), The growth of finance, *Journal of Economic Perspectives*, 27(2): 3–28.

Griffin, Penny (2009), *Gendering the World Bank: neoliberalism and the gendered foundation of global governance*, New York: Palgrave.

Griffith-Jones, Stephany, Ocampo, José Antonio and Stiglitz, Joseph E. (eds) (2010), *Time for a visible hand: lessons from the 2008 world financial crisis*, Oxford and New York: Oxford University Press.

Grocott, Chris (2015), Compromising liberty: Friedrich Hayek's *The road to serfdom* in practice, *Economy and Society*, 44(1): 140–64.

Grossman, Sanford J. and Stiglitz, Joseph E. (1980), On the impossibility of informationally efficient markets, *American Economic Review*, 70(3): 393–408.

Grullon, Gustavo and Ikenberry, David L. (2000), What do we know about stock repurchases?, *Journal of Applied Corporate Finance*, 13(1): 31–51.

Hacker, Jacob S. (2004), Privatizing risk without privatizing the welfare state: the hidden politics of social policy retrenchment in the United States, *American Political Science Review*, 98(2), 243–60.

Hacker, Jacob S. (2006), *The great risk shift: the assault on American jobs, families, health care, and retirement and how you can fight back*, Oxford and New York: Oxford University Press.

Hacker, Jacob S. and Pierson, Paul (2002), Business power and social policy: employers and the formation of the American welfare state, *Politics & Society*, 30(2): 277–325.

Hacker, Jacob S. and Pierson, Paul (2010), *Winner-take-all politics: how Washington made the rich richer and turned its back on the middle class*, New York: Simon and Schuster.

Hacker, Jacob S., Rehm, Philipp and Schlesinger, Mark (2013), The insecure American: economic experiences, financial worries, and policy attitudes, *Perspectives on Politics*, 11(1): 23–49.

Hacking, Ian (2002), Historical Ontology, Cambridge, MA: Harvard University Press.

Hagendorff, Jens and Vallascas, Francesco (2011), CEO pay incentives and risk-taking: evidence from bank acquisitions, *Journal of Corporate Finance*, 17(4): 1078–95.

Hall, Bronwyn H. (1993), The stock market's valuation of R&D investment during the 1980's, *The American Economic Review*, 43(2): 259–64.

Hall, Bronwyn H. (1994), Corporate restructuring and investment horizons in the United States, 1976–1987, *Business History Review*, 68(1): 110–43.

Hall, Peter A. and Thelen, Kathleen (2009), Institutional change in varieties of capitalism, *Socio-Economic Review*, 7: 7–34.

Halliday, Terence C. and Carruthers, Bruce G. (2007), The recursivity of law: global norm making and national lawmaking in the globalization of corporate insolvency regimes, *American Journal of Sociology*, 112(4): 1135–202.

Hambrick, Donald C., Von Werder, Axel and Zajac, Edward J. (2008), New directions in corporate governance research, *Organization Science*, 19(3): 381–5.

Hamel, Gary (2000), *Leading the revolution*, Boston: Harvard Business School.

Hammond, Thomas H. and Knott, Jack H. (1988), The deregulatory snowball: explaining deregulation in the financial industry, *The Journal of Politics*, 50(1): 3–30.

Handlin, Oscar and Handlin, Mary F. (1945), Origins of the American business corporation, *Journal of Economic History*, 5(1): 1–23.

Hansmann, Henry and Kraakman, Reinier (2000), The Essential Role of Organizational Law, NYU Law and Economics Working Paper No. 00-006; Harvard Law and Economics Discussion Paper 284; Yale ICF Working Paper No. 00-11, pp. 1–47.

Hanson, Norwood Russell (1958), *Patterns of discovery: an inquiry into the conceptual foundations of science*, Cambridge: Cambridge University Press.

Hara, Takuji (2003), *Innovation in the pharmaceutical industry: the process of drug discovery development*, Cheltenham, UK and Northampton, MA, USA: Edward Elgar Publishing.

Harcourt, Bernard E. (2011), *The illusion of free markets*, Cambridge and London: Harvard University Press.

Harriss-White, Barbara (1996), Free market romanticism in an era of deregulation, *Oxford Development Studies*, 24(1): 27–45.

Hart, Oliver (1995), Corporate governance: some theory and implications, *The Economic Journal*, 105(430): 678–89.

Harvey, Penny and Knox, Hannah (2010), Abstraction, materiality and the 'science of the concrete' in engineering practice, in Bennett, Tony and Joyce, Patrick (eds), *Material powers: cultural studies, history and the material turn*, London and New York: Routledge, pp. 124–41.

Hawley, Ellis (1966), *The New Deal and the problem of monopoly*, Princeton: Princeton University Press.

Hawley, James and Williams, Andrew (1997), The emergence of fiduciary capitalism, *Corporate Governance: An International Review*, 5(4), 206–13.

Hayek, Friedrich von (1944), *The road to serfdom*, Chicago: University of Chicago Press.

Hayek, Friedrich von (1949), *Individualism and economic order*, London: Routledge & Kegan Paul.

Hayek, Friedrich von (1979), *Law legislation and liberty, Vol. 3: the political order of a free people*, London and Henley: Routledge & Kegan Paul, pp. 76–152.

Henderson, Brian J., Pearson, Neil D. and Wang, Li (2014), New evidence on the financialization of commodity markets, *Review of Financial Studies*, 28(5): 1285–311.

Hermalin, Benjamin E. (2013), Corporate governance: a critical assessment, in Gibbons, Robert and Roberts, John (eds), *Handbook of organizational economics*, Princeton and Oxford: Princeton University Press, pp. 732–63.

Hiatt, Shon R. and Park, Sangchan (2013), Lords of the harvest: third-party influence and regulatory approval of genetically modified organisms, *Academy of Management Journal*, 56(4): 923–44.

Hillman, Amy J. and Keim, Gerald D. (2001), Shareholder value, stakeholder management, and social issues: what's the bottom line?, *Strategic Management Journal*, 22(2): 125–39.

Hilt, Eric (2014), History of American corporate governance: law, institutions, and politics, *Annual Review in Financial Economics*, 6(1): 1–21.

Himmelstein, Jerome L. (1992), *To the Right: the transformation of American conservatism*, Berkeley, Los Angeles and London: University of California Press.

Hirschman, Albert O. (1970), *Exit, Voice, and Loyalty*, Cambridge: Harvard University Press.

Hirschman, Daniel and Berman, Elizabeth Popp (2014), Do economists make policies? On the political effects of economics, *Socio-Economic Review*, 12(4): 779–811.

Hochschild, Arlie Russell (1997), *The time bind: when work becomes home and home becomes work*, New York: Metropolitan Books.

Howard, John L. (1991), Fiduciary relations in corporate law, *Canadian Business Law Journal*, 19(1): 1–27.

Huang, Laura and Pearce, Jone L. (2015), Managing the unknowable: the effectiveness of early-stage investor gut feel in entrepreneurial investment decisions, *Administrative Science Quarterly*, 60(4): 634–70.

Hughes, Everett Cherrington (1958), *Men and their work*, Glencoe: The Free Press.

Humphrey, Christopher, Loft, Anne and Woods, Margaret (2009), The global audit profession and the international financial architecture: understanding regulatory relationships at a time of financial crisis, *Accounting, Organizations and Society*, 34(6–7): 810–25.

Hunt, John Patrick (2009), Credit rating agencies and the worldwide credit crisis: the limits of reputation, the insufficiency of reform, and a proposal for improvement, *Columbia Business Law Review*, 109(1): 109–209.

Hyman, Louis (2011), *Debtor nation: the history of America in red ink*, Princeton: Princeton University Press.

Jackson, Ben (2012), Freedom, the common good, and the rule of law: Lippmann and Hayek on economic planning, *Journal of the History of Ideas*, 73(1): 47–68.

Jacobs, David (1988), Corporate economic power and the state: a longitudinal assessment of two explanations, *American Journal of Sociology*, 93(4): 852–81.

Jacobs, David and Myers, Lindsey (2014), Union strength, neoliberalism, and inequality: contingent political analyses of U.S. income differences since 1950, *American Sociological Review*, 79(4): 752–74.

Jacoby, Sanford M. (1985), *Employing bureaucracy: managers, unions, and the transformation of work in American industry, 1900–1945*, New York: Columbia University Press.

Jacoby, Sanford M. (1997), *Modern manors: welfare capitalism since the New Deal*, Princeton and London: Princeton University Press.

Jaques, Elliott (1951), *The changing culture of a factory*, London: Tavistock Publications.

Jarsulic, Marc (2013), The origins of the U.S. financial crisis of 2007: how a house-price bubble, a credit bubble, and regulatory failure caused the greatest economic disaster since the great depression, in Wolfson, Martin H. and Epstein, Gerald A. (eds), *Handbook of the political economy of financial crises*, New York and Oxford: Oxford University Press, pp. 21–46.

Jenkins, J. Craig and Brents, Barbara G. (1989), Social protest, hegemonic competition, and social reform: a political struggle interpretation of the origins of the American welfare state, *American Sociological Review*, 54(6): 891–909.

Jenkins, J. Craig and Eckert, Craig M. (2000), The right turn in economic policy: business elites and the new conservative economics, *Sociological Forum*, 15(2): 307–38.

Jensen, M. (1993), The modern industrial revolution, exit, and failure of internal control systems, *Journal of Finance*, 48(3): 831–80.

Jensen, Michael C. (1986), Agency costs of free cash flow, corporate finance, and takeovers, *American Economics Review*, 76(2): 323–9.

Jensen, Michael C. and Meckling, William H. (1976), Theory of the firm: managerial behavior, agency costs and ownership structure, *Journal of Financial Economics*, 3(4): 305–60.

Jones, Daniel Stedman (2012), *Masters of the universe: Hayek, Friedman, and the birth of neoliberal politics*, Princeton and Oxford: Princeton University Press.

Judt, Tony (2015), Downhill all the way, in *When the facts change: essays 1995–2010*, London: William Heinemann, pp. 13–29.

Jungmittag, Andre, Reger, Guido and Reiss, Thomas (2000), *Changing innovation in the pharmaceutical industry: globalization and new ways of drug development*, Berlin: Springer.

Kahle, Kathleen M. (2002), When a buyback isn't a buyback: open market repurchases and employee options, *Journal of Financial Economics*, 63(2): 235–61.

Kahneman, Daniel (2011), *Thinking, fast and slow*, New York: Farrar, Straus and Giroux.

Kalecki, Michał (1943), Political aspects of full employment, *Political Quarterly*, 14(4): 322–30.

Kaufman, Allen and Englander, Ernest J. (1993), Kohlberg Kravis Roberts & Co. and the restructuring of American capitalism, *Business History Review*, 67(01), 52–97.

Kaufman, Allen and Zacharias, Lawrence (1992), From trust to contract: the legal language of managerial ideology, 1920–1980, *Business History Review*, 66(3): 523–72.

Kaufman, Allen, Zacharias, Lawrence and Karson, Marvin (1995), *Managers vs. owners: the struggle for corporate control in American democracy*, New York and Oxford: Oxford University Press.

Kaufman, Jason (2008), Corporate law and the sovereignty of states, *American Sociological Review*, 73(3): 402–25.

Kedia, Simi and Philippon, Thomas (2009), The economics of fraudulent accounting, *Review of Financial Studies*, 22(6): 2169–99.

Kelly, Erin and Dobbin, Frank (1999), Civil rights law at work: sex discrimination and the rise of maternity leave policies, *American Journal of Sociology*, 105(2): 455–92.

Kerr, Ron and Robinson, Sarah (2011), Leadership as an elite field: Scottish banking leaders and the crisis of 2007–2009, *Leadership*, 7(2): 151–73.

Keynes, John Maynard (1953), *The general theory of employment, interest and money*, New York and London: Harcourt.

Khurana, R. (2002), *Searching for a corporate savior: the irrational quest for a charismatic CEO*, Princeton: Princeton University Press.

Kim, Jerry W., Kogut, Bruce and Yang, Jae-Suk (2015), Executive compensation, fat cats, and best athletes, *American Sociological Review*, 80(2): 299–328.

King, Robert G. and Levine, Ross (1993), Finance and growth: Schumpeter might be right, *The Quarterly Journal of Economics*, 108(3): 717–37.

Klausner, Michael (2013), Fact and fiction in corporate law and governance, *Stanford Law Review*, 65(6): 1325–70.

Kliman, Andrew and Williams, Shannon D. (2014), Why 'financialisation' hasn't depressed US productive investment, *Cambridge Journal of Economics*, 39(1): 67–92.

Knechel, W. Robert (2007), The business risk audit: origins, obstacles and opportunities, *Accounting, Organizations and Society*, 32(4–5), 383–408.

Knight, Frank H. (1938), Lippmann's *The Good Society*, *The Journal of Political Economy*, 46(6): 864–72.

Knorr Cetina, Karin D. (1981), *The manufacture of knowledge: an essay on the constructivist and contextual nature of science*, Oxford: Pergamon Press.

Kogut, Bruce M. (2012). *The small worlds of corporate governance*, Cambridge and London: MIT Press.

Kogut, Bruce and Macpherson, J. Muir (2011), The mobility of economists and the diffusion of policy ideas: the influence of economics on national policies, *Research Policy*, 40: 1307–20.

Konzelmann, Suzanne J. (2014), The political economics of austerity, *Cambridge Journal of Economics*, 38(4): 701–41.

Korpi, Walter and Palme, Joakim (2003), New politics and class politics in the context of austerity and globalization: welfare state regress in 18 countries, 1975–95, *American Political Science Review*, 97(3): 425–46.

Koyré, Alexandre (1959), *From the closed world to the infinite universe*, New York: Harper Torchbooks.

Koyré, Alexandre ([1968] 1992), *Metaphysics and measurement*, Reading: Gordon & Breach Science Publishers.

Krasna, Beth (2006), Enron revisited: what is a board member to do?, in Dembinski, Paul H., Lager, Carole, Cornford, Andrew and Bonvin, Jean-Michel (eds), *Enron and world finance: a case study in ethics*, New York and Basingstoke: Palgrave Macmillan, pp. 168–79.

Krier, Dan (2005), *Speculative management: stock market power and corporate change*, Albany: State University of New York Press.

Krippner, Greta R. (2005), The financialization of the American economy, *Socio-Economic Review*, 3(2): 173–208.

Krippner, Greta R. (2010), The political economy of financial exuberance, *Research in the Sociology of Organizations*, 30B: 141–73.

Krippner, Greta R. (2011), *Capitalizing on crisis: the political origins of the rise of finance*, Cambridge and London: Harvard University Press.

Kristal, Tali (2013), The capitalist machine: computerization, workers' power, and the decline in labor's share within U.S. industries, *American Sociological Review*, 78(3): 361–89.

Krome, Frederic (1987), From liberal philosophy to conservative ideology? Walter Lippmann's opposition to the New Deal, *Journal of American Culture*, 10(1): 57–64.

Kus, Basak (2012), Financialisation and income inequality in OECD nations: 1995–2007, *Economic and Social Review*, 43(4): 477–95.

Lambert, Susan J. (2008), Passing the buck: labor flexibility practices that transfer risk onto hourly workers, *Human Relations*, 61(9): 1203–27.

Lamont, Michele (1987), How to become a dominant French philosopher: the case of Jacques Derrida, *American Journal of Sociology*, 93(3): 584–622.

Lamoreaux, Naomi R. (1998), Partnerships, corporations, and the theory of the firm, *American Economic Review*, 88(2): 66–71.

Lamoreaux, Naomi R. (2009), Scylla or Charybdis? Historical reflections on two basic problems of corporate governance, *Business History Review*, 83(1): 9–34.

Lan, Luh Luh and Heracleous, Loizos (2010), Rethinking agency theory: the view from law, *Academy of Management Review*, 35(2): 294–314.

Landes, Elizabeth M. and Posner, Richard A. (1978), The economics of the baby shortage, *Journal of Legal Studies*, 7: 323–48.

Langston, Thomas S. (1992), *Ideologues and presidents: from the New Deal to the Reagan revolution*, Baltimore: Johns Hopkins University Press.

La Porta, Rafael, Lopez-de-Silanes, Florencio, Shleifer, Andrei and Vishny, Robert (2000), Investor protection and corporate governance, *Journal of Financial Economics*, 58(1–2): 3–27.

Latour, B. and Woolgar, S. (1979), *Laboratory life: the construction of scientific facts*, Princeton: Princeton University Press.

Lazonick, William (2013), From innovation to financialization: how shareholder value ideology is destroying the U.S. economy, in Wolfson, Martin H. and Epstein, Gerald A. (eds), *Handbook of the political economy of financial crises*, New York and Oxford: Oxford University Press, pp. 491–511.

Lazonick, William and Mazzucato, Mariana (2013), The risk–reward nexus in the innovation–inequality relationship: who takes the risks? Who gets the rewards?, *Industrial and Corporate Change*, 22(4): 1093–128.

Lazonick, William and O'Sullivan, Mary (2000), Maximizing shareholder value: a new ideology for corporate governance, *Economy and Society*, 29(1): 13–35.

Lenglet, Marc (2011), Conflicting codes and codings: how algorithmic trading is reshaping financial regulation, *Theory, Culture & Society*, 28(6): 44–66.

Lépinay, Vincent Antonin (2011), *Codes of finance: engineering derivatives in a global bank*, Princeton: Princeton University Press.

Lerner, Josh (2009), *Boulevard of broken dreams: why public efforts to boost entrepreneurship and venture capital have failed and what to do about it*, Princeton and London: Princeton University Press.

Le Roy Ladurie, Emanuel (1983), History that stands still, in Le Roy Ladurie, Emanuel, *The mind and the method of the historian*, trans. Siân and Ben Reynolds, Brighton: The Harvester Press, pp. 1–27.

Levitin, Adam and Wachter, Susan M. (2012), Explaining the housing bubble, *Georgetown Law Journal*, 100: 1177–258.

Levitt, Kari Polany (2013), From mercantilism to neoliberalism and the financial crisis of 2008, in Levitt, Kari Polany, *From the great transformation to the great financialization: on Karl Polanyi and other essays*, New York: Zed Books, pp. 137–79.

Lewis, C.S. (1942), *The screwtape letters*, London: Collins.

Lippmann, Walter (1937), *An inquiry into the principles of the good society*, Boston: Little, Brown and Company.

Lipton, Martin (1987), Corporate governance in the age of finance corporatism, *University of Pennsylvania Law Review*, 136(1): 1–72.

LiPuma, Edward and Lee, Benjamin (2004), *Financial derivatives and the globalization of risk*, Durham: Duke University Press.

Lo, A.W., Repin, D.V. and Steenbarger, B.N. (2005), Fear and greed in financial markets: a clinical study of day-traders, *American Economic Review*, 95: 352–9.

Locke, John ([1690] 2003), *Two treatises of government and a letter concerning toleration*, New Haven and London: Yale University Press.

Lopez, Robert S. (1976), *The commercial revolution of the Middle Ages, 950–1350*, Cambridge and New York: Cambridge University Press.

Lord, Richard A. and Siato, Yoshie (2010), Trends in CEO compensation and equity holdings for S&P 1500 firms: 1994–2007, *Journal of Applied Finance*, 3(2): 40–56.

Lubatkin, Michael H. (2005), A theory of the firm only a microeconomist could love, *Journal of Management Inquiry*, 14(2), 213–16.

Lynch, Michael (1985), *Art and artifact in laboratory science: a study of shop work and shop talk in a research laboratory*, London: Routledge & Kegan Paul.

Macey, Jonathan (2008), *Corporate governance: promises kept, promises broken*, Princeton: Princeton University Press.

MacKenzie, Donald (2004), The big, bad wolf and the rational market: portfolio investment, the 1987 crash and the performativity of economics, *Economy and Society*, 33(3): 303–34.

MacKenzie, Donald (2006), *An engine, not a camera: how financial models shape markets*, Cambridge and London: The MIT Press.

MacKenzie, Donald (2012), Knowledge production in financial markets: credit default swaps, the ABX and the subprime crisis, *Economy and Society*, 41(3): 335–59.

MacKenzie, Donald and Millo, Yuval (2003), Constructing a market, performing a theory: a historical sociology of a financial market derivatives exchange, *American Journal of Sociology*, 109(1): 107–45.

MacKenzie, Donald and Pardo-Guerra, Juan Pablo (2014), Insurgent capitalism: island, bricolage and the re-making of finance, *Economy and Society*, 43(2): 153–82.

MacKenzie, Donald and Spears, Taylor (2014a), 'The formula that killed Wall Street': the Gaussian copula and modelling practices in investment banking, *Social Studies of Science*, 44(3): 393–417.

MacKenzie, Donald and Spears, Taylor (2014b), 'A device for being able to book P&L': the organizational embedding of the Gaussian copula, *Social Studies of Science*, 44(3): 418–40.

MacKenzie, Donald A., Muniesa, Fabio and Siu, Lucia (eds) (2007), *Do economists make markets? On the performativity of economics*, Princeton and Oxford: Princeton University Press.

Maclean, Mairi, Harvey, Charles and Kling, Gerhard (2014), Pathways to power: class, hyper-agency and the French corporate elite, *Organization Studies*, 35(6): 825–55.

Madrick, Jeff (2011), *Age of greed: the triumph of finance and the decline of America, 1970 to the present*, New York: Alfred A. Knopf.

Major, Aaron (2014), *Architects of austerity: international finance and the politics of growth*, Stanford: Stanford University Press.

Mandis, Steven G. (2013), *What happened to Goldman Sachs: an insider's story of organizational drift and its unintended consequences*, Boston and London: Harvard Business Review Press.

Manne, Henry G. (1965), Mergers and the market for corporate control, *Journal of Political Economy*, 73(2): 110–20.

Manne, Henry G. (1967), Our two corporation systems: law and economics, *Virginia Law Review*, 53(2): 259–84.

Mannheim, Karl (1936), *Ideology and utopia*, London: Kegan Paul.

Mannheim, Karl (1986), *Conservatism: a contribution to the sociology of knowledge*, trans. David Kettler and Volker Meja, London: Routledge & Kegan Paul.

Mansfield, Bruce E. (1968), Erasmus in the nineteenth century: the liberal tradition, *Studies in the Renaissance*, 15: 193–219.

March, J.G. and Simon, H.A. (1958), *Organizations*, 2nd edn, Oxford: Blackwell.

Marris, Robin (1963), A model of the 'managerial' enterprise, *The Quarterly Journal of Economics*, 77(2): 185–209.

Marris, Robin (1964), *The economic theory of 'managerial' capitalism*, London: Macmillan.

Marron, Donncha (2007), 'Lending by numbers': credit scoring and the constitution of risk within American consumer credit, *Economy and Society*, 36(1): 103–33.

Martin, Felix (2014), *Money: the unauthorized biography*, London: Vintage.

Martin, Randy (2002), *Financialization of everyday life*, Philadelphia: Temple University Press.

Martinez-Moyano, Ignacio J., McCaffrey, David P. and Oliva, Rogelio (2014), Drift and adjustment in organizational rule compliance: explaining the 'regulatory pendulum' in financial markets, *Organization Science*, 25(2): 321–38.

Masten, Scott E. (1988), A legal basis for the firm, *Journal of Law, Economics, and Organization*, 4(1): 181–98.

Mayo, Elton (1946), *The human problems of an industrial civilization*, Cambridge: Harvard University Press.

Mazzucato, Mariana (2013), *The entrepreneurial state: debunking public vs. private myths in risk and innovation*, New York: Anthem Press.

Mazzucato, Mariana and Shipman, Alan (2014), Accounting for productive investment and value creation, *Industrial and Corporate Change*, 23(4): 1059–85.

McCarthy, Michael A. (2014), Turning labor into capital: pension funds and the corporate control of finance, *Politics and Society*, 42(4): 455–87.

McConnell, John J. and Buser, Stephen A. (2011), The origins and evolution of the market for mortgage-backed securities, *Annual Review in Financial Economics*, 3: 173–92.

McFall, Liz (2014), *Devising consumption: cultural economies of insurance, credit and spending*, London and New York: Routledge.

McGirr, Lisa (2001), *Suburban warriors: the origins of the new American right*, Princeton: Princeton University Press.

Merton, Robert K. (1957), *Social theory and social structure*, Glencoe: Free Press.

Mian, Atif and Sufi, Amir (2014), *House of debt*, Chicago and London: The University of Chicago Press.

Mian, Atif, Sufi, Amir and Trebbi, Francesco (2010), The political economy of the US mortgage default crisis, *The American Economic Review*, 100(5): 1967–98.

Milberg, William (2008), Shifting sources and uses of profits: sustaining US financialization with global value chains, *Economy and Society*, 37(3): 420–51.

Milberg, William and Winkler, Deborah (2010), Financialisation and the dynamics of offshoring in the USA, *Cambridge Journal of Economics*, 34: 275–93.

Mills, Charles Wright (1951), *White collars: the American middle class*, Oxford: Oxford University Press.

Mills, Charles Wright (1956), *The power elite*, Oxford and New York: Oxford University Press.

Minsky, Hyman P. (1980), Capitalist financial processes and the instability of capitalism, *Journal of Economic Issues*, 14(2): 505–23.

Minsky, Hyman P. (1986), *Stabilizing an unstable economy: a twentieth-century fund report*, New Haven and London: Yale University Press.

Mirowski, Philip (2005), A revisionist's view of the history of economic thought, *Challenge*, 48(5): 79–94.

Mirowski, Philip (2011), *Science-Mart: privatizing American science*, Cambridge and London: Harvard University Press.

Mirowski, Philip (2013), *Never let a serious crisis go to waste: how neoliberalism survived the financial meltdown*, London and New York: Verso.

Mizruchi, Mark S. (1983), Who controls whom? An examination of the relation between management and boards of directors in large American corporations, *Academy of Management Review*, 8(3): 426–35.

Mizruchi, Mark S. (2004), Berle and Means revisited: the governance and politics of large U.S. corporations, *Theory and Society*, 33: 519–617.

Mizruchi, Mark S. (2013), *The fracturing of the American corporate elite*, Cambridge: Harvard University Press.

Montgomerie, Johnna (2009), The pursuit of (past) happiness? Middle-class indebtedness and American financialisation, *New Political Economy*, 14(1): 1–24.

Moore, Marc T. and Rebérioux, Antoine (2011), Revitalizing the institutional roots of Anglo-American corporate governance, *Economy and Society*, 40(1): 84–111.

Moss, David A. (1996), *Socializing security: progressive-era economists and the origins of American social policy*, Cambridge and London: Harvard University Press.

Mowery, David C. (2009), *Plus ça change*: industrial R&D in the 'third industrial revolution', *Industrial and Corporate Change*, 18(1): 1–50.

Müller, Julian (2014), An accounting revolution? The financialisation of standard setting, *Critical Perspectives on Accounting*, 25(7): 539–57.

Neu, Dean, Gomez, Elizabeth Ocampo, Graham, Cameron and Heincke, Monica (2006), 'Informing' technologies and the World Bank, *Accounting, Organizations and Society*, 31(7): 635–62.

Niezen, Maartje G.H., Bal, Roland and De Bont, Antoinette (2013), Reconfiguring policy and clinical practice: how databases have transformed the regulation of pharmaceutical care?, *Science, Technology, & Human Values*, 38(1): 44–66.

Nik-Khah, Edward (2014), Neoliberal pharmaceutical science and the Chicago School of Economics, *Social Studies of Science*, 44(4): 489–517.

North, Douglass C. (1991), Institutions, *Journal of Economic Perspectives*, 5(1): 97–112.

O'Connor, Ellen S. (1999), Minding the workers: the meaning of 'human' and 'human relations' in Elton Mayo, *Organization*, 6(2): 223–46.

Orhangazi, Özgür (2008), Financialisation and capital accumulation in the non-financial corporate sector: a theoretical and empirical investigation on the US economy: 1973–2003, *Cambridge Journal of Economics*, 32: 863–86.

O'Sullivan, Mary (2000), *Contests for corporate control: corporate governance and economic performance in the United States and Germany*, New York and Oxford: Oxford University Press.

Ozment, Steven E. (1980), *The age of reform, 1250–1550: an intellectual and religious history of late medieval and Reformation Europe*, New Haven: Yale University Press.

Paine, Thomas (1995), *Rights of man, common sense, and other political writings*, Oxford and New York: Oxford University Press.

Palley, Thomas I. (2013), *Financialization: the economics of finance capital domination*, New York and Basingstoke: Palgrave Macmillan.

Palma, José Gabriel (2009), The revenge of the market on the rentiers: why neo-liberal reports of the end of history turned out to be premature, *Cambridge Journal of Economics*, 33(4): 829–69.

Pareto, Vilfredo (1901), *The rise and fall of elites*, New Brunswick: Transaction Publishers.

Partnoy, Frank (1999), The Siskel and Ebert of financial markets? Two thumbs down for the credit rating agencies, *Washington University Law Quarterly*, 77(3): 619–714.

Pascal, Blaise (1966), *Pensées*, London: Penguin.

Peck, Jamie (2010), *Constructions of neoliberal reason*, Oxford and New York: Oxford University Press.

Peñaloza, Lisa and Barnhart, Michelle (2011), Living U.S. capitalism: the normalization of credit/debt, *Journal of Consumer Research*, 38(4): S111–S130.

Perlow, Leslie A. (1999), The time famine: toward a sociology of work time, *Administrative Science Quarterly*, 44: 57–81.

Perrow, Charles (1984), *Normal accidents*, New York: Basic Books.

Perrow, Charles (2002), *Organizing America: wealth, power, and the origins of corporate capitalism*, Princeton and London: Princeton University Press.

Perugini, Cristiano, Hölscher, Jens and Collie, Simon (2016), Inequality, credit and financial crises, *Cambridge Journal of Economics*, 40(1): 227–57.

Petroski, Henry (1996), *Inventing unstable: how engineers get from thought to thing*, Cambridge: Harvard University Press.

Petryna, Adriana, Lakoff, Andrew and Kleinman, Arthur (eds) (2006), *Global pharmaceuticals: ethics, markets, practices*, Durham and London: Duke University Press.

Philippon, Thomas and Reshef, Ariell (2013), An international look at the growth of modern finance, *Journal of Economic Perspectives*, 27(2): 73–96.

Philips-Fein, Kim (2009), *Invisible hands: the making of the conservative movement from the New Deal to Reagan*, New York: W.W. Norton & Co.

Philips-Fein, Kim (2011), Conservatism: a state of the field, *Journal of American History*, 98(3), 723–43.

Phillips, Wendy, Johnsen, Thomas, Caldwell, Nigel and Chaudhuri, Julian B. (2011), The difficulties of supplying new technologies into highly regulated markets: the case of tissue engineering, *Technology Analysis & Strategic Management*, 23(3): 213–26.

Pierson, Paul (1996), The new politics of the welfare state, *World Politics*, 48(2): 143–79.

Pierson, Paul (1998), Irresistible forces, immovable objects: post-industrial welfare states confront permanent austerity, *Journal of European Public Policy*, 5(4): 539–60.

Pixley, Jocelyn (2012), *Emotions in finance: books, bust, and uncertainty*, Cambridge and New York: Cambridge University Press.

Polillo, Simone (2011), Money, moral authority, and the politics of creditworthiness, *American Sociological Review*, 76(3): 437–64.

Polillo, Simone and Guillén, Mauro F. (2005), Globalization pressures and the state: the worldwide spread of central bank independence, *American Journal of Sociology*, 110(6): 1764–802.

Pontusson, Jonas and Raess, Damian (2012), How (and why) is this time different? The politics of economic crisis in Western Europe and the United States, *Annual Review of Political Science*, 15: 13–33.

Posner, Richard A. (1973), An economic approach to legal procedure and judicial administration, *The Journal of Legal Studies*, 2(2): 399–458.

Posner, Richard A. (1974), Theories of economic regulation, *The Bell Journal of Economics and Management Science*, 5(2): 335–8.

Posner, Richard A. (1979), The Chicago School of antitrust analysis, *University of Pennsylvania Law Review*, 127(4): 925–48.

Posner, Richard A. (2009), *A failure of capitalism: the crisis of '08 and the descent into depression*, Cambridge and London: Harvard University Press.

Powell, Walter W. (2001), The capitalist firm in the twenty-first century: emerging patterns in Western Europe, in DiMaggio, Paul (ed.), *The twenty-first-century firm: changing economic organization in international perspective*, Princeton and Oxford: Princeton University Press, pp. 33–68.

Prechel, Harland and Morris, Theresa (2010), The effects of organizational and political embeddedness on financial malfeasance in the largest U.S. corporations: dependence, incentives, and opportunities, *American Sociological Review*, 75(3): 331–54.

Quadagno, Jill (1984), Welfare capitalism and the Social Security Act of 1935, *American Sociological Review*, 45(5): 632–47.

Quiggin, John (2010), *Zombie economics: how dead ideas still walk among us*, Princeton and London: Princeton University Press.

Reay, Mike (2007), Academic knowledge and expert authority in American economics, *Sociological Perspectives*, 50(1): 101–29.

Reay, Michael J. (2012), The flexible unity of economics, *American Journal of Sociology*, 118(1): 45–87.

Rhee, Eunice Y. and Fiss, Peer C. (2014), Framing controversial action: regulatory focus, source credibility, and stock market reactions to poison pill adoption, *Academy of Management Journal*, 57(6): 1734–58.

Rheinberger, Hans-Jörg (1997), *Toward a history of epistemic things: synthesizing proteins in the test tube*, Stanford: Stanford University Press.

Riskin, Jessica (2003), Eighteenth-century wetware, *Representations*, 83: 97–125.

Roberts, John, Sanderson, Paul, Barker, Richard and Hendry, John (2006), In the mirror of the market: the disciplinary effects of company/fund manager meetings, *Accounting, Organizations and Society*, 31(2): 277–94.

Robson, Keith, Humphrey, Christopher, Khalifa, Rihab and Jones, Julian (2007), Transforming audit technologies: business risk audit methodologies and the audit field, *Accounting, Organizations, and Society*, 32: 409–38.

Rock, Edward A. (2013), Adapting to the new shareholder-centric reality, *University of Pennsylvania Law Review*, 161(7): 1907–88.

Roe, Mark J. (1994), *Strong managers, weak owners: the political roots of American corporate finance*, Princeton: Princeton University Press.

Roe, Mark J. (2000), Political preconditions to separating ownership from corporate control, *Stanford Law Review*, 53(3): 539–606.

Roethlisberger, F.J. and Dickson, William J. (1943), *Management and the worker*, Cambridge: Harvard University Press.

Rom, Mark Carl (2009), The credit rating agencies and the subprime mess: greedy, ignorant, and stressed?, *Public Administration Review*, 69(4): 640–50.

Rona-Tas, Akos and Hiss, Stefanie (2010), The role of ratings in the subprime mortgage crisis: the art of corporate and the science of consumer credit rating, *Research in the Sociology of Organizations*, 30A: 115–55.

Rorty, Richard (2007), *Philosophical papers*, Vol. 4, New York: Cambridge University Press.

Rosett, Joshua G. (1990), Do union wealth concessions explain takeover premiums? The evidence on contract wages, *Journal of Financial Economics*, 27(1): 263–82.

Roy, William G. (1997), *Socializing capital: the rise of the large industrial corporation in America*, Princeton: Princeton University Press.

Rueda, David and Pontusson, Jonas (2000), Wage inequality and varieties of capitalism, *World Politics*, 52(3): 350–83.

Saint-Simon, Henri de (1975), From the government of men to the administration of things, in *Selected writings on science, industry and social organization*, trans. Keith Taylor, London: Croom Helm, pp. 157–222.

Salt, James (1989), Sunbelt capital and conservative political realignment in the 1970s and 1980s, *Critical Sociology*, 16(2–3): 145–63.

Sandefur, Rebecca L. (2015), Elements of professional expertise: understanding relational and substantive expertise through lawyers' impact, *American Sociological Review*, 80(5): 909–33.

Sarkar, Prabirjit (2013), Does an employment protection law lead to unemployment? A panel data analysis of OECD countries, 1990–2008, *Cambridge Journal of Economics*, 37(6): 1335–48.

Saxenian, AnnaLee (1994), *Regional advantage: culture and competition in Silicon Valley and Route 128*, Cambridge and London: Harvard University Press.

Schmidt, Vivien A. (2008), Discursive institutionalism: the explanatory power of ideas and discourse, *Annual Review of Political Science*, 11: 303–26.

Schneper, William D. and Guillén, Mauro F. (2004), Stakeholder rights and corporate governance: a cross-national study of hostile takeovers, *Administrative Science Quarterly*, 49(2): 263–95.

Schor, Juliet B. (1993), *The overworked American*, New York: Basic Books.

Schui, Florian (2014), *Austerity: the great failure*, New Haven and London: Yale University Press.

Schumpeter, Joseph A. (1942), *Capitalism, socialism, and democracy*, New York: Harper & Row.

Scott, Richard W. (2004), Reflections on a half-century of organizational sociology, *Annual Review of Sociology*, 30: 1–21.

Seeger, Matthew W. and Ulmer, Robert R. (2003), Explaining Enron: communication and responsible leadership, *Management Communication Quarterly*, 17(1): 58–84.

Selznick, P. (1949), *TVA and the grassroots*, Berkeley: University of California Press.

Seth, Anju (2001), The rise of fiduciary capitalism: how institutional investors can make corporate America more democratic, *Academy of Management Review*, 26(4): 668–70.

Shleifer, Andrei and Vishny, Robert (1997), A survey of corporate governance, *The Journal of Finance*, 52(2): 737–83.

Sikka, Prem (2009), Financial crisis and the silence of the auditors, *Accounting, Organizations and Society*, 34(6–7): 868–73.

Silvers, Damon (2013), Deregulation and the new financial architecture, in Wolfson, Martin H. and Epstein, Gerald A. (eds), *Handbook of the political economy of financial crises*, New York and Oxford: Oxford University Press, pp. 430–46.

Simakova, E. (2010), RFID 'theatre of proof': product launch and technology demonstrations, *Social Studies of Science*, 40(4): 549–76.

Simmons, Beth A., Dobbin, Frank and Garrett, Geoffrey (2008), Introduction. The diffusion of neoliberalism, in Simmons, Beth A., Dobbin, Frank and Garrett, Geoffrey (eds), *The global diffusion of markets and democracy*, New York and Cambridge: Cambridge University Press, pp. 1–63.

Simon, Herbert A. (1947 [1976]), *Administrative behavior*, 3rd edn, New York: Free Press.

Simon, Herbert A. (1957), *Models of man*, New York: Wiley.

Singer, David Andrew (2007), *Regulating capital: setting standards for the international financial system*, Ithaca and London: Cornell University Press.

Singleton, Kenneth J. (2014), Investor flows and the 2008 boom/bust in oil prices, *Management Science*, 60(2): 300–318.

Sinn, Hans-Werner (2010), *Casino capitalism: how the financial crisis came about and what needs to be done now*, Oxford and New York: Oxford University Press.

Smith, Wally (2009), Theatre of use: a frame analysis of information technology demonstration, *Social Studies of Science*, 39(3): 449–80.

Sockin, Michael and Xiong, Wei (2015), Informational frictions and commodity markets, *Journal of Finance*, 70(5): 2063–98.

Sorkin, Andrew Ross (2009), *Too big to fail: the insider story of how Wall Street and Washington fought to save the financial system – and themselves*, New York: Viking.

Spender, J.C. (1996), Making knowledge the basis of a dynamic theory of the firm, *Strategic Management Journal*, 17, Winter Special issue: pp. 45–62.

Spinoza, Benedict de (1670 [2009]), *Theologico-political treatise*, trans. R.H.M. Elwes, New York: Barnes & Noble.

State of Delaware (2015), Department of State/Division of Corporations/ About Agency, accessed 28 August 2015 at: http://www.corp. delaware.gov/aboutagency.shtml.

Stearns, Linda and Allan, Kenneth D. (1996), Economic behavior in institutional environments: the merger wave of the 1980s, *American Sociological Review*, 61(4): 699–718.

Stein, Judith (2011), *Pivotal decade: how the United States traded factories for finance in the seventies*, New Haven: Yale University Press.

Stigler, George J. (1971), The theory of economic regulation, *Bell Journal of Economics and Management Science*, 2(1): 3–21.

Stiglitz, Joseph E. (2010), *Freefall: America, free markets, and the sinking of the world economy*, New York and London: W.W. Norton.

Stiglitz, Joseph E. and Weiss, Andrew (1981), Credit rationing in markets with imperfect information, *American Economic Review*, 71(3): 393–410.

Stock, Brian (1995), Reading, writing, and the self: Petrarch and his forerunners, *New Literary History*, 26(4), 717–30.

Stockhammer, Engelbert (2004), Financialization and the slowdown of accumulation, *Cambridge Journal of Economics*, 28(5): 719–41.

Stockhammer, Engelbert (2013), Financialization and the global economy, in Wolfson, Martin H. and Epstein, Gerald A. (eds),

Handbook of the political economy of financial crises, New York and Oxford: Oxford University Press, pp. 512–25.

Stout, Lynn A. (2002), Bad and not-so-bad arguments for shareholder primacy, *Southern California Law Review*, 75: 1189–210.

Stout, Lynn A. (2004), On the proper motives of corporate directors (or, why you don't want to invite homo economicus to join your board), *Delaware Journal of Corporate Law*, 28: 1–25.

Stout, Lynn A. (2012), *The shareholder value myth: how putting shareholders first harms investors, corporations and the public*, San Francisco: Berrett-Koehler.

Styhre, Alexander (2015), *The financialization of the firm*, Cheltenham, UK and Northampton, MA, USA: Edward Elgar Publishing.

Suárez, Sandra L. (2014), Symbolic politics and the regulation of executive compensation: a comparison of the Great Depression and the Great Recession, *Politics and Society*, 42(1): 73–105.

Suárez, Sandra and Kolodny, Robin (2011), Paving the road to 'too big to fail': business interests and the politics of financial deregulation in the United States, *Politics & Society*, 39(1): 74–102.

Sundaramurthy, Chamu and Lewis, Marianne (2003), Control and collaboration: paradoxes of governance, *Academy of Management Review*, 28(3): 397–415.

Sunder Rajan, Kaushik (2012), Introduction: the capitalization of life and the liveliness of capital, in Sunder Rajan, Kaushik (ed.), *Lively capital*, Durham and London: Duke University Press, pp. 1–41.

Svetlova, Ekaterina (2012), On the performative power of financial models, *Economy and Society*, 41(3): 418–34.

Swedberg, Richard (2003), The case for an economic sociology of law, *Theory and Society*, 32(1): 1–37.

Tabb, William J. (2012), *The restructuring of capitalism*, New York: Columbia University Press.

Tabb, William J. (2013), The international spread of financialization, in Wolfson, Martin H. and Epstein, Gerald A. (eds), *Handbook of the political economy of financial crises*, New York and Oxford: Oxford University Press, pp. 526–39.

Tang, Ke and Xiong, Wei (2012), Index investment and the financialization of commodities, *Financial Analysts Journal*, 68(6): 54–74.

Teece, David J. and Winter, Sidney G. (1984), The limits of neoclassical theory in management education, *American Economic Review, Papers and Proceedings*, 74(2): 116–21.

Thornburg, Steven and Roberts, Robin W. (2008), Money, politics, and the regulation of public accounting services: evidence from the Sarbanes–Oxley Act of 2002, *Accounting, Organizations and Society*, 33(2): 229–48.

Tillman, Joseph A. (2012), Beyond the crisis: Dodd–Frank and private equity, *New York University Law Review*, 87: 1602–40.

Tomaskovic-Devey, Donald and Lin, Ken-Hou (2011), Income dynamics, economic rents, and the financialization of the U.S. economy, *American Sociological Review*, 76(4): 538–59.

Tomaskovic-Devey, Donald, Lin, Ken-Hou and Meyers, Nathan (2015), Did financialization reduce economic growth?, *Socio-Economic Review*, 13(3): 525–48.

Tourish, Dennis and Vatcha, Naheed (2005), Charismatic leadership and corporate cultism at Enron: the elimination of dissent, the promotion of conformity and organizational collapse, *Leadership*, 1(4): 455–80.

Trigilia, Carlo (2002), *Economic sociology: state, market, and society in modern capitalism*, Malden: Blackwell.

Tuckett, David (2011), *Minding the markets: an emotional finance view of financial instability*, London and New York: Palgrave Macmillan.

Tversky, Amos and Kahneman, Daniel (1981), The framing of decisions and the psychology of choice, *Science*, 211(4481): 453–8.

Urofsky, Melvin I. (1985), State courts and protective legislation during the progressive era: a reevaluation, *Journal of American History*, 72(1): 63–91.

Useem, Michael (1979), The social organization of the American business elite and participation of corporation directors in the governance of American institutions, *American Sociological Review*, 44(4): 553–72.

Useem, Michael (1990), Business restructuring, management control, and corporate organization, *Theory and Society*, 19(6): 681–707.

Useem, Michael (1993), *Executive defense: shareholder power and corporate reorganization*, Cambridge: Harvard University Press.

Useem, Michael (1996), *Investor capitalism*, New York: Basic Books.

Useem, Michael and Karabel, Jerome (1986), Pathways to top corporate management, *American Sociological Review*, 51(2): 184–200.

Van der Zwan, Natascha (2014), Making sense of financialization, *Socio-Economic Review*, 12(1): 99–129.

Van Horn, Robert and Emmett, Ross B. (2015), Two trajectories of democratic capitalism in the post-war Chicago school: Frank Knight versus Aaron Director, *Cambridge Journal of Economics*, 39(5): 1443–55.

Vaughan, Diana (1999), The dark side of organizations: mistake, misconducts and disaster, *Annual Review of Sociology*, 25: 271–305.

Veblen, Thorstein (1916), *The industry systems and the captains of industry*, New York: Oriole Chapbooks.

Velupillai, K. Vela (2014), Towards a political economy of the theory of economic policy, *Cambridge Journal of Economics*, 38: 1329–38.

Vinck, D. (eds) (2003), *Everyday engineering: an ethnography of design and innovation*, Cambridge and London: MIT Press.

Vogel, David (1983), The power of business in America: a re-appraisal, *British Journal of Political Science*, 13(1): 19–43.

Vogel, Steve K. (1996), *Freer markets, more rules: regulatory reforms in advanced industrial countries*, Ithaca and London: Cornell University Press.

Walkenhauer, Olaf (2001), Systems biology: the reincarnation of systems theory applied in biology?, *Briefings in Bioinformatics*, 2(2): 258–70.

Walker, Edward T. and Rea, Christopher M. (2014), The political mobilization of firms and industries, *Annual Review in Sociology*, 40: 281–304.

Walkling, Ralph August and Long, Michael S. Sr (1984), Agency theory, managerial welfare, and takeover bid resistance, *Rand Journal of Economics*, 15: 54–68.

Wallace, David Foster (2006), *Consider the lobster and other essays*, New York: Back Bay Books.

Watkins, Elizabeth S. (2001), *On the pill: a social history of oral contraceptives, 1950–1970*, Baltimore and London: Johns Hopkins University Press.

Watkins, Sherron (2003), Former Enron vice president Sherron Watkins on the Enron collapse, *Academy of Management Executive*, 17(4): 119–125.

Weber, Max (1949), *The methodology of the social sciences*, New York: Free Press.

Weinstein, Olivier (2013), The shareholder model of the corporation, between mythology and reality, *Accounting, Economics and Law*, 3(1): 43–60.

Werder, Axel von (2011), Corporate governance and stakeholder opportunism, *Organization Science*, 22(5): 1345–58.

Westphal, James D. and Bednar, Michael K. (2005), Pluralistic ignorance in corporate boards and firms' strategic persistence in response to low firm performance, *Administrative Science Quarterly*, 50(2): 262–98.

Westphal, James D. and Clement, Michael (2008), Sociopolitical dynamics in relations between top managers and security analysts: favor rendering, reciprocity and analyst stock recommendations, *Academy of Management Journal*, 51(5): 873–97.

Westphal, James D. and Graebner, Melissa E. (2010), A matter of appearance: how corporate leaders manage the impressions of financial analysis about the conducts of their boards, *Academy of Management Journal*, 53(1): 15–44.

Westphal, James D. and Khanna, Poonam (2003), Keeping directors in line: social distancing as a control mechanism in the corporate elite, *Administrative Science Quarterly*, 48(3): 361–98.

Westphal, James D., Park, Sun Hyun, McDonald, Michael L. and Hayward, Mathew L.A. (2012), Helping other CEOs avoid bad press: social exchange and impression management support among CEOs in communications with journalists, *Administrative Science Quarterly*, 57(2): 217–68.

Whalen, Charles J. (1997), Money-manager capitalism and the end of shared prosperity, *Journal of Economic Issues*, 31(2): 517–25.

Whalen, Charles J. (2002), Money manager capitalism: still here, but not quite as expected, *Journal of Economic Issues*, 36(2): 401–6.

White, Lawrence J. (2010), Markets: the credit rating agencies, *Journal of Economic Perspectives*, 24(2): 211–26.

White, Lawrence J. (2013), Credit rating agencies: an overview, *Annual Review in Financial Economics*, 5: 93–122.

Whitley, Richard (1986), The transformation of business finance into financial economics: the role of academic expansion and changes in the U.S. capital markets, *Accounting, Organizations, and Society*, 11: 171–92.

Whyte, William H. (1956), *The organization man*, New York: Simon and Schuster.

Williamson, Oliver E. (1975), *Market and hierarchies*, New York: Free Press.

Williamson, Oliver E. (1979), Transaction-cost economics and the governance of contractual relations, *Journal of Law and Economics*, 22: 233–61.

Williamson, Oliver E. (1981), The modern corporation: origins, evolution, attributes, *Journal of Economic Literature*, 19: 1537–68.

Wisman, Jon D. (2013), Wage stagnation, rising inequality and the financial crisis of 2008, *Cambridge Journal of Economics*, 37(4): 921–45.

Wolfson, Martin H. and Epstein, Gerald A. (eds) (2013), *Handbook of the political economy of financial crises*, New York and Oxford: Oxford University Press.

Wray, L. Randall (2009), The rise and fall of money manager capitalism: a Minskian approach, *Cambridge Journal of Economics*, 33(4): 807–28.

Zaloom, Caitlin (2003), Ambiguous numbers: trading technologies and interpretation in financial markets, *American Ethnologist*, 30: 258–72.

Zaloom, C. (2006), *Out of the pits: trading and technology from Chicago to London*, Durham and London: Duke University Press.

Zinman, Jonathan (2015), Household debt: facts, puzzles, theories, and policies, *Annual Review of Economics*, 7: 251–76.
Zorn, Dirk, Dobbin, Frank, Dierkes, Julian and Kwok, Man-shan (2005), Managing investors: how financial markets reshaped the American firm, in Knorr Cetina, Karin and Preda, Alex (eds), *The sociology of financial markets*, Oxford and New York: Oxford University Press, pp. 269–89.
Zuckerman, Ezra W. (1999), The categorical imperative: securities analysts and the illegitimacy discount, *American Journal of Sociology*, 104: 1398–438.
Zuckerman, Ezra W. (2012), Construction, concentration, and (dis)continuities in social valuations, *Annual Review of Sociology*, 38: 223–45.

Index

Adelstein, Richard P. 66, 67
agency costs 8, 116–18, 120, 130, 136,
        139–42, 144, 145, 148, 149, 155,
        159, 165–7, 169, 183, 196, 197,
        199–201, 208, 232
agency theory 23, 103
agency theory model 107–59
    contractarian view *vs.* corporate law
        view 122–7
    contractual theory inconsistencies
        127–32
    of corporate governance 112–22
    practical recommendations and
        policies 120–22
    team production theory 145–8
algorithmic trading 45
Almandoz, Juan 56
American Association for Labor
        Legislation (AALL) 65
American corporate law system
        109
American Housing Rescue and
        Foreclosure Prevention Act
        (AHRFPA) 43
American revolution 1, 34
Anglo-American corporate and
        securities law 173
Annales school 1
anti-collectivism 138–42
anti-takeover legislation 175
anti-trust legislation 40, 51, 53, 54, 61,
        62, 171
aristocracy 1
Aron, Raymond 73
Arrow, Kenneth J. 12, 92, 93
asset shielding 205
assumption 8
austerity 215

Babb, Sarah 47
Bainbridge, Stephen M. 197
Baker, George P. 117, 118, 152
Bank of Sweden's Prizes in Economic
        Sciences in memory of Alfred
        Nobel 75, 230
bankruptcy law 178
Baron, James N. 52
Baumol, William J. 90–92
Baysinger, Barry D. 123, 124
Bear Stearns 151, 194, 197
Bebchuk, Lucian A. 178, 197, 201, 202
Beckert, Jens 193
Bellow, Saul 68
Bendix, Reinhart 89
Berkeley, California 150
Berle, Adolf A. 23, 62–4, 71, 88, 102,
        111, 115–16
Bernanke, Ben 4
Bernanke, B.S. 4, 189, 230
Bertrand, Marianne 174–7
Blair, Margaret M. 38, 39, 41, 145, 147,
        148
Blau, Peter 89
Blauner, Robert 89
Blinder, Alan S. 3, 6
Block, Fred 82
Blyth, Mark 14, 188
bounded rationality 14, 92, 233
Bourdieu, Pierre 210
Bowen, Howard 55
Brahe, Tycho 10
Brandeis, Louis D. 60–62, 66, 101
Brandeisian progressives 70
Bratton, William W. 63, 64, 182
Bratton, William W. Jr. 36, 62, 107, 133,
        136, 139
Braudel, Fernand 5
Brownstein, Ronald 87

Brudney, Victor 127–30, 133, 134, 138, 146
Bryan, Dick 193
Burgin, Angus 76
Bush, G.W. 4
Business Behavior, Value and Growth (Baumol) 90
business charters 33–5
Butler, Henry N. 123, 124

Cambridge University *vs.* London School of Economics 82–5
Campbell, John L. 31, 32
Canguilhem, Georges 9, 14, 108
capital inflow and deregulation 189–92
capitalism 5
capital lock in 205
capital market efficiency hypothesis 131
Carlyle, Thomas 10
Carosso, Vincent 70, 71
Carruthers, Bruce G. 47, 48
Carter, J.E. Jr. 100, 189
Cassidy, John 76
Celler–Kefauver Act 110
Cheng, Ing-Haw 194
Cheung, Steven N.S. 123
Chicago law and economics school 123, 124, 126, 231
Choo, Jennifer 18
Clark, Cynthia E. 45
Clark, Robert C. 134, 143, 144, 146
Clayton Antitrust Act (1914) 40
Coase, Ronald 123
cognitive ideas 31
cognitive parading 31
Cold War rationality 222, 227
collectivism 23, 61, 62, 67–9, 71, 72–80, 85, 99–102, 107–9, 111, 158, 168–70, 188, 207, 209, 210, 232
Collins, Robert M. 84
Commodity Futures Modernization Act 191
Commons, John R. 65
Common Sense (Paine) 29
community logic 56

competitive capitalism 12, 32, 51, 108, 166, 219–20
complicit decoupling 45
Comte, A.M.F.X. 66
Conard, Alfred F. 184
Connecticut 104
conservatism 80–81
Conservatism 29, 30, 80–81, 88, 89, 99
The Constitution of Liberty (Hayek) 79
contract 112, 127, 128
    legal concept of 113
contracts *ex ante* 124
contractual arrangements 123
contractual rule making 143
contractual theory 125–7
contractual theory inconsistencies 127–32
contractual view, consequences of 148–58
corporate control, market for 95
corporate efficiency 118
corporate governance scholarship 196–202
corporate law 18, 29–57
    business charters development and 33–5
    fiduciary component of 55–6
    and innovation 44–7
    and regulations 42–7
    role of 35–42
corporate leverage 164
corporate proxy machinery 127
corporate restructurings 149–55
corporate system 8, 22, 33, 35, 37, 38, 41, 42, 89, 94, 95, 142, 143, 166, 196, 207, 234
corporate welfarism 65
corporation
    defined 37
    growth and differentiation of 39–42
    incorporators and 109
credit system 61

Daily, Catherine M. 20
Dalton, Melville 89
Dartmouth College 34
Davis, Gerald F. 12, 136, 193
Deal Decade 155

Dearborn Massacre 72
Debt-financed buyouts 155
default rules 37, 199
Delaware Chancery Court 163
Delaware General Corporation Law 39
DeMott, Deborah A. 128, 132
Deutsche bank 188
dialectical relationship 46
distribution rules 37
divine law 30
Dobbin, Frank 51–5
Dodd, Merrick 4
Donaldson, Thomas 183
Dowd, Timothy J. 53, 54
Downer, John 10
Dress to Kill (1998) 231
dual-class voting structures 179
Durcharbeitung 1–6

Easterbrook, Frank H. 123, 124, 127,
    141
economic freedom 5, 23–4, 55, 76, 79,
    81–2, 84, 126, 143, 209–12, 222,
    227, 231, 232
economic growth 85–7
economic ideas 13–22
    corporate governance and 15–22
    economic sociology view 17–19
    management studies view 19–22
    neoclassical economic theory view
        15–17
    policy-making and 13–15
economic organization 64
economic rationality 53, 224, 234
economic reasoning 220–22
economics, in books and real life 9–13
economic sociology 17–19
*The Economic Theory of 'Managerial'
    Capitalism* (Marris) 90
The Economist 150, 151, 153
Edelman, Lauren B. 48–50
efficiency theory 78, 109
efficient market hypothesis (EMH) 77,
    112–14, 120, 134, 145, 169, 230,
    231
Eisenberg, Melvin A. 37, 38, 41, 112,
    114–16, 120, 128, 129, 133–7, 182
Elijah complex 74

elite rule 142–5
Emergency Economic Stabilization Act
    (EESA) 43
enabling rules 37
The End of History for Corporate Law
    (Hansmann and Kraakman) 170
enforcement rules 92, 93
Englander, Ernest J. 154
English law 34, 38
Enron 43, 55, 58, 197, 213
Enron bankruptcy 43, 55
Enronitis 58
epistemic communities 31
epistemocratic fallacy 210, 211
epistemocratic sociodicy 210
Euclidean axiom 76
European feudalism 2

A Failure of Capitalism (Posner) 3
Faludi, S.C. 152
Fama, Eugene F. 111, 116–18
Family and Medical Leave Act (1993)
    53
Faulkner, Alex 44
Federal Reserve 4
Feldman, Martha S. 21
fiduciary duties 128, 130, 131
fiduciary law 129
fiduciary rules 37, 129, 134, 135
finance industry collapse 196–202
finance industry growth 184–9
finance market expansion 189–92
finance market pricing mechanism 135
finance sector, growth of 184–202
financial innovations 45–6
financial logic 56
financial market regulation 19
Financial Services Modernization Act
    191
FIRE (Finance, Insurance and Real
    Estates) sector 185
firm, governance 8–25
firm, nature of 8–25
first oil crisis of 1973 100
Fisch, Jill E. 200
Fischel, Daniel R. 123, 124, 127, 141
Fleck, Ludwik 76, 219
Fligstein, Neil 5, 18, 181, 191

Food and Drug Administration (FDA) 143, 144
Ford, Henry 65
Ford Motor Company 72
Fortune 79
Fortune 1000 companies 162, 206
Frame, W. Scott 45, 46
Franco-Prussian war 1
free market advocacy 60–103, 211
free market advocators 166
free-market capitalism 84
free market protagonists 107, 108, 110, 135
free-rider problems 146
French revolution 1
Friedman, Milton 82, 101
Fukuyama, Francis 170
Funk, Russell J. 46

Galbraith, John Kenneth 97
Gantt, H.L.L. 69
Gay, Peter 2
General Motors 60, 72
The General Theory of Employment, Interest and Money (Keynes) 209
Glass–Steagall Act 40, 46, 47, 110, 191
golden parachutes 156, 157, 199
Goldwater, B.M. 99
The Good Society (Knight) 73, 80
Google 179
Gordon, Jeffrey N. 88, 155, 165, 170
Gospel of Work 2
Gouldner, Alvin 89
Graebner, William 66
Gramm–Leach–Bliley Act 191
The Grapes of Wrath (Steinbeck) 68
Great Recession 1–6, 216, 230
Greenspan, A. 4, 188
Greenwood, Robin 187
Grocott, Chris 76

Habinek, Jacob 191
Hall, Bronwyn H. 205
Halliday, Terence C. 47, 48
Hambrick, Donald C. 20, 21
Handlin, Mary F. 34
Handlin, Oscar 34

Hansmann, Henry 170–74, 177, 179, 181
Hanson, Norwood 10
Harriss-White, Barbara 210
Hart, Oliver 16–18
Hawley, Ellis 69
Hayek, F. von 24, 73–83, 101, 102, 107–8, 166, 209
Hegel, G.W.F. 67
Heracleous, Loizos 182, 183
Herbert Simon tradition 19, 158
Hermalin, Benjamin E. 16
Hilt, Eric 41
Hirschman, Daniel 46
Hofstadter, Richard 66
holdup 125, 160
homo economicus 55
Hoover, Herbert 69
hostile takeovers 139, 148, 149, 155, 175
Howard, John L. 131
Hughes, Everett 89
human resource management 52–3

ideologies 14, 24, 25, 43, 62, 69, 74, 75, 97, 98, 100, 102, 137–9, 170, 183
Ideology and Utopia (Mannheim) 219
ideology of utopian capitalism 97
ING 188
Initial Public Offerings (IPOs) 37, 179, 199
institutional economic theory 30
institutional innovations 30–31
institutional investors 16, 151, 154, 206
institutional theory 109
insurance companies 151, 206
internal control systems 119
intraorganizational control 92
investor capitalism 13, 21, 22, 24, 165–211
    advancement of 184–202
    consequences of 203–7
Izzard, Eddie 233

Jacoby, Sanford M. 88
Jaques, Elliott 89
Jensen, Michael C. 111–14, 116–21, 169, 182

Jones, Daniel Stedman 83
junk bonds 149–51, 153, 154, 157, 159,
    167
juridical contract 112

Kahneman, Daniel 92
Kaufman, Allen 36, 70, 122, 125, 126,
    154, 156
Kaufman, Jason 33, 35
Kelly, Erin L. 51–3, 55
Kepler, Johannes 10
Kerr, Ron 56
Keynes, John Maynard 14, 81, 82–5,
    102
Keynesian economic model 103
Keynesian economic policy 74, 80–101
Keynesianism 85
    anti-statist critique of 99
    decline of 98–101
    see also Keynesian economic policy
Klausner, Michael 198, 199
Knight, Frank 73
Kogut, Bruce M. 20
Kohlberg Kravis Robert & Co (KKR)
    149–51, 154
Kolodny, Robin 46
Konzelmann, Suzanne J. 77, 83
Kraakman, Reinier 170–74, 177, 179,
    181
Krier, Dan 196
Krippner, Greta R. 189, 191
Kristal, Tali 86

Labor omnia vincit improbus 2
labour law 19
labour relations managers 89
Lambert, Drexel Burnham 150, 153
Lamoreaux, Naomi R. 34, 124, 125
Lan, Luh Luh 182, 183
Langston, Thomas S. 69
La Porta, Rafael 16
Lazonick, William 203
Le Colloque Walter Lippmann 73, 75
legal ambiguity 53
legal environment 18, 29–57, 107, 124
legal field 48
legal texts 49
legislation, empirical studies of 51–5

Lenglet, Marc 45
Le Roy Ladurie, Emmanuel 1
leveraged buyouts (LBOs) 119, 135–6,
    149–58
    managerial responses to 155–8
limited liability 38, 57, 58
LinkedIn 179
Lippmann, W. 72–4, 79–80, 104
Lipton, Martin 154
Locke, John 29
Long, Michael S. Sr. 155, 156
L'organization industrielle 64
Los Angeles Times 87
Lubatkin, Michael H. 182, 183

Macey, Jonathan 201
'Magna Carta of Liberalism' 74
management-centric system 168
management theory revision 181–3
managerial capitalism 11, 21–2, 25, 36,
    87–98, 102, 103, 110, 111, 117,
    148, 153, 159, 166, 168, 169, 180,
    184, 190, 195, 196, 207–10
managerial efficiency 19
managerial inefficiency 135
managerialism
    bounded rationality 92
    collectivism concept and 72–80
    decisions, framing of 92
    firm and 62–80
    free market advocacy 60–103
    neoliberal thought community 72–5
    New Deal and managerial capitalism
        64–71
    ownership and control 62–4
    principal–agent relations 60–103
    Roosevelt's New Deal 66–71
    trust *versus* contract 87–98
managerialist view 114
managerialization of law 49–51, 55
managerial malfeasance 157
managerial welfare hypothesis 155, 156
mandatory rules 37, 41, 129, 143, 145
Manne, Henry G. 94–6, 103
Mannheim, Karl 25, 29, 30, 219
market-based price system 92
market competition, virtues of 80–81
market efficiency 42

market failure, modality of 113
market for corporate control 57, 95, 96, 116, 121, 197, 200
market romanticism 210
Marris, Robin 11, 90, 92, 94, 97
Marshall, John 35
Martinez-Moyano, Ignacio J. 44–5
Massachusetts 34, 53, 104
Masten, Scott E. 127
Mayo, Elton 89
Means, Gardiner C. 62, 63, 102, 111, 116
Meckling, William H. 112–14, 116, 182
M-form 88
Mian, Atif 43, 44
Milken, M.R. 149–51, 153–5, 167
Mills, Charles Wright 97
mimetic isomorphism 53
Minsky, Hyman 14, 192
Mirowski, Philip 75, 76, 78, 99
Mises, Ludwig von 82, 108
Mizruchi, Mark S. 63
The Modern Corporation & Private Property (Berle and Means) 62, 63
modus tollens 117
money management capitalism 184, 192–6
    finance market actors 192–5
    sustainability of investor and 195–6
money trust, the 60, 101
Mont Pèlerin Society (MPS) 75, 82, 103
Moore, Marc T. 17, 62, 121
moral hazard 57, 58, 92–4, 175–7, 188, 189, 230
mortgage-backed securities (MBS) 186, 191, 193
Moss, David A. 87
Mullainathan, Sendhil 174–7
Müller, Julian 195
mythical transcendence 29

narcissistic leaders 56
National Industrial Recovery Act (NIRA) 67, 69, 107
Neeman, Zvika 202
neoclassical economic theory 15–17, 31, 122, 219–34
    theoretical realism of 227–30

neoclassicists 19
neoliberal thought collective (NTC) 76, 77
New Deal 22, 40, 47, 61, 63–72, 76, 79–81
New Deal programmes 61, 81, 110
Newell, Sue 45
New Hampshire 34
The New Industrial State (Galbraith) 97
nexus of contracts 109, 121, 133–7
    ideology of 138–42
    investor capitalism and 165–211
nexus of firm-specific investments 147
Niezen, Maartje G.H. 45
Nixon, Richard M. 100
Nobel, Alfred 75
non-infrastructure businesses 34
normalization of deviance 44–5
normative ideas 31, 32
North, Douglass 30

oligarchic managerial capitalism 168
operating rules 92, 93
option pricing theory 178
Orange County, California 99
organization routines 21
organized action 78
O'Sullivan, Mary 17, 18, 203
overbanking 184–202
ownership, separation of 118
ownership capitalism 65

Paine, Thomas 29, 30
Panglossian claim 141
pareto-efficiency 143
pareto-efficient rules 143
paternalistic elitism 142, 144–5
Peck, Jamie 3
pension funds 151, 174, 206
Pentland, Brian T. 21
performative theory 180
personal administration legislation 52
personal capitalism 65
Philippon, Thomas 185, 187
Philips-Fein, Kim 80, 81, 99
Phillips, Wendy 44
Pinochet, Augusto 77–8
poison pills 155, 156, 199

policy-making 13–15, 31, 32
policy paradigms 47
political liberalism 72
political mobilization 46
political rent-seeking 161
portfolio planning 110–112
positional conflicts 133, 137
Posner, Richard A. 3, 4, 6, 42
postcorporate economic organization 12
power balance 1
price function 76
price system 12, 92, 93, 161
price theory 77, 123, 124, 126, 165, 169, 201, 210, 212, 231, 232
price volatility 193
principal–agent relations 60–103
private equity firms 150, 151, 217
progressive era legal reform 64–71
propositions 8–9
public choice theory 227
public corporation 12
public good 29, 35, 138

Rafferty, Michael 193
railroad systems 53
rational choice theory 222–6
    tragic failure of 226–7
R&D investment 204–7
Reagan, R.W. 87, 99–101, 150, 189, 190, 212
real-life economics 9–13
Rebérioux, Antoine 17, 62, 121
regulatory environments 46, 49
rentier capitalism 209
Reshef, Ariell 185, 187
residual cash flow 16, 18
residual claimants 116–18, 124, 177–9
Rhode Island 34, 104
RJR Nabisco 153
The Road to Serfdom (Hayek) 74, 76, 78, 79
Robbins, Lionel 74
Roberts, Robin W. 43, 44
Robinson, Sarah 56
Rock, Edward A. 168
Rockefeller Foundation 89
Roe, Mark J. 139, 140, 142

Rogier, Louis 73
Roman law 38
Roosevelt, F.D. 61, 63, 66–72, 76, 79, 80, 102, 107
Röpke, Wilhelm 73
Rosett, Joshua G. 175
Roy, William G. 109
rules, categories of 37

Safeway 152
Saint-Simon, C. H. de 64, 66–7
salaried managers and directors 109–12
Samuelson, Paul 84
Sarbanes–Oxley Act 43, 197
savings and loans associations 190
scepticism 71
Scharfstein, David 187
Schmidt, Vivien A. 31
Schumpeter, Joseph 64
Securities Act of 1934 110
Securities and Exchange Commission (SEC) 40, 110, 143
securities industry 186
self-regulating contractual arrangement 125
Selznick, Philip 50
sexual harassment 51
shadow banking system 6, 7
shareholder democracy view 114
shareholder primacy 23, 169–70
shareholder primacy governance 172
shareholder primacy protagonists 170
shareholder welfare 170–74
    consequences of 203–7
shareholder welfare arguments 177–81
shareholder welfare hypothesis 155
shareholder welfare model 167
Sherman Antitrust Act 40
Shleifer, Andrei 15
Simon, Herbert 92
Simon, William E. 112
situation-specificity 132
Skilling, J.K. 58
Smith, A. 64, 65, 104, 190
Smith, George David 152
social democracy 139, 140
social democratic policy 139

Social Responsibilities of the Businessman (Bowen) 55
Social Security Act (1935) 79
Somers, Margaret R. 82
S&P 500 companies 194, 204
Spinoza, Benedict de 30
stagflation 87
stakeholder opportunism 20
Stalin, J. 72
state-level anti-takeover legislation 174–7
statutory corporate governance rules 131
Steinbeck, J.E. Jr. 68
Stigler, George 42
Stout, Lynn A. 55, 145, 147, 148, 177–82
Stout, Suzanne K. 136
structural rules 37
The Structure of the Corporation (Eisenberg) 112
Suárez, Sandra 46
Suchman, Mark C. 48
suppletory rules 37
Swedberg, R. 50, 51
systemic shock absorbers 193

Tabb, William J. 195
Taylor, F.W. 69
team production theory 145–8
Teece, David J. 9
theory-laden observations 10
Thornburg, Steven 43, 44
totalitarianism 100
tout court 119
Tversky, Amos 92
Two Treatises on Government (Locke) 29

Ulysses 224
Urofsky, Melvin I. 65
Useem, Michael 155
US Supreme Court 34, 35
utopian capitalism 97
utopian ideas 25, 219

varieties of capitalism literature 18
Veblen, Thorstein 60–61
vertical integration 97, 110
Vishny, Robert 15
Volcker, P.A. Jr. 189

Wachter, Michael L. 64
Walkling, Ralph August 155, 156
Wallace, D.F. 210, 211
Wall Street crash 6, 40, 61, 62, 64, 72, 101–2
Wall Street Journal 43, 152
Watkins, Sherron 55
Weber, Max 9, 10
Weinstein 180
Weinstein, Olivier 183
Weisbach, Michael S. 201
welfare capitalism 64–71
welfare state expansion 85–7
Werder, Axel von 20
Western capitalism 8
When the Music Stopped (Blinder) 3
White, Lawrence J. 45, 46
Williamson, Oliver 219
Winter, Sidney G. 9

Xiong, Wei 194

Zacharias, Lawrence 36, 70, 122, 125, 126, 156